TRANSFORMED

TRANSFORMED

Reinventing Pittsburgh's Industrial Sites for a New Century, 1975–1995

EVAN STODDARD

Harmony Street Publishers
Pittsburgh, Pennsylvania

Harmony Street Publishers, 192 South 17th Street, Pittsburgh, PA 15203
Harmony.Street.Publishers@gmail.com

ISBN (softbound) 978-0-9983996-0-7
ISBN (e-book) 978-0-9983996-1-4

Library of Congress Control Number: 2016919378

Maggie Diehl did developmental and copy editing.
Douglas Harper and Janet Stoddard enhanced the photographs using Adobe Lightroom and Photoshop.
Janet Stoddard made the maps.
Taylor Tobias designed the cover and text.

Map and photo credits:
Author: cover photo of the Pittsburgh Technology Center, and pages 6, 7, 25-2, 50, 52, 55, 57 (2), 59, 60, 63, 69, 74, 75, 113, 131, 150, 151 (1), 160, 165, 177, 180, 181, 185, 190, 191, 192
Classic Burgh Pics: page 10 (1)
Herb Ferguson: cover photo of the J&L Pittsburgh Works, and pages 70, 78, 79, 88, 91 (1), 133
Douglas Harper, page 151 (2)
Randolph Harris for RIDC: pages 142, 186, 197, 220, 239
Pittsburgh Department of City Planning: pages 51, 84
RIDC: pages 10 (2), 135, 136, 200, 218, 224, 234, 235, 237, 240, 244
Rivers of Steel: pages 158, 162, 164 (2), 168, 169
Janet Stoddard: pages 5, 26, 30, 36, 45, 57 (1), 73, 76, 101, 149, 152, 164 (1), 170, 176, 189, 206, 210, 223, 238, 365
URA: pages 19, 23, 24, 25-1, 29, 32, 38, 42, 46, 47, 48, 49, 54, 58, 62, 81, 82, 83, 86, 91-2, 98, 99, 100, 102, 107, 117, 118, 121, 127

This book is set in Permian typeface with Futura titles.

To Janet, for love, patience, and unswerving support

In memory of Roy Lubove, Pittsburgh historian

Night spread over the coal-town: its prevailing color was black. Black clouds of smoke rolled out of the factory chimneys, and the railroad yards, which often cut clean into the town, mangling the very organism, spread soot and cinders everywhere . . . Under such conditions, one must have all one's senses blunted in order to be happy; and first of all, one must lose one's taste. . . . Dark, colorless, acrid, evil-smelling, this new environment was. All these qualities lowered human efficiency and required extra compensation in washing and bathing and sanitation—or at the last extreme, in medical treatment.

Even after strenuous efforts to reduce smoke pollution, a single great steel plant in the heart of Pittsburgh still makes mock of these efforts at improvement—indeed, so heavy is the hold of paleotechnic tradition, that the municipal authorities only recently helpfully connived at the extension of this plant, instead of firmly demanding its removal. So much for pecuniary losses. But what of the incalculable losses through disease, through ill-health, through all the forms of psychological deterioration from apathy to outright neurosis? The fact that such losses do not lend themselves to objective measurement does not make them non-existent.

From Lewis Mumford, *The City in History: Its Origins, Its Transformations, and Its Prospects*, New York: Harcourt, Brace & World, Inc., 1961, pp. 470–72

CONTENTS

PREFACE

In this book I tell the stories of the earliest efforts to turn abandoned industrial sites in Pittsburgh to new productive uses. By the mid-twentieth century, following WW II, Pittsburgh was an industrial powerhouse where steel was dominant. Then, in the early 1980s, the bottom dropped out. Foreign competition, high labor costs, aging plants, and shifting markets combined to decimate Pittsburgh's steel industry. Other industries that had also been important to Pittsburgh, such as food and glass, fell on hard times as well. Within a generation the Pittsburgh region went from having the second-highest concentration of employment in manufacturing (after Detroit), to having one of the least.

This massive loss of industry devastated Pittsburgh's economy, leaving tens of thousands of workers without employment. Some scrambled to find new work locally or to be retrained. Wives who had been at home raising children suddenly had to find work outside the home. Many struggled to pay mortgages and other bills. Some pulled up roots, severed family and community ties, and left for better opportunities elsewhere. Many depleted their life savings or lost them when their houses suddenly lost their value.

Communities, too, felt the impact of the loss. Many of Pittsburgh's small municipalities were essentially company towns, dependent on a single plant for much of their revenue. The closing of that plant had dire consequences for schools and other public services. Community leaders and residents were desperate to replace the lost jobs with new ones. In addition, the shuttered factories quickly deteriorated, becoming unkempt and dangerous. Demolishing abandoned factories and replacing them with new uses became a top priority.

When private real estate companies failed to take on the task, apparently concluding the vacant properties held greater potential risks than rewards, local elected leaders and economic development officials took up the challenge. Beginning in the city of Pittsburgh, and then moving to surrounding Allegheny County, public officials led by trying, to the extent possible, to enlist private enterprises in the rebuilding effort.

Fortunately, Pittsburgh had a history of public-private partnership on which to build. Even before WW II corporate and civic leaders had foreseen the importance of diversifying Pittsburgh's economy and had joined hands to do so in a variety of ways. As a result, during the same time the steel industry was dying and other manufacturing declining, Pittsburgh's banking, healthcare, educational, and technology sectors were steadily expanding. Though the loss of steel was a terrible jolt for the region, other industries were rising to take its place.

Thus, by the time Pittsburgh hosted the G-20 summit in 2009, President Barack Obama could—and did—put the city's economic recovery on display for the world to see. Leaders of the world's economies saw for themselves Pittsburgh's transformation from a city on the brink of economic disaster to a city at the forefront of economic recovery.

Although the summit's activities took place in downtown Pittsburgh— itself the vibrant product of the renaissance that began at the close of World War II—if participants ventured out from downtown, they would have seen the impressive results of thirty years of sustained efforts by Pittsburgh's civic leadership to remake the city's built environment to accompany the changes in its economy. Their explicit goal in undertaking these projects was one important aspect of their larger goal of remaking industrial Pittsburgh for a postindustrial world.[1] Important among them:

- Derelict Herr's Island had become the fashionable Washington's Landing. Once the busy center of Pittsburgh's meat-packing industry, but largely abandoned by the 1970s, it was now the vanguard of public access to the rivers. A rowing club; a marina; a walking, jogging, and cycling trail; and classy residential and commercial buildings had taken the place of the unused corrals and rusting rail lines, a rail-repair scrapyard, one lone remaining slaughterhouse, and a rendering plant that had polluted the entire surroundings with a noisome stench.

- Along the Parkway East, where only a few years before the abandoned mill buildings of LTV Corporation's Pittsburgh Works greeted drivers just as the towers of downtown Pittsburgh came into view, now, Phoenix-like, the Pittsburgh Technology Center had emerged in its place.[2] The massive mill buildings had completely disappeared, replaced by distinctive, postmodern research facilities housing biotechnology, computer systems, and transit controls; public plazas; river overlooks;

lines of stately trees; and a "green river" of varied grasses and wildflowers.

- Even the site of what had been the largest steel mill in the world, USX Corporation's massive Homestead Works, was transformed beyond recognition.[3] One of the bloodiest labor battles of American history—the Homestead Steel Strike of 1892—had occurred on the site, but now all that remained of the enormous plant was a row of smokestacks, the historic pump house where the Battle of Homestead had occurred, and a handful of refurbished mill buildings. The remainder of the site had been reborn as Sandcastle (a water amusement park) and the Waterfront—260 acres of new riverfront housing, shopping, entertainment, and dining, with such "big box" tenants as Target and Lowe's; a town center with smaller shops like Barnes & Noble and Bed Bath & Beyond; a Loews Cineplex; and national and local restaurants.

- The companion Duquesne and McKeesport steel plants had been cleaned or selectively razed. Refurbished mill buildings housing new industrial and service tenants (including a giant call center) now stood next to new warehouses and manufacturing plants, as well as a new home for the Greater Pittsburgh Community Food Bank.

Reflecting on the choice of Pittsburgh as the location of the G-20 summit, a *Washington Post* reporter commented that G-20 "members are more likely to ask what Pittsburgh can teach them than why they had to come here."[4]

There undoubtedly are lessons others can take from Pittsburgh's experience and success. Some may lie in the very projects, listed above, whose stories I tell in this book. However, when others have urged me to make this book a how-to guide for other cities, I have found myself unable to do so. For one thing, time has passed and the world has changed. The demands of the time are different, as are the legal and regulatory environment and the level of knowledge. For another, every city has its unique history, demography, culture, economy, and market strengths or weaknesses—so many factors that make it impossible to lift an approach that is successful in one place and transfer it unchanged to another. I can, however, identify general principles that the stories illustrate in hope that others can learn something from Pittsburgh's experience that may be modified to benefit their changed time and circumstances. There are universal principles that apply in many situations.

I have a very personal interest in these projects because they became my professional concern for some twenty years, something my wife Janet and I did not expect when we first drove into Pittsburgh on a sparkling August afternoon in 1971. We had never been to Pittsburgh before, and now we were going to make it our home—at least for a time. As we emerged from the Fort Pitt Tunnel, the beautiful skyline before us took us completely by surprise. As we headed out the Parkway East, we were struck by the verdant hillsides to our left, the barge traffic on the active Monongahela River on our right, and LTV's enormous Pittsburgh and South Side steel plants that stretched out along the shore on both sides of the river.

Within weeks we had settled into a small row house in South Side, and I had begun my studies at the University of Pittsburgh's Graduate School of Public and International Affairs. At the time, South Side was still a steel town—hardly the entertainment center it is today. Our neighbors, almost all with Polish, Slovak, or Lithuanian surnames and many up in years, had close ties to the mill. They had worked there; their fathers or brothers had worked there; and many of their sons, now living in Brentwood or Baldwin, still worked there. Each day as I walked to school in Oakland, the working mill was a prominent feature of the landscape. The smell of sulfur was a constant reminder of its presence, and smog frequently obscured the green hills and grayed the air on humid summer days.

Fifteen years later all of this had changed. A long list of mills had closed: the Pittsburgh Works closed in 1981, the South Side Works in 1986. Upriver, USX closed its Duquesne Works in 1984 and its Homestead Works in 1986. USX's National Works in McKeesport closed in 1987, the same year as LTV's Aliquippa Works downriver. In a moment, as it seemed, Pittsburgh's renowned steel industry had practically disappeared. That is, the industry was gone—along with the smog and the smell of sulfur in the air—but the huge factories loomed as large as ever. Their funereal stillness was a perpetual reminder of what had been an entire way of life that had passed. At least three generations had made a living in the mills, through hope, toil, danger, and conflict. Now the great steel tradition was over and the jobs were gone.

After graduating from Pitt in 1974, I took a job in Pittsburgh's Department of City Planning. There, and after I moved to the Department of City Development in 1979, I took part in the earliest efforts to redevelop Herr's Island. When I moved to the Urban Redevelopment Authority of Pittsburgh (URA) in 1982, I continued to work on the Herr's Island project and then helped to plan and develop the Pittsburgh Technology Center.[5] From 1986 to 1993 I directed the Economic Development Department at the URA, which had responsibility to manage both projects. Although I did not participate in the projects outside the city, I kept abreast of them through my friends in County Development and my service on the board of Pittsburgh Countywide Corporation, which invested public funds in those projects.

After I went to work at Duquesne University in 1994, my interest in the projects continued. My history and the interest of others prompted me to write about what I had seen and experienced. I remember one conversation with a friend, a marketing professor at Wayne State, who asked why some tracts of land in Detroit, where houses and businesses had once stood, were left idle. Drawing from the stories I tell here and others like them, I explained the difficulties of land redevelopment in our nation's cities—the complexities and costs of assembling a city site; the effort involved in securing community support and consensus in an already developed city; and the uncertainties about what might lie below the surface of the ground.

I remember another conversation, with a bright and earnest public policy student who approached me at a reception to ask about Washington's Landing, which he was studying in class. Wouldn't it have been more effective, he asked in effect, to have taken the more than $25 million spent to redevelop the island—over half a million dollars an acre—and used it to strengthen or enhance important city neighborhoods such as Squirrel Hill or South Side? Yes, I admitted, it might have been, but that was not the decision public officials had faced. Rather, the question was what to do with a blighted, virtually abandoned island located only a 5- to 10-minute drive from downtown Pittsburgh. How could that island resource contribute to a new economy for Pittsburgh?

Although we could not predict the specific outcomes—and in retrospect had no idea of the costs that would be involved—the mission was clear: to make the island productive once again. We could not have imagined the complexity of issues or the costs involved. Nor could we have foreseen some of the most important benefits the effort would yield—the elimination of the stench from the rendering plant, the reclamation of polluted land, and the tremendous economic and recreational opportunities that emerged from the recovery of land along the river's edge. We could not and did not see where the road would lead us as we confronted one decision (and expenditure) at a time, weighed against uncertain future benefits, but we felt motivated by the clear goal of creating a new economy for a city in serious decline.

The answers to the questions I was being asked lay in the stories of the projects. Without knowing the stories, people would find it difficult to understand why the projects had been so important, how they had become what they had become, why developing them had been so problematic and taken so long, and what questions had been asked and answered along the way. I decided to tell the stories of the projects, as those of us involved in their development experienced them, so that others would be able to see and understand what was so clear to me.

In this book I tell about five projects. Choice of the projects was simple: they were the first major industrial redevelopment projects in Allegheny County and the only ones to begin before Pennsylvania changed the ground rules for redeveloping brownfields in 1995.[6] I have arranged the stories chronologically. Washington's Landing at Herr's Island was the first to begin, followed by the Pittsburgh Technology Center and Homestead; Duquesne and McKeesport were the last.

I tell each story from the beginning of efforts to recover the site until 1995, when Pennsylvania adopted the Industrial Site Recycling legislation that attempted to address many of the problems that were revealed in the course of developing these earliest projects. After telling about the first two, which were located within the city, I have inserted a short chapter that explains some of the circumstances surrounding the decline of Pittsburgh's steel industry. Some understanding of these forces and events is important to lay the groundwork for my explanation of efforts to redevelop the great steel mills of the Monongahela River Valley.

Since I was personally involved in the first two projects, as well as in the city's efforts to counter the impact of steel's decline, I was able to combine material from documents and the memories of others with my own personal records and memories, which meant injecting an element of personal reminiscence into those accounts. My purpose is to let each story unfold as it happened, to try to give the reader the experience of the participants themselves, who despite their careful planning could not predict from one day to the next what unforeseen events would occur. In fact, the unexpected is what made the projects so difficult and what makes their stories so fascinating.

Readers, however, do have the advantage of hindsight that the participants did not, and I, too, take advantage of hindsight here. Ten years after the end of my stories, in 2005, I visited and photographed the sites, which by that time had taken on their final character. I begin each project chapter with a timeline and an introduction that paints a picture of the project in its "finished" form. Next I flash back to the nineteenth century to explain briefly how the property first developed, its role and importance in Pittsburgh's industrial past, and how the site eventually fell into disuse. I devote the bulk of the chapter to telling the story of its transformation to what it has become today. At the conclusion of each account I highlight lessons the stories illustrate. I have framed each chapter to help illuminate a question or an issue that the particular project brings to the fore.

One issue deserves special mention here: environmental contamination— in the form of asbestos in the old mill buildings, contaminants found stored in barrels and other containers, and pollutants in soil and water. These are, by definition, an issue for every brownfield development. The stories I tell in this book illustrate abundantly the gravity of the questions and problems they pose and the difficulties of addressing them—difficulties that were particularly acute at the time about which I write, for then public policy to address problems of contaminated soil and water was still in its infancy. Indeed, the projects I have written about provided much of the data and experience on which environmental regulators in Pennsylvania, and elsewhere, drew in their efforts to develop effective approaches to preserve public health while at the same time encouraging efforts to recover derelict industrial sites.

Because environmental concerns figure so prominently in most of the stories and will almost undoubtedly raise questions in the minds of readers, in the concluding chapter, after commenting on the importance of the projects for Pittsburgh's recovery from the loss of industry, I attempt to place the projects in the context of the evolving environmental regulations of the time. Here I highlight some of the specific problems and challenges that those developing regulations raised for these projects and for others. I want to be clear, however, that this is not a book about the environment. My purpose is not to add to the literature on environmental policy but simply to help the reader better understand some of the forces that motivated participants in the stories and how those forces led them to make the decisions they did.

Finally, having told the stories of the projects, explained briefly their significance for Pittsburgh's recovery, and situated them in the environmental regime of the time, I return to the themes and lessons I introduced earlier and draw conclusions that I hope will help others in their efforts to replace the remnants of the old industrial world with new and vibrant uses. As the stories themselves should make clear, however, there can be no textbook approach to such undertakings. While some general principles may apply, each situation is as unique as the history and characteristics of a property, its community setting, the prevailing legal and regulatory context, and the individuals and organizations that set about to act on it. That, of course, is what makes for the adventure.

Evan Stoddard
Pittsburgh, Pennsylvania
December 2016

TRANSFORMED

The scrap yard at the lower end of Herr's Island before redevelopment began, with downtown Pittsburgh in the background

WASHINGTON'S LANDING TIMELINE

1903   Pennsylvania Railroad purchases much of Herr's Island for stockyards.

1959   Pittsburgh Department of Parks and Recreation recommends making the island a public park.

1965   Pennsylvania closes its Pittsburgh Joint Stockyards.

1975   Commonwealth of Pennsylvania proposes buying the island for a public park. Pittsburgh's Mayor Flaherty asks RIDC to study using it as an industrial park.

1978   The city unveils its first plan for the island, including both an office/industrial park and a public park, and engages the URA and RIDC to manage the development.

1980   City Planning Commission designates the island as a redevelopment area. Demolition begins.

1982   City Planning proposes mixed uses, including offices, a conference center, a marina, housing, and a public park.

1983   GAI completes an environmental investigation that reveals only minor problems. City Council approves the redevelopment plan; Jack Buncher opposes it.

1984–85 URA negotiates unsuccessfully with The Buncher Company.

1986   URA enters into a marketing and development agreement with North Side Civic Development Council. URA reaches an agreement with The Buncher Company and renames the island "Washington's Landing."

1987   URA agrees to buy out The Buncher Company. Washington's Landing Associates begins construction of the first office building. URA requests proposals to develop a marina.

1988	URA discovers PCBs on Buncher's property. Washington's Landing Associates stops construction.
1989	Three Rivers Rowing Association builds its rowing center. DER approves a containment cell on the island for the soil contaminated by PCBs. Construction of the containment cell uncovers animal waste. URA selects Haulover Resort Marina to develop the marina.
1990	Gamma Sports chooses the island for its new office and plant. The containment cell is completed. Construction begins on the marina.
1991	URA and DER sign a consent order and agreement. Construction begins on Gamma Sports. The marina opens. DER chooses the island for its new offices.
1992	Gamma Sports moves in. DER and Three Rivers Rowing Association occupy Washington's Landing Associates' second office building, and URA approves a third.
1993	The public park opens.
1994	Montgomery and Rust commit to developing housing.

1

WHAT SHOULD THIS BE?
From Herr's Island to Washington's Landing

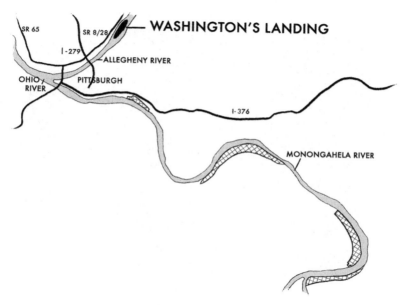

Washington's Landing

Manufacturing? Trucking and storage? Conference center? Park? What should this largely abandoned, blighted island known as Herr's Island become? Should it even continue as an island, or should the channel separating it from the mainland be filled to increase developable area and ease of access? These are some of the questions that confronted city officials as they contemplated redevelopment of the island—and they confronted them repeatedly as the project moved ahead.

INTRODUCTION

Billed as "the crowning achievement" for both the city of Pittsburgh and the Urban Redevelopment Authority (URA) in their campaign to reclaim Pittsburgh's many brownfields, Washington's Landing, formerly (and still to many) Herr's Island, was declared complete on September 30, 1999, twenty-four years after the city began its redevelopment efforts there.[1]

Herr's Island, one of only two islands remaining in the city of Pittsburgh, is about 2.5 miles above Pittsburgh's "Point," the location in downtown Pittsburgh where the Allegheny and the Monongahela rivers come together to form the Ohio. About 42 acres, the island is an elongated oval about 4,500 feet long and only 640 feet across at its widest point. It is separated from the north shore of the river by a narrow channel of the river, called a *back channel*, some 170 feet wide but only 6 feet deep.

Entrance to Washington's Landing, 2005

Today, Washington's Landing is a mixed-use development, including six office and industrial flex-space buildings totaling 227,500 square feet of space; a rowing club and its docks; a 150-slip marina and a 150-bay boat storage building; a small restaurant; ninety houses—some freestanding but most grouped in townhouse rows of several units; a public park with tennis courts; and a trail around the perimeter of the entire island, linked to the mainland by a repurposed rail bridge at the island's downstream end.

Only a few years after its completion, the island is settled and established, an attractive, peaceful refuge within the city limits. Today, street trees and other landscaping have matured. On a typical day, employees and visitors walk and jog along the trail. Residents and their dogs sun themselves in their backyards next to the edge of the trail. A group of young men work righting and repairing a boat at the marina. Waiters clean tables and straighten the bar in the restaurant. A small group chats on the sidewalk outside the restaurant. Cars and small trucks quietly come and go, dropping packages at businesses, entering or leaving the landscaped parking lots that border the smart-looking, one- or two-story office/industrial buildings. Only a couple of office parcels remain undeveloped, but they are simply grassy fields, and most visitors would probably overlook them. The overall atmosphere is serene and unhurried. The island seems far removed from the rush of the city around it. Indeed, there is little or nothing to bring to mind the difficulties and challenges that attended its redevelopment.

Redfin Blues at the Washington's Landing Marina, 2005

Gamma Sports' building, seen through the trees at the northern end of the public park, 2005

BACKGROUND

Benjamin Herr purchased the island in 1792 from its original owner, William Wilson, for residential and recreational use. By the mid-1850s it was laid out with streets and lots, and a bridge connected the island to the North Shore. By the 1870s, however, considerable industry had emerged on the island, and by the latter part of the nineteenth century a rail line served the Pittsburgh and Allegheny stockyards built by tanner James Callery in 1885 to serve his growing tanning business. By the turn of the century the island was almost entirely industrial.[2]

Back channel, looking upstream, with industrial buildings and an early bridge in the background

Industrial Herr's Island, looking upstream, covered with buildings, with what became the Buncher property to the right

In 1903, the Pennsylvania Railroad purchased a substantial portion of the island for use as a rest area for cattle shipped between Chicago and New York. From then until the early 1970s, the Pittsburgh Joint Stock Yards

Company owned and occupied the central and upper portions of the island. Federal law required that after thirty-six hours of shipping, cattle had to stop for rest, food, and water. To meet this need, as well as to supply meat to the local market, the company built cattle pens that covered the island, along with coolers, smokehouses, an engine room, and other assorted facilities for processing meat. The island boasted annual livestock shows, with roundups, prizes, and auctions. By the 1950s, however, faster trains could make the trip to the East Coast in less than thirty-six hours, and Herr's Island served only the local market.[3]

Herr's Island at mid-twentieth century, looking downstream

As early as 1959 the city's Department of Parks and Recreation urged that the island be converted into a recreation area. These plans never materialized, and by the mid-1960s Herr's Island had deteriorated and was largely abandoned. In early August 1965 Mayor Barr asked city council to approve a request for $1.25 million from the state's Project 70 fund to fill the back channel and preserve the island for future recreational use. Again, nothing came of the proposal.[4] Later that same month the Pennsylvania Railroad announced that it was closing the Pittsburgh Joint Stockyards, marking the end of livestock marketing on the island.[5]

Ten years later, in August 1975, the state of Pennsylvania announced plans to buy Herr's Island along with a number of other islands to create a string of island parks in the lower Allegheny River. Two months later, however, Mayor Pete Flaherty, concerned about the loss of industry and employment in the city, rejected the park idea. He "called on the RIDC to study the feasibility of using the island as an industrial park, with a small area set off for recreational use, possibly a marina."[6]

By this time the only active uses left on the island were a rendering plant owned by Inland Products, a packinghouse operated by Western

Packers (Herr's Island Packing Company), and a salvage yard owned by The Buncher Company. The city used a portion of the island, at its northern end, as an ash dump. The extensive stockyards and the railroad tracks, which covered roughly thirteen of the island's 42 acres, remained in the Penn Central Railroad's ownership and then passed to the Consolidated Rail Corporation (Conrail) in 1978, when Penn Central went bankrupt. The Chessie System (B&O Railroad) still had a right-of-way for its tracks, which crossed the island on a bridge and embankment.[7]

Herr's Island in 1981, with downtown Pittsburgh in the background. At the downstream (far) end of the island is Buncher's recycling plant, in the center the stockyards (to the left) and Herr's Island Packing (to the right), Inland Products on the near side of the B&O Railroad Bridge, and the former ash dump at the upstream end, in the foreground. Bridges across the back channel, from the top, are the Pennsylvania Railroad, 30th Street, 31st Street (connecting to Lawrenceville, across the river), Walker, and B&O Railroad.

DEVELOPING WASHINGTON'S LANDING

Regional Industrial Development Corporation's (RICD's) Plan – 1975–1976

RIDC's plan for a Herr's Island Industrial Park, with office, commercial, and industrial buildings, a marina, and a new bridge connecting directly to Routes 8/28

David O'Loughlin, a brash young staffer in Mayor Pete Flaherty's office, was the first in city government to champion converting Herr's Island into an office park, modeled after the successful RIDC Park in nearby O'Hara Township, just up the Allegheny River. In fact, RIDC had already investigated the feasibility of redeveloping the island in 1965. Their plan had also proposed filling the back channel to increase the size of the property and eliminate the need for a bridge. It was not difficult to convince the mayor that RIDC's concept had merit.

In 1976, in response to the mayor's request late the previous year, RIDC resurrected its plan and presented it to the city. It envisioned a combination of distribution services, light manufacturing, offices, a restaurant or a bank, a marina, terraces, plazas, and pedestrian walks. It described "a carefully designed, high quality, master-planned complex, based upon a set of protective standards and controls." They proposed a two-phase development: first to develop the island as it existed, which would require replacing a bridge; and second to fill the back channel, as earlier envisioned, to increase the development area to 70 acres. RIDC projected that the full development would bring 2,500 jobs.[8]

RIDC also recommended a strategy: put pressure on Inland Products and Western Packing to meet health standards as an inducement to get them to sell and relocate. On the other hand, they recommended trying to get The Buncher Company, led by its experienced and canny president Jack Buncher, to become the island's developer. In this scenario Buncher would buy Penn Central's property (which they had already been trying to do) as well as land that the URA would acquire from Inland Products, Western Packing, and the city. Buncher would then clear the island of the old industrial facilities (Buncher was in the demolition and salvage business) and develop it according to the master plan. The URA would construct a new road, sewer and water lines, and a bridge to make the development possible. In the second phase, the URA would acquire the land under the back channel from the state and convey it to Buncher in exchange for his doing the necessary dredging and filling. Using this approach, if the URA was wise and lucky, the net public investment could be as little as $2.9 million, and the return to the city on real estate taxes alone would be on the order of 11% per year.

We will never know if this plan would have worked, because no one ever tried to implement it. The city did not put pressure on Inland Products or Western Packing. Buncher did not buy Penn Central's property, and the city did not invite Buncher to become the island's developer. What is certain is that if Buncher had developed the island, it would be a very different place than it is today. There would be no rowing center, no housing, no park or walking trail, and likely no marina. In their place would be more industrial flex-buildings, warehousing, and probably continued rail access. In all likelihood the back channel would have been filled and the island would no longer exist as a distinct entity from the mainland. It also almost certainly would have developed more quickly and at less cost.

In the end, the public investment to redevelop the island was almost ten times as much as RIDC projected. The cost of the new road and bridge alone far exceeded RIDC's estimates. In their defense, RIDC could not have foreseen the environmental issues that would add major costs—although it is likely that a private developer like Buncher might never have discovered the contaminated soil on the island and might well have taken a different course if he had.

Would the loss of the island, public access to the riverfront, and a unique housing community have been worth the savings in time and public costs? Most Pittsburghers would probably say no. In addition, lessons learned in the process of developing the island would make an important contribution for years to come.

Early Delays – 1977

In 1977 newly inaugurated President Jimmy Carter invited Mayor Flaherty to become deputy attorney general, and Richard S. Caliguiri replaced Flaherty as mayor of Pittsburgh. This move initially created a setback for the project, because it would take time for the new mayor to take the lead of such a major development.

Despite this setback, Stephen A. George, executive director of the URA, remained optimistic: "Sometime next year, we hope to begin acquisition of property and get started on road building and site improvements." The *Pittsburgh Press,* however, was critical of the delay. "The Prolonged Transformation of Herr's Island" charged that "after nearly 20 years of talks, proposals and studies, the idea of turning Herr's Island into something more than a smelly, weed-ridden, junk-strewn piece of real estate is 'back in committee.' ... If you're waiting to park your boat at Herr's Island ... don't cut your engine. As Arthur V. Harris, president of TRIAD [Three Rivers Improvement and Development Corp.], put it four years ago: 'This is not an overnight proposition.'"[9]

The City's Plan – 1977–1979

The idea of using the island for economic development was compelling. The city's able planning director, Robert Paternoster, had become increasingly concerned about deterioration of the city's economic base. As his principal economic development planner, charged with devising ways the city could strengthen its economy, I was also worried. One of the city's major problems was stanching the exodus of firms leaving the city for suburban locations. It was difficult for the city to retain them because there were few sites in the city that could compare with the attractive and inexpensive sites in RIDC's suburban office parks. Herr's Island could help prevent the mass exodus to the suburbs. Under Paternoster's direction, Gary Fry and I researched and wrote a report of conditions on the island that the Planning Commission used to certify the island as a redevelopment area.[10]

The island also figured prominently in an application I wrote that year for the Community Economic Development Demonstration Program, a newly established competitive federal grant. When Pittsburgh won the award, it gave Mayor Caliguiri the resources to create a new Department of City Development and to hire Ed deLuca—the long-time economic development director in Baltimore, Maryland, but also a Pittsburgh-area resident—as director.

The island's development was also a central feature of the city's *Overall Economic Development Program,* which Paul Bödy and I wrote in 1978 to qualify the city for additional grants from the Economic Development Administration (EDA). A subsequent application for an EDA economic readjustment grant from the new Pittsburgh Countywide Corporation included a request for funding to build a new main street and bridge for the island.

The URA's board of directors first publicly unveiled plans for Herr's Island at its regular April 6, 1978, meeting, presided over by Jack Robin. Robin was the distinguished urban development expert who had served as the authority's first executive director thirty years before, under Mayor David Lawrence. Mayor Caliguiri had recently recruited him to return to Pittsburgh to head the authority's board. Robin "noted that today's meeting is very important in that it begins the actual realization of the Herr's Island Project which has been discussed for seven or eight years." The board approved the first acquisition of property on the island, Herr's Island Packing Company, for $650,000. The board also approved a six-month engineering design study, necessary to complete the application to the EDA. Employment projections, although lower than RIDC had forecast, were still optimistic. The Department of Development estimated that the project would create 2,000 new jobs and would cost $5 million, half of which could come from the federal government.[11]

Privately, Jack Robin was not as sanguine about prospects for the development. When my planning colleague Gary Fry and I presented a rough cost/benefit analysis of the project to the Mayor's Development Council in November 1977—suggesting that it would take decades to recoup the city's investment from new revenues—Robin accepted our analysis and recommended that we not proceed with the project. However, he was the only member of the council who did. As the years passed and costs continued to mount, Robin often reminded me that we had given fair warning, although both of us were proud of what the island eventually became.

The decision to use EDA funds—$2.27 million for site preparation, including a new street, bridge, utilities, and streetlights—effectively meant that the public, through the URA, would be the island's developer, rather than a private firm like Buncher, since EDA regulations prohibited grants to benefit a private developer, even to achieve a public purpose. As a result, the process would be much more complex than RIDC had originally envisioned. Under this public approach Buncher would acquire 25 acres from Penn Central and sell it to the URA—at a significant profit, of course. (Buncher always bought low and sold high and was highly successful as a result.) The city would transfer its former ash dump at the upstream end of the island to the URA, while the URA would begin designing the road in anticipation of receiving funds from the EDA. Buncher would develop his own property to "conform to the standards and controls of the Redevelopment Area Plan when it is prepared"—presumably for warehousing, which Buncher had experience in developing.[12] RIDC would get into the process as well, since it staffed Pittsburgh Countywide Corporation, which was the conduit for funds from the EDA. As a result, RIDC would actually negotiate and let the contracts for improvements. Hence, funds would flow from the EDA to Countywide to RIDC and finally to the URA.

On March 21 the URA entered into an agreement with RIDC to use EDA funds to contract with an engineering consultant. The consultant would undertake preliminary site planning and identify the permits the URA would need to begin the island's redevelopment. The URA selected GAI Consultants of Monroeville to perform this work, the first of many jobs GAI would perform on the island over the years. By August, less than six months later, the contract with GAI already had to be amended to include additional traffic analysis on the intersection of PA Route 28 and the 31st Street Bridge, which provided the main access to the island and was the most congested intersection in the city.[13]

As part of the initial planning the EDA required an "environmental

An accident at the intersection of the 31st Street Bridge and Routes 8/28, with Herr's Island's animal-holding shelters and corrals in the background

assessment"—not an assessment of soil and water conditions on the island, but an assessment of the development's impact on the natural and built environment. The report, submitted to the EDA in May 1979, optimistically predicted that the development would not create environmental problems.

By September 1979 the URA owned 70% of the island, a redevelopment plan was in preparation, funds from the EDA and the city had been committed to the project, and the URA was negotiating with the Pennsylvania Department of Environmental Resources (DER) and Inland Products to purchase Inland's rendering plant for reuse as a park. URA was also requesting bids to demolish the old cattle pens and slaughterhouse and clear the island to enhance its development prospects.

The pens, or corrals, were extensive, covering most of the central portion of the island. They must have been quite a sight when they held huge herds of cattle brought to the island for slaughter. While not on the scale of Chicago's stockyards, they had the same filth and vermin. When Jerry Dettore, the URA's director of planning and engineering, wrote to the Allegheny County Health Department seeking permission to burn the debris from the pens, the department's Daniel Cinpinski surveyed the island and noted, "Since a potential food source does exist at the Inland Products plant on the north end of the island, I would recommend that demolition begin at the north

15

end of the island and proceed southward to minimize driving rats toward a food source." He assured that "we will monitor rat activity during the demolition process."[14]

Planning and Engineering – 1980

The year 1980 was filled with intensive planning and engineering. By March GAI had completed its Herr's Island Engineering Planning and Design Study Final Report, although it proved to be nothing close to a final report. The city budgeted and the Department of City Development transferred $1.515 million to the URA for design and construction of the first phase of work, which was on the central portion of the island. Concurrently, the URA entered into an agreement with Pittsburgh Countywide Corporation to use the $2.27 million from the EDA for construction of the spine road.[15] The URA would use state funds to purchase Inland Products, the noxious rendering plant occupying 2.8 acres that created a noisome stench for residents of Troy Hill, above and across the back channel. The $2.3 million to buy Inland would come from the state's fund for island park acquisition.[16]

On May 5 the City Planning Commission declared the island and property across the back channel blighted, opening the way for the URA and City Planning to begin work on the redevelopment plan. The resulting plan again provided for filling the back channel to maximize the development area. However, since this would require approval both from the state and from the Army Corps of Engineers, it could not happen in time to eliminate the need for a new bridge to make redevelopment possible—as RIDC had foreseen. The plan also proposed a park on the Inland Products site, since park money was being used to buy it.[17] The URA would handle Inland's relocation and demolition. Relocation alone would likely take three years, since finding a new location for this malodorous use would not be easy. Although the city was anxious to retain employers, this was one company it did not care to keep.

The details of the redevelopment plan were not yet fully developed at this stage, but the outlines were clear: "The land use concept—an office/light industrial park developed in the context of [a] public river-oriented park—is firm, and its approval is needed to assure the State of the Authority's intent." The URA's board of directors adopted this conceptual land use plan, including the plan to fill the back channel. To meet another state requirement, the URA authorized GAI "to undertake a program of soil sampling, testing and evaluation in order to determine if any pollutants exist on Herr's Island."[18]

The city's proposed office–industrial use for the island reflected both the economic conditions of the time, that is, the steep loss of the city's industrial base, with its attendant jobs, and Ed deLuca's leadership of the project. Ed brought with him from Baltimore a long history of experience with industrial retention programs, along with ties to the EDA, which favored industrial development projects. Although the country at large was becoming more concerned with quality of life, Ed's experience and interests led him to think narrowly about the island's future. A park might be necessary to secure funding from the state, but housing and such amenities as a rowing center and marina were outside his ken.

That summer I moved from City Planning to City Development in order to take a more active role in the city's economic development. Having worked on the plans for Herr's Island as a planner, I would now be more involved in financing and development. In October the URA authorized the contract to demolish the buildings and cattle pens in the center of the island; from there, demolition on the island continued over many years. The Pennsylvania Department of Commerce made its first financial contribution to the project in 1982 to pay for the demolitions.

Proposal for a Steam Plant – 1980

Toward the end of 1980 a controversy erupted over a proposal from downtown business interests, including the Allegheny Conference on Community Development, Pittsburgh's premier organization of business leaders, which again brought into question how the island would be used. They wanted to build a waste-recovery plant on 15 to 20 acres of the island to replace the two ancient steam plants that heated and cooled downtown buildings. Apart from the age of the inefficient plants, the energy crisis was sending oil prices skyrocketing, and one of the two steam plants was oil-fired. The URA, recognizing the need, supported the concept of turning garbage into energy. But the proposal to put the plant on Herr's Island was in direct conflict with the city's plans as well as the concept the city had sold to the EDA.

Mayor Caliguiri tried to smooth over the issue, taking the position that there was room on the island for both a steam plant and a job-producing industrial park. He expressed the hope that in light of the energy crisis the EDA would recognize the importance of the steam plant. In an editorial the *Pittsburgh Post-Gazette* advocated the same position. However, in the end the plan to make steam from trash proved to be less economical than modernizing the old steam plant on the edge of downtown, and the idea of putting a steam plant on the island died.[19]

Access Problems – 1981

At the beginning of the project there were two decrepit bridges to the island: the Walker Bridge and the 30th Street Bridge. The upstream Walker Bridge belonged to Inland Products and had a severe weight restriction. Despite its condition, in January the URA agreed to accept the deteriorated bridge, with its accompanying liability, as an inducement to Inland Products to sell their property.[20]

The primary access to the island was via the 30th Street Bridge. This bridge crossed the back channel, connecting the island with River Avenue near the 31st Street Bridge, which in turn crossed the Allegheny River, linking Lawrenceville and East Ohio Street (State Routes 8 and 28). By 1981 it, too, had a serious weight restriction and needed to be replaced.

For a year or more, GAI and the URA explored every conceivable way of providing the best and least costly new access to the island. They finally concluded in July of 1981 that the budget would allow for only one new bridge to the island. A month later they decided that the best location for that bridge would be parallel to and upstream from the 30th Street Bridge. GAI completed a preliminary design report for the bridge and ramp in April 1982. It took into account the complex ramp system that connected River Avenue with the 30th and 31st Street bridges and East Ohio Street.

Unfortunately, both the Walker and 30th Street bridges were so deteriorated that neither could carry the demolition and construction equipment needed to work on the island before a new bridge could be built. The 30th Street Bridge would have to be repaired sufficiently that equipment could get onto the island. GAI agreed to design, inspect, and monitor those repairs, and it also won three contracts for grading, roadway construction, and utilities on the island itself. The URA and city officials expected that "upon completion of this work the property will be ready to put on the market."[21] GAI also received the award to design and oversee construction of the new bridge, a contract the costs of which grew threefold, to $734,000, before the year's end.[22]

Planning, engineering, and demolition continued through the following year. Meanwhile, the URA continued its negotiations to acquire Inland Products. On December 9, 1981, at a news conference in Pittsburgh, Governor Thornburgh finally announced the successful purchase of the Inland property. The company would have two and a half years to move from the island.[23] Their property would become a park and marina, part of the system of parks that city and county officials had for years hoped to develop along the county's riverfronts.[24]

Redevelopment Planning – 1981–1983

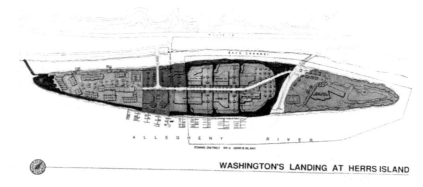

WASHINGTON'S LANDING AT HERRS ISLAND

1983 Preliminary Land Development Plan, showing, from left, park, housing, marina opposite the new bridge, flex-industrial/office buildings on the center of the island, and a corporate conference center on the upstream end

In early 1981 City Planning, now headed by Robert Lurcott, began working on a final redevelopment plan for the island. In May a team composed of Paul Farmer and Steven Branca of City Planning; David Libby, a planner at the URA; and me from City Development began meeting regularly to develop that plan. As the year progressed, Farmer and Branca became increasingly concerned that the benefits from a purely industrial project did not justify the projected costs.[25]

At the end of the year Mayor Caliguiri decided to streamline the organization of city development and precipitously eliminated the city's Housing and City Development departments, sending their staffs to newly created Economic Development and Housing departments at the URA. He appointed Paul Brophy, who had headed the city's Housing Department, to replace Steve George as the URA's executive director. Steve George and Ed deLuca of City Development, the two agency heads who had been most involved with the development of Herr's Island, were let go. I became part of the new Economic Development Department, under Gloria Fitzgibbons. Effective January 1, 1982, Paul Brophy and Gloria Fitzgibbons suddenly were responsible for Herr's Island and had to learn about the project from scratch.

During 1982 Paul Farmer of City Planning, seeking better uses for the island and emboldened by Ed deLuca's departure, visited waterfront industrial reuse projects on the East Coast looking for ideas. He brought back slides of mixed-use projects that he felt were more exciting and more appropriate and would lead to higher levels of investment on Herr's Island. He was convinced that strictly industrial uses were not ambitious or dense enough for what he considered an attractive and unique site.

Thus, in mid-December Bob Lurcott wrote to Jack Robin and Hiram Milton, president of RIDC and chairman of the city's Economic Development Committee, proposing a land-use study to reevaluate the uses the city had proposed in its application to the EDA.[26] Lurcott couched the argument in economic terms, however, saying that the "reason for reconsidering the EDA plan is the high public costs." The city should "provide the best return" on its substantial investment of public dollars. With some considerable reluctance, RIDC and Hi Milton, both of whose experience was in industrial development, went along.[27]

The Planning Department worked on the redevelopment plan throughout 1983, with substantial advice coming from The Harlan Company and architect Jonathan Barnett, both of New York City. In August, The Harlan Company delivered a report which concluded that "limited access makes manufacturing, warehouse and distribution facilities problematic" and the "proposed industrial uses do not give recognition to certain of Herr's Island's natural amenities: excellent views of downtown Pittsburgh, isolated rural atmosphere, [and] river frontage offering recreational opportunities." Harlan proposed a corporate conference center, a marina, an "office cluster of small, primarily single-tenant buildings," a public park, and residential development "at a point in time that the image of Herr's Island has been significantly improved and the Island's natural amenities have been indirectly marketed by means of the Phase 1 development."[28]

One problem with this plan, however, was Jack Buncher, with his rail-car repair facility on his 9.9-acre property near the island's southern tip. The earlier plan had envisioned industrial uses on Buncher's property, but the emerging idea was housing, since Buncher's property had the best views of downtown. Buncher had plenty of experience with industrial development, but no experience with housing and no interest in gaining it. Conversations between Buncher and the URA stalemated. In late September the URA's Jerry Dettore duly transmitted a copy of the draft plan to Jack Buncher for his comments. He did not expect a happy response.[29]

That same month of September 1983, GAI Consultants completed their environmental investigation for the URA. The investigation was limited to the central and northern portions of the island, which the URA controlled. GAI, using subsurface samples and trenching, "did not identify a hazardous waste disposal problem on Herr's Island. However, this result does not preclude the possible uncovering of minor quantities of hazardous materials during the development of the site." These words proved to be prophetic. Concerning the Inland Products property, they said, "A company

The Buncher Company's scrap and repair yard in operation, with Pittsburgh's downtown in the background downriver

representative knew of no hazardous material disposed of on the Island between 1960 and the present." The investigation did not include The Buncher Company's property because it was not under consideration for public acquisition, although in its survey of recent occupants of the island, GAI reported, "A [Buncher] company representative was contacted who was familiar with the Company's operations for the last 12 to 15 years. To the best of his knowledge, no toxic wastes were deposited."[30]

The Redevelopment Plan and the Redevelopment Proposal were completed by October. They called for 200,000 to 600,000 square feet of offices, research and development facilities, or light industry in the central part of the island. Public and private marinas would be built on both sides of the island for at least 200 boats, with services and a small commercial center of shops and restaurants near the terminus of the new bridge. Townhouses and condominiums and a 3-acre public park would go at the downstream tip, and a corporate conference center with 250 guest rooms at the upstream end. A pedestrian trail would encircle the island and cross the back channel to the North Shore.

The Planning Department estimated that the total public cost of developing the island would be just over $8.5 million. The net present value of tax benefits would exceed costs by a factor of 1.28 to 1.65. While this margin was not large, at least it was positive, and it gave the city an economic rationale to proceed with the plan. The Planning Department estimated that the plan would bring between 1,000 and 1,200 jobs to the island.[31]

The Buncher Problem – 1983–1985

While the rationale behind the plan seemed good, it did not address the problem of the mismatch between Jack Buncher's experience and interest in industrial development and the new plan's call for housing on his property. Buncher had agreed to develop in accordance with the previously adopted, industrial, plan. He had not anticipated an altered plan that called for housing, and he did not like it. He put the city in a bind, because if city council failed to adopt the new plan by the end of the year—just two months away—the URA's agreement with The Buncher Company to relocate its business from the island and for Buncher to develop his property in accord with the redevelopment plan would be void.[32]

City council met to review the new plan on November 17. According to the report of the meeting there was considerable discussion of the Buncher problem:

> Director [Paul] Brophy: [W]e are in discussions with the Buncher Corporation [regarding] a land swap so that the area ... which is owned by Buncher which is on that part of the island which the plan calls for residential would be moved so that we would own that and the Buncher Corporation would become owner of the middle piece of the island which is earmarked for industrial use. Those discussions are underway and they are far from concluded[,] however, but we are working under the assumption that we can arrive at an amicable understanding here so that our powers of condemnation would not be required for the Buncher properties, but rather we do an equitable transfer.

> Mr. Chairman [Robert Rade Stone]: Buncher in fairness has contributed to the city in its efforts, but if he decides here to get maximum dollar, it has blown our whole program. It would appear to me that we just can't let him run free; he's got to be working with the project[,] or else we are better to condemn them now and have full control of the island.

> Mr. [James] O'Malley: I think what Councilman Stone is saying is we work well with Jack Buncher and we expect Jack to work well with us.

22

On that hope, city council approved the plan and proposal on December 5 and required the URA to submit monthly reports of progress on the project.

By the end of 1983, the URA owned all property on the island except for The Buncher Company's 9.9-acre railroad salvage yard. Although Inland Products was still operating its rendering plant, it had agreed to cease operations by August and to relocate by November.

In his first report to City Council on February 1, 1984, Paul Brophy reported that The Buncher Company appeared to be in no hurry to complete a land swap.[33] Over a year later the Buncher problem was still not resolved. The URA expected to open bids March 22, 1985, for construction of the bridge and ramps. However, the URA did not own all the land to construct the bridge; it still needed a parcel owned by the recalcitrant Buncher. Although negotiations continued, the URA was stymied until it owned the land.

In April 1984, in a long and provocative article titled "A dream?: $5.2 million, decade later, Herr's still fantasy island," the *Pittsburgh Press* taunted: "A four-lane highway stretching about a quarter-mile between a junk-filled yard and a newly leveled lot is the only visible testament to more than $5.2 million in public funds and a decade of planning and re-planning that have been devoted to Herr's Island." The article reported growing dissatisfaction among members of the city council and quoted State Representative Tom Murphy's charge that "the delay reflects the URA's antiquated approach to development, at best, and the agency's muddled management, at worst."

Herr's Island, looking upstream, with Buncher's scrap and repair facility in the foreground and the new spine road stretching behind, under the 31st Street Bridge, with connections to the old 30th Street and Walker Bridges

The article went on to detail some of the challenges the URA had confronted and those it still needed to surmount to move the project along: the need to maintain the old bridge while raising funds for a new bridge, the higher-than-expected cost of consulting engineers, possible competition from a proposed conference center near the airport, traffic problems on Route 28 that limited industrial development, and sunken barges that would have to be removed.

Above all was the issue of Jack Buncher's ownership of the land for the planned marina and housing. Paul Brophy was hopeful of a swap. North Side interests, including Representative Murphy, thought that the URA should buy Buncher out. Murphy felt that "Herr's Island and the J&L property are two jewels in terms of the city's rebirth and should be used for a higher level of development." Buncher's position, however, was "We have no thought of being bought out. We plan to work with the URA and anyone else involved in developing Herr's Island," and Paul Brophy concurred: "It doesn't make sense to try and buy out a developer who already has expressed an interest on the island. We are trying to develop this island with a minimum expenditure of public funds." That being said, the URA had failed to negotiate a swap.[34]

In the meantime, City Planning and the URA engaged the Harlan Company, which had assisted in preparing the redevelopment plan, to undertake a market analysis and develop a marketing plan for the proposed conference center. Marketing of the conference center and a feasibility study of the market-rate housing, Paul Brophy explained to the URA's board in May, could occupy the year it would take to complete the new bridge. The bridge would be finished in 1986, the business park could begin development in the latter part of 1986 or early 1987, construction of the conference center, if feasible, in the first half of 1987, and the housing in 1987 or 1988.[35]

The new bridge under construction, seen from the Herr's Island side, with the old 30th Street Bridge behind

Assuming that the matter with Buncher would be settled by July, the URA ordered Crown Union, Inc., to begin construction of the bridge. The URA estimated that the cost of the bridge would be up to $4.6 million, including an assumed value of land that would still have to be purchased from Buncher.

Members of city council were growing increasingly frustrated with the delays. They wanted progress now, regardless of the problems. In approving a routine contract between the city and the URA in August, they added language requiring that "the Urban Redevelopment Authority shall develop a process and procedure to select a developer or developers for Herr's Island within 60 days of the approval of this Resolution by city council and the Mayor." Paul Brophy explained why the URA could not do what the Council had ordered: the URA did not own all the property needed to construct the bridge, the URA did not own The Buncher Company's property, and "it is beyond the URA's power to determine at present how the high-density downstream end of the island is to be developed. The developer is the Buncher Company, but the Buncher Company has no development plan." There would be no progress in resolving the impasse for another year.

The new spine road in 1985, looking north under the 31st Street Bridge

The same scene twenty years later, in 2005

A Development Partnership – 1986

By early 1986, city officials had concluded, based on the Harlan Company's work, that the market would not support development of a conference center. They decided to seek a single-tenant corporate office instead. In April, I became director of the URA's Economic Development Department.

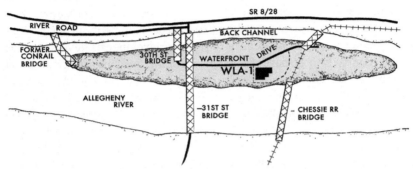

Washington's Landing Associates' first building

That summer a new factor in the development of the island came into play. North Side Civic Development Council's president, Tom Cox, and his assistant, Mark Schneider, proposed taking a role in developing Herr's Island's commercial and industrial properties through their new North Side Industrial Development Company.[36] The Council wanted to lay claim to Herr's Island for the North Side and to find ways to benefit financially from its development. The URA's top leadership wanted to have this influential community-based organization in its corner as development of the island proceeded.

Accordingly, at its June board meeting the URA approved a three-year contract with the council to market the island for light manufacturing, research and development, and office uses and to construct two buildings for lease. The council anticipated beginning construction of its first building by the end of the year. They introduced an unexpected partner, developer Dick Rubinoff.[37] Their choice of Dick Rubinoff was interesting, to say the least. Dick was the former son-in-law of Jack Buncher. In fact, Rubinoff had been with The Buncher Company at the time the URA had decided not to acquire Buncher's land on the island, based on Buncher's interest in participating in the redevelopment. However, after an acrimonious divorce and subsequent estrangement from his former father-in-law, Rubinoff had established his own competing industrial real estate development company.

Now a family feud escalated tensions and deepened Buncher's resistance. In September the North Side Industrial Development Company asked the City Planning Commission to rezone 27 acres of the central portion of the island for its development, and Buncher raised objections, arguing that the planned rezoning might affect development of Buncher's property on the southern end of the island.[38]

In a long letter to Paul Brophy, Jack Buncher offered both to swap the housing site he owned and could not develop for the industrial site that North Side wanted, and to develop the industrial site in partnership with North Side Civic Development Council. He offered to submit a development plan for one or two buildings within ninety days.[39] The following day The Buncher Company again asked the Planning Commission, without success, to delay the change in zoning. Given the URA's relationship with the Civic Development Council and the Council's relationship with Dick Rubinoff, the time for negotiating a simple swap of land between Buncher and the URA had vanished.[40] However, although Buncher's calculated delay had not worked out as he planned, he was still in control of the land needed to construct the bridge.

Then late in that year, a resolution was reached, only because the URA agreed to one of three things: Buncher would develop housing (unlikely, at best), or the city would rezone Buncher's property for office development (which City Planning would never agree to), or the URA would buy Buncher's property (increasingly likely, and costly, without doubt). In exchange, Buncher would agree to the rezoning of the central part of the island for office and industrial uses and would allow construction of the bridge to proceed. The November 25 negotiating session, in which the parties reached and signed this agreement (with much relief and some fanfare), was protracted and difficult. Ironically, the principal spokesman for The Buncher Company in these negotiations was Michael Rubinoff, vice president of The Buncher Company, Jack Buncher's grandson and heir-apparent, and Dick Rubinoff's son. Buncher himself did not attend. The meeting began in the morning, and a document was not signed until late in the day.

The URA's board meeting on December 11 confirmed these agreements, and finally the development of Herr's Island seemed to be ready to move forward. Symbolic of this hopeful moment, Jack Robin announced that the development would henceforth be known as "Washington's Landing," a reference to General Washington's having taken refuge on an island (somewhere in the vicinity of Herr's Island) when he crossed the Allegheny River during the French and Indian War. The board ratified the agreement that its new executive director, Ray Christman, had signed with Buncher and the North Side Civic Development Council, and it approved the council's proposed marketing plan and associated budget of $325,000 for the three years of its marketing contract. Further, Buncher and the URA announced their intention to enter into an option agreement that would convey a portion of Buncher's property, at its appraised value, to the URA for development of the marina and town center as soon as an appraisal could be completed.[41] With the URA's finally working out an agreement with Buncher, city council approved the necessary rezoning for the first phase of development.

Shortly after, the Howard Heinz Endowment, in a dramatic show of support for the development, made an unprecedented loan of $500,000 to the North Side Civic Development Council to help finance its first commercial building on the island. Construction was to begin in the first quarter of the next year, with occupancy scheduled before the year's end.

Development Underway, with Obstacles – 1987

In January 1987 the URA engaged a consultant to develop a housing marketing strategy for Buncher's property. RPR Economic Consultants' draft report, delivered in April, concluded that "residential development at Washington's Landing will be a pioneering effort. However, the lack of quality competitive sites in the city, the ability to offer a waterfront setting, and the security that could be offered at this isolated location should overcome that condition." RPR recommended that "residential development should tie directly into the marina." In short, housing was not impossible, but neither would it be easy. The plan called for housing, but it would be challenging to develop, and Buncher was still not interested. In February the URA approved the land lease for the first building on the island. Washington's Landing Associates—the joint venture of North Side Civic Development Council and the Rubinoff Company—leased 3.6 acres to construct a 45,000-square-foot flex-building with ninety-six surface parking places.[42]

During the summer of 1987 the URA took steps to address the problems in marketing the island. Despite the new bridge, access to the island was problematic because the only roads to get there, Route 8/28 and the 31st Street Bridge, were heavily congested, especially at rush hour. The URA commissioned GAI to determine whether improvements were possible. GAI concluded that significantly improving access to the island would be too costly to be considered seriously. The best the URA could do was to design and install new traffic lights at East Ohio Street, River Avenue, and the new bridge.[43] Another impediment to development was the cluster of fifty sunken and abandoned barges off the island's downstream end on city property on the North Shore bank. The URA authorized the Army Corps of Engineers to remove them, but first undertook to learn who owned the barges and then try to get the owners to remove them.[44]

Sunken barges off the downstream tip of Herr's Island, with downtown Pittsburgh in the left background

With development proceeding on the industrial part of the island, the URA wanted badly to move forward on the housing and marina. Having exhausted its efforts to get The Buncher Company to develop housing, the URA finally agreed to acquire Buncher's property, all 9.9 acres with the rail-car repair plant. With the URA over a barrel, Buncher negotiated a price of $2,691,086, or about $6.24 per square foot, almost five times the price the URA was getting for land in the central part of the island. On top of that, the URA agreed to pay up to $500,000 to relocate Buncher's rail-car business. In addition, Buncher got the option until the end of 1996 to develop two of the industrial parcels in the center of the island. (If Dick Rubinoff was going to have an option to develop two parcels, Jack Buncher wanted the same, no less.[45]) Before the end of the year, the URA applied for grants totaling $2.7 million—with half from the state's Department of Commerce and half from the Appalachian Regional Commission—to finance the purchase of Buncher's land.[46] Ground breaking for Washington's Landing Associates' first building, 44,500 square feet suitable for one to ten office or light industrial tenants, took place October 23.

29

Late in the year the URA issued a request for proposals to develop a marina for 200 boats and a town center, including a restaurant and other retail facilities. The URA expected the marina to "pave the way for the housing and park development, with selection of the marina developer in early 1988 and construction of the marina to begin in early 1989." The request for proposals anticipated that private investment on the island would reach $106 million and employment 1,300, with new city tax revenues to be in excess of $1.5 million annually. Concurrently, the URA engaged Environmental Planning and Design to create a master plan for the lower end of the island in preparation for the zoning approval that would be needed before development of the marina and housing could occur.[47]

At their first meeting of 1988 the URA's board saw a scale model of a proposed streetscape for the developing central portion of the island, including arbors, sidewalks, and street trees. Designed by architect Peter Bohlin, the plan had the support of the URA's staff and North Side Civic Development Council, whose property was directly affected. The board agreed to proceed with construction.[48]

PCBs – 1988

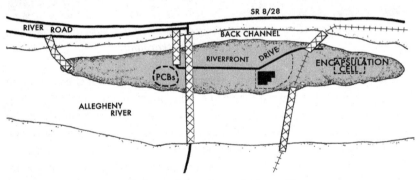

PCBs and the encapsulation cell

As the URA moved forward to complete its purchase of The Buncher Company's property, David Donahoe, the Authority's new executive director, made the decision to have the property tested for any possible environmental contamination. Although the URA had previously performed environmental tests on other parts of the island, the tests had not included Buncher's property, since it was not in the URA's hands. David Donahoe recalled the circumstances leading to that decision:

My recollection of it is that either in an anonymous correspondence or in a phone call from somebody, I was alerted to the fact that The Buncher Company had used a lot of the site as a direct dump. In other words, stuff was just poured out the window.... That's when I began asking questions which I had not asked at that point since I assumed that this was all done. But I said, are we sure about the environmental?... That's my recollection, that I got this information surreptitiously. I did follow it up just to make sure and was surprised by the answer.[49]

The URA engaged ICF Kaiser Engineers to perform an environmental assessment, which consisted of testing a limited number of soil and groundwater samples. To the URA's shock, ICF found that the site was contaminated with heavy concentrations of two known carcinogens, PCBs (polychlorinated biphenyls) and PAHs (polynuclear aromatic hydrocarbons).[50] While the PAHs were an understandable byproduct of the operation of the railroad and rail-car facility, the presence of PCBs was altogether unexpected and far more serious. These liquid compounds were used as cooling agents in electrical transformers and related equipment, but how they got on the island was unclear. David Donahoe remembered the day Jerry Dettore walked into his office to tell him about the discovery. "I remember the look on his face. It was not a mission that he wanted to perform."[51]

The discovery of contamination created a terrible dilemma for the URA and raised many questions. Was contamination limited to Buncher's property, or was it more widespread? How extensive was it on Buncher's property? Should the URA proceed to acquire Buncher's property or leave Buncher with the liability? If the URA backed away from the purchase, would Buncher remove the contaminated soil and develop the property, or simply fence it off and leave it undeveloped? If that were to happen, would tenants be willing to lease space anywhere on the island? Would anyone be interested in developing the remainder of the island? Would investors finance their developments? If, on the other hand, the URA were to purchase the contaminated property, what costs and liabilities would the Authority incur? Even if the contaminated soil were removed, could that site ever be developed? Moreover, could it be developed for housing? Clearly, the URA "had to develop quickly a strategy for saving the project," but the existing plan might have to change considerably.[52]

The fact that development was already underway on the island was a complicating factor. Steel was going up for the office building. How would Rubinoff respond to the discovery of the contamination? David Donahoe remembered the scene well even years later:

> Dick Rubinoff ... came into my office and Joe Gariti and I were there
> and we had to break this news to him. He had already put out
> considerable money and so his first reaction was to ask to be
> excused. ... We told [him] and he said, "Look, I need to be excused."
> And he left the room, for the men's room, I suppose. We didn't know
> whether to follow him or what was going to happen. He eventually,
> of course, came back. It was about 15 minutes before he entered the
> room, and we were thinking about going down. I think I didn't, but
> Joe might have gone in just to make sure he was all right and, anyhow,
> he came back. He just excused himself and he said, "What does this
> mean? What are you going to do?"[53]

Rubinoff and his partners were adamant that the URA should proceed
to buy the property. Buncher's property, or at least an easement across it,
was necessary to bring utility lines from the 31st Street Bridge to their
construction site and ultimately to serve the finished office building. At the
same time, they expressed grave concerns about the possibility of
undiscovered contamination on their own site. Since there were no answers,
the discovery of the PCBs brought all work on the island to a halt, and the
steel framework of the building sat untouched for months.

Washington's Landing Associates' first building, with construction brought to a
halt by the discovery of contamination on Buncher's property

The URA called a special board meeting in late April for the sole purpose of announcing the "discovery of unsafe levels of hydrocarbons and biphenyls, including PCBs, in soil samples taken from approximately three acres of the Buncher property at the southern end of the island." The URA estimated that containment or cleanup could cost anywhere from $100,000 to nearly $3 million dollars, quite a range. Had the URA completed the purchase as initially planned, the agency would have been liable for the entire cleanup. Now the URA could try to renegotiate with Buncher after it had a better estimate of the costs. The URA decided to proceed with the purchase—believing that the remainder of the island could not be effectively developed if the "toxic waste" were not contained or removed—but renegotiate the price.[54] The board authorized additional tests of the Buncher property. SRW, Inc., agreed to move a laboratory onto the site to speed up the process of analyzing samples as they were taken and to deliver a report to the board in early July. In the meantime, since development was already underway and the URA's acquisition of Buncher's property would now clearly be delayed, the board authorized the executive director to obtain easements through Buncher's property to get utilities to the properties upstream.[55]

Choice of the date for the special board meeting was not entirely arbitrary. David Donahoe remembered

We decided to make this a story on [a primary] Election Day so that it would not become the lead story of the day. If we told a reporter on Election Day, the lead story the next day was going to be the election. We wanted to make it public, but we wanted to do it in a way that wouldn't blow the project away.[56]

Still, the story appeared on page one of the *Pittsburgh Post-Gazette*, under the headline, "Toxic waste found on river island."[57]

One outcome of the newspaper coverage was an alarm sounded by the DER. Three days after the URA's announcement, Jerry Dettore received a call from an inspector in the Bureau of Waste Management whose supervisor had asked him "to investigate the situation on Herr's Island." Jerry reported, "I explained our 1983 program, our 1988 work with GAI, and our ICF/SRW work.... [The inspector] stated that due to the level of PCBs in excess of 50, EPA will likely get involved in the process." It was an odd call, given the extent of DER's previous involvement, and a daunting, if inaccurate, prediction.[58]

The publicity also prompted another significant call to the URA. A former Buncher employee had seen the articles and called to report that electrical transformers had come to Buncher's scrap operation on the island beginning in 1974. They were stored in the open yard, and the internal oils (which contained the PCBs) were dumped on the ground. The transformers were then moved by crane to another area for disassembly for scrap. Most of that operation had decreased in 1980, when refurbishment of rail cars began, but even after that, the operation continued to some extent in the open yard.[59]

With this information the URA debated whether a case existed against The Buncher Company: whether they might have violated environmental laws for which they could now be held liable. Consultation with outside environmental counsel quickly convinced the URA that it would be difficult and probably fruitless to pursue a suit. A suit would be problematic, since Buncher had ceased its operations with the transformers at about the time that regulation of the disposal of PCBs first began. Besides, pursuing a legal remedy would inevitably throw the development into a state of uncertainty for months or years. URA officials decided to avoid becoming distracted from pursuing the principal objective of redeveloping the island.

The Buncher Company, meanwhile, minimized the significance of the problem. Tom Balistrieri of Buncher even suggested that the URA simply dispense with the problem by bringing in 3 feet of topsoil to cover the contaminated area. The URA's Joe Gariti wryly responded that "this would not be acceptable because of the requirement that the PCBs be removed from the premises."[60]

David Donahoe observed

> The Buncher Company's success has been because they, either accidentally or with amazing foresight, I don't know which it is, buy land that eventually people have to have. They need it for something they want to accomplish, and you can just go around the city and figure out where that is, and obviously the acquisition of their property on this island was critical. And they're prepared to hold on to it until you do what they want you to do.... You think, well why'd you pay for it at all? Their allegation is ... that they had not caused the damage and therefore should not be held liable for the damage, and if you wanted this property that's what you would have to do. And ultimately the URA did pay for the property. Ultimately you have to decide, okay, well what are we trying to do here? We just had to decide how valuable it was to the development and reach a price. They're a real estate development company; they

are not a civic player; they're not involved in the civic community. Their interest is in return on their real estate investment, period.[61]

The Buncher Company also steadfastly continued to refuse to allow the URA or Dick Rubinoff access across their property to bring utility lines from the 31st Street Bridge to serve the northern portion of the island. They would not budge even after Chairman Jack Robin wrote to his former grade-school friend Jack Buncher to request his reconsideration.[62] The old boy network had failed.

David Donahoe ascribed the following motives to Buncher:

> There was always in the back of my mind, that Buncher would have been happy if we'd have just turned the whole thing over to him and said, "Okay now, you develop it or do something with it." In which case we would have had some aluminum warehouses, that's what Herr's Island would be . . . instead of this . . . kind of yuppie housing, rowing . . . and so I think that was just kind of, "Okay, you want to do that? You're going to pay for it, and I'm not going to make it easy." . . . They were going to get their pound of flesh out of them.[63]

The URA engaged ICF Kaiser to test the rest of the island to explore whether there were PCBs elsewhere. Fortunately, none were found. The URA also asked them to explore the extent of the contamination on Buncher's property and sent the resulting report to the DER's Pittsburgh office, along with ICF's thoughts about paving over the contaminated soil in lieu of removing it. ICF recommended "consolidation of the contaminated soil in an already contaminated area which would then be paved for roads, tennis courts, etc.," ideas that had already been explored in a meeting with the DER.[64]

A response took two months. Although the state had no existing cleanup standard for soils contaminated with PCBs, the DER said they would require cleanup to the high standard of 2 parts per million (ppm). Further, the DER indicated, "As the Department's mandate is to protect current and future generations, Central Office has indicated that removal of the contamination rather than containment would be necessary in order to guarantee that exposure to such wastes be reduced permanently."[65]

Finally, a Positive Development: A Rowing Center – 1988

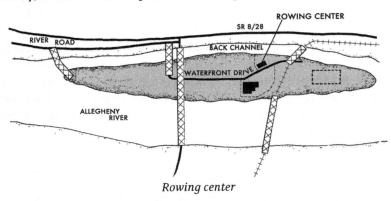

Rowing center

In the midst of this problematic period, Michael Lambert, director of the new Three Rivers Rowing Association, called me. The association was looking for a site to build a boathouse and rowing center. They were familiar with Herr's Island because they had used an abandoned mooring cell at the island's northern end as a starting point for races in their new annual Head of the Ohio regatta. The back channel would be an ideal location for a boathouse because it offered protection from weather and powerboats for launching the delicate rowing shells. The ideal site was also far enough away from Buncher's contaminated site to be safe. I immediately recognized the value of putting a rowing center on the island. Where toxic contaminants suggested sickness and danger, a rowing center would suggest health and youth. It would promote recreational use of the waterfront. A rowing center would also bring many people onto the island, serve as a marketing tool, and help overcome any stigma or fear of the contamination, which was localized and regardless would have to be thoroughly corrected.

David Donahoe was initially skeptical. He was understandably focused on the PCB crisis. In addition, a nonprofit organization like the rowing center would not pay property taxes. In addition, introducing it would require yet another amendment to the plan, since the entire central portion of the island, where the Rowing Association wanted to build, was zoned for office and industrial use. My idea was to designate the rowing center as a piece of the public park that the URA had promised the state. Although it would not be in the exact location of Inland Products, it might still satisfy the state's intent. Furthermore, if the city retained ownership of the land under the rowing center and leased it to the Rowing Association, it would cut the center's cost and hasten its construction. Thus persuaded, Donahoe became more open to the idea and eventually agreed.

In September 1989 the URA approved a cooperation agreement with the city to accept land for the rowing center to lease to the Rowing Association. In exchange for the lease the Rowing Association agreed to undertake a public rowing program. The proposed boathouse would consist of 14,000 square feet on two levels, with four bays for storage of boats: one each for Carnegie Mellon University; Duquesne University; the University of Pittsburgh; and the Rowing Association, with its 100 members.[66] The following month the URA approved the final plans, drawings and confirmation of financing, allowing construction of the rowing center to proceed.[67]

How to Dispose of PCBs – 1988–1989

In the meantime, ICF Kaiser was conducting more extensive tests of Buncher's property to determine the extent of the contamination and to develop alternative cleanup plans and cost estimates. By early October they had found that levels of PCBs were predominantly less than 50 ppm, which put the site under DER's (rather than EPA's) jurisdiction. The contamination was isolated to approximately 3 acres of the land that was slated for residential use. There was no evidence that the contamination was being released into the river or into groundwater. PAHs were scattered throughout the area, but in relatively low concentrations. Removing the soil with the PCBs would also eliminate the PAHs.[68] ICF explored two cleanup strategies.

One strategy would entail removing the contaminated soil from the island and disposing of it in the nearest landfill that would accept such material—in Louisiana. This option had a number of serious drawbacks. It would involve transporting the soil by rail a great distance, with all the attendant liability and publicity. It would also give the URA long-term liability. Since federal law assigned full and several liability to any polluter of a site, and since, in the government's view, the URA would become a polluter of any site where the waste was taken, the URA theoretically would be liable for cleanup of whatever dump accepted the waste, yet it would have no control over how that site was managed. Finally, moving and storing the waste off the island could cost up to $6 million.

The other option would entail constructing an engineered disposal cell on the island itself. The continued presence of the contaminated soil on the island held the risk of dampening enthusiasm for development there but would place the contamination where the URA could control its future liability. In addition, the estimated cost was much lower: $1 to $2 million.

Under either option, the URA, by excavating the contaminated soil, would become a "generator" of pollution and therefore liable for proper disposal of the "generated" (i.e., excavated) contamination. The URA decided to try, with ICF Kaiser's help, to sell the idea of constructing a disposal cell on the island to one arm of the state (the DER), while approaching other arms of the state (the departments of Commerce and Community Affairs) to finance the cleanup.

Buncher's idled facility, fenced off to prevent contact with the PCB-contaminated soil

New problems multiplied almost immediately. In a conversation with DER's Chuck Duritsa in late November, ICF's Jim Nairn learned that the DER defined on-site disposal as disposal on the very location of the contamination, and it said that removing the contaminated soil to, say, the River Avenue site across the narrow lower back channel, would require a permit. Obtaining a permit would result in a long and public process. At the same time, regulations that the DER was promulgating for disposal of residual wastes such as soil with the PCBs would require disposal above the level of the 100-year floodplain, eliminating the Buncher site itself. In a subsequent conversation with Chuck Duritsa and Tony Orlando, however, Nairn was encouraged to learn that the DER would consider any location on the island itself as contiguous to the contaminated area and would not require a permit, even though removal from the island across the narrow back channel would require one. A solution appeared possible.

David Donahoe attributed this softening attitude to intervention from the state's Secretary of Commerce, Ray Christman, who had previously led the URA, and from his friend Art Davis, Secretary of the DER: "I think the encapsulation solution forced the normal career people out of the box, and I don't think they would have done that unless they were told, Get out of the box. That isn't the same as saying, Do something wrong; do something that violates. It's just, let's take a hard look at this, because, remember, the state had an enormous investment in this site."[69]

However, Chuck Duritsa, who headed DER's Pittsburgh Regional Office at the time, disagreed. He recalled the matter differently and did not believe that Christman's personal friendship caused the unusual and creative problem-solving.

> Art was my boss, and I know Ray Christman fairly well, also. That was not the case. We had historically worked with sites, mostly on active sites with active industries, and worked through the cleanup they needed. So this was just kind of a variant to what we had been doing, for myself, for over 20 years. So we were quite willing to work with the URA to find an avenue where they could manage the waste on site. So my recollection is it was something that we decided, in shop, in Pittsburgh, as a way to help move the process forward.

> When they said to get out of the box, the building of the landfill requires a permit under the Solid Waste Management Act. That landfill, that's now under the tennis courts, legally should have had a permit. We didn't do that. We used an instrument, a consent agreement, to allow that to happen. So we were bending, quite frankly we were bending a lot, to get this done. But it was done and it was done properly. It was constructed to meet all the standards that the landfill had to meet. But it was something we were comfortable with doing because it moved the project along.

> Art Davis quite frankly was one of the secretaries who was not the type to put pressure on you. So I don't recall it that way at all.[70]

During this generally bleak period, one other hopeful sign of progress in the island's redevelopment was the groundbreaking for the rowing center, which took place on January 13, 1989. Despite the cold, wet weather, the event was well attended. Rowing supporters from throughout the region came to celebrate this beginning of a promising new chapter for the sport of rowing in Pittsburgh.[71]

Early in 1989 the URA began to renegotiate the terms of its acquisition of Buncher's property and budget for disposal of the contaminated soil. After investigation, ICF Kaiser estimated that the cost of disposal on the island would be $820,000, less than originally estimated. On the other hand, estimates of the cost of disposal off the site had climbed to between $6 million and $8 million.[72] ICF presented the URA's proposal to the DER on February 14, and on March 1 DER's Tony Orlando wrote to the URA granting conceptual approval, with final approval contingent on submission and approval of more specific plans.[73]

On March 9 the URA's board promptly approved the new terms for purchasing Buncher's property and approved the plan to dispose of the contaminated soil on the island. Under the new agreement the URA would pay $2.77 million for the site (down from $3.2 million), effectively splitting with Buncher the projected cost of cleaning up the site, now estimated to be $850,000. Buncher would receive credit for this reduction on his projected future purchases of the two parcels in the central portion of the island.

Despite the unforeseen increase in the project's cost, money was being saved because, as Donohoe commented, the DER had agreed to a "completely safe and more cost effective solution," that is, encapsulation. Donohoe explained, "[that] was a very difficult and time-consuming effort; however, it was both instructive in terms of dealing with old industrial land in the future as well as constructive, in terms of understanding that hazardous waste is a fact of life and can be dealt with logically and that the existence of waste products should not deter people from development on older industrial sites."[74]

The URA immediately contracted with ICF Kaiser to prepare project specifications and construction drawings for the proposed soil encapsulation cell, together with guidelines for the excavation and confirmatory testing of the contaminated soil. The costs rose again: Kaiser's services alone would cost $250,000.[75]

The encapsulation cell, or landfill, would have to be placed at the island's northern end, where the city's former ash dump had created a large hill. This location was the only one high enough such that a hole for the cell could be excavated and still be above the 100-year floodplain. The URA proposed to amend the redevelopment plan to relocate the main public park here, atop the encapsulation cell. This amendment would have the advantages of protecting the cell, of conserving land on the lower part of the island (where the park had originally been planned) for other uses, and of complementing the adjacent rowing center. The placement would still allow development of a single office or industrial building north of the Chessie System's rail line, in accordance with the plan. The URA explored various recreational uses for the park and settled on a tennis complex as the most advantageous.

At the same time as the URA was managing these problems on the island, it was moving forward with other aspects of the development. July saw dramatic, visible progress on many fronts. The URA had the old scrapyard across the back channel on the North Shore demolished and cleaned up over the summer, in the process removing an underground storage tank. In its June meeting the URA's board authorized a request for qualifications from developers for the housing, marina, and town center and appointed a prestigious committee to review the submissions. The request went out in late July, supported by local and national ads, including in the *Wall Street Journal* and various engineering and construction periodicals.

Also in July, as the URA and DER negotiated over disposal of the contaminated soil, Governor Robert P. Casey visited the island to present the city with a grant of $3 million from Community Affairs' Housing and Redevelopment Program. The money was to help finance improvement of the riverfront and development of the public park that would cover the encapsulation, an indirect means of paying for disposal of the contaminated soil. Meanwhile, the URA extended the North Side Civic Development Council's marketing contract for the island for another year, to October 1990, a move necessitated by the delay caused by discovery and disposal of the contaminants. This was not a propitious time to be marketing the island.[76]

The same month of July, ICF (now named ICF Technology, Inc.) submitted specifications for the soil encapsulation cell to the DER.[77] On July 31 the URA and DER agreed on the plan to encapsulate the contaminated soil on the northern end of the island. On August 18, less than a month later, the DER's Tony Orlando wrote to the URA approving the construction details with only minor comments and a request for additional drawings.[78] With the DER's approval the URA could engage Environmental Planning and Design to draw up the new master plan and a detailed development plan for the northern end of the island. It also authorized bidding and award of a contract to build the encapsulation cell and secure the contaminated soil in it. Construction was expected to begin October 1, with the project to be completed by the end of the year.[79]

In the meantime, the rowing center was nearing completion. Work had not resumed on the office building, however. Its developer was waiting to assess the impact of the contamination on his project. To this point the URA had spent $15.6 million in public funds on the island, and another $9.3 million was committed. Yet little of the immense effort and expense had yet paid off.

Given the DER's concerns for safety and environmental protection and the URA's concerns for liability and marketing, both agencies were anxious to enter into a binding agreement to resolve these issues. The agencies began working on a consent order and agreement that would accomplish their respective goals.[80] It needed to set forth the URA's obligations to clean up the island and monitor and protect the encapsulated waste and, at the same time, reassure prospective developers that they could purchase and develop property on the island without fear of liability for the island's past environmental problems. The DER drafted the document, which the URA's Jerry Dettore and Joe Gariti then reviewed in late September.

That same month the Three Rivers Rowing Association dedicated its new rowing center, the first completed building on the island, and immediately put it to use at the beginning of October as the hub for that year's Three Rivers Regatta.

Three Rivers Rowing Association's new boathouse, the first building completed on Washington's Landing

Three Rivers Rowing Association's new boathouse, from the back channel side, with the dock to the left

On September 28 the URA awarded the contract for the soil encapsulation cell to Atlas Services Corporation. The contract amount was $994,717, somewhat higher than the URA had estimated.[81] Construction started a month later on October 24, with the removal of vegetation from the northern end of the island, where the cell was to be constructed. That same day, the

URA received submissions from five prospective developers for the lower portion of the island. One of them, Haulover Resort Marina, was interested exclusively in the marina.[82] The committee selected three others—Lincoln Property of Dallas, Parencorp of Massachusetts, and Zeckendorf of New York—to interview later in the year.[83] The developers proposed a range of housing types and styles, some integrated with a marina. However, they all required very high public subsidy because of problems the URA had already encountered on the island and the island's pioneering location. As a result, the URA rejected the housing proposals, deciding instead to try to develop the island first as a destination for work and recreation in the belief that once the island was used for those purposes, housing could follow later on at a lower public cost. With this strategy in mind the URA decided to explore moving forward with Haulover Resort Marina's Pittsburgh partner, Dick Gregory, who had proposed building a marina without any accompanying housing.[84]

At the same time as work was about to begin on the encapsulation cell, the Authority and the DER completed their negotiations on a consent agreement. The agreement would obligate the URA to complete its cleanup of the contaminated site, monitor the disposal site quarterly, and provide for continued monitoring if the site were ever sold.[85]

Consequences of the discovery of contamination continued to accumulate. At the urging of the North Side Civic Development Council, in October the URA agreed to apply for an Enterprise Zone competitive grant to reimburse the Council for $273,702 of additional carrying costs it had incurred because of the resulting delay.[86] In early November the URA presented its revised plan for development of the island's northern end to the City Planning Commission but had a mercifully brief setback when the commission initially refused to approve the plan. The URA had proposed to put a day-care center in the recreational building adjacent to the encapsulation cell. The idea of having a day-care center next to the stored contaminants—sealed though they might be—was more than the Commission could stand.[87] Once the URA had eliminated the center from its proposal, the Commission quickly approved the plan.[88]

Despite this temporary setback, the URA proceeded with the plan to transfer the parcel for the park atop the future encapsulation cell to the city. As planned, the park would include a pedestrian trail, up to twelve tennis courts (five to be built initially, designed so that they could later be covered by a bubble for year-round play), a clubhouse of 800 square feet, a par course, and parking for sixty cars.

Another Shock – 1989–1990

Meanwhile, Atlas Services Corporation began excavating for the encapsulation cell. As they did, they made a second disturbing discovery—greasy material that at first the workers could not identify. Gradually it became apparent that they had discovered partially decayed animal carcasses, apparently buried by Inland Products, the rendering plant that had by now relocated from the adjacent site. Indeed, back in 1983 GAI Consultants had identified rendering wastes in their early investigation, but the URA had removed what was uncovered at that time. Now, the further Atlas dug into the hill, the more animal carcasses they found, including parts of a giraffe, apparently brought from the zoo.

The contractors brought dumpsters onto the island to hold the animal waste until they could assess the extent of the problem. Soon much of the island was covered with dumpsters. Ultimately, every available dumpster in the region was brought to the island and filled with decaying animal parts. The smell was terrible. What could not be placed in dumpsters was placed in a temporary earthen structure lined and covered with plastic sheeting. In a November 16 letter to the DER, ICF reported the discovery and their attempts to manage the emerging problem.[89]

In preparation for the URA's December board meeting, the Authority's new Executive Director, George Whitmer, wrote to the board to alert them to the problem. He described the contractor's unearthing "oily putrid waste" of a "greasy lard-like nature," stopping work and calling in ICF to examine the waste. It would take three to four weeks to get results from a testing laboratory. He explained that the URA had requested DER's permission for excavation and temporary storage to allow the contractor to move forward as quickly as possible, and also explained the discovery that there was much more waste than had originally been thought. Whitmer concluded that while "dealing with unanticipated work items and change orders is normal business in construction management . . . it is not unreasonable to suggest that the extra costs to be borne on the project could approach $500,000." Actually, the URA would have been fortunate had the additional costs been that low. "Unfortunately, what appeared initially to be a small amount of waste product and a manageable contract change order evolved into a major on-site construction operation." In the end the contractor removed 8,350 tons of organic waste, at a cost of over $660,000.

Construction on the encapsulation cell came to a halt while the URA worked to remove the animal waste. The resulting delay breached Atlas's contract and would add a premium to the cost of constructing the cell, an additional unanticipated cost, but there was no alternative. The carcasses had to be disposed of before the cell could be built or soil moved from the Buncher site. A contract that was originally less than $1 million dollars had grown to almost $1.5 million.[90]

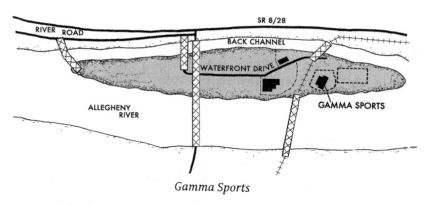

Gamma Sports

On a positive note, despite all the difficulties, the island attracted its first industrial tenant. Gamma Sports, a manufacturer of tennis equipment, decided to build its office and manufacturing facilities directly adjacent to the park and tennis courts and, of course, the containment cell. For this company the presence of the planned tennis courts and the island's other features were attractions that outweighed concerns about possible environmental problems. Gamma was a division of Michigan-based Ferrari Importing Company, Inc., founded by Pittsburgher Harry Ferrari and operated from Penn Hills (although its manufacturing facilities were in Royal Oak, Michigan). The entire operation would be consolidated on Herr's Island. At its January 1990 meeting the URA's board approved the sale of property to Gamma at the price of $2.29 per square foot. Gamma's building would be 36,000 square feet and bring fifty employees to the island. Gamma expected that number to grow to 100 within five years.[91] Bringing Gamma to the island, given the environmental issues, was a tremendous coup.

Other costs kept mounting: costs for engineering services, redesign of the encapsulation cell (due to introduction of the park and tennis complex), more testing because of the animal waste, and discovery of a leaking fuel tank on Buncher's property.[92] The URA also increased Schneider Engineers' testing program across the back channel, where the DER had requested two more monitoring wells and soil sampling. George Whitmer commented, in wry understatement, "Even though the testing program is more extensive than originally envisioned, it is in the Authority's best interest to secure DER's approval of the program."

45

To maintain its progress despite all these distractions, delays, and costs, the URA simultaneously engaged Environmental Planning and Design, which had done the master plan for the northern end of the island, to complete detailed planning and construction documents for the park and tennis complex, and it authorized the staff to advertise for bids and award a construction contract. To help meet the unbudgeted costs of preparing the northern end of the island for development—for Gamma Sports and the park—the URA again turned to the state, applying for, and later receiving, an additional $1 million grant from the Department of Commerce's Industrial Communities' site preparation program.[93]

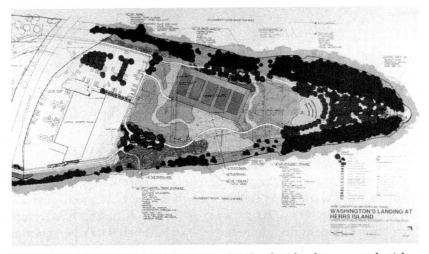

Environmental Planning and Design's plan for the island's upper end, with tennis courts (over the containment cell), amphitheater, woods, and trail

In the meantime, ICF analyzed the animal remains that the contractors had uncovered. They found them to be nonhazardous but still a "special waste" due to their noxious odor. ICF proposed on-site disposal. The DER rejected that proposal on February 20, requiring instead that the material go to a special landfill. Three days later URA and DER officials met to discuss the island's mounting problems. Included among those in attendance were the DER's Gale Campbell and the URA's Jerry Dettore. The meeting was not happy. Jerry's explanation of the circumstances surrounding the unexpected discovery of the animal waste and the dramatic financial impact it had had on the project did not have the desired effect. "Gales states that it may be in the URA's interest to consider that some of its property and the Herr[s] Island site as not being developable due to past usage. Gale . . . states that an investigation should be done prior to the development or purchase of such a property as most large corporations do before committing to a purchase or development." What was Dettore to say? The best he could do was to say that it would never happen again: "Jerry states that the URA has learned its lesson and presently does that prior to any commitment to develop a site. Jerry states that the Herr[s] Island site was purchased in the early 1970s prior to these concerns existing."[94]

Excavating for the containment cell

Laying the containment cell's plastic liner

Completing the containment cell in preparation for filling

Finally, on March 12, after the URA had agreed to remove the rendering waste from the island, construction resumed on the encapsulation cell. Ironically, the next day members of the city council criticized the pace of development at Washington's Island at a public hearing on the rezoning for the encapsulation cell, the park, and Gamma Sports. "There's something seriously wrong that there's nothing happening," Council President Jack Wagner was quoted as saying. "We've been dropping the ball somewhere. We've been putting all kinds of money into this island for years and nothing's happening." Councilman Jim Ferlo concluded, "It's a bad project."

George Whitmer responded by saying that the URA had worked hard to lure developers, but that the toxic waste problem "has created an atmosphere that is not conducive to development. . . . I think there's always a sense of impatience when you don't see buildings being built. Until we get all the environmental problems corrected, we're going to have problems." Whitmer also described the URA's success and good fortune in having found Gamma Sports and lured them to the island in part because they could share use of the tennis complex that would sit atop the encapsulation cell, not to mention attractive public financing.[95]

Although frustrated, later that month city council approved the zoning for the island's upper end. I represented the URA at that meeting. In giving approval, Council President Wagner told me he wanted to see significant development as soon as possible. "Tomorrow isn't soon enough. I'm tired of hearing development is on the horizon. It's about time we get something back for the money spent over there." I did not say, but felt like asking, What more could we do?

Filling the containment cell

Once the containment cell was ready, on April 4, Atlas Services began to excavate the contaminated soil from the Buncher site, transport it by truck, and deposit it in the cell on the other end of the island. Tarps on the trucks prevented the wind from carrying contaminated soil to uncontaminated areas. Decontamination pads at both the northern and southern ends were used to remove soil that had collected on the equipment. Over the next two and a half months Atlas excavated and eventually moved a total of 17,962.69 cubic yards of contaminated material, consisting of all the soil that contained over 2 ppm of PCBs.

Cleanup underway at the Buncher site, April 1990

Then, on April 26, during the removal and relocation of the contaminated soils, ICF, doing routine sampling to guide the excavation, took a sample at another location on the Buncher property and found that it was also contaminated with PCBs above 50 ppm. On examination, the contractors discovered a dozen small capacitors and a small transformer that were leaking PCBs. On May 10 they found still another concentration over 50 ppm.[96]

The new discoveries prompted additional involvement of the regulators. Because of the extremely high concentrations of PCBs around the leaking capacitors, the EPA took jurisdiction, ruling that the most contaminated soil would have to be incinerated, while soils with levels between 50 and 500 ppm would have to be moved to an EPA-approved landfill in Idaho. Since the URA had to wait for the availability of containers approved by the U.S. Department of Transportation to carry the contaminated soil, the last shipment did not leave the island until the end of the year.[97]

Tennis courts, field, and amphitheater over the completed containment cell, 2005, with Gamma Sports and downtown Pittsburgh in the background

Meanwhile, the decaying rendering waste sat in dumpsters all across the upper end of the island waiting for URA to find a landfill willing to accept it. In late April the URA finally received notice that American Waste Services of Youngstown would accept it at its Breitenstein, Ohio, landfill if it contained no infectious agents. Fortunately, none were found, and on May 16 the DER gave the URA its approval to ship the rendering waste to Ohio. Over the next month the waste was deodorized and moved by truck to that landfill, with the last loads leaving the island June 11.[98] That environmental nightmare was finally over.

Visible Progress at Last – 1990

In May the URA sealed the deal with Washington's Landing Marina, Inc., an outgrowth of Jim and Dick Gregory's Haulover Resort Marina that the URA had been working with since the previous fall to develop the marina complex. It would include a full-service marina for 450 boats, with adjacent restaurants and a commercial center, on 4 acres. They proposed to build 175 wet slips, a dry-stack building to house 150 additional boats ("You might call it valet parking for boats," George Whitmer explained), a marina store, a members' lounge, and a repair facility across the back channel on the mainland within a year, in time for the following summer season.[99]

Throughout that spring Atlas Services continued to fill the containment

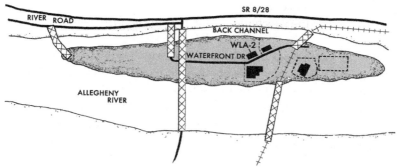

Washington's Landing Associates' second building

the skepticism that had greeted the original proposal for the boathouse, the Association's request for more room met no objection. The boathouse had been a great success. The issue was how to accommodate both expansion of the boathouse and the second building for the DER, since both wanted the same property. The idea occurred to me to build the boat storage bays underneath a portion of the second DER building's parking area, behind the building and along the back channel. While this construction would complicate ownership of the property, it would have important benefits: it would give the Rowing Association the additional space they needed for boat storage, and it would create a level parking lot for Rubinoff's building and solve the problem of the slope down to the back channel. I approached Dick Rubinoff with the idea, and the parties worked out an agreement that enabled both to use the parcel efficiently and that benefited all concerned.[117]

Three Rivers Rowing Association's expanded storage area, under the parking lot of 500 Waterfront Drive, 2005

Chuck Duritsa remembered an interesting incident that occurred as construction on the new building and parking lot proceeded:

> I recall looking out my office window, which looked directly onto the area where they were going to excavate for the foundation. I happened to be looking out the window the minute that a large backhoe started digging one of the first holes in the area. And I recall the backhoe operator jumping off his backhoe rig and running over and looking into the pit he was just constructing. And in fact what they had found I believe was a 10,000-gallon underground storage tank, which had not been found in any of the other environmental evaluations. They uncovered it and what made the matter worse for the people in the rowing club, who just thought the world was going to come to an end, and the other developers, was that my staff—we had just developed an underground storage tank staff—and for a practice, for an educational exercise, the lady who headed up that section took all of her employees across the street to let them watch the tank being uncovered, to see how it was done, what it looked like, which put even more fear into the folks from the rowing club and others.
>
> But as it turned out there, in that instance, I do recall that many phone calls were made to higher-ups, saying, you know, do what you can to work with them, but it never was a big environmental problem. In fact, there was no oil left in it, there was very little residual contamination under it, and quite frankly all it amounted to was removing the tank and a small amount of contaminated soil, but from the other side they thought the world was going to come to an end when they found that tank. But in fact it worked out very, very simply, very easily.[118]

Washington's Landing Associates' first two buildings, 400 and 500 Waterfront Drive, with the boathouse to the left and Gamma Sports behind

500 Waterfront Drive, 2005

Park, Trail, More Development, and "The Smell of Success" – 1993

With the coming of spring and the new construction season, work began in earnest on the site improvements that—finally—would change the entire face of the island. Demolition and clearance of the unsightly Buncher buildings began, and John Zottola Landscaping began construction of the park and of the river trail that would encircle the island, a contract of over $1.1 million.[119] In May 1993 Gamma Sports finished and took possession of its new building—37,000 square feet on 2.45 acres completed at a cost of $2.26 million.

Gamma Sports, 2005

59

Washington's Landing Marina had had a successful first year of operation. Sales had been brisk: 260 boats were docked at the marina, and

Gamma Sports, 2005

Gamma Sports, 2005

Gamma Sports, 2005

there was demand for more slips. In June the URA approved the marina's proposal to add twenty-seven more wet slips; build the ship's store and members' lounge; improve the existing parking lot; and add a second, temporary, lot. Due to its success, the marina had stabilized its financing as well. The owners extended their land lease with the URA from twenty-eight months to twenty years, increased and extended the term of their loan from the URA from twelve years to twenty-five, and leased an additional parcel for the new uses.[120]

Late in the year, on the basis of the success of its first two buildings, the Rubinoff Company proposed and received the URA's approval to build a third building, 30,000 square feet in size, on the parcel adjacent to its first building. Rubinoff planned to begin construction in the spring and to have the building occupied within a year. Although they had no tenant identified for the building, they were now confident about the market for office space on the island.[121]

By March of 1993 the park and trail were nearing completion, and the URA turned its attention to long-term ownership and maintenance. The URA had no interest in managing parkland or maintaining a trail, and they had no resources to do so. Following the precedent that had been established with the parcel for the Rowing Association, the URA turned title to the park, which encompassed some 7.5 acres with five tennis courts, over to the city. The URA decided that it would also convey title to the land over which the trail passed to the owners of the adjacent parcels, with a public easement for the trail. The URA developed a plan and guidelines for, and then created, an association of all property owners on the island—Washington's Landing Association—that would maintain both the park and the trail. The association would use a formula to assess property owners a fair share of the cost of maintenance.[122]

On a beautiful day in early October the URA held a ribbon-cutting ceremony "to mark the official opening of the park and tennis courts and to show off the renewal work complete so far." A feature article announcing the event appeared on page one of the *Pittsburgh Post-Gazette,* carrying the headline "Washington's Landing: The Smell of Success." The article quoted me as saying, "Let this be a lesson to all of us that public real-estate development of old industrial sites isn't easy. We need to be patient."[123] I had worked on Herr's Island for sixteen years. No one looking at Washington's Landing after it was completed would suspect how much patience had been required.

Northern end of Washington's Landing, 1994, the woods, amphitheater, tennis courts, Gamma Sports, and the perimeter trail

Housing – 1993–1994

Tom Murphy was elected mayor of Pittsburgh in November 1993. Before the year's end and before he took office, the URA entered into exclusive negotiations with a partnership of the Rubinoff Company and Montgomery and Rust, the local housing developers who had built Perry Point in the North Side and the Village of Shadyside in the East End. The goal was to determine the feasibility of building between 100 and 130 housing units at the tip of the island, adjacent to the marina.[124]

In July 1994 Mayor Murphy announced that, as part of his larger effort to see 600 new housing units built along the rivers to attract people to live in the city, construction of ninety to one hundred townhouses would begin in the fall, on 7 acres at the downstream end of the island. The first phase would include twelve townhouses. To support the development, the city would invest $2.9 million in road improvements, a park, and continuation of the riverfront trail. Private investment in the one hundred houses was expected to be $17 million. The new houses at Washington's Landing were expected to sell for between $140,000 and $211,000, far above the median $57,600 price of a house in the city or even of the $80,000 median house price in the metropolitan area. Still, realtors felt that the houses, with their riverfront location and proximity to downtown, would sell well.[125] They were right.

Housing, Washington's Landing, 2005

Housing, Washington's Landing, 2005

Housing, Washington's Landing, 2005

In light of all the complications that had slowed the island's development, the timing, scope, and quality of the housing took some of those who had been involved in the island's earlier history by surprise. David Donahoe, who had stepped down as the URA's executive director only five years before, commented

> I thought—it was my absolute belief—that the housing component ... was going to have to be abandoned. ... I didn't think you would ever be able to sell residential property on that island and I think, my recollection is, we actually developed alternate plans, that we would amend the development plan and have it become all commercial or some other use. That ultimately, and this was long after I left, was not the case. They were able to bring, very successfully, housing, although it's high-scale housing; it's become outrageously high-scale housing. My wife just told me the other day that she saw [one] for sale [for] four hundred and some thousand dollars, which surprised me.[126]

Housing on the island—expensive housing, at that—was a vindication of the views of those who, over the years and through many difficulties, had maintained that an island in the city is a singular resource and that a mixed-use development in a park-like island setting, so close to downtown Pittsburgh, but so tranquil and made so lovely, would succeed and would sooner or later be sought after as one of the most distinctive and desirable places to work and live that the city offered. In the end this, in fact, was what occurred at Washington's Landing.

LESSONS

Perhaps the first and most obvious lesson to take from the story of Washington's Landing is that recovering an old industrial site takes time and money—more of both than the average reasonable person would predict. The unexpected is bound to occur. There is simply no way to know what is under the ground short of drilling and testing the entire site. There is no way to anticipate changes in market demands. In addition, the human factor, in the form of diverging interests and concerns—of planning versus development, of the public interest versus the private, of the regulators versus those being regulated—inevitably leads to delay and expense. For Washington's Landing each of these considerations was significant and led to a much more protracted process than any of the actors could have imagined.

A corollary lesson is that elected officials are impatient for progress and have difficulty accepting how long redevelopment takes. They are looking for a ribbon to cut, a success they can trumpet before they face the next election. With Washington's Landing, members of the city council were the most vocal critics. The staff at the URA regularly kept the mayor informed, and the URA published a regular quarterly progress report of its development projects. While this report, together with an occasional tour, seemed to suffice for state legislators, on whom the city relied to support the significant investments the state made in the project, it clearly didn't satisfy the city council. Perhaps there was nothing the URA could have done to make council members happy about the project's fits and starts, though regular briefings might have made them better allies. In the end, despite their bluster, they supported the project when they needed to.

More problematic were the URA's relations with the environmental regulators at the DER. A lesson to be learned here is that regulators are police, not colleagues, and must be expected to act like police. Their job is to keep bad things from happening. They have a responsibility to control and the power to punish. Their role is inherently adversarial. The developers at the URA thought of themselves as good people doing a good work, putting a blighted, unproductive property back into productive use while creating ancillary benefits of public access to the river and enhancing the region's network of walking and biking trails. They expected that other progressive people would laud and support their efforts. Especially they expected this of other public officials, who shared their ethic of public service. However, regulators have a different responsibility. Where the URA was the gas, the DER had the responsibility to be the brakes. Though officials at the DER undoubtedly were as desirous as any others to see the region's abandoned industrial sites restored to usefulness, their role in safeguarding public health demanded conservative action, particularly in light of the prevailing laws and regulations. I will have more to say about this in the concluding chapter of this book. While more, and more frequent, conversations between leaders of the URA and the DER may have helped each better understand the goals and concerns of the other, and may have avoided some of the tense moments and shortened some of the delays, it is unlikely that the eventual outcome would have been much different given the DER's responsibilities and constraints.

What ultimately worked to allay concerns about environmental liability and bring the parties together was the consent agreement between the DER and the URA. The agreement acknowledged the site's environmental legacy; recognized the investigations and cleanup the URA had undertaken to protect public health, as well as its future monitoring responsibilities; and sought to ease the anxiety of future developers about investing in the island. The agreement helped both parties achieve their goals. This lesson learned for Washington's Landing found application again at the Pittsburgh Technology Center and in other parts of the state. Likely every brownfield development will need some instrument of this sort to satisfy its environmental issues.

In the meantime, environmental problems can loom large. The discoveries of PCBs and then of animal waste were enormous shocks. Could the URA have anticipated them? In retrospect the answer is probably yes. After all, once the PCBs were discovered, former Buncher employees explained their source. Employees of Inland Products surely knew of the company's burying animal remains. However, neither the URA nor its consultants did research that identified these contaminants. In the end perhaps the only difference knowing would have made was a better initial price for Buncher's property (though given Buncher's negotiating skills that is by no means certain!). A lesson from this history is to do more thorough historical research beforehand to identify possible environmental problems.

Discovery of the PCBs almost derailed the project. The URA could have chosen to focus (more than it did) on Buncher's liability. Wisely, in retrospect, leadership of the URA set aside the issue of Buncher's negligence and instead stayed focused on developing the island. They rightly went back to Buncher and negotiated a better deal for his property, but they did not allow the environmental problem or Buncher's responsibility for it to distract them from pursuing their goal. They followed the same course when their contractors uncovered Inland Products' deposit of animal waste. Here, too, the URA avoided becoming mired in a legal back-and-forth with the polluter, a discourse in which they may or may not have prevailed. Rather, they pushed ahead, returned to the state for additional support, which the state generously gave, and cleaned up the problem.

The solution to that problem brings another lesson to mind: the value of hiring good professional advisors. The URA's Planning and Engineering Department, headed by Jerry Dettore, an engineer himself, and the RIDC, headed by Brooks Robinson, an architect, hired excellent technical help. It is practically impossible for a public-service agency of the URA's or RIDC's size to have the variety of skills required for the magnitude of a project like Washington's Landing in-house. Getting good outside help is essential. In the case of Washington's Landing the URA worked closely with its contracted engineers. It was Jim Nairn of ICF who came up with the idea of building a containment cell on the island and who sold it to the DER. The Planning

Department, for their part, retained forward-thinking planning and urban design professionals in Jonathan Barnett and the Harlan Group to advise on land use.

Perhaps the most significant lessons to take from Washington's Landing relate to land use. At the beginning of this chapter I suggested that the issue of land use—what the island should become—was perhaps the defining issue of the project. In a way, it is almost miraculous that the island ended up being the beautiful, mixed-use project it did. Several powerful forces were pulling toward industrial and commercial development, a cheaper and much easier alternative. That was RIDC's original plan. It was the premise of the early grant from the Economic Development Administration. It would have addressed very directly the pressing need for jobs at a time when the Pittsburgh region was losing thousands of manufacturing jobs. Jack Buncher was prepared to develop it, and very much wanted to. In fact, not ceding to Buncher's desire stalled the project for years. Almost without question, had the city enlisted RIDC to pursue its original plan, with Jack Buncher's involvement, the island would have been back in productive use years before it was.

However, choosing industrial and commercial development would have been going backward. While almost undoubtedly it would have succeeded, it would have done little to add to Pittsburgh's vibrancy or attractiveness as a place to live or visit: it would not have contributed to what the city was becoming. It also would not have taken advantage in the least of Herr's Island as an island, the only developable island in the city, so close to downtown Pittsburgh and with such spectacular views of the city. In fact, it likely would have had the island cease to be an island, with the back channel filled to add land for development. In addition, full industrial and commercial use would have increased an already difficult problem of access onto and off the island, and, finally, it is likely the environmental contamination would not have been discovered or addressed.

Paul Farmer of City Planning had a different vision for Herr's Island, based on his visits to mixed-use, oceanfront properties on the East Coast and his conviction that quality of life was essential to the future of cities. Though, granted, Pittsburgh was a different market from the East Coast, a much weaker one, Farmer was convinced that similar development could succeed in Pittsburgh. Jonathan Barnett agreed, and the planning director, Bob Lurcott, backed him up. Jack Robin and others, including myself, though intrigued, were skeptical. However, Mayor Caliguiri was swayed. Twenty-five years later the wisdom of the decision to hold out for a mixed-use, river-oriented development is evident in the constant activity in the rowing center, the robust use of the trails, the popularity of the marina, and the high value of the housing, all of which only add to the attractiveness of the island's office uses.

The lesson here is not to choose the most obvious land use reflexively but to weigh options and consider emerging trends and market forces. Forecasting what the site will contribute a generation ahead is probably the correct perspective, despite current pressures. Ideally, the use will be visionary but realistic. All this suggests patience. In fact, as Washington's Landing demonstrates, the market may take time to develop, even when the goal is sound. For example, an additional lesson from Washington's Landing is that housing in a pioneering location like the island is likely not going to work, without large subsidies, until surrounding amenities (like the park, the trails, and the marina) are first in place.

Finally, once the goal is clear, it pays to be alert and opportunistic in working toward it. Taking advantage of Three Rivers Rowing Association's interest in the island, though unexpected and though initially the proposal seemed a bit wild, advanced the city's purposes tremendously. Likewise, George Whitmer's dogged pursuit of the DER, once he became aware of their interest in new office space, was brilliant. Their presence on the island said louder than words, this place is safe. The partnership that allowed the Rowing Association to expand into space under Washington's Landing Associates' second building was another creative and opportunistic solution that advanced the city's development goals for the island.

Housing, Washington's Landing, 2005

J&L's Pittsburgh Works, with the site of the Pittsburgh Technology Center in the foreground, west of the Hot Metal Bridge

PITTSBURGH TECHNOLOGY CENTER TIMELINE

1900–1905   Jones and Laughlin (J&L) merge and expand steel operations on both sides of the Monongahela River.

1974   LTV Corporation purchases J&L Steel.

1981   LTV closes the Pittsburgh Works. Park Corporation purchases the property.

1983   Park sells the site to the URA with an agreement to demolish and scrap the mill buildings.

1984   As demolition proceeds, URA brings fill to cover the old foundations. An Urban Land Institute panel recommends RIDC as the developer of a center for advanced technology firms.

1985   The City Planning Commission designates the site as a redevelopment area and approves a master plan for a center for research and advanced technology. The University of Pittsburgh (Pitt) and Carnegie Mellon University (CMU) express interest in developing portions of the site. A phase 1 environmental study identifies no concerns.

1986   URA gives RIDC the right to purchase or lease the property and names the project the Pittsburgh Technology Center. Construction of improvements begins.

1987   The universities negotiate a role in developing most of the site, reducing RIDC's role. A phase 2 environmental study, undertaken at the universities' request, identifies no serious problems.

1988   A new master plan reflects the universities' development plans. Building plans are underway for the universities' first buildings.

1989   URA approves plans for Pitt's first building. Discovery of cyanide prompts DER to request more environmental study and the universities to lose interest in development.

1990	URA makes and loses bids for Pittsburgh National Bank and Legent Corporation.
1991	Construction begins on Pitt's Center for Biotechnology and Bioengineering and the first public open spaces. URA makes and loses a bid for "Corporation X." URA formally assumes development responsibility.
1992	URA makes and loses a bid for American Thermoplastics. URA leases space for surface parking to serve downtown Pittsburgh.
1993	Union Switch & Signal chooses the Pittsburgh Technology Center for its Systems and Research Center after URA offers to use tax increment financing to build its parking garage. Pitt occupies its building. URA and DER sign a consent order and agreement. CMU and Union Switch begin construction of their buildings.
1995	CMU occupies its new building, housing the Carnegie Mellon Research Institute. A consortium of public-service organizations dedicated to advancing high-technology companies announce they will occupy a new RIDC building.

2

HOW SAFE IS SAFE ENOUGH?
From the LTV Pittsburgh Works to the Pittsburgh Technology Center

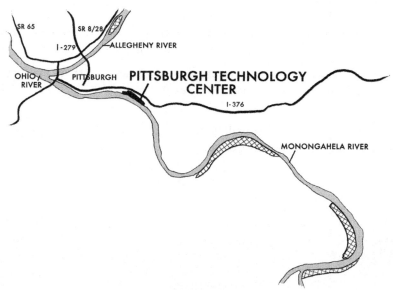

Pittsburgh Technology Center

Loss of industry from American cities and subsequent efforts to put abandoned industrial properties back into use coincided with the emergence of the environmental movement. The Environmental Protection Agency was formed in 1970; however, the first national legislation to address the problem of land that had been polluted by industrial development (CERCLA, commonly known as Superfund) was not adopted until 1980. By that time, work on Herr's Island was well underway, and only three years later the

URA began its efforts to transform LTV Corporation's shuttered Pittsburgh Works into the Pittsburgh Technology Center. Not until 1988, six years after the project had begun, did Pennsylvania adopt its Hazardous Sites Cleanup Act.

As a result, Pittsburgh's early industrial redevelopment projects, with similar projects across the country, became the means through which the country came to terms with questions such as the following:

- How clean must a site be to be considered safe?
- How far must a party that is cleaning a polluted industrial property pursue the diminishing benefits and increasing costs of making the site ever cleaner?
- At what point will the government sign off on cleanup efforts and say that a property is clean enough?
- How can an owner that has cleaned up a property become free of future liability for past pollution it may not have caused?
- How can future occupants of a property be assured that a property is safe enough to purchase and occupy?

Such questions dominated the attention of those who sought to develop the Pittsburgh Technology Center.

INTRODUCTION

Pittsburgh Technology Center, 2005

The Pittsburgh Technology Center is a planned research, office, and light manufacturing center built on the 49-acre site of the former hot-strip mill of the LTV Corporation's Pittsburgh Works, a long, narrow piece of land between Second Avenue and the Monongahela River less than 2 miles east of downtown Pittsburgh. Railroad tracks run the length of the property along the river.

Plaza, hedgerow, green river, and buildings at the Pittsburgh Technology Center, with the Hot Metal Bridge in the background, 2005

The master plan provided for a campuslike setting combining a river walk, tree-covered walkways, and a greensward consisting of a variety of grasses and wildflowers that would meander, riverlike, through the property. Carnegie Mellon University and the University of Pittsburgh developed the first buildings at the Pittsburgh Technology Center, housing research centers for biotechnology, bioengineering, artificial intelligence, robotics, and computer applications.[1]

With those developments in place, it is difficult to imagine the former presence of the enormous steel mill that had once covered the entire property. The site has become an open, suburbanlike campus, an oasis of green within its urban setting. The planned tree-lined hedgerows (lines of trees and walks), a serpentine walkway along the river, and a curving river of grass and wildflowers break the expanse.

Open space and buildings at the Pittsburgh Technology Center, with downtown Pittsburgh in the background, 2005

Ten years after the events related in this chapter, there are already seven large, beautifully designed buildings, comprising 683,000 square feet of space, scattered along the length of the site on the river side along Technology Drive, which was built parallel to Second Avenue to diminish traffic congestion. Space remains for the expansion of the Carnegie Mellon Research Center and for Union Switch & Signal. At the center of the development, a large parcel between Aristech and the University of Pittsburgh's Center for Biotechnology is still available for future use. The parking garage for Union Switch & Signal is still the only structure along the Second Avenue side of the site. Since the development has not yet achieved its planned density, areas reserved for parking structures are still surface lots, largely serving both the Technology Center and downtown workers. Activity is largely inside the buildings, although during warm weather it spills over onto the decks and patios of the offices with views of the river below.

BACKGROUND

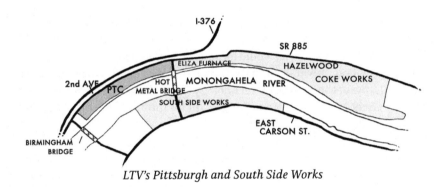

LTV's Pittsburgh and South Side Works

Early activities on the property were a sawmill and metals operations. The Pittsburgh and Boston Copper Smelting Works (later C.G. Hussey & Company), established in 1849, was just east of the bend in Second Avenue (then Braddock Street) where Union Switch & Signal's parking garage is now located. The copper works continued in operation until J&L acquired their property in 1963, dismantled the plant, and made a parking lot. In 1859 Moorehead & Company opened its Soho Iron Works, located on the quarter of the site that was nearest the city. Manufacturing small products such as nails and chain, Morehouse built their production facilities close to the river to take advantage of barge transportation.

Other early companies were J. Matthews's Soho Coke Works, which occupied the land west of Hussey and east of the Soho Iron Works; McClaren and Company's Eureka Steel Works; the Keystone Rolling Mill Company; and W.J. Ritchie's sawmill, planing mill, and box factory. From the 1880s until approximately 1920, a manufactured gas plant operated on the portion of the site between the University of Pittsburgh's and Carnegie Mellon University's current buildings.

J&L, the firm that grew to encompass the entire site, had its origins in 1859. James Laughlin, an Irish immigrant who became a Pittsburgh banker, formed Laughlin and Company and built the Pittsburgh area's first two blast furnaces—the Eliza furnaces—and also several beehive coke ovens just southeast of the current Pittsburgh Technology Center. Laughlin developed a working relationship with Jones, Lauth and Company, located on the south side of the river. Iron produced in Eliza's furnaces was taken across the river and rolled on the South Side. It was transported first by ferry and later by rail after the Hot Metal Bridge was built in 1877.

The two companies merged in 1900 to become Jones & Laughlin, Ltd., and later the Jones and Laughlin Steel Corporation, known as J&L Steel. Between 1900 and 1905 the new company expanded on both sides of the river. Since at the time the riverbanks sloped down to the river, and since J&L needed flat land for its steel-making facilities, it placed fill—up to 20 feet comprising primarily slag, cinders, and building rubble—to make the site flatter and less prone to flooding.[2] By 1916 there were six blast furnaces at the Eliza site that could produce 1.7 million tons of iron a year. J&L built Bessemer and later open hearth furnaces, and later still electric arc furnaces to produce steel, thereby becoming the major competitor to Carnegie Steel (which later became U.S. Steel and then USX). A former worker at the plant described how the plants on the two sides of the river worked together:

> The Eliza blast furnace shop made molten iron, which was poured into large railroad cars that we called submarines or torpedoes. The cars carried the iron across the river on tracks to the Southside, where the iron was poured into open-hearth furnaces and processed. From there the molten iron was poured into ingots, which were lowered into soaking pits to stabilize temperature before being sent to the blooming mill. At the blooming mill the ingots were squeezed, turned, and rolled into long slabs of various widths. These slabs were run through a shear to cut them to size and taken outside to cool before being reloaded onto railroad cars and returned to the Pittsburgh Works.[3]

The primary operations performed in the part of the mill that would later become the Pittsburgh Technology Center included hot and cold rolling of steel, pickling or finishing, and storage. The Pittsburgh Works' primary products were structural steel pieces such as angles and beams, bars, and steel pilings.

View of the site of the future Pittsburgh Technology Center, left center, covered by mill buildings, with the Eliza furnaces behind and the South Side Works across the river

Throughout much of the twentieth century, employment in the mills on both sides of the river averaged about 12,000. The workforce in the Pittsburgh Works alone reached up to 8,500. Then in the 1960s employment began to decline as the plant aged, the population of the country moved west, and competition in the world's steel market increased. LTV purchased the controlling interest in J&L in 1968 and took full control in 1974. By the following year the workforce at the Pittsburgh Works was down to 3,604, and only the largest furnaces remained in operation. Eliza produced her last iron on June 22, 1979, and in 1981 LTV shuttered the Pittsburgh Works, leaving only the coke works in Hazelwood and the power plant in the South Side still in operation for a few remaining years.[4]

In 1981, the same year the Pittsburgh Works shut down, the Park Corporation, a privately owned Ohio-based corporation founded and owned by Raymond P. Park, purchased the 49-acre site on the downtown side of the Hot Metal Bridge that would become the Pittsburgh Technology Center. Ray Park had been active in recycling abandoned industrial facilities for twenty-five years. At the time Park purchased the site, they did not make their intentions clear, although presumably they planned to make a profit from the sale of equipment and scrap from demolition, followed by sale or development.[5]

Vacant mill buildings on the site of the future Pittsburgh Technology Center, seen from the South Side, across the river

DEVELOPING THE PITTSBURGH TECHNOLOGY CENTER

A Public Initiative – 1982–1984

In 1982 the collapse of the steel industry in Pittsburgh hit hardest. Unemployment reached its highest point in the region, and community leaders were anxious to pursue every possible way of replacing the lost employment. The idle and now vacant and deteriorating Pittsburgh Works, so close to the heart of the city, loomed before every traveler along the Parkway East, a constant and painful reminder of the region's loss. In fact, the hulking remains of the Eliza furnaces and mill buildings of the former Pittsburgh Works were in the foreground of their first view of the Golden Triangle.

Site of the future Pittsburgh Technology Center in the foreground, with the Eliza furnaces and the Parkway East to the left and the South Side Works across the river

Brooks Robinson, President of RIDC, was the first to conceive of a public initiative to redevelop the Pittsburgh Works as a modern industrial park. He raised the idea with Mayor Richard Caliguiri, who liked it from the start. He gave the Urban Redevelopment Authority (URA) the task of exploring ways of acquiring the site.

The city sought support for the project from Governor Thornburgh and Allegheny County's state legislative delegation, which, in the final stages of deliberation on the state's 1983–84 budget, introduced legislation to grant $1 million to the URA toward the site's acquisition. The legislation passed, and the URA's board authorized a grant agreement with the Commonwealth on August 25, 1983.[6]

On September 30, the URA quickly signed an option agreement with the Park Corporation to acquire the property, and it exercised this option a month later, on October 28. The purchase price was $3,429,000. The purchase agreement provided that Park would be responsible for the demolition and removal of all improvements on the property, including buildings, fixtures, machinery, and equipment. Park would make a profit both on the sale of the property and on proceeds from selling machinery and scrap from the site. The URA's interest was the potential for the development itself. At the time the URA's board approved the acquisition, Jack Noonan, the Authority's director of real estate, told the board, "The proposed development of the site is projected to generate [in] excess of $15 million in private investment and create 1,100 new jobs."[7]

The city matched the state's contribution of $1 million toward the purchase price. The URA took the remainder from funds it had on hand for land purchases.[8] From the start it was clear, however, that the city's support for the project would necessarily be more moral than financial. Federal regulations required that the city's Community Development Block Grant be used to assist low- and moderate-income people, who would likely not be the primary beneficiaries of the new development. Other demands on the city's bond funds made that source politically risky. Instead, the URA would have to rely primarily on the state to finance improvements to the property. Over the succeeding years the URA would return again and again to the state's Department of Community Affairs and Department of Commerce to fund redevelopment of the property, just as it had with the Herr's Island redevelopment.

With strong support from the legislative delegation and the obvious need to address the economic crisis in western Pennsylvania, the legislature and governor approved repeated investments in the project: the first a grant of $1,859,800 from Community Affairs in early 1984 for design and site preparation, followed by a second $1 million from Commerce, which the Authority sought in late 1984, that would also leverage a grant from the U.S. Economic Development Administration.[9]

The URA struggled with who should develop and market the property. While the URA had experience in developing industrial property, especially the Chartiers Valley Industrial Park in the West End, RIDC had far more. Indeed, RIDC dominated Pittsburgh's industrial and office park market. RIDC also had the advantage of being a state-licensed Industrial Development Corporation, which gave it access to low-cost state financing through the Pennsylvania Industrial Development Authority for both building infrastructure and constructing buildings.

Given these strengths, in March the URA agreed to give RIDC a ten-year option (at the cost of one dollar), with the possibility of a five-year extension, to develop the property for "small and developing businesses." RIDC agreed to invest $1.3 million in site improvements. Brooks Robinson noted that a number of businesses, either in Oakland or associated with the health center, had approached RIDC looking for space. They were candidates for the new development.[10]

An important early question for the URA and RIDC was whether to attempt to remove the massive foundations that covered most of the site. Estimates to remove them seemed prohibitively high. Fortunately, engineering studies suggested that bringing in fill to raise the elevation above the 100-year floodplain would also provide enough depth to run gravity sewers. The URA decided to leave the foundations in place and to build on top of them. Although this approach would require special foundations and thereby raise the cost of buildings, the public cost would be much less. Thus, beginning in early 1984 and continuing through much of 1985, as the Park Corporation proceeded with demolition, the URA sought fill from construction projects throughout the region to raise the elevation of the property.[11]

Foundations of the demolished mill buildings, with downtown Pittsburgh in the background

Chapter 2

Advice from the Urban Land Institute – 1984

Believing that the site offered the city a truly unique and historic real estate opportunity, Rebecca A. Lee, the young and energetic director of the URA's Economic Development Department, approached local foundations for grants that, together with public funds, would allow the URA to bring in a distinguished panel of real estate experts from the Urban Land Institute's Panel Advisory Service to evaluate the site, its market potential, and the overall development strategy.[12] Steven Zecher and I wrote briefing documents for the panel and arranged for them to meet with city officials, the RIDC, and university representatives, among many others. Lodged at the William Penn Hotel, the panel worked feverishly, and with little rest, from Sunday evening, November 11, when they arrived, until Friday the 16th.

After their week of intensive examination, the panel issued a press release and held a press conference in which it presented its findings and recommendations to Mayor Caliguiri. They confirmed that the site presented a unique opportunity for Pittsburgh to foster significant growth in employment in advanced technology firms. The major attractiveness of the site was its proximity to the university and health center, "where many young advanced technology firms already thrive." They recommended that the URA finalize its draft agreement with RIDC to develop the site, suggesting that the development should have high standards of design, use the riverfront as an amenity, and provide a convenient, campuslike, urban setting. Finally, they warned that "the public sector must be prepared to make substantial initial investments in roads, utilities and site preparation. However, this work may result in land values significantly higher than in suburban office parks."[13]

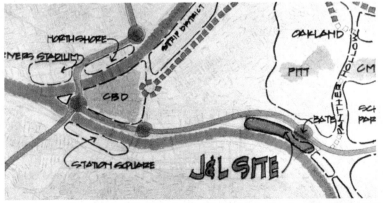

Advantageous location of the J&L site, in the ULI Panel's view, November 1984

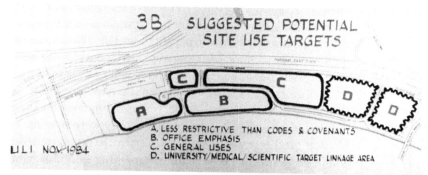

ULI Panel's recommendation for uses for the J&L site, November 1984

The issue of RIDC's involvement with the project was significant. The URA had already struggled with the pros and cons. Most of the panel members, being for-profit developers and potential competitors, began the week with a clear prejudice against RIDC. Their week in Pittsburgh did not change their philosophical opposition to a nonprofit developer: they firmly believed that competition in the private market produces the best, most efficient outcome. But they soon discovered that RIDC so dominated Pittsburgh's industrial real estate market as essentially to control it. All other developments were judged against RIDC's suburban office parks. In addition, RIDC's sponsorship by Pittsburgh's corporate elite made it a powerful force to reckon with.

One panel member made an unfortunate and rather overblown allusion to the panel's views in the press conference. The newspaper quoted him as saying, "RIDC is a monster out of control. It is eating its own children." Brooks Robinson, president of RIDC, was understandably outraged at such a statement. He wrote to the president of the Urban Land Institute, Claude M. Ballard, early the following week, defending the RIDC and complaining about the remark. Ballard duly replied three weeks later, apologizing for the panel member's criticism and reiterating the panel's conclusion: "The Panel recommends that RIDC, with its recognized success in developing industrial/business parks and its catalytic role in bringing the potential of the J&L site to the attention of the city, be responsible for developing the property."[14]

Asbestos and the Health Department – 1984

As the Park Corporation began selling off machinery and preparing the mill buildings for demolition, the Allegheny County Health Department staged a surprise inspection. Seeing the activity on the site, and aware that the mills would be full of asbestos, they went to investigate. They found "a warehouse full of bags" of asbestos but no permit to actually remove it. Nor was Park complying with the county's stringent requirements for asbestos removal. The Department put an immediate stop to what was happening. Duly corrected, Park quickly changed their procedures and complied with regulations. Don Horgan of the Health Department remembered, "They were basically doing it the way EPA would require. They were wetting it, but they weren't doing it the way we would require, which is containment, negative air, double-bagging, you know, sealing everything up, and as soon as we saw it they quit what they were doing and fulfilled everything we asked them to do. They ended up working with us and getting the permits."[15]

The enormous size of the buildings, however, required modifying the Health Department's normal procedures. "[W]e learned that you couldn't contain a whole boiler the size of a city block long; that we had to do it in sections." The new techniques that the Health Department and contractor developed on this project became the standard for later demolitions in Homestead and other old steel facilities.[16]

Studies and Plans – 1985

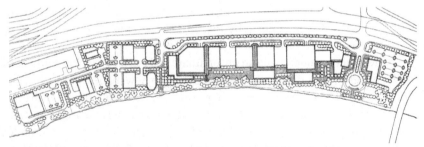

1985 Preliminary Land Development Plan for the Pittsburgh Technology Center

It was clear early on that problems of access to the site would limit the scope of the development, just as access problems had been an issue for Herr's Island. Second Avenue was a narrow tunnel between a stone wall supporting a rail line on one side and the monstrous mill buildings on the other. Although the demolition of the mill would open the vista toward and across the river, it did nothing to widen the street to improve access. Early in the year, therefore, the URA requested and received proposals from three engineering firms to conduct a traffic study to address this difficulty.

At its board meeting in March 1985 the URA authorized site planning to begin through a supplemental agreement with RIDC. The agreement provided $50,000 "to allow RIDC to enter into contracts for the preparation of the development plan for the Pittsburgh Technology and Industry Park," the URA's new name for the project.[17] While planning was underway, work continued on preparing the site.

In May, RIDC, acting on the URA's behalf, authorized Advanced Environmental Consultants, Inc., to undertake a "phase 1" environmental reconnaissance of the site. In its report the consultants stated that "though it is evident the area does not pose a significant environmental problem, additional work . . . should be performed."[18]

The URA felt it would be on stronger ground to finance improvements if the site were certified as a Redevelopment Area under state law and if it were thereby acknowledged as an area that warranted the URA's involvement, even though no condemnation of property was needed. Accordingly, the URA asked City Planning to study the area to determine whether it met the conditions of blight set forth in the state's redevelopment law. The Planning Commission certified the site as a Redevelopment Area on July 23.

At the same meeting, the Planning Commission also approved a master plan, termed a Preliminary Land Development Plan under the city's zoning code, for the site to be developed as an advanced technology, research, business, and manufacturing center for "firms specializing in research development and applications for robotics and bio-medical technology, computer software and hardware, related commercial research and development, and office and business services and support." Fully developed, the 51-acre site was expected to accommodate 800,000 square feet of building space.

It was at this early stage of planning that the universities began to lobby for a role in developing the site. The URA's quarterly newsletter for legislators alluded to these discussions and described development plans in the following words:

The Regional Industrial Development Corporation (RIDC) of Southwestern Pennsylvania will guide the development and market and manage it. Discussions are continuing with both Carnegie-Mellon [sic] University and the University of Pittsburgh about portions of the site. Carnegie-Mellon University has expressed interest in developing a national center for robotics and computer research, development and manufacturing firms, while Pitt would like to develop bio-medical engineering research and development laboratories. Development costs for site preparation are estimated

85

to be nearly $17 million; in turn, the project should generate more than 1,600 jobs, $70 million in private investment, and nearly $1.5 million in annual tax revenues.[19]

The roles of RIDC and the universities would continue to evolve as time went on.

Keeping the project in the forefront of state legislators was important. By this time the Commonwealth had granted a total of $4 million to acquire and prepare the site, including $2 million from Commerce that had been approved with the new budget in June for additional site preparation, engineering, and construction.[20] Much more would be needed to complete work on the site. One approach the city decided to try was to request funds from the state's capital budget through Strategy 21, the framework through which the city, Allegheny County, and the universities regularly lobbied for funds from Harrisburg, an approach that proved successful as time passed., bringing support for projects that ranged from the old mill sites to the new Pittsburgh International Airport and the Andy Warhol Museum.

In August 1985 the RIDC and URA solicited engineering proposals to fill and grade the site to raise the elevation 4 feet; construct a two-lane road, including utilities; widen and place traffic signals on Second Avenue to provide for new entrances to the site; and stabilize and landscape the embankment above the river. In early September they selected the firm of Wilbur Smith.[21]

Demolition of the mill buildings, 1985

All this time, Park had been demolishing the emptied mill buildings to foundation level. Then the massive foundations were cleaned and backfilled, and in the process oil-contaminated soil and water were removed. The foundations were then filled and covered to a depth of 10 to 20 feet with the clean fill the URA had contracted to bring in from construction projects throughout the region. Securing the site from scavengers was a challenge throughout the process.[22]

Start of Site Development and a Universities Initiative – 1986–1987

On April 21, 1986, following the Urban Land Institute panel's recommendation, the URA and RIDC signed the agreement giving RIDC "the exclusive right or option to purchase or lease the Property or any portion thereof" for consideration of one dollar. The term of the agreement would be ten years, with the right of RIDC to extend the agreement for an additional five years, assuming that performance measured up to the URA's standards.[23]

At the URA's May board meeting Chairman Jack Robin announced that the project would now be called the Pittsburgh Technology Center. The board authorized an agreement under which the Pittsburgh Water and Sewer Authority would provide $2.4 million to finance public water and sewer costs both on the site and along Second Avenue. RIDC, as the project's developer, would be the URA's agent to carry out the improvements.[24]

Work on the water and sewer lines was to begin in July, but the URA and RIDC were not fully in control of the timing.[25] By early June, although the engineering was complete, the URA was predicting that work would not start until September because it could not get an important sewer permit from the DER.[26] Through a conversation with a DER employee in early July, the URA's John Coyne learned that although the DER had received the URA's sewer application, with a favorable recommendation from the Allegheny County Health Department, and although it appeared complete, "they are so backlogged that our module hasn't even been recorded. . . . I should check back with them in about three weeks."[27] The result was a frustrating delay, to say the least, the first in a project that thus far seemed streamlined compared to the challenges with Herr's Island, where URA was at the same time confronting conflict with Jack Buncher.

In the meantime, the URA pursued other sources of financing for the project. In June it applied for a grant of $438,000 from the Appalachian Regional Commission for additional grading, backfilling, and excavation. In October it received an additional $2 million from the Pennsylvania Department of Commerce for the reconstruction of Second Avenue, and $400,000 from the city for site improvements.[28] In September, in anticipation that work would soon begin, the URA authorized RIDC to award a $2,457,161 site preparation contract to Casciato Brothers for backfilling of pits; site grading; and construction of the roadway, curbs, utilities, and drainage systems.[29]

Cleared site of the future Pittsburgh Technology Center, with the Eliza furnaces in the foreground, the South Side Works across the river, and downtown Pittsburgh behind

Finally, on October 10, the URA held an official groundbreaking to mark the start of public construction.[30] Both Governor Thornburgh and House Speaker K. LeRoy Irvis spoke, since the state, having already contributed $6 million to the project, was the prime source of financing to move the development ahead. The URA reiterated its expectation that "by its 1995 completion" the development would bring $70 million of private investment, 1,600 permanent jobs, and 4,400 related jobs.[31] In retrospect, these were highly optimistic goals to reach in such a short time, but both universities had ambitious plans to attract private development that would follow their initial, publicly funded investments on the site. The two venerable presidents of those institutions, Dr. Richard Cyert of Carnegie Mellon and Dr. Wesley Posvar of Pitt, touted the research strengths of their respective institutions and assured everyone that there were companies that would seek to benefit from proximity to their research facilities at the Center.[32] "We held the program under a big circus tent," I recorded after the event, "[and] then hoisted a flag symbolic of the project's official transformation from former steel mill to high tech. center. All went without a hitch, and everyone seemed pleased."

Cyert and Posvar took seriously what the Urban Land Institute panel had said about the importance of the universities as the new economic generators for the region. But they went a step further, believing that there could be financial benefits to the universities in developing the land themselves. They met privately with Mayor Caliguiri and convinced him of the merits of their cause. With his endorsement the universities began working with the URA on development policies that would put the universities squarely in charge of developing the site, effectively supplanting the RIDC. By the end of the year demolition of the old mill structures was nearly complete, and the URA was stockpiling more fill to grade the site.

Early in 1987 newly elected governor Robert P. Casey toured the site and announced that the state would invest $14 million for the University of Pittsburgh's facility for biotechnology and health-related research. At its May meeting, the URA's board with that assurance reserved 8.85 acres for Pitt and the Pennsylvania Department of General Services (DGS, which would build and own Pitt's building) "for development by DGS of a Biotechnology Center and the construction by Pitt of 3 building modules" for the private companies that would be attracted to locate next to Pitt's facility.[33]

Environmental Questions – 1987

To this point neither the URA nor any of its partners had reason for concern about the environmental condition of the property. The URA had tested twelve pits and four monitoring wells; taken ten soil borings; and analyzed water, sediment, and sludge samples—all with no significant findings.[34] Notwithstanding, concern about environmental liability was generally running high at that time. Public bodies and developers were learning that brownfields often contained significant contamination, and great care was needed to discover and ameliorate them according to evolving regulations.

In March, when Wilbur Smith Associates, in the process of preparing bid specifications for the road, noticed various oils, sludge, and liquids in pits in the proposed construction area, they thought that the substances should be analyzed. The universities also began to raise questions about environmental contamination and asked whether the URA would certify the site as free of hazardous waste or indemnify them against any environmental liability, which the URA was not willing to do. Concern also arose over statements made by former J&L employees, reported in Advanced Environmental Consultants' 1985 study, that suggested that J&L had had a waste dump for excess oils and other materials on the site, generally located in the area of the new western entry where a storm sewer was being constructed.[35]

These various concerns led RIDC, acting on behalf of the URA, to commission ICF/SRW as a subcontractor to Wilbur Smith, to undertake a "phase 2" environmental assessment, making additional tests of groundwater and soil over the entire site and recommending appropriate treatment where necessary. Summarizing the prospects for the study, Deborah Barman, the URA's project manager, observed, "The environmental investigation is a laborious task which will continue . . . and more than likely result in the finding of no hazardous waste on site."[36] In fact, after preliminary examination, ICF/SRW found the oils and sludge to be refined lubricating products containing few, if any, priority contaminants. They tested for but found no PCBs and only limited amounts of phenols. They recommended that the oils be removed and recycled.[37]

On May 21, along with its report of the studies performed to that point, Wilbur Smith gave RIDC its proposal for the additional environmental studies to alleviate what appeared to be minor concerns of workers involved in construction on the site. A comprehensive review would be done in two phases: a sampling and testing phase, followed by refined investigations, removal, and correction.[38]

Wilbur Smith initiated interviews of former employees of J&L Steel, C.G. Hussey Corporation, and Park Corporation who were familiar with the history of the site after WW II. Aerial photos greatly assisted these efforts. RIDC also contacted Advanced Environmental Consultants in an effort to obtain additional information. The interviews, in conjunction with the review of the aerial photos, led the consultants to conclude that "there is only limited likelihood that this or any other location on the J&L site . . . was ever used as a permanent dump site."[39]

Wilbur Smith and ICF/SRW used all this information to design a three-pronged program of testing and sampling "which when combined with the efforts to date . . . would represent a diligent effort . . . to identify environmental hazards at the former J&L site." First, four monitoring wells would be located along the railroad tracks, including one on the site of the reputed material dump. If nothing turned up in the groundwater, it would be an excellent indication of favorable environmental conditions on the site. Second, borings would be used to locate and analyze the cyanide-cleaning tank shown on the Hussey site plan. Third, Wilbur Smith would try to realign the new sewer to eliminate any remaining concerns contractors might have about the supposed material dump site, which, although apparently nonexistent, had already led one contractor to walk off the job.

In retrospect, this level of concern about contamination may now seem exaggerated and out of balance. As time has passed, we have come to expect that older industrial sites most likely will be contaminated, and we take that in stride as a routine feature of the development process. However, at that time even recognition of the problem of contaminated soil was still relatively new. The federal Superfund law was only seven years old. That law had made every party that ever owned a parcel of contaminated land liable for its complete cleanup. Liability could also extend to financial institutions that came into possession of contaminated land and to contractors who worked on it. Laws and regulations were evolving, and courts at the state and federal levels were interpreting their application. Both regulators and those they were regulating were trying to find their way through this uncertain and unsettled legal and regulatory environment. These conditions—these fears and this uncertainty—dramatically colored the history of the Pittsburgh Technology Center.

Cleared site of the Pittsburgh Technology Center, ready for development, June 1987

The Universities as Real Estate Developers and a Clean Environmental Report – 1987

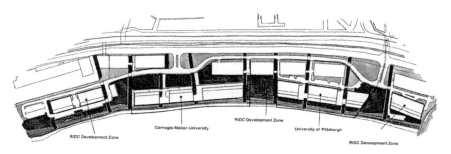

The two universities' development zones in the center of the site, Pitt's to the right (east), CMU's to the left (west)

In July of 1987 the URA received another infusion of funds from the Pennsylvania Department of Commerce. This $2 million grant (bringing Commerce's total contribution to $8 million) was to complete the site improvements on the eastern portion to support the University of Pittsburgh's proposed development. In addition, the URA received word that it would receive from the Department of Community Affairs $6.732 million through Strategy 21 for Second Avenue and the eastern portion of the roadway. The city contributed another $400,000, bringing its total contribution to date to $1.2 million.[40]

The same month, the URA, RIDC, and the two participating universities agreed to formal development policies for the Center. The document gave the universities a greatly expanded role. It outlined the universities' development plans; provided for development zones for each university; described the planning and design efforts that the city, URA, and RIDC had undertaken; outlined the URA's commitments to improve access; addressed responsibilities for developing and maintaining open spaces; and outlined ways of providing parking. All in all, it was a comprehensive, if brief (eight pages, minus the signatures), statement of the partners' expectations, roles, and plans for the development. It was based on the assumption that the universities would be the principal, perhaps exclusive, developers.

Both universities planned to develop initial buildings of between 75,000 and 150,000 gross square feet. Pitt's would "house university-related biotechnology, bioengineering and medical research and development activities." Carnegie Mellon (CMU) would build two buildings, one to house the Center for Advanced Manufacturing and Software Engineering and the relocated Mellon Institute, and the other a joint venture with the Carley Capital Group for speculative offices and research space. Both universities were to begin construction by the end of 1990. By 1996, CMU was committed to developing a total of 300,000 square feet, and Pitt 250,000 square feet. The URA agreed to provide land for these developments at no cost. The universities would also have the right to develop the remainder of the site—an estimated 410,000 square feet beyond their initial commitments—before the URA could market it to others. The RIDC or URA would reserve 40,000 square feet of space for site amenities (although a bank was the only amenity specified.)

This approach to developing the project was dramatically different than either the RIDC or the Urban Land Institute had envisioned. It was evidence of the universities' rising importance to Pittsburgh's economy after the decline of industry. It was also evidence of Dr. Cyert's and Dr. Posvar's ambitions for their universities—ambitions that would prove to be overreaching but reflected their entrepreneurial personalities. Public officials, who were desperate to find champions to lead the region out of its economic doldrums, were only too happy to believe they had found an answer in the universities.

To accommodate the universities' proposed developments, the policies initially gave Pitt 9.2 acres immediately west of the eastern entrance where Pitt's Center for Biotechnology and Bioengineering now stands, and CMU received 10.8 acres in the general area of the site's western entrance, the location where the Carnegie Mellon Research Institute was later built. The universities were to submit proposals showing their schedule and financing plans for parking structures, which would be the responsibility of developers or occupants (with a preference that they work through RIDC to assure uniform design).

The URA would develop the public open spaces, including the riverfront, a green river (a band of grasses and wildflowers), and plazas, and they would transfer ownership of those public open spaces to the city. Developers, including the universities, would have the responsibility to own and develop open space on their own parcels. The URA and developers would have responsibility for developing hedgerows that penetrated their respective developments. Maintaining all the open spaces, regardless of ownership, would be the responsibility of a tenants' association, membership in which would be required by the disposition agreements between the URA and individual developers. The document ended with a statement of "special concerns" that made clear that the universities' performance was conditioned on the URA's completion of the site improvements, satisfactory "environmental and floodplain conditions," "adequate and economically feasible parking facilities," and "satisfactory covenants and restrictions."[41]

In summary, the new development guidelines, instigated and indeed demanded by presidents Cyert and Posvar, neither of whom was known for making modest plans, set the development on a course that tied its success to the universities' success in attracting commercial tenants to their buildings. The presidents were certain they could do this. However, city and URA officials should have been more skeptical of their claims. In fact, universities are neither established nor organized to be real estate developers. Despite the presidents' confidence, they proved unable to deliver on their promises.

By August the URA had worked out an agreement with the city and the Pennsylvania Department of Transportation to reconstruct and widen Second Avenue for the length of the site. The same month, Wilbur Smith and ICF/SRW carried out their groundwater monitoring program and soil tests. The tests showed high levels of PAHs, a byproduct of coal combustion, which was no surprise. The tests also showed low levels of cyanide (slightly above drinking water standards), but no PCBs, heavy metals, or pesticides.[42] Their report of August 14 concluded that "a purposeful and diligent effort to identify environmental hazards at the site of the PTC has been performed and that, with the exception that the ground water is not suitable for potable use without treatment, we have found no significant environmental hazards. Further review and investigation is not warranted."[43] Their reassuring conclusion would prove very premature.

A Reduced Role for RIDC – 1987

With the universities' having put themselves forward as real estate developers, RIDC's role had to change. Where the RIDC had previously been charged with marketing and developing the property, the universities had effectively supplanted RIDC as developers, having now assumed primary responsibility for identifying tenants for the new buildings they would develop. Consequently, on August 18 Brooks Robinson wrote to the URA's general counsel, Joseph Gariti, sending him a proposed amendment to the contract between the two organizations that took the new circumstances into account. Referencing the development policies that had been signed the previous month, he concluded, "This document effectively places the allowable development capacity of the site under the control of these universities.... [While] RIDC stands ready to assist the URA with development of both infrastructure and individual projects, the Development Policies . . . render portions of the Agreement between URA and RIDC dated 4/21/86 inoperative."[44]

The new development policies also necessitated new plans to activate the Specially Planned District zoning that the city had adopted for the site. The minutes of the URA's August board meeting noted that "within the next two or three months each university will be hiring an architect to design its first buildings.... In the meantime, it is essential that the Authority and RIDC hire a site planner to work with the universities' architects to create a site plan and Final Land Development Plan" that could be "completed and approved by the City Planning Commission in time for the building permits to be issued to the universities."[45] In October the URA, through RIDC, contracted with Urban Design Associates to prepare these plans.[46]

RIDC's role had been reduced to being a contracting agent and a conduit for funds for the URA, which was now working directly with the universities. For the URA, which had ultimate responsibility for developing the project, the resulting arrangement became difficult and troubling. David Donahoe, who became URA's executive director in December 1987, recalled

> I just don't think [the universities] were used to being developers, and the structure that had been agreed to by somebody, certainly wasn't me, where you had them and then you had RIDC who was in charge, and then suddenly Oxford appeared [as a partner to CMU, engaged to construct and lease their buildings] and they were in the middle of it. . . . I remember saying several times, although the mayor just would not, "Can't we get the universities out of this? Just get them out of it, because it's not going to happen." . . . You know, it's just not in the natural sense of a university to be a developer and therefore just, it was too hard to deal with them because they didn't talk the same language. And it seemed like you were always dealing with the president of the university, really. You need to deal with people who get the job done, but everything had to be cleared with the president of the university.[47]

Forward Movement – 1988

The state granted $17,002,195 from the capital budget for CMU's first building—a Strategy 21 request—through a January 20, 1988, agreement between the Department of Community Affairs and RIDC. The new development plan was also coming along. On January 28 I wrote, "Urban Design Assoc. has done a fine job with the Pgh. Tech. Center master plan. I am thrilled with the outcome and just want to get it set now." However, less than a month later, on February 12, I wrote, "I spent practically all afternoon at Urban Design Associates with the two recalcitrant universities trying to reconcile their impossibly opposite views of a master plan for the Pgh. Tech. Center." And on February 18, I reported, "We came to a decision on the Pgh. Tech Center master plan, going as far as we could to accommodate the universities." Working with the universities was not easy.

In April 1988 the URA and RIDC awarded the contract to reconstruct Second Avenue to Golden Triangle Construction Company.[48] The problem of access to the site was a major concern to the Planning Department. In fact, zoning of the site, on Planning's insistence, limited development so that no more than 730 vehicles per hour would enter or leave the Center, a figure the Planning Department felt would not overburden the intersection of Second Avenue and Bates Street, where the entrance to Interstate 376 already brought considerable traffic. Widening Second Avenue would ease the problem, but other steps would also be needed. In July the URA applied to the U.S. Economic Development Administration for a grant to study extending the city's light-rail system to Oakland, via the Center, to increase access from both downtown and the universities.[49]

By summer, design of the universities' buildings was progressing well. The University of Pittsburgh had settled on a name for its facility: the University of Pittsburgh Center for Biotechnology and Bioengineering. Carnegie Mellon was designing its proposed two buildings. Groundbreaking for both universities' buildings was expected to occur in 1989. Despite his reservations about the universities' abilities as real estate developers, the URA's David Donahoe was quoted as saying, "This is truly a cooperative effort, involving City and State government, Pittsburgh's two major research universities and the private sector. It is an outstanding example of the effectiveness of our public/private partnership."[50]

Behind the scenes was a different reality. I recorded the following on June 28: "Today the City Planning Commission adopted the master plan for the Pittsburgh Technology Center, on which we have been working steadily for months and which we were still unsure until yesterday whether it would have the final support of the two universities and their developers. The day before presenting it to the Commission two weeks ago, we were meeting with them up until 4:30 to negotiate the final points of disagreement. Then after the public presentation they threatened to withdraw support. Fortunately the compromises held."

As development plans moved forward, provisions for parking became an increasingly important issue. The development plan set aside areas for structured parking between the building zone, which fronted the river, and Second Avenue. To reach the site's full development potential, the plan required that two-level parking be built on lots near the center of the site, with multifloor garages at either end. The universities and their developers wanted to defer building structured parking as long as possible, so as to minimize cost, and instead build temporary surface lots throughout the site, including on parcels scheduled for later development. The URA, for its part, did not want to see parcels outside the universities' development zones used for temporary parking, fearing that parking would become an obstacle to marketing and developing those other sites. Still other issues relating to parking were control and parking fees. Who would manage those services? How would fees be kept consistent across the site?

My department proposed a single parking organization to develop and manage parking, thereby centralizing control and allowing parking fees to be uniform across the site.[51] At our regular project coordinating meeting at the URA, our proposal got support, but David Donahoe thought we could not pull it off with the universities. While CMU agreed with this approach, Pitt wanted to control its own parking on its development zone. The URA proposed another alternative that we believed would be acceptable to both.[52] Pitt acceded, with requests for only minor amendments.[53] CMU's partner, Oxford Development Company, however, was not satisfied. David Matter of Oxford, after going over the proposal in detail with the URA's new project manager, Rebecca Flora, wrote to David Donahoe that "while we are grateful for the time and effort you and your colleagues have devoted to the resolution of this issue . . . , unfortunately, even with the latest modifications . . . , we do not believe that parking costs have been sufficiently reduced to make the project competitive in the marketplace and, therefore, economically viable."[54] The URA compromised further by agreeing to put off construction of structured parking as long as possible.[55] Essentially, the URA had backed down.

In September the URA approved the conveyance of property to the Pennsylvania Department of General Services for construction of Pitt's building. Dr. Jack E. Freeman, who made the presentation to the URA's board on behalf of the university, explained that the building would be four stories high, contain 80,000 square feet, and house research and development for biotechnology and bioengineering. Construction was to begin in the spring of 1989 and be completed by April 1991. He predicted that the building would be "a magnet for a series of commercial developments" and stated that the university was "in the final stages of negotiating with a private developer" to construct the additional buildings Pitt envisioned.[56] Although not named at the board meeting, that developer was National Development Company (NADCO), which was exploring the market for a second building, next to Pitt's. If that were successful, others would follow.

New Environmental Questions – 1988–1989

In the meantime, during the same year that PCBs were found on Buncher's site on Herr's Island, a series of seemingly insignificant events in late 1988 raised environmental concerns among personnel at General Services, which was to construct the state-owned building for Pitt's occupancy. First, although agreeing with ICF/SRW's environmental findings, Pitt's environmental consultant recommended additional testing and placement of additional monitoring wells to confirm past findings and create long-range monitoring capabilities.[57] ICF/SRW found that the stockpiled waste that had been accumulating from construction of infrastructure on the site (composed of rubble, slag, and soil) contained high levels of lubricating and cutting oils, grease, and PCBs. They reported this finding at the end of October and then wrote to the URA, recommending that contractors take precautions while performing test borings or pile or caisson work at the Center. The URA forwarded the warning to Bohlin Powell Larkin & Cywinski, the Pittsburgh architectural firm that was designing Pitt's building. In turn, the architectural firm wrote to General Services requesting that the state directly contract for subsurface investigations rather than through the architectural firm, since the latter's insurance did not cover environmental problems.[58]

Meanwhile, Pitt had never given up on its desire to have the URA indemnify the university from environmental liability, which the URA had said it would not do. As a compromise, the URA agreed to contribute $10,000 for additional environmental testing "conditioned upon the University and NADCO agreeing that the Authority will have no further obligation in assessing environmental conditions."[59] Pitt immediately informed General Services of the plan for additional testing.[60]

More Movement Forward – 1989

As designs for the buildings moved forward, the URA needed to do more-detailed site planning and succeeded in obtaining a grant of $300,000 from the Richard King Mellon Foundation for that purpose, $75,000 of which was to go to each of the two universities for their site plans.[61] With the grant, Urban Design Associates continued to work with the URA and with the universities' architects and development partners on refinements to the master plan and the detailed site plans for each development. Meanwhile, Bohlin Powell Larkin Cywinski was proceeding with the design for Pitt's building, which would be clad with metallic panels and feature an atrium with views of both the river and downtown Pittsburgh.

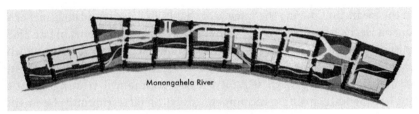

Urban Design Associates' plan for the Pittsburgh Technology Center, 1989

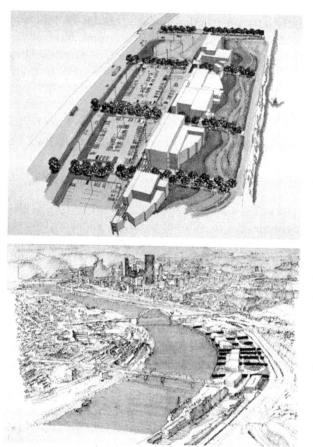

Urban Design Associates' perspective and rendering for the Pittsburgh Technology Center, 1989

The state's grants to the universities came with an obligation to match the grants with an equal private investment. But from the standpoint of financial risk, CMU was in a slightly different and more problematic situation than Pitt. Whereas Pitt's building would be built and owned by the state, with only a moral obligation on Pitt's part to match the state's investment, CMU would be contractually obligated to match the state's grant, and they viewed its partnership with Oxford Development Company as crucial to meeting that obligation.

Carnegie Mellon and Oxford had engaged the noted but controversial architect Peter Eisenman to design their buildings. According to their master plan, their first university building, a joint venture of CMU and Oxford (which would handle construction management, leasing, and maintenance), was to be 90,000 square feet, expanding in a second phase to 120,000 square feet. This plan was to be accompanied by an initial Oxford building of 110,000 square feet that would be followed by four additional Oxford developments that would bring Oxford's total square footage to 540,000 square feet of building space.

Eisenman prepared an elaborate marketing brochure for the Carnegie Mellon–Oxford project early in the year to explain the logic of his design in terms of a challenge from Richard Cyert, president of Carnegie Mellon, to Eisenman:

THE CYERT CHALLENGE:
I want the design to symbolize man's capacity to overcome knowledge. I do not want you to decorate a facade with a computer chip. I want something far more significant. I want something that challenges man's very occupation of space, not just the surface of that space. And I do not think that you can do it.

THE EISENMAN RESPONSE:
As the architectural discourse changes its focus from nature to knowledge, a far more complex object emerges. This requires a more complex form of architectural reality. By allowing scientists to occupy buildings that are shaped like Boolean cubes—the models for computer design in the field of artificial intelligence—we are symbolizing man's capacity to control knowledge. At the same time, we are giving the buildings a strong sense of movement and dynamism.[62]

Peter Eisenman's model for CMU's Research Institute, 1989

"According to the plans [for the first building], as many as 18 seven-story segments could join together in a structure of shapes and hues that change with the perspective of the viewer," the URA reported. I remember asking in the meeting at which Eisenman presented his conceptual plans to the URA whether rectangles placed at apparently random locations on the elevations were windows. "They might be," Eisenman replied. David Donahoe remembered the mayor's reaction to the proposed design: "[The architect] had this solution where there would be sort of little valleys in this development. And the mayor looked at this and said, 'What are these ditches over here?' And the design people almost had a heart attack, that the mayor was referring to these elaborate treatments as ditches."[63] To eyes and minds untrained in such architectural innovations, the building looked strange, to say the least.

On July 25 the Planning Commission approved the Final Land Development Plan for Pitt's building, clearing the way, from the standpoint of local regulations, for construction to begin. I made the presentation on behalf of the Authority and wrote a little later that their action was "a great relief after weeks of preparation, discussion and negotiation." Jack Robin commented afterward that "it was not the finest hour of either Pitt or the Planning Commission."

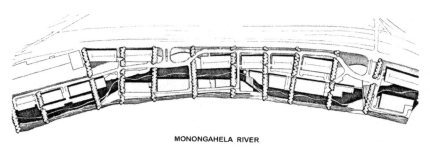

MONONGAHELA RIVER

1989 Final Land Development Plan, showing the two universities' development zones (Pitt's to the right, CMU's to the left) and Pitt's proposed first building (second building from the right)

With all the planned development (Pitt's building plus National Development Company's second building in Pitt's zone, and Carnegie Mellon's building plus Oxford's buildings in its zone), the URA was projecting larger development outcomes than previously—$260 million in private investment, nearly 11,000 direct and spin-off jobs, and more than $3 million in new annual tax revenues for the city.[64] Two days later we had a "summit meeting" with Mayor Sophie Masloff (who had assumed the office upon Mayor

Caliguiri's unexpected death in May 1988), Jack Robin, President Cyert of CMU, and others at which the universities reported progress to the mayor. The same evening I went with Pitt representatives to make a presentation to the Oakland community organization. Because the Center was removed from Oakland, the community was generally uninterested, but it was important to keep people informed.

An Environmental Roadblock – 1989–1990

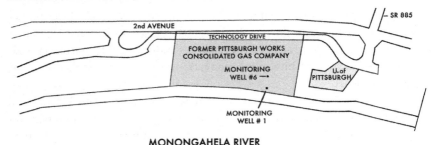

Cyanide on parcels 3 and 4

In March 1989, ICF/SRW commenced the additional environmental testing.[65] On June 13 they reported that after they had made fifty-two borings, taken ten soil samples, and installed four monitoring wells on the University of Pittsburgh's site, their findings were negligible except for elevated levels of cyanide in the water.[66] On August 22 William Kosko of the Department of General Services wrote to Ana Guzman, Pitt's project manager, requesting that ICF/SRW's report be submitted to the Pittsburgh Regional Office of DER for formal review before the land was transferred to the state. General Services acknowledged that doing so might delay the start of construction, which turned out to be prophetic.[67]

On September 5 Jerry Dettore sent a copy of the report to Tony Orlando at DER for review and requested a meeting to discuss it.[68] During the months of September and October, Jim Nairn of Civil and Environmental Consultants discussed the various environmental studies with DER's staff on the URA's behalf and, at the URA's request, provided DER with copies of the earlier studies.[69] The requested meeting at DER's Pittsburgh office, held October 19, resulted in a request for still more information, which Jerry Dettore sent the following day. At the end of the month he wrote again, clarifying the exact parcels that were planned for Pitt's building and that therefore DER was being asked to evaluate.[70]

DER's Gale Campbell responded on November 7. Whereas the URA and their consultants had felt that there was no contamination on the site that even warranted notifying DER, DER disagreed. To the contrary, they concluded that further study was now required on parcel 4, west of Pitt's proposed building.[71] DER noted that depending on the findings, steps might have to be taken to ensure the safety of workers. On the other hand, parcel 2, where Pitt's building was to be located, was acceptable. The URA contracted with Civil and Environmental Consultants to perform the additional testing at a cost of $40,000.[72] Their report, dated December 20 and transmitted to DER the next day, stated that total cyanide levels ranged up to 130 ppm in the groundwater, and free cyanide to 1 ppm.[73]

The presence of cyanide was puzzling because the steel-rolling operations did not involve cyanide. Only later would the partners come to identify the source and extent of the problem. DER's reaction was not encouraging. Gale Campbell wrote on January 12 that because of the presence of cyanide in the samples, DER wanted the groundwater monitored for a year, at which time they would determine whether continued monitoring would be necessary. DER also recommended additional soil borings on parcel 4, west of Pitt's site, and concluded they could not recommend construction there at this time. Finally, DER would insist on deed restrictions that would recognize the existence of the contamination. They stated in conclusion, "The DER has serious reservations concerning the use of this property for anything other than an open space, parking lot or similar use."[74]

Despite the discouraging developments on the environmental front and the inevitable delay these developments caused, the URA continued to move the project forward. Representatives from DER's Pittsburgh office and the URA met on February 5 to discuss the additional testing. Also in February, in preparation for the construction season, the URA retained architects GWSM, Inc., to design the open space just to the east of Pitt's proposed building, the landscaped buffer along Second Avenue, and both the eastern and western entrances, and to oversee construction, which was to begin mid-year.[75]

Later that month the URA and General Services closed in escrow on the parcel for Pitt's building contingent on the DER's final approval, and the following month the URA approved the final drawings for Pitt's building.[76] As proposed, the University of Pittsburgh Center for Biotechnology and Bioengineering would encompass 91,000 square feet with 100% devoted to laboratory uses. It would have four floors plus a basement and a penthouse. Its financing of $14 million would come entirely from the state. Pitt would contribute in-kind and additional expenses as a match. Pitt projected that the building would house sixty new research jobs and lead to creation and expansion of a new industry, leading in turn to additional private investment and diversification of Pittsburgh's economy. Construction was to begin in the summer if DER signed off by May, with completion eighteen months later.[77] On April 9 Jerry Dettore sent the DER Civil and Environmental Consultants' report of the soil borings on Pitt's parcel and the results of their tests for cyanide contamination, which confirmed elevated cyanide levels west of Pitt's planned building.[78]

DER took months to respond to the report, a fact that was puzzling and frustrating to the URA. On the one hand, the Department of Community Affairs and Department of Commerce were pouring state funds into the project—only to have development meet a stalemate at the DER.[79] On May 18, I wrote to Ray Christman, who had become the Secretary of Commerce after leaving the URA, and who, coincidentally, had worked for the DER's secretary, Art Davis, early in his career. I thought that perhaps with Ray's commitment and understanding and his personal relationship with Davis, he could get the DER to soften its stance. I asked Ray to meet with Davis in an effort to dissuade the DER from requiring deed restrictions on the contaminated sections of the site. The URA was concerned that such restrictions would deter private development on the site by frightening financial institutions regarding the possibility of then-unknown future liability.[80] It would take some time before Ray would feel able to respond to my request.

On May 24 Jim Nairn of Civil and Environmental Consultants summarized his firm's conclusions about the environmental situation at the Center for the URA's new executive director, George Whitmer. The tests had detected total cyanide in concentrations in excess of 50 ppm in several borings on parcel 4 and in one boring on parcel 3, but reactive cyanide was not detected in any sample, indicating that the form of cyanide present would not release hydrogen cyanide gas, particularly under the environmental conditions prevalent at the site. Determining whether the materials containing cyanide at the PTC site were "hazardous wastes" had required a review of federal law because of the complexity of making the determination. Although the materials were not among the hazardous wastes enumerated in the law, Nairn felt they should be tested for reactivity and toxicity, which could lead to their being considered hazardous. Finding that they were not hazardous, the consultant classified them instead as residual wastes under Pennsylvania regulations: "The bottom line conclusion of this report was that cyanide at the PTC site poses no substantial risk to human health or the environment."[81] The consultant had not found hazards at the Pittsburgh Technology Center.

Despite this judgment, the URA had significant concerns about what the DER's letter would say when it finally came. The DER might make a different judgment. The URA worried about how it would affect the willingness of the private sector to invest on the site.

The URA as Developer – 1990

By this time, three years after the universities had put themselves forward as developers of the project, it had become clear that they would not be the answer to attracting private development, as their own developments had languished and demands from private firms to join them had not materialized. Pitt's plan to begin construction on its building in the spring was now mired in the environmental clearance process. Carnegie Mellon's design, when submitted to cost analysis, had proved to exceed by far the amount of the state's grant, and after all the fanfare CMU had dismissed Peter Eisenman as their architect.[82]

Gradually, the staff of the URA came to the realization that the city would have to take the lead through its own marketing and contacts, principally referrals of companies that sought help from the mayor's office or from the URA directly to locate in the city. If the DER's letter raised uncertainty about the environmental safety of the site, it could prove a powerful dissuasion to private investors and make private development on the site impossible.

To get a sense of the magnitude of the potential problems of financing private development on the site, George Whitmer asked David Matter of Oxford to explore the mood of institutional investors. Whitmer and Matter were old friends, having worked together in Mayor Caliguiri's office, and Matter was very familiar with the site because of Oxford's involvement as CMU's development partner. Through Oxford's broker, Matter asked for a response from one of its lenders, Aetna, Inc. Aetna was one of the world's largest commercial real estate lenders, and Oxford was one of Aetna's largest borrowers in western Pennsylvania (with $300 million outstanding).

Matter's inquiry produced a discouraging response. Rachel Handel of Aetna wrote that "it would be very unlikely that Aetna would ever be able to make a loan on this particular piece of property given the environmental issues raised in the draft May 14, 1990 letter report to J. Dettore." Handel also expressed concern about the impact of the area that contained the cyanide on the remainder of the Center.[83] Matter concluded that the language in Aetna's response, if strictly applied, would effectively eliminate Aetna as a possible permanent lender.

Chapter 2

The Environmental Bottom Line – 1990

The DER's long-awaited and long-negotiated letter finally arrived at the URA in August. Dated August 8, from Gale Campbell to Jerry Dettore, it summarized the DER's review of the consultant's April 9 *Report of Findings—Contamination Assessment—PTC*. Noting that "the additional data indicates that cyanide waste is present 15–20 feet below the surface over most of parcels 3 & 4," DER concluded that "a notice referencing the presence of these conditions . . . is essential to ensure that waste materials will not be disturbed and ground water will not be used." DER requested quarterly monitoring of groundwater for an additional year and beyond, if warranted.[84]

In an August 7 interoffice memo, George Whitmer commented that the DER's letter had been "long anticipated." It is "not quite what we would have liked," but there were at least positive changes from the initial draft. By that time the URA had already concluded, "The letter doesn't make much difference with respect to financing private development, an issue we are going to have to overcome in the future."

Not long after, the question of the source of the cyanide that had caused so much trouble and delay was answered. Notwithstanding all the paid consultants and experienced regulators who had been on the case, it was Dr. Richard Luthy, a chemical engineering professor at CMU with expertise in environmental engineering and water quality, who was able to explain its presence. Because CMU's first building had initially been planned to go near to Pitt's building, on the very location where the highest concentrations of cyanide were found, officials at CMU had enlisted their own expert, Dr. Luthy, to explore the matter further. Using old Sanborn Insurance maps, Luthy documented the presence of a manufactured gas plant at that location from the 1880s until about 1920. Iron cyanide, a "comparatively non-toxic" compound, was a by-product waste of the manufacturing process.[85] The cyanide had been present throughout the steel mill's existence, buried under its massive 10- to 12-foot-thick foundations. Tens of thousands of mill workers had labored on top of the cyanide-contaminated soil for decades with no ill effects because the cyanide had been encased far below the surface of the ground.

Luthy concluded, "There is no indication that the contaminants pose a risk to the environment or human health."[86] He noted, however, that property further to the west had not been developed until later and "will probably show comparatively low levels of cyanide contamination," which in fact proved to be the case.[87] This was the site where CMU then insisted on locating, carefully avoiding the site of the manufactured gas plant, which was benign even though cyanide may have been present.[88] The presence of the cyanide accounts for the fact that the universities' buildings were not built side by side and explains why a large gap remained between Pitt's and CMU's buildings for many years.

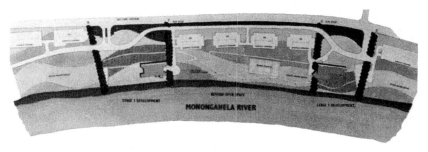

Preliminary Land Development Plan adopted in January 1992, showing Pitt's building on the right and CMU's on the left, with the cyanide-contaminated parcels separating them

Moving Forward under the New Order – 1990

Finally, on August 16, 1990, months later than expected, the Department of General Services opened bids for the University of Pittsburgh's building. Tedco Construction Corporation's bid of $7.52 million was successful, and it became the general contractor.[89] Over $26 million had already been invested in the site, most of it public money, with nothing yet to show for it. The first buildings were to have been started in 1986, but lack of interest by tenants and discovery of the cyanide had pushed the development back four years.

Then another concern arose. Without a recommitment from CMU, the state was reluctant to proceed with Pitt's facility, fearing that they would be building the only building on the site. However, in late November, after CMU reaffirmed its commitment—having dismissed its original architect and moved its location—the state awarded the contracts to build Pitt's building.[90] With Pitt's building committed, attention turned to public spaces. Pitt, reluctant to spend their state money on landscaping, was looking for ways to cut costs. In one incident, Ana Guzmán, Pitt's Director of Facilities Planning, complained that the black mondo grass (an expensive plant often used as a groundcover) that the architects had included in the landscape plan would cost $200,000, which far exceeded their budget. The URA backed off from insisting on that type of grass.[91] On another front, the URA contracted with the firm of Adam Filippo & Associates to design signs for the Center.

The URA and its partners continued to struggle with how to obtain private development. The URA pitched the Center to Pittsburgh National Bank (PNB), which was looking for a location for its data center. Pittsburgh National had looked for sites throughout the region. Although PNB's use was not compatible with the Center's research focus, the URA and universities felt that any private investment would help the universities with their required matching private investments and would encourage other private tenants to consider the site. Ultimately, PNB narrowed its choices to a location near the airport, a choice that the bank's management favored. The Technology Center, which the bank continued to consider only because George Whitmer pressed its upper management to do so, was unsuccessful in the end.

On October 29 Ray Christman at Commerce, perhaps responding to my request some months earlier, wrote to George Whitmer and Joe Gariti seeking their "best judgment" in preparation for a meeting with Art Davis of DER and the Governor's Office to discuss a proposed approach to resolving the Technology Center's environmental questions. Although the state could neither provide indemnification nor back away from its regulatory responsibilities, he outlined a number of steps that might raise confidence for prospective investors.[92]

Despite the evident problem the environmental situation had created, the state was not willing to relax its requirement for private development. When Dr. Robert Mehrabian arrived in Pittsburgh in the summer of 1990 to take the presidency of CMU, the *Pittsburgh Press* noted his immediate concern about this problem and, at the same time, his optimism about the project. "How many [university research parks] have a prime real estate plum in the center of a major city?" Mehrabian asked.[93] Still, the requirement remained a constant concern for the university. In a November 11 letter to George Whitmer, Secretary Karen Miller of Community Affairs stressed that if non-state participation in CMU's project failed to reach 50% within five years of the time CMU secured an occupancy permit, "the grantee will be required to return the Commonwealth funds equal to the amount by which the contribution failed to meet the necessary total."[94] This was certainly an incentive to keep trying to bring private investment to the Center.

A Bid for Legent – 1990

It was in this context that the URA made a valiant effort to bring Legent Corporation to the Center. Formed in 1989 by a merger of Pittsburgh's prominent Duquesne Systems with Marino of Vienna, Virginia, Legent at the time was a leading Pittsburgh independent systems software company whose market was in IBM mainframe computers, networks, and applications systems. Legent's management had made the decision to leave their leased headquarters in Allegheny Center on the North Side and build their own facility. Initially, Legent's officers and their real estate agent, Oliver Realty-Grubb & Ellis, had not considered any locations in the city. In fact, they had already spoken with National Development Company about their property on the Parkway West. The URA, however, learning about the company's plans to relocate, quickly made a forceful presentation of sites in the city. The URA's first recommendation was the North Shore, but Legent's officers were not enthusiastic. Washington's Landing was also a possibility, but the size and configuration of parcels there were severe constraints.

The Pittsburgh Technology Center best met Legent's requirements, but when George Whitmer and I first met with Legent's management in July, the site was difficult to sell. Since we still had not heard from DER, the URA could not give any assurances about environmental concerns. On August 9 Steve Zecher and I met with Carolyn Vetovich of Legent and their Oliver Realty advisors. She had not been happy about scheduling the meeting. I promised I would take no more than half an hour. As we talked, however, she became very interested and had many questions. Oliver began to take our side somewhat, and we stayed over an hour, leaving on a very cordial note.

By September the environmental situation was clearer, and we promoted the Center heavily.[95] In late September Legent's Realtor issued a request for proposals that included this promising provision: "Legent has requested that we evaluate the J&L site, along with several other alternatives." The company required an assurance that it could take occupancy of a new building by June 1, 1992, when its lease at Allegheny Center expired.[96] At the end of the month Neal Pollon, Legent's executive vice president, toured the Technology Center with George Whitmer.

As possible developers for Legent at the Technology Center, David Matter of Oxford Development and Richard Irwin of National Development wrote to the city and the URA, outlining what they thought would be required to win in this "highly competitive process." Besides the free land and free parking that Legent had already requested, the developers asked for an environmental indemnification that would cover the entire site and pass to future owners; they required a letter from the DER "stating that there is no known health hazard and no cleanup required"; they wanted evidence that the state would in fact build the new ramps to the Parkway from Second Avenue that had been under investigation for some time; they required zoning for general office use, a "firm commitment to provide food service and fitness facilities" on free land to be provided by the URA, and an option for a second building—extraordinary demands, some of which the URA simply could not meet.

In a progress report to Legent's realtor at the end of the month, Richard Irwin gave his opinion that from an environmental standpoint a building on the site could be financed. He assured that an amenities center, consisting of a restaurant, a banking machine, a fitness facility, and a day care facility, would be built on the designated site between Pitt's and CMU's development zones.[97]

Pulling out all the stops, George Whitmer wrote to Legent's realtor, committing that the URA would "provide land to the Legent project at no cost to Legent" and would "work with the developer to construct parking on the site at no cost to Legent."[98] The URA projected that they could finance the $4.5 million cost of a garage and three tiered lots to support Legent's first building (225,000 square feet on five floors, a projected investment of $27 million), using a combination of a Business Investment Fund loan from the state, project funds that the URA had on hand, and tax increment financing.[99]

Despite these heroic efforts, Legent decided to move to the Parkway West area near the airport. Shortly thereafter, however, the company moved its headquarters to its offices in Vienna, Virginia, although it made a point to advertise its continued presence as a Pittsburgh employer. Only five years later, in September 1995, Legent was acquired by Computer Associates, and within a few years only a small number of the 2,500 people who had worked for Legent at the time of its acquisition were still employed there. What had been a serious disappointment at the time meant, in the end, that the Technology Center had dodged a bullet.

Environmental Denouement – 1990–1991

Interestingly, in October 1990 state senator Jack Wagner proposed that to improve traffic to and from the South Side, the state should acquire the rail bridge across the Monongahela that marked the southeastern boundary of the Technology Center. At that time, however prescient, the proposal came to nothing. Although LTV indicated that it was willing to consider a sale, the company still used the bridge for steam and electric lines, and there were higher priorities for the state's development funds. Years later, public acquisition of this Hot Metal Bridge— which had once carried hot steel from the furnaces on the South Side to the rolling mills across the river—and its conversion to an automobile, bicycle, and pedestrian bridge, would support development of South Side Works from LTV's former mill on the South Side.[100] It also would allow bikers and walkers to cross the river to use the trails that now run along both sides of the river.

In early December the URA reported to the DER that there had been no significant change in the condition of the groundwater on the parcels west of Pitt's site over the stipulated year of testing. The URA wanted the issue of groundwater quality settled for good. Dettore asked for discussion and offered the services of the URA's consultant, Jim Nairn.[101]

The DER concurred that CMU's development of parcel 4 was not a problem so long as there were provisions for the safety of workers and proper disposal of any waste encountered during construction. They also agreed that even though the groundwater was only somewhat contaminated, treating it was not feasible because the contamination was so far below the surface, under the foundations of the old mill. The groundwater could not be used. Fortunately, it did not seem to be affecting water in the Monongahela River, so it was deemed not to be problematic. The DER asked for continuing quarterly monitoring to detect any deterioration in water quality.[102]

In the end the alarm over possible contamination on the site had been much ado about practically nothing. The URA's original contention that there was no hazardous waste on the site had been verified, but the heightened awareness created by the DER's involvement; the time-consuming, expensive, and inconclusive testing; and the resulting delay of almost two years had increased rather than diminished environmental concerns and had marked the site as an environmental problem, with the unintended effect of dampening private interest.

Carnegie Mellon, whose contract with the state required dollar-for-dollar matching of local funds, despaired of the potential for private development and began to account for—and asked the URA and RIDC to account for—every hour spent by employees on the project in order to apply the hours toward their obligation. Pitt, which had only a moral commitment to generate matching private development, had gone from confidence that it would quickly and easily exceed it to disclaiming it entirely.

Chapter 2

University Research Centers – 1991

Construction finally began on the University of Pittsburgh's Center for Biotechnology and Bioengineering in February 1991. Preparations also were underway to begin construction of the site's first public open spaces, the park immediately adjacent to Pitt's building, and the hedgerows on either side.[103] By the beginning of May, excavation for Pitt's building was 90% complete, and the piling 80% complete. Tedco had encountered no unusual site conditions. Their only problem centered on their inability to get a city building permit.

Meanwhile, CMU was moving forward with its plans. Ties between the URA and CMU had grown stronger with George Whitmer's appointment to direct the URA. He and Steve Schillo, CMU's budget officer, had worked together in Mayor Caliguiri's administration. In addition, Whitmer had forged a friendly relationship with Pat Keating, assistant first to President Cyert and then to President Mehrabian. Pat heavily felt the pressure to recruit private development to satisfy CMU's commitment to the state. Together, he and Whitmer avidly pursued every possible private interest in the site. The friendly collaboration between CMU and the URA led CMU to a formal decision to work directly with the URA, rather than through RIDC, on developing its building.[104]

The *New York Times* of Sunday, July 28, 1991, ran a story in its "Northeast Notebook," reprinted the next month in the *Chicago Tribune,* reporting on the Technology Center's evolution. The story noted progress on Pitt's building, the delay caused by the discovery of cyanide in the soil, and the universities' scaled-back plans and their collaboration with the URA to market the site.[105]

CMU's efforts moved forward steadily. In August they settled on the scope of work for an environmental investigation of their new site, which was to include core borings and soil samples, at a cost of $72,717. One important feature of that work was to determine as precisely as possible the western boundary of the site formerly occupied by the Pittsburgh Gas Works, the source of the cyanide. CMU did not want to incur any liability for the cyanide, regardless of how safe the levels might be. There was no way to assure that at some later date a regulator might not require that it be removed, and CMU did not want to be responsible. It would not build its building on that property.[106] The best uses that could be imagined for the parcels contaminated with cyanide were as tennis courts to serve the universities' athletic programs and as an amenity for workers in the technology companies that all parties hoped would be attracted to the site.

*Cyanide-contaminated site, still undeveloped in 2005, viewed from the
University of Pittsburgh's building*

That same month, Gilbane Properties of Providence, Rhode Island, and ORS of McLean, Virginia, approached the URA regarding a client, "Corporation X," which was interested in relocating to Pittsburgh and for which they were serving as site selection specialist and developer. The firm was involved in research and development and was looking for approximately 250,000 square feet, which could double to 500,000 square feet, for a North American headquarters facility. The URA made a proposal and attempted to follow up, but nothing developed because other locations apparently proved to be more suitable. The URA never did learn the identity of the mysterious client.

In October, City Council authorized the URA to apply for Strategy 21 funds, in the amount of $17,002,195, from the Pennsylvania Department of Community Affairs for the design and construction of CMU's much-delayed 80,000-square-foot research facility. CMU assured that an equal amount of private funds would be invested at the Center as a matching share, although there was a great deal of anxiety at CMU about how that would be accomplished. Construction of CMU's building was now scheduled to begin in mid-1992 and to be completed in early 1994.[107]

Another Framework for Development – 1991

Given the environmental cloud hanging over the site, attracting private development was clearly far more difficult than the universities or the URA had foreseen. The URA concluded that it would need to continue to take the lead, but it would also need to work in close collaboration with both universities, which were motivated to attract private development because of their legal or moral commitments. In addition, the presence of the universities and their buildings on the site was still clearly the most powerful marketing advantage the Center had.

By now, the university presidents who had originally met with Mayor Caliguiri had left. Dr. Richard Cyert, who had presided over CMU since 1972, had retired in 1990 and had been succeeded by Dr. Mehrabian. Pitt's Dr. Wesley Posvar retired in 1991 and was succeeded by Dr. Dennis O'Connor. These changes in leadership opened the opportunity for a more collegial and cooperative relationship to develop between the two universities. The growing strength of the relations among the universities and the URA finally made the RIDC's role in marketing the Center superfluous.

In September 1991 the URA's board, recognizing the new relationships, authorized the URA to execute a memorandum of understanding with the universities for joint marketing and development. The memorandum called for the creation of a tripartite organization comprising the URA, Pitt, and CMU to market the site to private developers. It would replace the 1987 agreement signed by the URA, RIDC, Pitt, and CMU, which was outdated both because of elimination of the universities' development zones and because of the change in roles. Essentially, whereas in 1987 the universities had wanted the privilege of developing the entire site, they were now reluctant to take title to any part of it and wanted no responsibility for its development. Yet because of their obligation to satisfy the state's requirement for matching investment, they agreed to do their best to help the URA market the site to any private developer. The URA and Pitt agreed to count all non-state expenditures, starting with 1991 and moving forward, toward CMU's obligation, which was the most pressing.[108]

The new development scenario and the memorandum also replaced the 1986 agreement between the URA and RIDC, which had designated RIDC as the master developer prior to the universities' involvement, although in reality RIDC had not had that role for some time.[109] Whitmer suggested that the development partners continue discussions with RIDC about developing a building on the site, a role proposed for the RIDC from the time of the first agreement, although Whitmer doubted that private financing could be found because of the poor real estate climate and the environmental problems.[110]

The URA and CMU pushed forward on CMU's building plan. In November the URA assumed the contract with Urban Design Associates for site planning and engaged UDA to complete the Final Land Development Plan for CMU's site (parcel 1-west) at a cost of $45,000. After its disappointing experience with Peter Eisenman, CMU had retained Bohlin Powell Larkin Cywinski architects, a known quantity because of their success in designing the University of Pittsburgh's building.

The foundation for Pitt's building was completed in early summer, and erection of structural steel in July. The entire project was approximately 50% complete. The structure was in the process of being enclosed, after which work would concentrate on the interior spaces, with completion still expected by early fall of 1992. The URA continued to work with the Department of Transportation on concepts to improve access by adding ramps to and from the Parkway East. Although alternative designs had been under consideration for some time, there was no resolution, and the earliest time they could possibly be completed was 1997.

In late 1991 the URA reported that a total of $56,303,654 had been committed to the Center, $49,330,000 of which had come from the state, $2.28 million from the city, $2.9 from the Pittsburgh Water and Sewer Authority, $1.5 from the URA, and $330,000 from the Richard King Mellon and Pittsburgh foundations.[111] The first building was still not complete.

Renewed Efforts to Secure Private Development – 1992

Amid doubts about the prospects for private development of the site, Brooks Robinson received an inquiry from Penn State about the possibility of using a portion of the site for leaf recycling, hardly a high-tech use. Fortunately, Maribeth Rizzutto, the city's recycling coordinator, determined that the DER required that leaf recycling sites be at least 300 feet from a public water source, precluding the Center from eligibility for this use and settling the issue without controversy.[112]

Design and preparations continued for CMU's building. In March George Whitmer received word that the Department of Community Affairs would contract with the URA for CMU's building for $16,107,195, the original amount of $17,002,195 less the $895,000 that CMU had already used up on their aborted first design.[113] CMU continued to feel great and justifiable concern about their obligation to match the state's funds with an equal amount of private investment. They had not yet found a source. One approach was to commission RIDC to develop a speculative building, assuming that financing could be found. A possible tenant was the Mine Safety and Health Administration, which was being displaced from a building CMU had acquired from the federal government. The URA asked Urban Design Associates and RIDC to make a preliminary proposal, which they did in April, although George Whitmer expressed his opinion that even for a building fully leased by a government tenant, "there is certainly a question as to the current ability to finance in the private market." To overcome that problem, Brooks Robinson suggested a novel way of financing the building—recoverable grants that would be replaced by conventional financing as the building was leased. This idea sounded doable. The URA commissioned Urban Design Associates to develop a preliminary design for the building.[114]

Meanwhile, the DER continued to complain about the site and to ask for a formal agreement with the URA to place restrictions on its development. In an April 3 letter, Gale Campbell sent to Jerry Dettore a copy of the DER's *Ground Water Quality Protection Strategy*, which set forth the DER's general position on sites such as the Pittsburgh Technology Center, where cleanup to background standards was not achievable for technical or economic conditions; "the overall strategy requires, at a minimum, on going monitoring and restrictions regarding the use of ground water for sites which cannot be adequately remediated." Campbell noted that while the cyanide waste appeared to be "relatively stable and not highly toxic," it had contaminated the groundwater, and thus the groundwater could not be used. He also repeated DER's concern about contamination of groundwater with organic compounds at the northern end of the site, near MetalTech. That concern had not been resolved, and monitoring of wells would need to continue there. Ultimately, the DER wanted a binding legal document that would commit the URA to take the actions that the DER required in exchange for assurances from the DER. Campbell advised the URA to consult its attorneys and advise him of the URA's intentions.[115]

On April 15 personnel at the URA, including George Whitmer, Joe Gariti, Jerry Dettore, Dana Michael, and I, met to discuss the DER's latest letter. Jerry and Joe felt that the DER was pushing for a consent order that would require cleanup of the area near MetalTech, which Jerry estimated would cost some $100,000, take several years, and require the setup and maintenance of a pumping station. On the other hand, if worded properly, a consent order could assist in marketing the site because it could certify some parcels as clean for development. A danger that I feared, however, was that a consent agreement could call for still additional testing on the parcels that had not already been tested thoroughly, and that such a provision, together with the DER's usually acerbic language and the presence of the agreement itself, might be detrimental to or possibly delay development further. George observed that any potential developer would review the DER's entire involvement anyway. His fear of an agreement was that because of the presence of cyanide on a portion of the site, the DER might apply restrictions to the entire site.

The group finally decided that Joe and Jerry should begin discussions with the DER regarding a consent agreement. At least with an agreement, the URA would have certainty about what cleanup the state would require, and it would also know what sites could be developed. Meanwhile, the URA's Economic Development Department would apply to the Department of Commerce's Industrial Site Recycling Program to cover any resulting cleanup costs. Joe and Jerry would try to get the DER to limit any restrictions on development to the area containing the cyanide; they would request an acknowledgment that the area with the cyanide had in fact been treated, at least partially, by covering it with fill. They would also try to persuade the DER to declare other areas "clean"—thus allowing for development—and to agree to a reasonable treatment plan for the area near MetalTech.[116] URA would then agree to build parking on that site in the hope that it would permit a less aggressive treatment plan.

Regardless, the URA pushed forward with development, convinced that the environmental problems could be solved in the end. It announced that it would begin construction of additional open spaces, including entry signs, lawns, and tree-lined walkways. Construction of the University of Pittsburgh's Center for Biotechnology and Bioengineering was nearing completion. Carnegie Mellon still hoped to begin construction on its building before the end of the year.[117]

University of Pittsburgh's Center for Biotechnology and Bioengineering,
the first building at the Pittsburgh Technology Center, 1992

University of Pittsburgh's Center for Biotechnology and Bioengineering, the first building at the Pittsburgh Technology Center, 1992

Another candidate emerged for the Technology Center when I learned, too late, that American Thermoplastics, a dynamic plastics manufacturing company located in old warehouses on Second Avenue only a block from the URA, had been working with RIDC on planning new headquarters and a plant in RIDC Park in O'Hara Township. Not surprisingly, RIDC, whose role in redeveloping the PTC had diminished, had not shared the information with us. As a result, the URA had not had the opportunity to propose alternative locations in the city. I hurriedly enlisted my staff to help, and we pasted together information on a number of sites—not including the Technology Center—for Steve Silberman, the company's young president. I knew him slightly from having interviewed him some years previous about his company and from frequent greetings as we passed one another on the street as I walked to work each morning. Silberman accepted the information graciously, but the only city site that interested him at all was the Technology Center. However, despite our desire to get private development at the Technology Center and despite the fact that we hated to lose another firm from the city, American Thermoplastics did not fit the research and development profile the zoning required. Silberman also found the land at the Technology Center to be "very, very expensive" compared to land in the suburbs. In April 1993 American Thermoplastics announced that it was leaving the city for RIDC Park.[118]

Toward the end of 1992, in an effort calculated more to introduce the public to the Technology Center than to realize an income from the property, the URA decided to develop and lease surface parking at the Center for commuters working downtown. A request for proposals issued in October produced proposals from four parking operators. The URA selected Golden Triangle Parking, the bidder that offered the best financial return, and in December it authorized a lease of six lots, spanning practically the length of the property, on the properties designated for parking in the master plan.[119]

Finally, a Private Commitment – 1992–1993

Unbeknownst to the URA, in mid-1992 Union Switch & Signal was looking for a new site to consolidate and expand its operations.[120] Years previously it had closed its historic plant in Swissvale and moved its headquarters and production to South Carolina while relocating its research operations to McCandless Township in Pittsburgh's North Hills. Joyce Gannon of the Pittsburgh *Post-Gazette* reported how the search began:

> Real estate broker Jon Harrigan was on his way home to Allison Park one day last April when he noticed that the parking lot at Union Switch & Signal's McCandless office building was jam-packed. He pulled his car into the lot, walked into the building and asked to see the company's facilities manager, Harry Sampson. Through that cold call, he learned that Union Switch was talking about finding a new home where it could expand.

> Coincidentally, executives from the firm's Italian parent, Ansaldo Group, were scheduled to arrive in Pittsburgh within weeks to explore the possibility of moving the company to the RIDC Thorn Hill Industrial Park in Marshall. About a month later, Sampson called Harrigan to say that Ansaldo wasn't totally sold on the Thorn Hill site and that Union Switch could use his help.[121]

Harrigan and his partner, Greg Black, of Pennsylvania Commercial Real Estate ultimately considered forty-two possible sites for Union Switch.

Once the prospect came into view at the URA, we did everything possible to answer Union Switch's questions and meet their needs. The fit with the Technology Center seemed ideal.

When the critical factors in their deciding on the Center proved to be the cost and availability of parking, I revived the idea of the URA's financing the cost of a parking structure. I proposed that, for the first time in Pittsburgh, the URA take advantage of the state's relatively new tax increment financing statute, which would make the site no more expensive to the company and its employees than the competing suburban sites. I made it my personal mission to educate the members of the city council, the school board, and county officials on this new form of public financing, since all three bodies would have to pass legislation to approve its use for the proposed garage. Given the novelty of the approach and the potential difficulties that might be involved in securing agreement from the taxing bodies, George Whitmer, who had in the meantime moved from the URA to the mayor's office and been replaced at the URA by Mulugetta Birru, again approached his friend David Matter of Oxford Development and asked him to work with the URA and the city to shepherd the tax increment plan through its many required steps.

To improve the possibilities for quick retirement of the tax increment bonds, the URA included the entire Pittsburgh Technology Center in the tax increment district so that taxes from any development on the site would be directed to repay the bonds used to finance the garage. For good measure, the URA also included the expected payments for governmental services from Pitt's and CMU's buildings. At the end of the day, the URA would own the garage free and clear. If this approach would bring this substantial and symbolically important business to the Pittsburgh Technology Center, it seemed well worth the public contribution.

In the end, with this incentive the company chose the Technology Center, citing affordability, access to research at Pitt and CMU, and the capacity to expand onto adjacent land. Union Switch's building, to be built and owned by RIDC, would take advantage of low-interest Pennsylvania Industrial Development Authority financing available only through a state-designated Industrial Development Corporation like RIDC. The building was to be 175,000 square feet and cost $20 million. Union Switch expected that 450 people would work in the facility and wanted to provide room for up to 700. The state of Pennsylvania would contribute heavily to financing the building, with funds coming from the Industrial Development Authority, the Pennsylvania Economic Development Finance Authority, and the Sunny Day Fund. At a press conference in Mayor Sophie Masloff's office on March 3, Union Switch & Signal announced their decision to build their new Systems and Research Center at the Pittsburgh Technology Center. It would be the first private investment in the Center. Although the URA and the universities were understandably pleased, especially since Union Switch's decision to build on the site immediately satisfied CMU's obligation to match the state's investment in its building, the response from the public was not unmixed. The *Pittsburgh Post-Gazette* editorialized that "it would have been better if an out-of-state firm had been attracted,"[122] even though selection of the Pittsburgh Technology Center was returning one of the company's principal functions almost to its original home.

MONONGAHELA RIVER

First buildings at the Pittsburgh Technology Center, with Pitt on the right, CMU on the other side of the parcels with the cyanide, which in this plan have surface parking and tennis courts, and Union Switch and Signal on the left

MONONGAHELA RIVER

Plan for the ultimate build-out of the Pittsburgh Technology Center, with buildings arrayed along the river, parking structures along Second Avenue, hedgerows crossing the site, and the "green river" running through it

Good Outcomes – 1993

That same month, Pitt's Center for Biotechnology and Bioengineering was nearing completion. Donald Miller, the *Pittsburgh Post-Gazette*'s art and architecture critic, was complimentary, calling the building "a major step for this post-industrial city, . . . [a] silvery European-looking building, a postmodern grandchild of Swiss architect Le Corbusier." Jon Jackson of the architectural firm that designed the building commented, "The building is

obligations. Therefore, there is no basis for the Department to require, and the Department will not require, anyone to perform any response, removal, remedial and/or monitoring activities with respect to the Development Parcels based on the environmental review." However, it continued, "unknown, undisclosed or changed facts or conditions, or . . . unforeseen or changed circumstances" could cause the department to require additional action.[131] Relief at executing this document, despite its limitations, cannot be overstated.

Inquiry from Another University – 1993

In July, Duquesne University, through Ann Gleeson of U.S. Congressman Bill Coyne's office, approached the URA about the possibility of developing a building at the Center to house its growing environmental science programs. In turn, the URA approached RIDC to serve as the developer, asking them to revive the concept of the building they had begun to design the year before for the eastern part of the property. Considering that the state had fully financed the cost of Pitt's and CMU's buildings, the URA began to explore the possibilities for state financing for this building. In a September 16 letter, I suggested the possibility of finding funds that had been authorized in an earlier state capital budget, such as a 1988 authorization of "Monongahela Valley redevelopment projects," and offered the URA as an applicant for the funds. The state would require 50% non-state participation.[132]

RIDC's proposal, received in mid-September, included a building of approximately 80,000 square feet on 4 acres of property, which RIDC would purchase for $200,000 an acre. The project would include two towers with a winter garden between them: one tower for Duquesne and the other for lease. The development cost would be $16.2 million. Financing might include a grant from the state, state loans, a loan from the URA, and some conventional financing. The Duquesne University Environmental Research and Education Center would house the Chemical Analysis and Automation Research Institute, the Applied Biology Research Institute, the Environmental Science and Management Program, and a child care facility to serve the entire Technology Center.

The URA, RIDC, and Duquesne wrote back and forth about various details of the proposal, but ultimately Duquesne lost interest in the site, preferring to concentrate on developing its own campus— another disappointment in efforts to attract significant, appropriate developers to the site.

Conclusion of a Development Chapter – 1993–1995

In August, after my presentations to the school board, city council, and county officials, the URA approved the tax increment plan to finance construction of the five-level parking garage that would contain 561 spaces for Union Switch. The plan would entail issuance of some $5.7 million in revenue bonds that would be repaid primarily by taxes that the RIDC would pay to the three taxing bodies on the Union Switch building, estimated to be $527,500 annually. The taxing bodies would have to agree to the plan in order for it to take effect, and each of them did agree over the succeeding months.[133] During the same period, the URA approved RIDC's final drawings for Union Switch's 174,000-square-foot building, which ultimately would be built with financing from Dollar Bank and the state.[134]

Carnegie Mellon broke ground for its building in September. Union Switch followed shortly thereafter, on September 23, with the intent to occupy the building in 1995 and with high hopes for future expansion. One of Union Switch's officers predicted, "If our growth plan continues at the rate in which we grew in the past, we'll have the need of raising another facility." The plan the parties had agreed on provided for that possibility by reserving land for Union Switch to expand downriver.[135]

With Pitt's building in use and other buildings underway, the URA and developers had the incentive to conclude their negotiations to form an association to maintain the Center's extensive open spaces, including the riverfront, the green river, hedgerows, and plazas. Discussions had gone on for months, but without tenants the discussions were all theoretical. The URA calculated assessments on the basis of what the universities' developments would have owed on the land had they been taxable (which, of course, they were not). The universities understood from the start that they would share in the cost of maintaining open spaces at the Center, and the URA was able to secure their agreement, along with RIDC's and Union Switch's, to both a formula and actual assessments, which the URA then presented to City Council for approval. Some members of the council criticized the assessments for being too low: $8,000 from CMU and $6,400 from Pitt. Ultimately, however, the council approved the proposal.[136]

In an editorial on Pittsburgh's economic development conditions near the year's end, the *Pittsburgh Post-Gazette* commented in passing on the slow progress at the Pittsburgh Technology Center. Robert Mehrabian, CMU's president, came to the project's defense in a subsequent letter to the editor. He acknowledged that "the pace of development at the PTC was slowed by environmental concerns raised by the state. But we meticulously examined the area and proved that there are no health risks associated with the site." He praised Union Switch's "relationship with Carnegie Mellon and interest in our high-technology capabilities as key elements in the decision to build in Pittsburgh. . . . This development," he said in conclusion, "is a shining example of how industry, civic and government organizations and universities can achieve great things by working together."[137]

By mid-1994 construction was in full swing on the Carnegie Mellon Research Institute, Union Switch & Signal's building, and the parking garage. The *Post-Gazette's* real estate writer, Ron DaParma, wrote that "lofty expectations long held for a grand, suburban-style high technology park in Pittsburgh are coming ever closer to fruition at the Pittsburgh Technology Center. . . . Now that the . . . project is finally moving forward, more developments are sure to come, according to officials."[138]

Another firm had expressed interest in a large research use. Discussions were also active to move several prominent nonprofit business service organizations, organized as the Oakland Consortium, from their location in an RIDC building on Henry Street in Oakland, adjacent to the old Mellon Institute and the Software Engineering Institute, to a new building that RIDC would develop as a center for entrepreneurship "to provide services to new and developing applied research firms in the area."[139]

Although the Pittsburgh Technology Center had cost close to $40 million in public funds to develop and was nowhere near to meeting original projections of employment, officials continued to speak in its defense. For Brooks Robinson the Center was "important, if for no other reason than its symbolic purpose. Our feeling when we were first considering this project was that the site was so strategically located, and visually so important to the city, that it had to be cleared to make way for new development."[140]

By early 1995 the new Carnegie Mellon Research Institute building was sufficiently complete that research units could begin to occupy their new space. Over a four-month period some eighty-five researchers moved into the new building. Dr. William Kaufman, CMU's vice president of applied research and the Institute's head, was enthusiastic about the new building. Noting the informal areas for conversation and the flexibility of movable partitions to enclose laboratory workspaces, he observed just prior to the dedication in April that the building "gives you the opportunity for a cross-fertilization of ideas that is very beneficial."[141]

Carnegie Mellon University's Research Institute, the second building at the Pittsburgh Technology Center, 1995

An editorial in the *Pittsburgh Business Times* praised the Institute's "stunning, five-story headquarters in the Pittsburgh Technology Center," noting that it provides a "higher profile in the local corporate community."

> In a spacious laboratory off one of the new building's fifth-floor corridors, a robotic inspector answers . . . commands, crawling across a lengthy hunk of aircraft skin with a metallic "thwump" of small, suction-cup feet. . . . In other laboratories throughout the new institute, researchers pound computer keys, cook vats of industrial waste, improve the annealing of steel, and craft lighter, stronger magnets. The goal of all of these projects is to apply tomorrow's technology to today's problems in industry.[142]

Program for the opening of the Carnegie Mellon Research Institute, 1995

Just over a month later, on May 19, the Oakland Consortium—consisting of the Enterprise Corporation of Pittsburgh, the Ben Franklin Technology Center of Western Pennsylvania, the Pittsburgh High Technology Council, and the Southwestern Pennsylvania Industrial Resource Center—announced that they would occupy a new four-story, 70,000-square-foot building, bringing some ninety employees to the Center and occupying about half the space in the building. RIDC would develop the building, and other familiar players in the development of the Pittsburgh Technology Center would also be involved: Oxford Development Company as the construction manager and leasing agent, and Pennsylvania Commercial Real Estate as tenant consultant.[143] The building would occupy 4 acres at the extreme western end of the site. The URA agreed to provide a loan of $2.2 million toward the $8 million cost of the building.[144]

It seemed fitting that the announcement of this building should come on the same day that Governor Tom Ridge signed the landmark Industrial Land Recycling legislation. Frustrations and delays in developing the Pittsburgh Technology Center, among other important industrial land redevelopment projects in the Pittsburgh area, had forcefully brought to the attention of state officials over a period of many years the necessity of resolving the tension between addressing legitimate environmental concerns and moving forward critical economic revitalization. The new awareness of the need to resolve the tensions thus played an important part in the passage of that legislation. The process was neither short nor simple, as economics and environmental realities intervened, but the outcome was a dramatic change, both physically and economically. It replaced decaying, outmoded industrial hulks with a center for technological and scientific research that helped advance Pittsburgh's efforts to build a new economy out of the remains of the old. How the Pittsburgh Technology Center would evolve over time would depend on future realities and considerations, but at the time it was considered "one of the best examples of brownfield redevelopment in the nation."[145]

Lessons

The experience of developing the Pittsburgh Technology Center reinforces many of the same lessons that can be gleaned from Washington's Landing and suggests some others.

Like Washington's Landing, the first and most obvious lesson is that developing the Pittsburgh Technology Center took far longer than anyone imagined it would. One after another problem and surprise impeded its progress. Here again, the delays resulted from discoveries of unsuspected environmental contamination, from bureaucratic reviews and approval processes, and from sheer human pride and obstinacy, among other factors. We should expect that all public efforts to renew old, abandoned industrial properties will run into similar setbacks. We should not be surprised either by delays or by impatience with the delays.

That said, as with Washington's Landing, holding out for an ideal use can pay off in the end, though doing so will likely delay the project further when the market is weak, as it was for housing on Herr's Island and as it appears to have been for private, university-affiliated research space at the Technology Center. In fact, the Urban Land Institute's panel apparently miscalculated the strength of the universities' ability to attract commercial partners. Indeed, despite their best efforts over a period of many months, two of the best private real estate developers in Pittsburgh, National Development and Oxford Development, working closely with Pitt and CMU, were unable to attract any private development to the universities' development zones. Nonetheless, in the end the basic premise of the project, that there was a market for private research and development space in Pittsburgh, proved sound, given enough time.

Along the way, however, Pittsburgh learned that universities make poor real estate developers. When their private real estate partners lost interest because the universities oversold their abilities, development became even more problematic. Universities lack the expertise and the focus, they are bureaucracies, and they have a different mission. Let them educate, perform research, generate patents, and spin off new companies, but, at least from the experience of the Pittsburgh Technology Center, don't rely on them to develop commercial real estate.

Another lesson the Pittsburgh Technology Center reinforces is that environmental regulators cannot be and will not be development partners; they wield police powers and they use them. Their role is inherently conservative since they are responsible for securing health and safety, and they are justifiably criticized and held liable if they do not. It is to be expected that they will press for studies, scrutinize methods and results, set and enforce high standards, and generally paint the most negative picture of environmental conditions so that no one can come back to say, "I was not warned."

Are they always right in their cautious, conservative stance? The Pittsburgh Technology Center amply illustrates, even more than Washington's Landing, that they are not. In response to the query at the beginning of this chapter, "How clean is clean enough?" the answer is likely not rooted in science. In retrospect, the actual danger to humans from environmental contamination at the Pittsburgh Technology Center was minimal. True, no one should drink groundwater from the site, but likely no one ever contemplated doing so. The most significant contamination found was inert cyanide buried below the massive foundations of the mill (still in place), which had been there for close to a hundred years while thousands of steel workers apparently suffered no adverse consequences. Yet the presence of this harmless substance proved to be a major obstacle to development because of the DER's regulatory cautiousness, together with ignorance about the source of the contamination, fear of potential liability in the face of the unknown, and the general environmental anxiety of the times. Even once the source and true nature of the cyanide was known, the other factors kept the property from being developed for many years. How clean must property be? The answer to that question is often far more a matter of social and cultural factors than a matter of health or science.

Pittsburgh Technology Center, 2005

3

THE RISE AND FALL OF STEEL IN THE MONONGAHELA RIVER VALLEY

The Monongahela River was the backbone of Pittsburgh's steel industry, its working river. For most of the twentieth century the largest steel mills in the world lined its banks. The J&L plants straddled both sides of the river close to the Point in downtown Pittsburgh where the Monongahela flows into the Allegheny to form the Ohio River. These plants included the enormous furnaces and rolling mills that would be abandoned and then razed to become the Pittsburgh Technology Center and the mixed-use South Side Works. Upriver other massive plants founded by Andrew Carnegie marched in a riverside row of smoky giants: the Homestead Works, the largest integrated steel mill in the world; the Edgar Thomson Works in Braddock; the Duquesne Works; the National Works in McKeesport; and the Clairton Coke Works. Today, only the Edgar Thomson and Clairton works remain in operation. The other three, Homestead, Duquesne, and National, all closed in the mid-1980s, to be transformed into other uses, other identities, as American steel died and Pittsburgh's economy changed.

The causes for the decline of American steel were both national and international. Dumping from countries where government-subsidized steel production and much lower labor costs was a major contributor. Changes in technology allowed modernized Pittsburgh plants to operate with many fewer workers. Then mini-mills in other regions, using completely different processes, made the Pittsburgh operations obsolete. These newer mills were much less costly to run and thus more able to compete with foreign steel.[1]

The story of what happened to steel-dominated communities outside Pittsburgh is different from the stories of Herr's Island and J&L's Pittsburgh Plant. At the city sites the primary challenges to redevelopment were organizational, financial, and environmental. In contrast, the Monongahela Valley towns faced all these plus the loss of their principal employer and their tax base.

HOMESTEAD

The Homestead Works encompassed 380 acres, stretching 3.5 miles along the river. The bulk of the mill was on the southern side of the river in the boroughs of West Homestead, Homestead, Munhall, and Whitaker. Homestead and Munhall housed most of the mill, with some 130 acres of the mill in each community. The Carrie blast furnaces were across the river in Swissvale and Rankin.

Andrew Carnegie purchased the Homestead Works in 1886 from the group of investors that had built the plant earlier in the decade. At the time it was the most modern steel plant in the world. Initially built to produce steel rails, Carnegie adapted it to make structural steel and enlarged it in later years. In 1892 it became part of the consolidated Carnegie Steel Corporation, which also included the Duquesne and the Edgar Thomson works managed by Henry Clay Frick. The bloody Homestead Strike also erupted in 1892 when Carnegie left Frick to confront protesting workers.[2] The Homestead Works, along with Carnegie's other steel holdings, became part of the United States Steel Corporation formed by J. P. Morgan in 1901. In 1941 the U.S. Defense Plant Corporation expanded the Homestead Works to increase its output to meet the Allies' needs for steel to fight World War II. That expansion meant demolishing 1,225 buildings and displacing 3,500 people, another hardship for that community.[3]

U.S. Steel's Homestead Works, 1983

133

At its height during World War II, the Homestead Works employed 15,000 workers, making up to 3 million tons per year of structural steel used in heavy construction, railroad cars, tunnels, bridges, ships, and machinery. The Homestead Works produced the structural steel for the Empire State Building in New York City; the Sears Tower in Chicago; the USX Tower in Pittsburgh; and major bridges, including the Verrazano-Narrows Bridge in New York City. But by the 1970s, the U.S. steel market had shrunk, and the number employed in the mill had dropped to 6,000 employees. When the plant closed in 1986, only 600 people still worked there.[4] From a deadly strike to torn-down homes to lost jobs, the residents of Homestead suffered one hardship after another. The fluctuations in steelmaking dominated their lives for generations.

DUQUESNE AND NATIONAL

The Duquesne and National works were partners, facing each other from opposite sides of the Monongahela River, just as the Pittsburgh and South Side sites of J&L Steel did in Pittsburgh. Together, the two sites operated as a fully integrated mill, primarily producing pipe, with the production of hot metal centered at Duquesne and the rolling and finishing operations at McKeesport. The nearby, supporting Clairton Works supplied necessary coke for these processes.[5]

The Duquesne Steel Works began when a group of experienced iron and steel owners bought farmland along the river and started constructing a mill in 1886. Disagreements among the partners delayed construction, but by 1888 the mill was manufacturing steel rails. Utilizing a process learned from other plants that eliminated a costly step, the Duquesne mill was able to undercut Carnegie's prices in Homestead. Carnegie alleged that the product from Duquesne was inferior. That charge, together with labor difficulties and a shortage of capital, weakened the company. In 1889 Henry Clay Frick purchased the Duquesne Works for the Carnegie interests at a bargain price.[6] Between 1890 and 1910 the plant expanded to include six blast furnaces and additional mills. In 1901 it, too, became part of the newly formed U.S. Steel Corporation.[7]

The program for the city of Duquesne's Silver Jubilee in 1916 poetically described the development and impact of the mill on the town:

Like the meteor the town of Duquesne has darted out of space and cut a brilliant path across the horizon. Unlike the meteor it remains in the horizon, more lustrous than ever, and constantly growing in intensity of beauty and attractiveness.

It is the acknowledged Young Giant of the unconquered and unconquerable Monongahela Valley.

Thirty years ago the site of the Duquesne of today was covered with fields of waving grain and orchards of ripening fruit. Today the scene is changed. Pasture fields have given way to monster workshops; the plow and other agricultural implements have yielded to the rolls and electric traveling cranes of wonder-working mills; the fresh, balmy breezes of the open country have surrendered to the clouds of smoke and steam and graphite of world-renowned industries; the quiet of hill and vale is broken by the fierce lungs of modern mechanical devices and the thunderings of innumerable trains of cars; . . . the babbling brook has hushed its song and now mingles with the contents of great underground sewers—as if by magic all is changed, and the foundations of a great little city are laid.

All forms of twentieth century blessings, comforts and conveniences combine to make it an ideal place of residence, business and work.[8]

During World War II the Defense Plant Corporation erected additional shops at Duquesne, and the plant continued to grow after the war with the construction of new furnaces, including a blast furnace named Dorothy Six.

U.S. Steel's Duquesne Works

In 1870 the Flagler Company purchased the partially rebuilt works of the Fulton-Bolman Company in the city of McKeesport, then a little town with only 200 people, located across and just up the Monongahela River from Duquesne at the confluence of the Monongahela and Youghiogheny rivers. Shortly thereafter, the Flagler Company incorporated as the National Tube Works. In 1899, thirteen major tube and pipe producers, including the National Tube Works, consolidated and formed the National Tube Company. On March 1, 1901, the National Tube Company became a subsidiary of the U.S. Steel Corporation.

Originally, the National Tube Works was an integrated steelmaking facility lacking only a coke plant. It served as the "mother plant" of U.S. Steel's eastern tubular products section for the next eighty years. Throughout the 1900s, the National Plant produced steel tube and pipe of various sizes and characteristics.[9] When the mill was booming, McKeesport was the second largest municipality in Allegheny County after Pittsburgh.

U.S. Steel's National Works, with McKeesport behind

In 1969 the National Plant merged with the Duquesne Plant across the river. Following the merger, many of the operations at the National Plant closed, including the blast and open-hearth furnaces and the blooming mill and rolling mills. The Duquesne Plant thereafter supplied all rounds, blooms, and bars.[10]

STEEL'S DECLINE

Over the years the changing fortunes of the steel industry had an enormous impact on the towns where the plants were located. First, technological improvements reduced the number of workers needed to produce the same output of steel. Productivity improved with increased mechanization, and new technologies emerged for making steel. Constructing and operating a new mini-mill, which used the newer technologies, became far cheaper than modernizing Pittsburgh's old integrated mills. A second major change was the increasingly high wages of union steel workers, combined with the rise of automobile transportation, which made it possible for workers to move out of old and often substandard housing in the mill towns for newer suburban areas. The communities surrounding the mills began to empty. Finally, the downturns in domestic steel production led to severe cutbacks in employment in the mills and, ultimately, to their closing. Thus, population and economic conditions in the mill towns declined steadily.[11]

U.S. Steel (which changed its name to USX Corporation in 1986) closed the Duquesne Works in 1984, the Homestead Works in 1986, and the National Plant in 1987.[12] Other important manufacturing plants in the Mon Valley also closed. Copperweld Corporation's Plant in Glassport closed. (Southwestern Pennsylvania Economic Development District later redeveloped it as the Glassport Industrial Center.) The enormous Westinghouse Plant in Turtle Creek was shuttered. (RIDC later acquired and developed it as Keystone Commons.)

Some people in the valley foresaw the closings. Some even welcomed an end to the smoke-belching mills. Mel Achtzehn of Duquesne remembered

We could see what was happening. The mill at one time, during the war years, they had up to 15, 16 thousand employees, and then they dropped down to around 4500, at that particular time. You can see that the mill being old, and the new processes coming in, made it kind of hard for this mill down here to show a profit. Now we did have some good areas. Number 6 blast furnace, which they called "Dorothy," which was the last one that came down, that had the record of iron-making. It was an excellent furnace. But that was just the one item there. Our rolling mills and things like that that we had here at the time weren't big enough or large enough to do the work that was needed for the new special-type metals.

A lot of people were upset. However, there was a certain group who said they were glad it's gone; we will not have a dirty city any longer. I can remember sweeping the sidewalk in front of the store and we had a lot of graphite at this particular time, and a man coming down, he says, boy, look at this filth on the street. And I said, when

I don't sweep this street any more you're going to be out of a job. Lo and behold, we don't have the filth on the street and the mill's no longer here.[13]

To others the closings felt sudden and unexpected, and to them the impact of the closings was devastating. Although improvements in productivity had led to loss of employment, the plants were operating efficiently, and it seemed inconceivable that USX would simply abandon them. Lou Washowich, mayor of the city of McKeesport from 1980 through 1994, told this story:

I took office in 1980, and actually the budget was already in place from the previous year, so I worked the year under the previous budget of the mayor that was there before me. So in '81 that was our first budget. I developed a relationship with a guy named Al Voss, who was the superintendent or general superintendent of Duquesne-McKeesport Works, very nice guy. And naturally we relied on the steel mill; it was a big contributor to the revenue of the city. And I believe it was in 1981 or 1982, I'll never forget that it was April when the announcement come out. Formulating that budget, starting in August or September, I had called Al and the mill was working. They were booming. And I said, Al, we're getting ready to prepare our budget. What do things look like for next year? And he said, Mayor, I can see us working at 110% capacity. And knowing this guy—he was not the kind of guy, I mean he was a down-to-earth guy—and if he had other facts I'm sure he would have said, Lou, be careful. I took that information, and naturally we ran with that information. And it was in April that I got a call from the *McKeesport Daily News* that U.S. Steel had made the announcement that they were going to phase out the National Works. Now that's the first time that I heard that, from the newspaper. Al didn't even get a chance to call me, which I'm sure he would have, but naturally he didn't make that decision. That decision was made by U.S. Steel.[14]

The closing of these local plants reflected national trends in the steel industry. Between the mid-1950s and 1987, when the National Plant closed, employment in the primary metals industry nationally had fallen by almost half, dropping from 1.2 million jobs to 700,000. In the Pittsburgh region, however, the losses were much more severe, with employment in primary metals falling from 129,000 to 21,000. Mounting losses were already severe by the early 1970s.

The results in the Monongahela River Valley were catastrophic. Workers and their families felt betrayed by the companies for which they had worked all their lives and by the nation that had depended on their industry to save the free world in two world wars. Mayor Washowich described the impact on his city and its families:

> I think one of the things people never realized about the steel industry, as long as it existed, that they contributed so much to the other small stores and industry around, that they kept them going. And pay days, the workers taking their checks and walk into the bank, the card shops and the dollars that just flowed off of that National Tube site. So from then on it was a complete change for us.

> I don't think anybody really understands the heartache, people losing jobs, closing down, losing houses, and families splitting, the whole cycle of what takes place in families that were once structured with an income and doing things, that all of a sudden became dysfunctional families. That had a devastating effect on the entire valley.[15]

As problems began to emerge in the steel industry, Jim Flaherty, then chairman of Allegheny County's Board of Commissioners, convened leaders from steelmaking regions around the country under the auspices of the Steel Communities Coalition. Flaherty did much of the work of organizing the coalition, contacting the other cities and urging their participation. Jim Smith of United Steelworkers also played a leading role. The Steel Communities Coalition met regularly between 1977 and 1980, twice in Pittsburgh, with good representation. Mayor Richard Caliguiri served as chair one year.

I was working as principal economic development planner at City Planning in 1980 when I got a call the afternoon of September 9: would I attend the meeting of the Steel Communities Coalition representing Mayor Caliguiri at 4:00 P.M. at the airport? "Accordingly," I wrote later, "I took the limousine out, and spent 2½ hours in earnest conversation with this small and rather select group, sitting next to former county commissioner Jim Flaherty and only a couple of seats from chairman Tom Foerster, current county commissioner. I found both of them to be intelligent and informed." I had seen but not really known them before.

The coalition was successful in calling attention to the plight of the steel industry, and it made some progress in countering the dumping of foreign steel. The International Trade Commission invited Commissioner Tom Foerster, who was a member of Allegheny County's Board of Commissioners throughout the 1970s and became chairman in 1980, to testify on the matter, and the commission subsequently issued sanctions.[16]

Popular concern over the condition and decline of the mills in the Mon Valley coalesced into a coalition of Pittsburgh's steel communities that organized in 1979. Known as the Tri-State Conference on Steel, they gathered to fight the corporate disinvestment that, in the minds of the participants, was the reason the mills could not compete with foreign steel and led to the closures.[17]

When USX announced in October of 1984 that it was planning to demolish the Dorothy Six furnace and related facilities at Duquesne, the Tri-State Conference on Steel, United Steelworkers, and other groups came together to try to find a way to reopen the plant, perhaps with employee ownership.[18] USX agreed to hold off demolition until a feasibility study could be completed. Commissioner Foerster agreed to find money from the county's Department of Development to study the feasibility of preserving Dorothy Six. "The situation in Duquesne was very tender," Foerster remembered.

In May 1985 the Tri-State Conference on Steel and United Steelworkers, joined by other supporters of efforts to reopen the mill, held a "Rally to Save Jobs, Families and Communities" in the Monongahela and Ohio river valleys. An aide to U.S. Senator John Heinz read a letter in which the senator said, "There are those who think that the Mon Valley is dead and that steel making has no future. They are wrong. I join you in calling on U.S. Steel to abandon its plan to dismantle Dorothy Six. For my part, I will use every means at my disposal to assist in attracting the investment needed to ensure a prosperous future for Dorothy Six and a return of hope and steel jobs to the Mon Valley." *The Pittsburgh Press* reported that "Tri-State and the union are promoting creation of a municipal authority that would have eminent domain power to purchase closed steel mills or industrial sites, and sell the properties to workers or another manufacturer."[19] But none of this would materialize.

It was difficult for people whose families had worked in the mills for generations to accept that they were closing forever. Lou Washowich observed, "It probably was no different than any other time that they threatened to shut it down. The biggest majority of the people that worked there and lived in the city of McKeesport, they'll never close it down. This is the best pipe manufacturing plant in the country. I mean a whole gamut of things, until they literally closed it down."[20]

In the latter part of 1984 Commissioner Foerster asked Governor Thornburgh to form a commission in the Mon Valley and asked the state for $50 million for industrial redevelopment in the valley. When the funding was denied, the county commissioners formed their own Mon Valley Revitalization Commission in May 1986. Commissioner Foerster asked James R. Taylor, chairman of Three Rivers Bank of McKeesport, and Joseph M. Hohman, director of the Allegheny County Department of Development, to cochair the commission, which was composed of sixteen members representing a wide variety of interests.[21] The county commissioners gave the commission an open charge to bring in any recommendations they felt would alleviate conditions in the valley. Although the new group was not intended to become an operating entity, it worked to issue a report and monitor improvements, and it organized seven task forces to study and make recommendations on different facets of life and the economy of the valley.

In the meantime, community leaders in Duquesne made concerted attempts to market the idled mill site. They sent letters to 250 companies, inviting them to consider the site, and by 1985, a year after the plant had closed and the feasibility study of restarting the plant was proceeding, they had identified fourteen interested firms. Not all members of the community were supportive of efforts to find new uses. Many still believed that the mill would reopen, and they doubted that the identified companies were truly interested. In any case, since USX still owned the property, redevelopment could not proceed.[22]

Augie Carlino, who became a leader in planning for the future of the mill sites, described how acceptance of change slowly developed:

> Early on, when these mills closed down, all these communities, they're all the same, there was a false belief that these mills would reopen. So in that belief there was nothing more that they wanted to hear than RIDC, somebody else, was going to actually come in and come up with a plan to reopen those mills. And that's all based on a mindset that these people had lived with, them and their ancestors, for a hundred years. The mill was their bread and butter, job-wise and revenue back to the community. And there was literally a dependency upon that. They couldn't think beyond that.
>
> So we come in with alternative plans, and that probably met the greatest resistance at the local government levels. So initially I would say I was highly dissatisfied with the local governments

because there was no ability for them to think beyond—there was no thinking, put it like that. And there was no ability for them to be visionary, to see what other types of opportunities lay for that mill. That was forced upon them more and more as the mills began to be torn down because that set in stone for them the realization that, one, their false hope was just that, and, two, if they couldn't be visionary they were going to become unelected because the community was growing restless with what happened at these mill sites.[23]

The study of Dorothy Six, released in January 1986, concluded that preservation was not feasible, but Commissioner Foerster never considered the study to be wasted because it had helped the community to come to terms with the inevitable.[24] The furnace came down August 1, 1988.[25] Reflecting on that day, Mel Achtzen said

Yeah, U.S. Steel blew it over, because it was too much of a headache. They didn't want this any more, so we got up one morning and there it was, lying on its side. I can understand that. At that time we didn't know they were going to blow it over, but I can understand why. I can understand their reason, because of the hassles they were getting. And U.S. Steel was getting a black eye. Of course, they were the culprit; they were the bad guy, and everything. And the people who were after the plant, after the portions of the plant, of course they were the good guys; they were the white hats, you know. U.S. Steel had the black hat, but then they just ended it real quick, blew it over.[26]

Dorothy Six, in the background, the emblematic furnace whose demolition August 1, 1988, came to symbolize the end of steelmaking in Duquesne

The Homestead Works closed in 1986. A note on the last work schedule given to the workers read, "The 100 mill will shut down after the 7-3 turn on Saturday 6/29/85 [sic] and temporarily cease operations. When operations resume, scheduled personel [sic] will be contacted the week prior to start up."[27] But the mill never started up again.

The steel industry was in a national, not just a local, crisis. On August 1, 1986, 22,000 USX workers in nine states went on strike. Officials grew anxious when the strike continued into October, prompting Commissioner Foerster, Mayor Caliguiri, Mayor Harold Washington of Chicago, Mayor Wilson Goode of Philadelphia, and Beaver County Commissioner Joseph Widmer to appeal to U.S. Secretary of Labor William Brock to intervene to help resolve the dispute.[28]

The crisis in the valley and the failure of initial efforts to revive steelmaking in Duquesne prompted leaders of the Tri-State Conference on Steel to push state officials to charter the Steel Valley Authority. Formed in 1986 under the Municipal Authorities Act of 1945, the authority had the power to use eminent domain to take over plants that were threatened with closure and to float bonds to finance a project in an effort to save them. In the wake of the studies that ruled out reopening the Duquesne Works, the Steel Valley Authority turned its attention to the Homestead Works and LTV's South Side Works, which seemed to offer greater potential for reopening.[29] One after the other, however, these possibilities vanished.

Other ideas were put forward. In 1986, as hopes grew dim for any revival of steel, County Commissioner Barbara Hafer proposed converting the McKeesport property into a recreational and entertainment complex, River City Park, with a dog racing track as the major draw. The Mon Valley Commission included that idea in their thinking about development of a service industry in the valley to replace the manufacturing base that had died.[30] The state directed a grant of $60,000 from its new Renaissance Communities Program in October 1986, following Duquesne's designation as a State Enterprise Zone. The grant was intended to support new development in the valley.[31]

Meanwhile, the closed mills were both attractive and dangerous to scavengers. When USX closed the plants, the corporation essentially abandoned them as they were. Mark Patrick, who worked for the Allegheny County Department of Development at the time, remembered touring the mill sites shortly after they closed. He described

> buildings full of brand new equipment, but just left and you'd kind of walk into offices throughout the building. It was eerie, because

you would walk in, and the electricity was still on, and you would walk into offices and they would be disheveled but—coffee cups on desks, fans running—I mean it was like the neutron bomb. And like I said, there was—I remember one building that was just almost floor to ceiling with jack hammers, brand new, in the box, jack hammers, just stacked to the ceiling, and, you know, just buildings and buildings full of that type of thing. Like, boy, they really did walk away, lock, stock, and barrel.[32]

Vandalism resulted, leading to concern that historically valuable materials and valuable equipment might be destroyed.[33]

Another concern that emerged was the real danger the shuttered mills posed to trespassers, especially desperate unemployed people, who broke into them to scavenge materials and equipment. A jury awarded $1 million from USX to the family of one man who was electrocuted at the Duquesne site in 1986, apparently trying to scavenge copper wire. A young man from Penn Hills perished in a similar accident the following year, prompting his mother to say, "He was desperate with no job. . . . It's very disturbing how they're leaving mills and mostly in black neighborhoods with low-income, nonworking people. It's set up like a trap because black people don't have jobs and they scuffle and try to make money any way they can. If they'd taken precautions none of this would've happened."[34]

As the mills closed, the towns that had depended on them for tax revenues felt the loss. In 1986 several of the communities, under the auspices of the Steel Valley Council of Governments, commissioned a study of their financial situation. In that year, revenues in Clairton, Duquesne, Munhall, and West Elizabeth failed to meet expenses. Those municipalities began to think about layoffs and sharing of services to adjust to the new reality of life without steel.[35]

The magnitude of the problems facing the valley and its communities was difficult to fathom for those who did not witness it. As Dennis Pittman of McKeesport described

On the government side one of the major components was education. [State representative] Tom Michlovich was one that early on orchestrated a bus ride. He literally loaded legislators in Harrisburg on buses, drove them here from Harrisburg. And it was like going to Jurassic Park. I don't mean that to be dramatic. Folks from Philadelphia and Scranton and the eastern part of the state heard about the demise of the steel industry and all that kind of thing, no concept of what that meant till they got here. And when you got here you saw these huge expanses of land, at that time many covered with buildings that might have reminded you, if you were an old western movie fan, of Dodge City, with the tumbleweed on the gates, doors slamming. And the mass of these buildings! The pipe mill here would have fit Three Rivers Stadium a couple of times—inside—inside. The legislators had no idea what they read about and heard about, until they came and saw it. And when you walk in you realize if you're from New York it could have been Yankee Stadium, it could have been Wrigley Field, inside, a couple of times, that big.

And then you kind of wonder, if you didn't read the history, what did they do here for a hundred years? They literally made all the pipe for the Alaskan pipeline. If not two world wars certainly the Second World War, they made all the steel for all the battleships, all the merchant marine, all the guns and then rebuilt, under the Marshall Plan, Japan and Europe.

The jobs that were lost in this valley, not just in McKeesport, but Homestead and Rankin and Duquesne, and up and down the valley, from the metals industry and the directly related industries, so it might be trucking, it might have been the coal industry, those jobs that were lost totaled about 100,000. If those were normal families of four, dad, and two kids and mom, that's like 400,000 people going away. Some retired. Some went to take jobs in other areas. God knows. That's like dropping a bomb on Hiroshima. It really is. 400,000 people suddenly couldn't afford a house, couldn't afford a car payment, couldn't feed themselves. Crazy. And now mom and dad go to work, at minimum wage, no fringes. I mean everything changed. So that learning curve was very difficult for everybody.[36]

Rolling Mill at the USX Homestead Works

SANDCASTLE AND THE WATERFRONT TIMELINE

1886	Andrew Carnegie purchases the Homestead Works.
1892	Henry Clay Frick crushes the Homestead Strike.
1901	The Homestead Works becomes part of United States Steel Corporation.
1941	The U.S. Defense Plant Corporation expands the Homestead Works.
1971	U.S. Steel renovates the Big Shop.
1986	USX closes the Homestead Works.
1987	USX puts its Homestead property up for sale. Kennywood purchases a portion of the site to develop the Sandcastle water park.
1988	Park Corporation purchases the remainder of USX's Homestead site, almost immediately begins to sell machinery, agrees to study the possibility of reopening the Big Shop and the 160-inch plate mill, and begins demolition. The Remaking Cities Conference convenes in Pittsburgh. The Steel Industry Heritage Task Force organizes.
1989	Sandcastle opens.
1990	Park donates the Homestead Strike property and the 48-inch rolling mill to the Steel Industry Heritage Task Force and demolishes the Hole in the Wall and the roll shop.
1992	Park completes renovation of selected old mill buildings and announces development of the Eighth Avenue property for a grocery store, pharmacy, and offices.
1994	Park demolishes the Big Shop. Construction begins on the new Shop 'n Save grocery store.

1995 Construction begins on a new access bridge at the site's eastern end. Park restores the historic pump house and water tower when the Steel Industry Heritage Task Force fails to come up with funds to do it. The new Shop 'n Save opens.

4

LOOK BACK, OR LOOK AHEAD?
From the USX Homestead Works to Sandcastle and the Waterfront

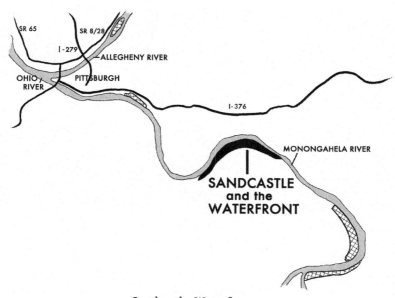

Sandcastle–Waterfront

It was probably inevitable that when the giant steel plants closed, people in the affected communities, where families had worked in the mills for generations, would react in disbelief and would make every effort to restart them, to recreate the high-paying jobs they had lost, and to maintain their accustomed way of living. When that failed, they looked back nostalgically on what they had contributed to the country and to their communities. Some made efforts to memorialize the sacrifices, contributions, and culture

149

the mills represented. Others, sensing that the world was moving on and feeling that the old mills and people's nostalgia for them retarded the work of creating a new economy and culture, were impatient with efforts to try to hold onto the past, the old buildings, the old machinery, the old way of life. Efforts to recover, memorialize, or reuse the abandoned USX Homestead Works highlight the issues and problems of reconciling these two points of view.

INTRODUCTION

Sandcastle is Pittsburgh's only water park, created on the site of the Homestead Works' former rail yards in the borough of West Homestead. Sandcastle offers its customers pools, fourteen water slides, the world's largest hot tub, food concessions, gift shops, an arcade, and a boardwalk.

Housing at the Waterfront, 2005

The Waterfront, developed primarily on the Homestead portion of the old Homestead Works, is a mixed-use development of big-box retail stores, smaller shops in a New Urban town center, restaurants, offices buildings, and housing. Industrial uses in rehabilitated mill buildings are on the eastern part of the site, mostly in Munhall.

Visiting the Waterfront is very similar to visiting any other large, fully developed, contemporary U.S. shopping center. There is little on the site, very little, to remind visitors of the enormous mill that occupied the entire property only fifteen years ago—just a line of a dozen tall stacks standing to the side of the western entrance; two large mill buildings, refurbished and repainted, at the opposite end of the site; and a couple of small historic structures tucked away in a corner of the property near the river.

Retail shops at the Waterfront, 2005

The traffic, the substantial stores stocked with tremendous inventories, the buzz of commercial activity, the nightlife, the housing complex with its pool and activity center, and the landscaped parking lots and "town center" are all so fully developed that it seems as if they have existed forever. It is difficult to imagine that any other use was ever there, let alone a massive steel mill that employed thousands of workers and saw important historical events.

Lighted stacks, 2005, among the few reminders at the Waterfront of the great steel works that preceded it

151

than Park, has threatened to seize the mill by eminent domain to stop USX Corp. from selling it to Park." The Authority's Bob Erickson said that the public would be "at least two years ahead" in developing the J&L site if Park hadn't come in. "These communities are distressed," Erickson said. "They can't wait for seven or 10 years for the type of process occurring at the Hazelwood [Pittsburgh Technology Center] site."

Park, however, claims that almost any old industrial site requires years of renovation. Old steel mills have to be torn down because they cannot serve any other purpose than to make steel, and are too dilapidated to be renovated, [Park Corporation's vice president William] Cook said. The demolition process is time-consuming, and more expensive than renovating.

"There aren't many quicker than we are," Cook said.

"I can understand the SVA saying that J&L will take 10 years to develop. Sure it will. But remember, you're completely recycling a piece of land. We don't really like to tear anything down," he said. "If you tear something down, the payoff is far in the future. If somebody wants to lease or purchase a building, it's to our advantage to talk to them because it would bring profits and revenues to us immediately.

"We appreciate the dramatic change in the Mon Valley. It makes us sick every time we hear a mill going down; that's one less customer for WHEMCO (West Homestead Engineering and Machine Co.), after all," Cook said.

"Change is difficult. We know that. We're just trying to do the best we can for the communities, ourselves and the people who work there."[4]

Simultaneously, another party also was negotiating with USX for a different portion of the property. Kennywood, the historic Pittsburgh amusement park located in nearby West Mifflin, was interested in developing the western 42 acres of the site, along the river and behind WHEMCO, for a water park, marina, and nightclubs, to be known as Sandcastle. Park's interest was in the other 300 to 310 acres of the site.

The Steel Valley Authority's Attempts to Intervene – 1987-1988

The Steel Valley Authority asked USX for a ninety-day freeze on the sale to both Kennywood and Park. While the SVA did not object to the sale to Kennywood, it still had concerns that Park would simply liquidate the property instead of developing it. USX denied the authority's request in a November 30 letter, citing a letter of intent from Park and extended negotiations with Kennywood. The authority, however, continued to threaten to take the property by eminent domain and on December 9 asked the councils of its ten member-municipalities to take the preliminary step of designating the Homestead Works an "economic development project."[5] "We envision ourselves as being the overseer of all development on the site," the authority's solicitor, Jay Hornack, said. "It is very much our development project."[6] The municipalities, however, had questions or reservations and took no immediate action.[7]

On December 10 the authority convened a hearing at Steel Valley High School and invited presentations from four interested developers: Park; Kennywood/Sandcastle; Carnegie Mill Group (the newly named Innovative Technologies, with the addition of Pittsburgh industrial real estate developer Jack Buncher); and Allegheny Recycling Corporation, a subsidiary of Glenshaw Glass Corporation. Estimates of attendance ranged from 200 to over 400 people. The meeting was in essence an orchestrated protest to USX's proposed sale to the Park Corporation, with the threat of eminent domain behind it.

The Carnegie Mill Group's David Lichtenstein stated that they had been taken by surprise by USX's announcement of a deal with Park, because they thought that USX still had their proposal under consideration. He presented a five-year plan for a mix of commercial, industrial, residential, and recreational development "to begin 100 acres at a time, immediately upon land acquisition." Carl Hughes, president of Kennywood Park, received support for Sandcastle's proposed recreational development, since the site they were proposing had no buildings that had been used in steel manufacturing. He projected that Sandcastle would be in operation by mid-1989.

Drew Orient of Allegheny Recycling proposed to turn the Carrie Furnace site in Rankin into a recycling center and referred to recycling legislation then being considered in the Pennsylvania legislature. He indicated that USX had refused to discuss their proposal, and he supported the plan to use eminent domain to take the property from USX.

USX, in light of the tentative sales agreement with Park, chose not to speak at the meeting.

SVA members Mike Stout and [state] Rep. Michael Dawida said they oppose the sale to Park Corp., claiming the company will act as liquidators who would raze the mills without a plan for redevelopment.

In calling for eminent domain, Dawida said, "Never beg for what you have the power to take. You have the legal power to take the Homestead Works of U.S. Steel and the moral and economic power to make it work.

"Steel Valley Authority is attempting to reorganize industrially to create an American capitalism in which people matter and the community takes economic responsibility.

"USX property belongs to the people of Munhall and Homestead. SVA is asking USX to give the authority the plant, or it has to be taken by eminent domain."[8]

Exercising eminent domain, however, would not be easy. The authority would need to have the support of a majority of its ten member-municipalities and the approval of the municipalities in which the property was located, not to mention the money to compensate USX. "There's no magic wand," authority member Chuck McCollester said. "There is no white knight here. There are no guarantees that the companies coming in are going to be any more enlightened than the one that left."[9]

On Friday, December 11, USX announced that it had closed the deal with Kennywood's officers for their proposed Sandcastle development. The same day, USX officials met with state representatives David Levdansky and Thomas Michlovic, who suggested that USX give the remainder of the property to the SVA. USX replied that because of its responsibility to its shareholders, it could not give its property away.[10]

In a weekend editorial the *Pittsburgh Press* voiced its opinion:

Taking the eminent domain route would be legally complex, time-consuming and costly in itself, with no guarantee that the courts would go along. Even if approval were given, a fair takeover price would be set and the authority then would have to come up with the money, possibly by floating bonds. The cost of the property could be in the millions of dollars.

And then what? Predictions that parts of the old steel mill would be quickly reopened, which otherwise would be dismantled by Park Corp., or that developers would suddenly appear to transform the area are too far-fetched to be credible.

The Steel Valley Authority ... is making the argument that its birds in the bush are better than the bird in the hand. That seems a dubious proposition.[11]

State Senator James Romanelli also voiced support for Park's plan, telling local officials at a meeting on January 22, 1988, that the sooner Park closed on the property, the better. At the same meeting, Park's Bill Cook said that Park and USX were working on final details of their agreement and that he believed Park was making a far better offer to USX than the other proposers, which accounted for USX's interest.[12] "'The business deal has been made,' Cook said a couple of days later. 'The Park Corp. does have an agreement with U.S. Steel. I would say to everyone that the thing to do now is to work with us to make sure it is a successful development.' Cook said Park would be 'very disappointed' if it didn't have some kind of development on the land within a year of buying it."[13]

The RUDAT (Regional/Urban Design Assistance Team) and Prince Charles in the Valley – 1988

Concern for the future of the communities in the valley was widespread. Seeing this concern as reflective of a crisis in industrial communities worldwide, David Lewis proposed an international conference, using the Mon Valley as a case study. Lewis was the founder of Urban Design Associates, an architectural firm in Pittsburgh, and a professor of architecture at Carnegie Mellon University; he lived in West Homestead. The Allegheny Conference on Community Development and local foundations responded to his proposal and agreed to sponsor an American Institute of Architects Regional/Urban Design Assistance Team (RUDAT) February 25–29, 1988, followed immediately by a Remaking Cities Conference, March 2–5.

The team, with expertise in labor relations, environmental law, real estate development, industrial economics, transportation, and urban design, focused on developing new ideas for the Homestead, Duquesne, McKeesport, and East Pittsburgh (Westinghouse Electric Plant) sites. Using the redeveloped Bishop Boyle Center in Homestead as its base, the team interviewed residents, public officials, technical experts, and others and held an open hearing before presenting its findings at a public meeting.[14]

Reporting on the team's experience, architect Charles Zucker said

> In meeting with many people, we came up with what we call the "myths of the Mon." There were myths we kept hearing that may have been true but not any longer. The first is that there is some sort of magic key. For example, that improving the highway network will save the Valley—the highway as savior. Second, that the steel industry will come back and re-employ, reinvest, and redevelop. The third is the white knight myth: that some savior is going to come in and scoop up these sites, and redevelop them to the same job intensity. Another myth is that the towns are unable to control their own destinies—that they've been so much under the mantle of the steel industry, their sense of being a company town is so great, that there is little way that they could control life for themselves within the new economy.[15]

The team, which formed the working part of the conference, advised leaving the steel industry behind, which helped change people's attitudes. Whereas people had previously clung to the steel industry, they began to say, let's forget about the steel industry.[16]

Two days after the meeting in Homestead, the conference convened at the Vista Hotel in downtown Pittsburgh. The conference brought Prince Charles of England and notable architects and developers from throughout the world to discuss the problems of old industrial cities. The conference proved to be a second occasion through which the valley's residents began to come to terms with the loss of the steel industry.[17] Out of the conference came the idea for the Mon Valley Initiative, a consortium of community development organizations in the valley, created with organizational and financial assistance from the Allegheny Conference and local foundations.[18]

45-inch rolling mill and stacks

158

Without any action, the abandoned mill buildings had begun to deteriorate. Officials in West Homestead expressed concern about the condition of the 45-inch and 100-inch mill buildings, adjacent to where work on Sandcastle was underway. Mayor John Dindak commented, "They have been sitting there for more than two years, and they are getting worse and worse." The RUDAT report had called for cleaning up industrial property. Emboldened by the report and his recent luncheon with Prince Charles at the conference, Mayor Dindak called for action on these deteriorating buildings in his municipality. "This is prime, choice property and it is sitting there idling and wasting away." Councilman Ray Siniawski joined in: "There are no fences or security. People have been going in and removing wiring to get copper. A young man was electrocuted doing the same thing at the Carrie Furnace in Rankin."[19]

Park's First Steps – 1988

USX completed its sale of some 300 acres to Park on March 31. Park paid close to $3 million for the land and buildings and an undisclosed amount for the equipment left in the plant. By this time Park's general approach to developing the site was well known: sell or scrap steelmaking equipment, raze facilities that had no usefulness other than for making steel, reuse buildings that could be adapted to other uses, and find new uses for vacant land. "We're not going to sit around," said Raymond P. Park, chairman. "We'll start immediately. Sometime this summer we'll have fairly concrete plans on how to attack the property, what buildings we're going to save and what buildings will have to come down."

Officials of the SVA and Tri-State Conference on Steel restated their concerns about the loss of productive capacity, since they still clung to the idea that steelmaking could be revived in the valley. "We are still concerned about the development of that site as to its potential for creating jobs."[20] Park responded, "I can understand just about any kind of rehabilitation or development, but it's beyond me what their concept is."[21]

The Regional/Urban Design Assistance Team and the Re-making Cities Conference had confronted the community with the reality of the permanent loss of the steel industry, but many could not see another vision yet. George DeBolt, who served as the local chair of RUDAT, related

> Our vision for the mill site assumed that the mill was gone, that they weren't going to make steel there any more. And when we made our presentation to the community we got creamed. We got

159

hammered by former steel workers, retired steel workers, union members, who said, "Bring back the mills. Bring back the mills." We said, "Folks, the mills aren't coming back, so let's look ahead, let's see what else we can do." So the biggest step in the 1980's was to get the community to think of this mill site as someplace other than a mill, because the mind set was, that's a mill. It's been a mill for a hundred years. It's been a mill for four generations. And we kept saying, "Hey, folks, the mill's gone. The buildings are still there, but the mill's gone. We've got to look ahead." So we got creamed—in the press, by everybody. "Jobs! We want jobs! You're taking away our mill jobs!"[22]

The Tri-State Conference on Steel and the Steel Valley Authority, concerned about the loss of steelmaking capacity, asked Ray Park for the opportunity to tour the mill to assess the condition of the remaining equipment. Park agreed, but he did not believe that Pittsburgh would ever again be a steel town. He felt that it was in everyone's interest to scrap obsolete steel equipment and move on. "In my opinion, you have to ask how many steel mills do you need standing by idle?" he said.[23] Editorializing, the *Pittsburgh Post-Gazette* agreed, concluding, "It is a sad ending for a mighty facility, but it seems at this point that there is no escaping the necessity for putting this part of the past behind in order to make room for new possibilities for the Monongahela Valley."[24]

Still others, however, led by Pittsburgh History & Landmarks Foundation, at least wanted to preserve reminders of the region's steelmaking past. They were encouraged by one recommendation of the Urban Design Team that

Carrie Works, 2005

blast furnaces three and four at the Carrie Works be preserved as an "interpretive historic center" because of their connection with the Homestead Strike and labor history; because of their "monumentality and scale"; and because such a center would give closure to the era of steel in the Valley. They organized a Steel Industry Heritage Task Force, which held its first meeting at Pittsburgh History & Landmarks Foundation's Station Square in Pittsburgh the first week of April, and invited Ray Park to attend.[25]

Over the next couple of weeks, Ray Park and his associates met with some of the concerned parties and tried to allay fears. The first week of April, Park and Bill Cook toured the site with Commissioner Foerster and county development director Joe Hohman, who left the meeting satisfied that Park was interested in development of the site and would cooperate with the county in developing it.

Similarly, Park reassured Tom Croft of the SVA that they would work with the authority on ideas to reopen the Big Shop. Park also allayed the concerns of the mayors of West Homestead and Munhall that he would take immediate steps to improve the appearance of the property by razing buildings that had no value for reuse; installing fencing, paving, landscaping, and lighting; and making improvements to some of the buildings, especially at the Munhall end.[26]

Less than two weeks after Park's purchase of the property, Jim Roddey, a politically connected advertising executive and later the county's first elected executive, made a public proposal to use the bulk of the site to develop an Olympic sports training facility, with an indoor swimming pool, a gymnastics training center, a hotel, and other supporting businesses. Noting that the United States had only one major Olympic training facility, in Colorado Springs, Roddey suggested that a facility in the East would improve the country's competitiveness and be a regional attraction. Roddey had been considering the idea for some years, and he had found support among former Olympic athletes with Pittsburgh connections, including Allegheny County Commissioner Barbara Hafer's husband, John Pidgeon, a 1948 Olympic swimmer who was headmaster of the Kiski School in nearby Indiana County, and Bob Mathias, two-time decathlon gold medal winner who had attended the Kiski School. Roddey had also spoken with prospective investors to explore financing for the project.[27] However, all this was academic, because by this time Park Corporation had taken control of the property and had its own ideas.

Park moved forward quickly with activities to prepare the site, as it had promised. By mid-April it began advertising to sell machinery and buildings. The Steel Valley Authority responded by again decrying selling off steelmaking facilities. The *Pittsburgh Press*, however, commented that "if the Steel Valley Authority or anyone else knows of prospective buyers or users of the complex for steelmaking, the time is at hand for bringing them forward. It would be unrealistic to expect Park to wait indefinitely on those who talk about reviving steel but cannot produce any private investors willing to risk their money to do it."[28]

Trying to Save the Big Shop – 1988

The Big Shop

At the end of the month the Park Corporation neutralized concerns for a while by announcing that it would undertake a study to explore the potential for reopening the Big Shop to serve remaining USX plants in Braddock, Clairton, and West Mifflin and other customers that might be found. At its peak during WW II the Big Shop had employed 574 steelworkers. Over 500 had still worked there in 1982. In 1971 USX had spent millions of dollars to renovate it. There was popular interest in seeing it back in operation.

Ray Park and Bill Cook both expressed optimism that it could reopen profitably but said that with the proposed study "the possibility of making a mistake becomes less likely." Strategic Management Advisors of Houston, Texas, which had advised Park on reopening other manufacturing facilities, would perform the study, which was expected to take two to three months. Park also asked Homestead mayor Steve Simko, who had been the shop's superintendent for seventeen years until USX closed it in 1984, to assist. Simko had advised USX when they were negotiating to sell the shop to Innovative Technologies and had subsequently joined that group and then its successor, the Carnegie Mill Group. Simko expressed surprise that Park invited him to take part but said, "I'll do anything as a mayor to help our communities to get some work in here. I'll join anybody. Yes, I'll help them to get the big shop started. I worked there. I built that shop. Nobody knows it better than I do. My gut feeling is that [Park] can make it go." Simko led a tour of the Shop on May 2 for officials of the Steel Valley Authority, United Steelworkers, the municipalities, and possible investors.[29]

George Merrick, the president of Strategic Management Advisors, reported progress on the study in early June at a meeting of the Steel Valley Regional Planning Commission. He indicated that if there were a problem, it would likely be finding workers. "I am inclined to believe there is a need," he said, and the shop "can be restored and the equipment can be reconditioned. But the key ingredient that would make this option work is people. We are concerned about whether there are still enough skilled people in the Monongahela Valley to operate this shop. We are concerned that they may have moved away." He expected that it would take another six weeks to finish the study and that, at best, opening the shop would require federal, state, and local aid.[30] A month later Merrick was still optimistic, saying that equipment appeared to be in good shape but that a final decision would not come for another month, after utilities were reconnected and a market study was completed. He predicted that it would be six months before production would begin.[31]

Interested local representatives of various groups toured the mill site again on July 22. At a meeting organized by the Tri-State Conference on Steel the following day, hopes for development of portions of the mill were still high. Mike Stout of the Steel Valley Authority reported that in response to a survey sent to 2,100 United Steelworkers, 475 former steel workers had expressed interest in returning to work in Homestead, 234 of whom were unemployed. Stout announced that in addition to its work toward reopening the Big Shop, Park was considering restarting the 160-inch plate mill, which also had employed over 500 workers during its best days and as many as 300 just before it closed. Ray Park's son Kelly reiterated the Park Corporation's interest in working with local officials on the redevelopment and said they had consultants who were studying future uses. Community groups discussed forming a task force to work with Park to bring together all the varied interests in the valley to support reopening of mill facilities.[32]

Demolition or Preservation? - 1988

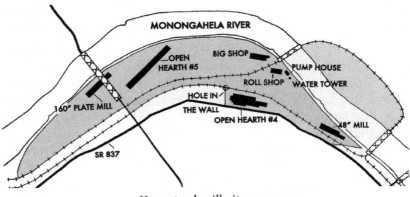

Homestead-mill-site-map

Concurrently, Park announced that demolition of many of the old steelmaking facilities would begin within a month and continue for three or four years. Park had hired about sixty workers for a demolition crew, including residents of the valley and former steel workers. Park would start toward the eastern end of the site, in Munhall, and then work its way west through Homestead to West Homestead. First to go would be two open hearth furnaces, numbers four and five.[33]

Open hearth furnace five

Advocates of preservation, however, did not want to see the open hearth furnaces demolished. On the tour, they had found the furnaces to be in very good condition, and they were considering a recommendation that the furnaces be preserved, along with the Carrie blast furnaces across the river.

164

At the Tri-State meeting a representative of the Steel Industry Heritage Task Force reported the group's efforts to obtain funds to establish a Mon Valley Heritage Park, similar in concept to heritage parks in Lowell, Massachusetts, that preserved the history of New England's textile industry, and in Birmingham, Alabama, that preserved the history of that city's steel industry. The National Park Service had agreed in April to give advice, and the task force, which now represented over thirty groups, including the Allegheny Conference on Community Development and the Historical Society of Western Pennsylvania, had been awarded $350,000 in federal funds for planning. The group believed that a museum preserving the history of Pittsburgh's steel industry would serve as an important tourist attraction and contribute to the region's economy.[34]

Consultants retained by the Historical Society toured the Homestead, Duquesne, and National works on July 27 and 28, specifically to assess historical resources. They found Homestead, with its combination of both open hearth and blast furnaces, to be the most promising of the three former mill sites for preservation. The Carrie Furnace "drew raves from members of the team," who "said it looks much the way it did when it was brand new, . . . 'an incredible site and amazingly well preserved.'"[35]

Carrie Furnaces, viewed from between refurbished mill buildings across the river, 2005

Unfortunately, federal legislation proposed by U.S. representative John Murtha of Johnstown to develop national parks in nine western Pennsylvania counties failed to include Allegheny County. United States senator John Heinz began efforts to include Allegheny County in the bill to fund preservation of portions of the mill sites and development of a heritage museum. Heinz's press secretary commented, "Without the coal mines and steel plants of Western Pennsylvania, I don't think America would have had its industrial preeminence. We wouldn't have been able to fight and win two wars. The mills provided great strength and they are important to us."[36]

Chapter 4

Out with the Old, In with the New – 1988-1989

By mid-October, Strategic Management Advisors' study of the Big Shop was still not complete, but Park was proceeding as if it would reopen the facility. Sixteen people were working on a $1 million shop restoration program, reconnecting utility lines that ran for over a mile and rehabilitating both equipment and the building itself. The company planned to operate the Big Shop as a division of WHEMCO. Despite protests, Park had begun to demolish the open hearth furnaces, and Park was actively marketing both buildings and land that he was clearing to industrial firms, including a number of possible tenants in the metals industry "that [had] the potential of creating several hundred new jobs."[37]

One of the problems for any development was lack of access. The one entrance to the site was a ramp off the Homestead High Level Bridge. Otherwise, the site was cut off from the communities by the rail line that ran the length of the property, parallel to Eighth Avenue. Park hoped to extend at least four existing roads into the mill property all the way to the river, using overpasses and ramps, but demolition would have to come first. The county had agreed to try to obtain federal and state funds for the road extensions.[38]

Meanwhile, spring rains in 1989 impeded construction on the Sandcastle water park, delaying its opening until July 15, well after school was out for the summer. When it opened, however, the park, with its fourteen water slides, was a novelty for Pittsburgh. It was especially remarkable for having the tallest water slide in the country, the 85-foot-tall Lightning Express. In its first season the park drew 85,000 visitors.[39] It was a success from the time it opened.

After months of study Park finally concluded that reopening the Big Shop did not make sense after all. Instead, the company planned to move about two-thirds of the equipment from the shop over to WHEMCO, which had much more space—1.5 million square feet—compared with the Big Shop's 40,000 square feet.

On the other hand, Park was continuing to study the possibility of reopening the 160-inch plate mill, which experts estimated would cost between $10 and $35 million to restart. Mike Stout and others who were hoping to restart steel production at LTV's former South Side Works' electric arc furnaces were delighted with the thought that the Homestead Mill could serve as a market for steel produced in the South Side Works. "Not all were ready to endorse the possibility until they saw more detailed plans, however. George DeBolt, president of the Homestead Area Economic Revitalization

Corp., said, 'My primary concern would be that any activity in the 160-inch mill not impede other types of development on the site.'[40] Park ultimately spent some $5 million to explore restarting the 160-inch plate mill before finally tearing it down, in the meantime having developed alternate plans with and without the mill.[41]

Park's Approach – 1989-1990

Ray Park summarized his view of the development in late 1989, saying, "This is going to be a real showplace, with heavy and light manufacturing and some commercial and recreational ventures." Park Corporation planned to invest over $50 million in the property. Spread over the 320 acres of the development, the cost was approximately $156,000 per acre, far less than the public expenditures for Washington's Landing or the Pittsburgh Technology Center, although Park expected public funds for access improvements to supplement its own investments and thus reduce its costs for developing the property.[42]

Park kept costs low in several ways. Among them, the company worked hard to sell machinery and equipment from the sites. The toughest aspect of that was identifying what was still usable. "You can't start scrapping it until you know its value." These scrap sales did help to offset the demolition costs. Park had some ten people selling used machinery from the property before demolition began. The first two years of effort focused on equipment sales.[43]

By early 1990, Park was projecting that it would retain and renovate a million square feet of building space for industry, while the rest of the site would be cleared.

Preservation Pressures – 1990

On February 1 Governor Casey announced grants for site clearance and infrastructure improvements for four Mon Valley developments, including $2.1 million for the Homestead Industrial Park and for an extension of Martha Street in Munhall at the eastern end of the site, to provide better access.[44]

The grant for Homestead, however, became a rallying point in a growing dispute between the Park Corporation and the Steel Industry Heritage Task Force over development of the task force's proposed steel heritage center. Members of the Task Force wanted Park to sell them, or at least give them an option to buy, some 32 acres, including the Carrie furnaces across the river in Rankin and Swissvale, and some 8 acres in Munhall, the site of the

167

landing of the Pinkerton police during the Homestead Steel Strike in 1892. This site included the pump house, the water tower, and the roll shop, all of which the task force hoped to use for exhibit space for the museum. The task force had also been negotiating with the Park Corporation to save the "Hole in the Wall," a pedestrian underpass that workers had used for access into the mill, and the 48-inch universal plate rolling mill, the last remaining steam-powered mill in the world. The mill, which could produce plates as wide as 48 inches, had operated at the Homestead Works for over eighty years, from July 1899 until it shut down in December 1979.

Hole in the Wall in the 1980s

For its part, the Park Corporation was skeptical that the task force could raise the funds to develop the park and museum. Through the efforts of Senator John Heinz and Representative John Murtha of Johnstown, the federal government had appropriated funds for studies of the proposal—$350,000 in 1988 and $535,000 in 1989. However, the group was far from its goal of having the property designated as a national park. The Park Corporation estimated that a steel heritage park and museum would cost some $35 million to develop. The task force was offering Park only $50,000 for a two-year option to purchase the property, with seemingly little assurance that it could raise the funds necessary to carry through with development.

Ray Park took the position that he would be willing to sell the land only if the task force could come up with a "substantial amount" of the $35 million to develop it. "We don't want something to sit there for years and years with nothing done with it," Park said. "We don't believe they can do it. We don't believe it's feasible." The task force countered that without control of the property, donors were not interested in contributing to the project.

The issue came to a head at a meeting June 14 between officials of Park and members of the task force, including state legislators.[45] At the meeting Park's representatives stated that "they had 'irrevocably' decided not to sell any of the property," although they "agreed to donate the water tower, pump house and eight surrounding acres to the task force—and [would] restore the area itself if the task force cannot, because of the site's historical value." Park also agreed to donate the 48-inch rolling mill to the task force.[46] By the end of the year the task force had found a temporary storage place for the disassembled mill in RIDC's Keystone Commons—the renovated Westinghouse Plant in Wilmerding—and had begun to dismantle, clean, and move its components there in hope that eventually they would return to Homestead.[47] On the other hand, Park announced its decision to demolish the wall containing the famous Hole in the Wall. Two weeks later, to the consternation of members of the task force, Park demolished the roll shop, which the task force had hoped would house exhibit space for the museum.[48]

48-inch rolling mill in 1988 and 2003

While the offer of the donation of the rolling mill and the land was positive, these by themselves did not meet the task force's goals. Without the Carrie furnace property, any thought of a national park would be squelched because the project would lack both the size and the fundamental elements that could attract the federal government's interest. As Jo DeBolt, the task force's executive director, explained, "We can't build a program off fixing two little buildings [the water tower and pump house]."

Park's unwillingness to go along with the task force infuriated state legislators who attended the meeting. Representative Tom Michlovic

By early 1991 Park had removed nearly 900 tons of equipment from the site and demolition was well underway. From their experience on the J&L Hazelwood site, Park was already well familiar with Allegheny County's requirements for asbestos removal, which was a major aspect of the demolition process. "When Homestead came up they knew exactly what they were going to have to do," the county's inspector reported, adding that Park complied fully with the County Health Department's requirements, doing whatever they were asked.[54]

With demolition in progress Park appealed to have the property's assessed value lowered in order to decrease its tax liability. While the company had paid only $3 million for the land and buildings and subsequently had begun demolishing buildings, the county had assessed the property at $14 million, and the county's Board of Assessment Appeals and Review had upheld that assessment. Unsatisfied, Park appealed to the Court of Common Pleas. To avoid a prolonged legal battle, the Steel Valley School District, joined by the boroughs of Munhall, Homestead, and West Homestead, negotiated an agreement with Park to lower the assessment to $12 million for 1989 and to $9.5 million beginning in 1990. The taxing bodies agreed to subtract Park's overpayment in 1989 and 1990 from their 1991 tax bill.

The agreement would be painful for the taxing bodies. In fact, it would leave Homestead with a shortfall, even after they had raised garbage and sewage fees and borrowed funds to balance the budget. However, it seemed the best they could do. Without relief, Park threatened to "demolish everything and let it sit, sell it to some developer and leave." The tax revenues to which the taxing bodies were accustomed, and which they felt they needed, would come only once the property was developed, and not before then.[55]

Zoning also continued to be an issue. The Regional Planning Commission's subcommittee had finished its work and sent proposed ordinances on to the boroughs' planning commissions. The Park Corporation continued to oppose the ordinances, saying that they "would be far too rigid for prospective companies or developers."[56] Hearings and discussions continued throughout the year.[57]

In February 1992, the Park Corporation announced that it planned to develop some 15 acres fronting East Eighth Avenue, Homestead's main street, for a large grocery store, a pharmacy, and office buildings. This property, straddling Homestead and Munhall, was on the town side of the rail line that separated the bulk of the site from the community and that related more to the town than to the rest of the site. Homestead had no grocery store, and interest by the owner of the Shop 'n Save in West Homestead to build a new store on the mill site was viewed as a major step toward redeveloping the property, even though it was not in the main part of the site.

When Homestead's council, over the mayor's veto, passed the new zoning and subdivision ordinances recommended by the Regional Planning Commission, Park and the broker for the grocery store charged that the new zoning might pose an obstacle to the development, but the Homestead Borough Council stuck to their guns, retaining the new zoning, with its more restrictive standards.[58]

Time in Slow Motion – 1992-1993

The pace of development seemed slow to people on the outside. Confidence was low. Edward Lapko, who owned Lapko's Bar and Grill on East Eighth Avenue, lamented, "Progress is in slow motion. Everything that Park Corp. suggests—it looks good on paper, but when will it materialize?"

Looking back in January of 2000 on the progress of the project in those days, West Homestead Mayor John Dindak said

> Park Corporation would have had this property, grounds, ready for development, probably, three, four years ago. But there was a lot of contamination in the ground from the kind of business that the steel mills did, the open hearth ones that had a lot of grease, oil, and stuff like that. They spent a ton of money and a ton of time, and they had to clean all that out. And the mills, a lot of them had asbestos in it, stuff like that, so it was an environmental problem that they did not encounter, because Park never ever had such a major project like this. They always were little. This was the biggest he ever had.[59]

Park's work on the Technology Center, however, had taught them significant lessons and skills. The company felt that it was the unrealistic local dreams for the return of steel and governmental inefficiencies that were the major causes for delays, in addition to the environmental issues. Park saw itself as competent, efficient, and realistic in the way it tackled this project, despite the problems that kept emerging as the work unfolded.

Compared with Duquesne and McKeesport, however, Park's progress in Homestead seemed rapid. Betty Esper, the new mayor of Homestead, thought that those projects were two or three years behind Homestead. Kelly Park explained that "Park Corp., which has its own demolition and excavation crews, engineers and architects, has been able to move faster than RIDC. 'It's a matter of us going down to the site and deciding what we want to do and it gets done. . . . We can make a decision in a day and go do it.'" [60]

Park did its own environmental cleanup, including removal of asbestos and tanks both above and below ground. Park's motto, according to chief engineer Jack Bell, was "renovate instead of litigate." Park's strategy was to "get rid of it, bury it, document it, and pay one person to verify" that it was done. Park had its own people remove asbestos, with inspection done by Allegheny County. They turned "stacks of manifests" into the state and found that they got no inspection visits as long as the state got its paperwork. [61]

"Governments," said Bell, "hire consultants to watch consultants to hire consultants. We say we'll go in and do it. We're a family-owned business. There are no layers. We are our own demolition company. There are so many pitfalls that it's impossible to do it efficiently through government. The key is specific oversight by qualified personnel." Mellon Bank was Park's creditor. If Park needed to buy a $3 million machine to assist with the demolition, it was done. Ray Park wanted to "fix it, get rid of it." According to Bell, the Homestead project was the largest demolition project in history. [62]

By this time Park expected to demolish all but 2 million square feet of the more than 7 million square feet of buildings that had been on the site at the time of their purchase. By fall of 1991 about 75% of the demolition was already complete, and Park planned to have its first renovated building, 250,000 square feet, ready for occupancy in early 1992. [63]

Development could not come soon enough for the region. Closed mills and greater efficiency in those that remained resulted in out-migration, falling demand for housing, higher vacancy rates, and demolition, all of which depressed property values in the Mon Valley communities. Late in the year Allegheny County projected that the value of property in Homestead would fall by 7.7% in the following year, the steepest drop in the county. [64] Political leaders in Homestead began to consider asking the state to designate the borough a "distressed municipality" under Pennsylvania law, which would entail appointment of a financial overseer but would give the borough access to special loans and grants from the state. [65]

Park projected that the two large refurbished buildings at the Munhall end of the site would be ready for industrial occupancy by summer of 1992.

Taking a different approach from that in Duquesne and McKeesport, where the RIDC was hiring a marketing firm, Park planned to market its property on its own. The new zoning in Homestead, however, continued to be an issue for Park. It did not permit any uses by right but instead required a public hearing to secure a conditional use for each individual prospective development. To the Park Corporation, that was onerous. Munhall was just beginning to address the issue of zoning, and, seeing the conflict in Homestead, officials there hoped to strike a better balance between ensuring quality and encouraging development.[66]

Reacting to the situation in Homestead, Park again appealed the tax assessment for the Homestead portion of its property, claiming that the new laws "substantially decrease[d] the value of [their] property."[67] Homestead council members, however, still held fast, despite Mayor Esper's opposition. They had become convinced that "future development at the old USX site should create an attractive—and not just industrial—Homestead" with "a diversity of [business] uses." On the other hand, Mayor Esper, with other "ordinary Homestead residents," was skeptical about redevelopment plans required by the new zoning. In disgust, they brought up an earlier proposal from the Remaking Cities Conference to plant flowers temporarily on the mill site, an idea which was long dead but which they viewed as representative of the planners' ridiculous mentality. "Why can't they [the Park Corporation] do what they want?" Esper said. "Let's get on with development."[68]

Demolition and cleanup continued. Early in 1993 Park's Jack Bell estimated that demolition would likely take another two years, and grading and cleanup another two years beyond that. These delays resulted from the complications of many utility lines and the "labyrinth of underground tunnels" on the site, with some buildings having three or four stories underground.[69] Starting with 7.5 million square feet of buildings—172 acres—Park had by midyear demolished 80%, or 6 million square feet.[70]

Because of its desperate financial situation, the state of Pennsylvania accepted the borough of Homestead into its Municipalities Financial Recovery program on March 22 and appointed Joe Hohman, former Director of Allegheny County's Department of Development, as the borough's financial coordinator. Hohman was hopeful that development of the mill site would help extricate Homestead from its financial problems. In the meantime the borough would have to economize.[71]

Access Issues - 1993

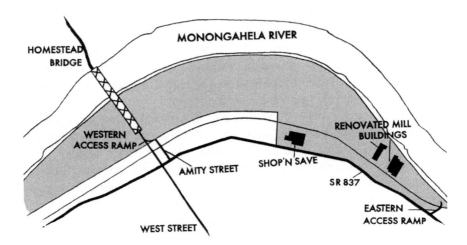

*First developments on Park's property, and new access ramps at
both ends of the property*

In July the Steel Valley Enterprise Zone received the first installment of a
$110,000 grant from the state, in part to fund a traffic study for a new
westbound ramp from the Homestead High Level Bridge to provide access
to the new development.[72] Park was hoping that the county, which owned
the bridge, would build the ramp to connect to the proposed spine road
that would run the length of the site, roughly 3.5 miles.

Access to the eastern end of the site was also a concern. This problem
was solved by award, in August, of the first publicly funded improvement
on the site, the state grant of $2 million toward the cost of a new concrete
bridge across the rail line, replacing an old rail bridge, that would connect
the site to East Eighth Avenue near the Rankin Bridge.

Park was actively marketing this eastern end of the site, beginning
with the supermarket and strip shopping center planned for the small
portion of the property on East Eighth Avenue. Park planned a harbor
facility near the Rankin Bridge and manufacturing or distribution in the
few mill buildings it had retained and rehabilitated at the Munhall end of
the main property.[73]

Refurbished and repurposed mill buildings in Munhall, with the eastern access road on the right, 2005

More Contention over Preservation – 1994

The issue of preservation continued to be contentious:[74] 1994 began with an escalating controversy over Park's decision to proceed with demolishing the Big Shop, which the Steel Industry Heritage Corporation (the now-incorporated task force) had been hoping to acquire to house the 48-inch rolling mill. Demolition began January 26, without notice and without a demolition permit. The Steel Industry Heritage Corporation was taken by surprise.[75] "'We were in the midst of negotiating with them to buy the building,'" said August Carlino, the corporation's executive director. For its part, Park officials contended there had been no agreement on a purchase price for the property. "'We had an asking price that they (the foundation) didn't like and they had a buying price that we didn't like,'" and Park had notified the foundation six months beforehand that the "'rapidly deteriorating'" Big Shop was coming down. The Heritage Corporation had not negotiated directly with Park, since Park had made the decision not to negotiate with parties—including the Heritage Corporation—that had no money to buy property at Park's prices. Jack Bell, Park's engineer who was spokesman on the issue, summarized, "'We are not, and have not, and will not negotiate with the local group. These people have no money, unfortunately. We have an objective to develop this site.'"[76] "'There must be a commitment to build a museum from a group that can supply the funds in a reasonable time schedule or the property won't be sold,'" Bell explained. "'It's hard enough to get funding when you own the property. It's even more difficult when you don't own it,'" responded the Heritage Corporation's Carlino.[77]

The day after demolition had begun, municipal officials stopped it because Park did not have a permit.[78] With the building partly demolished, however, Park immediately applied for a permit, which the borough solicitor said the municipality would have to grant. The Park Corporation was adamant that they could not "wait forever for buyers who would establish a steel heritage museum. The Big Shop 'is right in the middle of our development,' Bell said. 'The idea of someone taking forever to improve the appearance of these buildings was not acceptable.'" With permit in hand, the Park Corporation proceeded to complete demolition of the Big Shop in late February.[79]

At this juncture, however, efforts to develop a steel industry heritage park were still stalled. Governor Casey did include $18.9 million for the museum in his capital budget, but it was contingent on the Steel Industry Heritage Corporation's raising an equal amount in matching funds. The Park Corporation had agreed to preserve the water tower and pump house, the only two buildings remaining from the strike era. The Howard Heinz Endowment had made a commitment for a grant to the Western Pennsylvania Conservancy to acquire historical property from the Park Corporation, including 12 acres of the Pinkerton landing site on the Homestead side of the river and the 60 to 65 acres of the Carrie furnace site on the other side. According to some, Park had agreed to a price of $1.5 million, but the foundation refused to provide funds for the purchase until the Heritage Corporation could demonstrate that it could carry the project through to completion. That meant a buy-in by the National Park Service, which would then require a recommendation by the Secretary of the Interior and an act of Congress.[80]

Development Possibilities – 1994-1995

In actuality, however, two messages were coming from the community: we want preservation, and we want development. The municipalities were hurting and were growing impatient with the combination of demolition and the slow pace of development, which together were undermining property tax revenues. "We're trying to emphasize that this is a bigger issue than just this one building," said Randy Harris, a Steel Industry Heritage spokesman. "There's less and less taxes coming off the property every year because there's no development."[81] Bill Davis, a community activist and council president in Munhall, voiced the opinion that the state should buy out the Park Corporation to hasten development.[82]

Finally, April 1994 brought the announcement that construction would begin on the first new development on the site, the 39,000-square-foot Shop 'n Save grocery store, to be developed by SuperValu of Minneapolis. They would move the existing Shop 'n Save from West Homestead into expanded space on 4 acres of the site on East Eighth Avenue. Response from the community was positive, especially since the design of the new supermarket was sensitive to its surroundings.[83] Buoyed by the announcement, the Homestead Area Economic Revitalization Committee announced $3.5 million in street improvements that summer, including new lights and benches, for East Eighth Avenue.[84]

Throughout 1994 an entirely separate issue came into play. Speculation was intense that riverboat gambling would come to Pittsburgh, as it recently had to a number of cities on the Mississippi River and the Gulf Coast. Sandcastle was among the many sites mentioned, and Harry Henninger, president of Kennywood Entertainment Company, the owner of Sandcastle, admitted to exploring the possibility. In fact, by July he estimated that twenty casino operators had "approached him about the possibility of establishing gambling operations at Sandcastle." He felt he had to consider it out of self-defense, noting that "plans by other developers for riverboat gambling in Pittsburgh 'will have a definite effect on other forms of entertainment,' including on Sandcastle. The water park could ensure its survival by offering gambling, Henninger noted."[85] Governor Casey, however, was staunchly opposed to introducing casino gambling into the state, and legislation to authorize it eventually died in the legislature.

By 1995 the Park Corporation had torn up nearly 1 million cubic yards of concrete, and had nearly finished leveling the Homestead Works.[86]

Access Improvements – 1995

In spring 1995 Mellon Stuart Construction Company began to build the $3.6 million new bridge at the eastern end of the site.[87] So far, however, there had been no movement on improving access to the western end of the site, where the Homestead High Level Bridge crossed the property. That bridge would be the means by which the relatively wealthy communities of Squirrel Hill, Shadyside, and Greenfield in the city of Pittsburgh would have access to the new development. Ray Park wanted a ramp built from the High Level

Pump house and water tower, 2005, near the landing site of the Pinkerton Police during the Homestead Steel Strike of 1892

Bridge that would bring customers directly onto his property. Mark Patrick, who worked in the county's Department of Development at the time, remembered how this came about: "Ray Park took Tom Foerster for a ride on the site and said, 'We have the idea that we're going to do something here. We have one very narrow, inadequate ramp here, and we'd like to have a second ramp.' And somehow Foerster used county bond money to build a ramp and, I mean, it's a nice ramp. And that's how it happened, 3 million dollars. 3.3 million."[88] Funds for the ramp appeared in the county's capital budget, survived cost-cutting measures even when Commissioner Foerster failed to be reelected, and Republicans took control of the Board of County Commissioners in 1996. The county's Department of Public Works was able to begin construction of the ramp that summer.[89]

Progress on Preservation and the First Opening – 1995

In May 1995 Park announced that it would begin restoration of the historic pump house and water tower with its own resources, since funds from the federal government had not been forthcoming. The fate of the Carrie blast furnace, however, remained uncertain. Although the Department of Community Affairs had approved a $2 million grant to build a bridge to connect the historic sites on the two sides of the river, and a grant of $1.5 million from the Department of Commerce had helped pay for construction of an access road to the Pinkerton landing site, there was still no progress on preserving the blast furnace.[90]

On the positive side, however, in addition to Park's offer to restore the pump house and water tower, the state, acting on a request from Allegheny County, had approved $2 million under Strategy 21, the city's, county's, and universities' joint request to the state for financial support of their most important, major economic development projects. The Heritage Corporation planned to use Strategy 21 funds to restore the historic Bost Building and another adjacent building on East Eighth Avenue to serve as the main visitors' center for the Steel Heritage Center. Plans included a theater and exhibits that would document the history of industry and labor in the region, including the role of the Homestead Works.[91]

New Shop 'n Save, 2005, opened in 1995

181

At the end of May the new Shop 'n Save opened for business. About three times the size of the old store it replaced in West Homestead, it was the first new construction project in Homestead in twenty years and the first new, productive use on the Park Corporation's portion of the former Homestead Works, which had closed ten years earlier.[92]

With its arrival, a new era for the tax-poor municipalities began. The groundwork was in place for the mall, office, and housing development that was just around the corner. The site was ready, as ready for development as an unused site in the suburbs or a rural location. The task now was simply to identify and attract the right mix of stores and businesses to this favorable location, one that had the advantages of being close to both city and suburban communities. For the most part, the jobs at the Waterfront and at Sandcastle would not match the pay or benefits of those at the vanished steel mill. The mill was gone, but efforts to keep its memory alive continued, while new uses and a new way of life began to emerge to replace it.

LESSONS

While Washington's Landing and the Pittsburgh Technology Center are some distance from a neighborhood, the Homestead Works had been the economic and geographic focus of a community for a century. Understandably, therefore, public opinions about its redevelopment were far stronger than for the sites in the city. Hence, the burden on the developer to engage members of the community in conversation about the future of the site was significantly greater in Homestead. This entailed communication, selling, and negotiation both with leaders—local elected officials (who would approve development standards and could rally their constituents to support the project), other opinion leaders, and the general public.

The Park Corporation was attentive to this need, and as a result things went generally well for them. While they held firm to their own interest, they met frequently with community leaders and the public at large. They listened to community concerns, for example, in the matters of reopening the Big Shop and preservation of historically important buildings. Although they didn't always accede to the community's requests, in significant instances they did, including in donating and preserving the historic buildings and site associated with the Homestead Strike Pinkerton landing.

In one respect, however, the public exercised legitimate control. As with Washington's Landing and the Pittsburgh Technology Center, this was in setting standards for land use and development. In this case, as noted, the developable portion of the Waterfront site spanned three municipalities. Having one municipality's zoning ordinance be more lenient than the others would have led to a distorted development pattern, with development concentrating in the municipality that had the laxest standards. Therefore, it was important that the three municipalities collaborated to adopt similar development standards, which is what happened. The Park Corporation objected that the resulting standards were too restrictive and costly; however, the municipalities generally held firm and reaped public benefits, such as views of and access to the riverfront.

Perhaps the most significant lesson to be drawn from this project, however, is the importance of seeking to accommodate people's often conflicting desires to return to the safety of a familiar past—or at least to memorialize it—and to move forward, often impatiently, to grasp an unknown but hopeful future. People hold on to what they know, and they take pride in having prevailed over difficult challenges and dangers. Although Homestead's past was ugly, a history of danger, oppression, conflict and death, it was also glorious in its accomplishments—the building of the Brooklyn Bridge and the Empire State Building, the winning of world wars. It had also been the means of many families' achieving middle-class prosperity in America's mid-century. Yet people are also realistic. Once they have accepted that old ways will never return, they are anxious to move forward, while at the same time giving due respect to past sacrifices and accomplishments.

In my view the leaders involved in redeveloping the Homestead Works deserve high marks for working carefully through these conflicting pressures of revival, preservation, and replacement for new uses. Both public leaders and Park made extraordinary efforts and expended considerable time and capital to explore the possibilities of bringing back some of the old uses on a firmer financial base. None proved successful. They then came to understand and honor the significance of preserving some of the most important symbols of the past struggles and accomplishments. Likely, a shrewd economic calculation was a significant part of Park's motivation: he would gain community support for his larger project if he conceded minor preservation victories. However, public support for preservation, from state legislators who saw preservation as part of the price Park needed to pay in exchange for the state's financial support for the project, was probably a larger factor. Once there was clarity on the scope of preservation—the stacks, the pump house and water tower, the salvaged rolling mill—the community's attention naturally and rightly focused on quickly realizing the benefits it stood to gain from quick redevelopment of the mill property, and conflict subsided.

Shops at the Waterfront, 2005

Idle stoves at the USX Duquesne Works

CITY CENTER OF DUQUESNE AND INDUSTRIAL CENTER OF MCKEESPORT TIMELINE

1870   The Flagler Company purchases the Fulton-Bolman Company and shortly after incorporates it as the National Tube Works.

1886   Construction begins on the mill in Duquesne.

1888   The Duquesne mill begins manufacturing steel rails.

1890   Carnegie Steel Corporation purchases the Duquesne mill and expands it over the following years.

1899   Thirteen tube and pipe producers, including the National Tube Works, form the National Tube Company.

1901   The Duquesne Works and the National Tube Company become part of the U.S. Steel Corporation.

1969   The Duquesne Plant and the National Plant merge into a single operation.

1984   The Duquesne Works close.

1986   U.S. Steel Corporation becomes USX Corporation.

1987   The National Plant closes. The Mon Valley Commission releases its report and recommendations for revitalizing the Monongahela River Valley. USX Corporation agrees to turn its Duquesne and National plants over to Allegheny County for redevelopment.

1988   Duncan Lagnese and Associates completes a first environmental study of the two sites, including estimated costs of cleanup. USX demolishes Dorothy Six in Duquesne. The Allegheny County Industrial Development Authority acquires title to the property, releases USX from responsibility for environmental conditions, and contracts with the nonprofit Regional Industrial Development Corporation (RIDC) to act as developer.

1989	Allegheny County's planning consultants unveil plans for the sites. The county and RIDC give them new names.
1990	RIDC Growth Fund assumes title to the properties. Environmental problems surface, resulting in additional investigations. RIDC hires ICF Kaiser as its environmental consultant. Construction begins on a new plant for Aluglas (later renamed Metallized Paper Corporation) in McKeesport. Road construction begins.
1991	Environmental cleanup and demolition begin. Metallized Paper Corporation and Camp-Hill Corporation begin production in McKeesport. RIDC submits its environmental cleanup plan to the DER and the Health Department and receives responses. RIDC accomplishes a swap of land with the Union Railroad. Earth Products Recycling occupies space in Duquesne.
1992	Allegheny Recovery Corporation commits to the Duquesne site. Environmental cleanup and demolition continue.
1993	Allegheny Recovery Corporation begins operations in Duquesne. RIDC completes environmental cleanup.
1994	McKeesport Industrial Manor II, a renovated mill building, attracts its first tenant.
1995	Duquesne Industrial Manor, another renovated mill building, goes on the market. Pennsylvania approves legislation creating the Industrial Site Recycling Program.

5

PUBLIC, OR PRIVATE?

From the USX Duquesne Works to the City Center of Duquesne;

From the USX National Plant to the Industrial Center of McKeesport

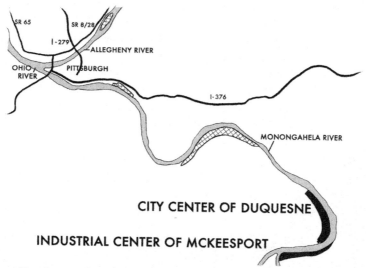

City Center of Duquesne and Industrial Center of McKeesport

What are the relative advantages of public and private corporations for converting abandoned industrial sites to new, productive uses? Does private enterprise, acting on the profit incentive, perform best, or should the government step in to assure development that best fulfills a community's desires for their reuse? The history of the transformation of two giant steel plants in Pittsburgh's Monongahela River Valley—the sister plants in Duquesne and McKeesport—sheds light on these questions.

189

INTRODUCTION

City Center of Duquesne is an industrial park built on the site of the former USX Duquesne Works, which closed in 1984, comprising 220 acres some 5 miles up the Monongahela River from Homestead. Like the Homestead Mill site, it lies between the river and State Route 837, which in Duquesne is called Duquesne Boulevard. Railroad lines run its length along both the river and the road. The homes and commercial center of the city rise above the hill across the Boulevard.

Industrial Center of McKeesport is another industrial park, developed on the site of the former USX National Plant, which closed in 1987, on the other side of the river. The mill property, approximately 1.3 miles long and 0.16 mile wide, encompasses 135 acres, bordered on the north by the Monongahela River and on the south by the Union-McKeesport Connecting Railroad and Conrail tracks. Beyond these is Lisle Boulevard, lined with businesses, the main thoroughfare of McKeesport's commercial district. The Youghiogheny River runs along the site on the west, while the tapered east end of the property is bordered by railroad tracks, yards, and property owned by the Dravo Corporation.

Unlike in Homestead, reminders of these projects' industrial past are still present everywhere. Stoves and a blast furnace still loom over the southern end of the Duquesne site, next to the cavernous open ore pit, which is surrounded by a fence and barbed wire to deter trespassers.

Abandoned ore pit at City Center of Duquesne, 2005

The majority of the old mill buildings are gone at both Duquesne and McKeesport, and in their place are vast vacant tracts. These lots are not blessed with proximity to universities as is the Pittsburgh Technology Center, and they are unlike the Waterfront or Sandcastle, which have proximity to an affluent market. In addition, they have poorer access to highways. As a result, development here has come much more slowly.

Vacant land at City Center of Duquesne, 2005

Vacant land at Industrial Center of McKeesport, 2005

Since the aim was to create industrial parks, those of the old mill buildings that could and might yet be adapted for modern industrial or office uses have been retained. They stand as reminders of their steel heritage. New, bright green, metal roofs at Duquesne, blue at McKeesport, and new roadways, street trees, and entrance signs, all present immediate visual cues that the properties are in the process of becoming modern industrial parks, but the projects are plainly far from finished. In fact, they are clearly still in their earliest stages of redevelopment. Duquesne, which is closer to Pittsburgh and where development is more compact, seems further along. Both sites house a number of productive businesses, yet one has the sense that years will pass before these properties are again filled to capacity.

Renovated mill buildings at City Center of Duquesne, 2005

Renovated mill buildings at Industrial Center of McKeesport, 2005

DEVELOPING THE CITY CENTER OF DUQUESNE AND THE
INDUSTRIAL CENTER OF MCKEESPORT

The County Steps In – 1987

The day before Governor Dick Thornburgh left office in January 1987, the county received the bad news that the Department of Community Affairs had denied its $6.8 million grant request under Strategy 21 to fund infrastructure projects in Duquesne, McKeesport, Glassport, and Wilkinsburg. The county had expected the state's support of this joint annual city–county application for state capital funding first instituted in 1985. The state said the proposed projects did not meet the guidelines of the program under which it had applied. In vain, county officials appealed to the governor to reverse the department's decision. They were told that the county would have to reapply under other programs. However, the hopes of county and local officials were renewed when incoming Governor Robert P. Casey visited the valley on his first day in office and said, "I have a commitment to help here." In fact, it took almost a year for the county to get the funds that it both needed and had expected, with a resulting delay in the projects.[1]

On March 25 the Mon Valley Commission released the report they had worked on since the commission's formation the previous spring—a $335 million plan to revitalize the Mon Valley—and presented the first copy to Governor Casey. An estimated $307 million of the total cost of the plan was proposed to come from the state, the bulk of that for road improvements, not including the proposed Mon Valley Expressway.[2] In releasing the report, Joe Hohman, the commission's cochair and director of the county's Department of Development, made the surprise announcement that USX had agreed to turn its McKeesport and Duquesne sites over to the county for redevelopment. While acknowledging that developing the sites would likely take ten to fifteen years, Hohman stated, "This is definitely the key ingredient to the whole program."[3]

Reception to the announcement in the valley was enthusiastic. Mayor Louis Washowich of McKeesport commended the county commissioners for their "bold move" in proposing to take over the mill properties and said, "It allows us to determine what direction we want to go. It gives us a chance to control our own destiny. We sure don't need another 10 years of vacant, rusted steel plants."[4] Mayor Raymond Terza of Duquesne added, "We all feel good because there will finally be some motion there."[5]

Governor Casey was also enthusiastic. "I pledge my personal commitment to work with the groups and organizations involved in making this report a reality," he said after hearing a review of the commission's recommendations. "We have to invest in this valley if our future is going to exist. Working together there is nothing we can't do."[6]

Behind the scenes Brooks Robinson at RIDC and the county had both worked to secure the chance to develop the sites. Commissioner Foerster had gone to David Roderick, president of USX, and explained that the people did not want the steel properties sold off to just any purchaser.[7] Foerster proposed that USX turn control of the Duquesne and McKeesport properties over to the county at no cost.[8] By the time the commission released its report, the county had reached an agreement with USX in principle to acquire the properties on the conditions that USX would be paid a predetermined price as development occurred and that the county would lease back any portions that USX continued to use. In fact, hope lingered that USX might restart portions of the plants or be directly involved in their redevelopment. Regardless, the county and RIDC would work together to plan, redevelop, and market the sites.[9]

Negotiations – 1987-1988

Formal negotiations between the county and USX proceeded during the summer of 1987. The county proposed to pay USX $10,000 per acre as parcels were sold to new businesses.[10] The county also asked USX to make payments in lieu of property taxes for a period of time. Roderick agreed, as did the board of USX.

The county's administrators were not unified in how they thought development should be handled. Steve Barrouk, Jack Exler, and others who had responsibility for the county's economic development activities wanted to manage the projects themselves. However, Joe Hohman and Jim Dodaro (the County Solicitor, a resident of White Oak, adjacent to McKeesport, and a Pennsylvania Turnpike commissioner) believed that the county did not have the capacity to manage so large a project. He had urged Foerster to recruit RIDC to manage redevelopment on the county's behalf, hoping that the RIDC would jump in and accelerate the projects' development.[11]

Pursuant to this thinking, Foerster and Hohman began serious discussions with Brooks Robinson about taking on the Mon Valley properties. Tom Foerster remembered it as an easy sell; Joe Hohman remembered otherwise. Robinson was willing to be involved and to lend his time and expertise as long as there was no expenditure or liability for RIDC. Accordingly, the county agreed to provide $400,000 per year for the first three years through its Industrial Development Authority to cover insurance and security costs.[12] It was, after all, a project that the county, not RIDC, had initiated, and Robinson insisted on establishing a separate fund to keep moneys for the Mon Valley projects from commingling with RIDC's other funds. As resources became available, RIDC would move forward. While the county was already seeking $16 million from the state under Strategy 21 to help prepare the sites for development, Robinson predicted that it would take fifteen years or more to redevelop them.[13]

In early 1988, while the county was pursuing these negotiations, the Park Corporation and USX concluded their agreement of sale for the Homestead Works. At the same time, the city and county submitted a new Strategy 21 request to Governor Casey for $156 million, including $16 million toward what was estimated to be an $83 million cost to prepare the Duquesne and McKeesport sites. The county hoped to see 4,500 workers employed there after redevelopment.[14] On receiving the request, however, the governor responded that "we already have made a substantial commitment." (The state had approved $181.8 million of the original 1985 Strategy 21 request of $425 million, the bulk of which was for the new Pittsburgh airport.[15]) In an editorial titled "Ditching the Dinosaurs," the *McKeesport Daily News* explained that the new Strategy 21 request "is concentrating on sweeping away the dinosaur remains of this area's heavy-manufacturing past as the best way to pave the way for an economic future." The editorial also acknowledged the realization that the region "must cut its losses, clear away the debris of the past, and prepare the old sites for the next stage. . . . a shedding of the past, a realization that it isn't coming back."[16]

The same forces behind redevelopment of the abandoned steel sites were also the impetus behind the Mon Valley Expressway, a proposed 54-mile expansion of the Pennsylvania Turnpike between Pittsburgh and West Virginia that valley leaders believed would improve access and stimulate development. The proposal had a thirty-year history, but the economic crisis in the valley gave it new urgency. Governor Casey and Turnpike Commissioner Jim Dodaro, knowing that the expressway could not pay for itself with tolls alone, thought it should be viewed as an economic development project. Dodaro suggested raising the state's gasoline tax to raise funds.[17] The Mon Valley Commission included building the expressway as one of the recommendations in its report.[18] Although he opposed raising the gasoline tax to fund it, Governor Casey became an important supporter of the expressway, calling it "the best long-term investment we can make for the future growth of the Mon Valley," and he sped its design and development as funds became available to do so.[19] In the meantime, the state moved other, smaller, road improvements forward, including reconstruction of Lyle

Boulevard in McKeesport, along the front of the shuttered former steel plant.[20]

Over the spring and summer of 1988, negotiations continued on the agreement that would convey the former mill properties to the county's Industrial Development Authority. While these negotiations were underway, Camp-Hill Corporation came forward with a proposal to lease and reopen the electrical weld resistance line in McKeesport to manufacture carbon and alloy pipe.[21]

As these negotiations neared an end, Duncan Lagnese and Associates, retained by RIDC to do an environmental study of the sites, discovered possible problems of water contamination from ammonia at McKeesport and from halogenated methane at Duquesne. Neither appeared to be serious, but as a representative of the consultant stated, "Just the fact there is a detectable quantity is cause for concern."[22] In the same report Duncan Lagnese estimated the cost of environmental cleanup of the two sites to be $14 million, mostly for removal of asbestos. Brooks Robinson hoped to use proceeds from selling scrap and equipment, valued at between $7 million and $13 million, to pay the cost of environmental cleanup.[23]

Preservation Out – 1988

In April 1988, with leadership from the Allegheny Conference on Community Development, the Steel Industry Heritage Task Force formed. In July the task force toured the McKeesport, Duquesne, and Homestead sites, examining possibilities for historic preservation in those communities. The group concluded that Homestead had the best resources, and the demolition of the Dorothy Six blast furnace on August 1 eliminated Duquesne as an option.[24] Thereafter, the task force focused its attention on Homestead.

The demolition of Dorothy Six represented a major turning point in the community's acceptance that steel was gone and was not going to return. As Dennis Pittman, who served as McKeesport's Community Development Director and later as a member of RIDC's Policy Committee, explained

> The local folks, very frustrated. I mean they had candle light vigils. "Don't tear the mills down. They're gonna reopen. Yes, they are. They've always done this. They went on strike. They banked the furnaces. You don't understand." It wasn't until physically, and that interesting enough was one of the main decisions—tear some of this crap down. Get it gone. And the minute it falls over—wow!

Remains of Dorothy Six. Her stove lingered on the site for some years after demolition of the main tower.

The removal of that blast furnace . . . clued everybody, we have to go on with our lives. Something has passed. Grandpa died, and we have to go ahead. We're not going to forget him, but we've got to go forward. That event chronicled as well as anything where we were headed.[25]

A Three-Way Contract – 1988

As the agreements to transfer the land from USX to the county concluded, some were excited that a county agency—the Industrial Development Authority—was to be the owner of the property. County Commissioner Barbara Hafer voiced such confidence and optimism, stating that with that arrangement "development and recruiting of companies will be well planned and organized" and "planners will be able to screen the types of companies and the by-products they produce when the developments are planned. Sometimes we get so desperate to get jobs we take any type of company but not here."[26] Government control appeared to strengthen future benefits going to the communities, not just to corporations seeking profit.

The Industrial Development Authority (IDA) acquired title to the two properties on August 10, with RIDC designated as master developer. Encompassing a total of 360 acres, 230 in Duquesne and 130 in McKeesport, this was believed to be "the largest single transfer in the country of industrial property to a local government for redevelopment."[27]

Under the agreement, USX would be paid $10,000 per acre at the time land was sold or used, plus half the difference for any land sold for over $30,000 an acre. Potentially, USX could receive a minimum of $3.6 million for the 360 acres. In the interim, USX would make a payment in lieu of real estate taxes, equivalent to the taxes on the land—but not the buildings—for up to fifteen years.[28] Harold C. Haase, president of USX Realty, commented, "From our standpoint, I think it's more of a community support project."[29] In his view, Commissioner Foerster said, "The county is taking a risk. Our neck is way out on the line because now it's up to the county to develop that property. We thought it's time government took a risk."[30] His perspective proved to be more realistic than Barbara Hafer's in his consciousness of the risks that go along with control and responsibility.

The agreement also made reference to Duncan Lagnese's environmental report and provided that RIDC and the IDA would "assume all the responsibility and cost of the remediation of all environmental conditions and materials in or on the Premises in accordance with the Report" and "release USX from all past, present and future claims . . . for environmental conditions under Federal, State or local law and regulations." While in light of subsequent events, some would later be critical of this release, the county and RIDC did not believe they could gain control of the properties and redevelop them without it.[31]

Planning Begins – 1988-1989

The county and RIDC quickly engaged L.P. Perfido Associates, a Pittsburgh architectural firm, to work with Grad Partnership, a New Jersey architectural firm, to do site planning and make recommendations for road construction or upgrading, propose phasing of demolition, and identify buildings to be retained for renovation.[32] The expectation at the time of purchase was that RIDC would keep five buildings at McKeesport and fourteen buildings at

Duquesne for reuse.[33]

Joe Hohman characterized the project as "a complex and multi-year effort to transform those properties into a mixed use to serve existing and new businesses and to create jobs."[34] He estimated that it would take up to three years to clear and prepare both plants for development.[35] At the same time, however, the county already was talking with fifteen to twenty prospects, some of them sizable companies that were interested in the sites. Steve Barrouk, the IDA's executive director, gave his opinion that "all we have to do is get it started and it will move forward on its own momentum."[36] Work was already underway to convert U.S. Steel's former plant headquarters office building, just across Duquesne Boulevard from the Duquesne site, into a business innovation center.

The county initially hoped to raise $45 million for the projects, $15 million each from the federal and state governments and $15 million from the county's Community Development Block Grant. In addition, Foerster wanted to invest $3 million per year of county money, and the county did so the first year. Subsequently, Foerster was unable to get a second vote from either of the other two county commissioners to continue the policy. Foerster recalled that the county had promised Moody's and Standard & Poor's that the county would not issue more bonds than it could retire in six years, which also eliminated that possibility of county support. On the positive side, the state, including both governors Thornburgh and later Casey, was very supportive.[37]

The IDA planned to retain a contractor to perform both demolition and environmental cleanup, giving the contractor the right to the resale value of the materials recovered from the sites. Sale of scrap metal, estimated at 200,000 tons, and equipment could potentially offset the entire $14 million cost of demolition and cleanup.[38] The county expected to award a contract by May of 1989.[39]

To help oversee progress on the many efforts to revitalize the valley, County Commissioners revived and expanded the Mon Valley Commission, which had been dormant since issuing its report. So many groups were interested in developments in the valley that a body like the commission was needed to disseminate information and coordinate action. The commissioners raised the size of the commission to thirty-four in an effort to include all the interested constituencies. As the Commission prepared to unveil redevelopment plans at its first public hearing some nine months later, Joe Hohman reminded everyone that patience would be necessary: "There's been a lot of activity, but we're looking at a 15-year, 20-year game plan. There won't be drastic changes overnight."[40]

By early 1989 the county had requested and received proposals to provide security for the sites and statements of qualifications from fifty-seven firms interested in bidding on demolition and environmental cleanup.[41] That number grew with another five late entries.[42] By February the county had run into bonding problems with the low bidder for the security contract, but it had managed to make a short list of twenty qualified demolition and cleanup contractors.[43]

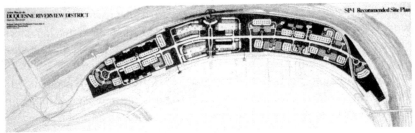

1989 plan for Duquesne

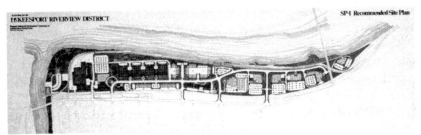

1989 plan for McKeesport

On June 13, 1989, Grad Partnership and L.P. Perfido Associates, the county's site planners, unveiled plans for the sites at a sparsely attended public meeting at McKeesport High School. Both sites would have a mix of office, research and development, and industrial and light-industrial space. Both would have new public access to the river through a marina in McKeesport and an overlook pavilion in Duquesne. Both would be connected to their respective communities through extensions of city streets into the developments, six in McKeesport and three in Duquesne. About 25% of the buildings on both sites would be retained and renovated for small tenants. Each site would have about 1.8 million square feet of new office space. The plans recommended moving rail lines on both sites from their interior locations to the riverfront, to allow circulation through the sites. This plan would require land swaps with Conrail at Duquesne and

CSX at McKeesport. Finally, in both cases the planners identified portions of the sites for early development, with demolition following in stages on the remainder of the sites.

The goal in both communities was to revive the industrial job base. Mel Achtzehn of Duquesne, who was then serving on the city council, explained, "Our goal was to put this into production, jobs. We did not want it to go into a retail item, like Homestead did. We felt that it would be more beneficial to the city and the people to provide better-paying jobs."[44]

The plan for McKeesport included a site for Aluglas of Pennsylvania, which was proposing to build a $40 million plant to manufacture aluminized paper for chewing gum wrappers and beer bottles. Aluglas was expected to be in operation by April and to employ 300 workers.

Contracting Problems – 1989

The plans for the two developments did not include cost estimates or timetables, but demolition and cleanup alone were expected to take two years.[45] The county had expected to award a contract for that work in May but then pushed the date to July. It had received bids from eight firms, all to accomplish the work in either two or three years, but the range in the financial offers was staggering.

The wide range of the bids reflected not only the differences in the amount of effort the bidders had invested in preparing them but also the difficulty of estimating the amount of work involved and the associated costs. Another reason for the differences may have been that some firms were demolition experts whereas others specialized more in environmental cleanup. Only two of the bids estimated that proceeds from the sale of scrap, machinery, and equipment would cover the cost of demolition and cleanup. American Atlas Corporation of Michigan expected profits of over $5 million from the job. In contrast, the other six contractors expected that the costs of demolition and cleanup would exceed sales proceeds, but the range of the estimated gap ranged from $200,000 to over $27 million, with an average expected gap of $15.5 million.[46] "I'm baffled," Joe Hohman was quoted as saying. "When somebody says they will charge you $26 million and someone else says they will pay you $5 million, I don't know what it means. That's a difference of $31 million, and that's a lot of money in my neighborhood."[47]

The county analyzed the companies and worried over the selection, but it finally awarded the contract to low bidder American Atlas in early July. On the surface there was every reason to believe that American Atlas could do the job. They had extensive experience in demolishing plants, including Jones & Laughlin Steel Corporation's plants in Youngstown, Ohio. They had spent $40,000 in preparing their bid and had had a team on the site for six weeks as they prepared their estimate. They expected to hire some 300 workers for the first six months of work and retain about half of them throughout the two-year project. "It's the best job we've ever seen," co-owner Marty Haitz was quoted as saying. "Everything about it is perfect. We're going to make a wonderful profit," and he expected that Allegheny County would also.[48]

A problem quickly arose, however. American Atlas could not meet the county's requirement to secure a $28 million performance bond and claimed that a bond for that amount could not be secured for a demolition project. The county, recognizing the difficulty but feeling the need to have insurance if the contractor should fail to carry out the project, decided to re-bid the contract, giving more alternative means of having contractors provide security for their work.[49]

Although twenty-five firms requested bid documents, in the end, when the county received bids in October, American Atlas was the only bidder. The amount they offered to pay the county had dropped to $1.6 million, due, they said, to a fall in the price of scrap steel and an increase in the scope of environmental work the county was requesting. Hohman feared that other potential bidders dropped out because they had become alarmed by the possibility of environmental liabilities they would incur if they uncovered unexpected asbestos, PCBs, or other hazardous materials—concerns that were not surprising.[50]

In the end, however, American Atlas was unable to meet even the county's reduced bonding requirements. Deciding that their own public bidding requirements were creating an obstacle, the county reluctantly began discussions with RIDC about assuming title and full management responsibility for the projects.[51] Joe Hohman ventured that "'it's the most prudent thing to do to expedite the project.'"[52] Given the difficulties they had experienced in getting started with the demolition and cleanup, the county and RIDC concluded that they should try a different approach and retain a construction management firm to oversee those activities. They identified and interviewed several local firms.[53]

While plans for cleanup evolved, community leaders sought additional financial help with the escalating costs of cleanup from the federal government. Mel Achtzehn of Duquesne and Lou Washowich of McKeesport together went to Washington and tried, unsuccessfully, to find officials who would be sympathetic and responsive. Although they got a hearing, nothing came of their efforts. It was a frustrating experience.[54]

Aluglas, meanwhile, was proceeding with its plan to develop 5 acres of the McKeesport property. By November they had secured commitments for the $40 million needed to construct their proposed 70,000-square-foot plant, none but the equity from conventional sources. Over half was to come from the state of Pennsylvania. The company planned to begin construction in February and to occupy the plant by late summer, initially with 70 workers, projected to grow to 360 within four years.[55]

In December the county's Department of Development, in association with the Mon Valley Commission, the IDA, and the RIDC, unveiled new names and logos for the two development sites: Industrial Center of McKeesport and City Center of Duquesne. The Department of Development noted, "The new names and their logos symbolize the transition the Mon Valley is making from the economic tragedies of the past to the new opportunities that beckon in the nineties."[56]

The RIDC Growth Fund – 1990

In January 1990 the IDA voted to pass title to the properties to the RIDC Growth Fund. RIDC had formed this affiliate to shield RIDC itself from any liability that might come from the projects. On February 1 at Keystone Commons, Governor Casey presented the county with a check for $15.6 million for four development projects in the Mon Valley. The funds included $4.97 million for construction of access roads, environmental cleanup, and site preparation at the Industrial Center of McKeesport, and $3.75 million for access roads and bridges, water and sewer line improvements, and other site improvements at the City Center of Duquesne.[57]

Commenting on the grants from the Commonwealth, the *Pittsburgh Post-Gazette* editorialized, "Certainly there has been a temptation to [write off the Mon Valley], rather than spend a great deal of state money. As the experience in clearing the former Jones & Laughlin steel plant in Hazelwood for the Pittsburgh Technology Center has shown, it's not just a matter of razing structures. The problems of clearing the site of old, buried toxic wastes to the point of satisfying state Department of Environmental Resources standards for office buildings and light-industry structures are not only costly but seemingly endless."[58]

Upon accepting responsibility for the developments in Duquesne and McKeesport, Brooks Robinson described the scope and complexity of directing them and clearly indicated how responsibility was to be shared among interested parties:

The purpose of the conveyance was to facilitate the scrap sales, remediation, demolition and redevelopment of the properties as two urban industrial centers which will restructure the economy of the communities and serve as an example of the recovery of the Mon Valley Region. The progress of the work is being undertaken by the RIDC Growth Fund through a Policy Committee that is comprised of the mayors of both McKeesport and Duquesne; a community member appointed by each mayor; the chairperson of the Mon Valley Commission; Allegheny County Departments of Planning and Development; state representatives and senators from these communities; and RIDC.[59]

RIDC formed a management team to oversee and plan the decommissioning and demolition of the sites. In April, RIDC contracted with Turner Construction Company to serve as the construction manager and project coordinator for both sites, including the responsibility for demolition, cleanup, and liquidation of equipment.[60] National Industrial Services, Inc. (NISI), nationally recognized in this regard, was hired to market and sell the scrap and machinery.[61]

Environmental Questions and Investigations – 1990

Shortly after RIDC took over, Killam Associates Consulting Engineers (the former Duncan, Lagnese and Associates, Inc.) met with David Barto of the EPA at the Duquesne site to conduct an inspection in order to assess compliance with EPA's standards for regulating PCBs. The inspection included a review of documents in which USX had detailed the presence of equipment containing PCBs. Unfortunately, the records were incomplete. The review failed to locate half of the thirty transformers that had been identified, and EPA requested documentation of their disposition. They wanted to know where those transformers had gone and also wanted other documents in the form of registrations, inspection reports, and annual reports. RIDC asked USX for these documents. Following EPA's regulations, RIDC also solicited help from Killam to develop a plan to track all equipment that contained PCBs. RIDC had not attended to that plan in the short time they had owned the property, which had resulted in the missing transformers.[62]

By August, Killam had concluded definitively that removal of the PCBs at the Duquesne site would lead EPA to classify RIDC as a "Generator with Onsite Storage," requiring "Notification of PCB Activity." Killam completed the required form for RIDC.[63] Even though RIDC was cleaning the property, the act of removing the PCBs made RIDC a polluter, according to the vagaries of the law. Despite their efforts to protect themselves, there was no avoiding the liability that came with owning contaminated property.

In June RIDC contracted with ICF Kaiser Engineers, chosen for their experience with cleaning and demolishing other steel facilities, to serve as their environmental consultant. Kaiser would handle environmental assessments; planning and design; specifications for cleanup; bidding and awarding environmental contracts; and overseeing the environmental contractors, coordinating their work with Turner and NISI.[64]

During the months of July, August, and September, Kaiser performed an environmental survey of the sites to verify all the environmental problems previously documented by Killam in their earlier work for the IDA in 1988.[65] They investigated eighty-one structures and areas at McKeesport and an unspecified number at Duquesne. They surveyed each for specific concerns, including drums, suspected PCB-containing electrical equipment, asbestos, tanks or vessels, solid waste and raw materials, residual waters, and liquid waste.

More problems turned up. On July 3 the Pennsylvania Department of Environmental Resources' Gale Campbell wrote to RIDC after reviewing Killam's earlier environmental assessment and study of groundwater contamination. His response was sharply critical:

> We find these documents to be inadequate for purposes of defining the extent of environmental problems at the captioned facilities or mitigating same. The contract bid specifications place the responsibility for compliance with all applicable environmental regulations on the contractor. We sincerely doubt that a qualified contractor can be found with sufficient expertise in the various environmental regulations such as the Pennsylvania Clean Streams Law, Pennsylvania Solid Waste Management Act, Federal Toxic Substance Control Act, RCRA, Clean Air Act, and OSHA to insure compliance with these various statutes and their supporting regulations.

In conclusion, Campbell indicated that the DER "would be pleased to meet with you and/or your consultants to discuss this matter. It appears that extensive remediation is needed and this should be performed prior to further site development."[66]

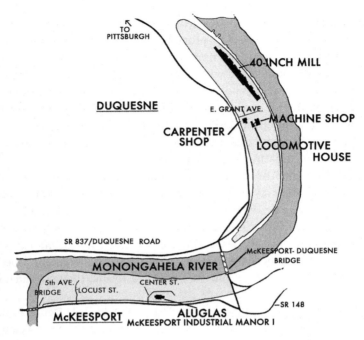

First construction in Duquesne and McKeesport

RIDC was disturbed by both the criticism and the delays that the letter's demands would entail. RIDC felt pressure to seize the moment to move development forward rather than waiting for all cleanup to be accomplished first. Work had already begun. Construction on Aluglas's new building in McKeesport was in full motion, with completion scheduled for October. To meet that reality, therefore, RIDC awarded a contract of $380,000 in late July to Tedesco Corporation to widen and extend Center Street from its entrance to the site on Lysle Boulevard, across the railroad to the new plant—even though the Pennsylvania Utility Commission still had not approved the widening of the crossing, a request that had been pending since November.

Work was also scheduled to begin in Duquesne in time for Duquesne's centennial in September 1991.[67] The first buildings needed to be demolished, including the 40-inch mill building, where the new South Linden Street was to be constructed, and the locomotive house. Other planned work included renovation of the brick machine shop and carpenter shop and extension of Grant Avenue into the mill site to the waterfront.

Responding to the DER – 1990

Robinson did not respond to the DER's critical letter until late August. His apologetic and conciliatory letter began by explaining RIDC's involvement with the properties and the process it was following to re-use them. RIDC was expecting Kaiser to complete the preliminary phase of its evaluations in approximately three weeks. Those evaluations would expand their earlier work. Kaiser had the responsibility to prepare the specifications and make recommendations that the RIDC Growth Fund and its Policy Committee would review before entering into a contract. "The program is recognized to be complex and as such will take place in phased and managed segments consistent with the equipment/scrap sales and possible development," Robinson explained. Robinson apologized a second time for the length of time it had taken him to respond, as well as for the length of his explanation. He requested the opportunity to meet with the DER once Kaiser had finished its assessment in order to review the study and to develop the procedures for appropriate contracting, supervision, and certification of the cleanup to achieve their goals at the sites.[68]

In fact, the number of environmental concerns Kaiser had just identified significantly exceeded those identified in the previous report. The most widespread environmental problem was asbestos, but two other issues were actually more pressing. The first was a large number of drums scattered throughout the sites. The second was discovery of a large amount of PCB-contaminated electrical equipment. RIDC decided to remove them from both sites on an accelerated time frame. The other environmental issues—asbestos, tanks, vessels, solid and liquid wastes, and residual waters and soils—would be handled one area at a time.

To this end, over the subsequent weeks Kaiser and RIDC reviewed each area for potential environmental concerns; estimated the costs of cleanup, demolition, and accessibility to new roads and site entrances; and designated four areas consisting of ten to twenty buildings or sites in each project. They then assigned priorities to the areas in each project, from 1 through 4, with project 1 having the highest priority. In each area they would begin with asbestos abatement, followed by environmental cleanup and finally demolition.[69]

The meeting between RIDC and the DER occurred on October 29, following RIDC's internal briefing meeting four days earlier. The RIDC had invited others as well, so the meeting included representatives from Turner, Kaiser, RIDC, the Allegheny County Department of Development (Joe

Hohman), DER (Chuck Duritsa and Joe Chnupa), DER's Waste Management Division (Gale Campbell), and the Allegheny County Health Department (Dave Piposzar and Al Brunwasser).

Robinson began the meeting by summarizing the project's background and emphasizing RIDC's desire to be a responsible owner. He explained that the two sites comprised a significant part of a recovery strategy for the Mon Valley, along with the URA's Pittsburgh Technology Center and RIDC's Keystone Commons. The goal was to reestablish an industrial job base in the valley. He also described the process RIDC was using, including oversight by the Policy Committee; development of master plans; and the roles of Turner, National Industrial Services, and Kaiser. "We think we have a strong, experienced team in place," he said. "We know the task is complex. We plan to do the job properly and by the regulations, but we do not expect to be placed under a special focus, and we hope to have support for imaginative and economic processes. Our target is to develop properties and buildings that serve industry." Altogether, the meeting was surprisingly smooth and harmonious.

During the meeting, Robinson emphasized that Killam's phase 1 evaluation was a preliminary survey. For purposes of cleanup the regulators should look to Kaiser's materials. The strategic plan would identify specific sources of contamination and support RIDC's plans to remove buildings and encourage early new developments, with priority placed on any source of contamination that posed serious health or migration problems. The parties agreed to meet regularly until DER and the Health Department were comfortable with the plans. Robinson expressed interest in establishing an agreement for the cleanup, including both a scope of work and a schedule. The DER hesitated at first but agreed to negotiate. After asking, the DER was informed that USX would become involved in environmental cleanup only if the assessment revealed a large environmental condition not identified by Killam or if the cleanup costs extended beyond agreed-upon limits.

Relating to the EPA – 1990

The main concern of all parties was that the intentions of the EPA were unknown. Given the volatile nature of environmental concerns, no one knew how flexible or cooperative EPA would be. Although the McKeesport site appeared on EPA's list as potentially contaminated, the group had no idea of its exact status with EPA. The group decided that Kaiser should do a quiet investigation to find out. The parties agreed that Kaiser would also prepare and submit a strategic plan for cleanup to DER and the Health Department over the next several weeks. With a plan agreed upon, the EPA might be encouraged to step back. USX was asked to advise RIDC promptly of any contact by the EPA.[70]

A few days later, Albert Brunwasser, Director of the Allegheny County Health Department, wrote to Joe Hohman to express his thoughts about the matter of EPA's involvement. He suggested obtaining a legal opinion of USX's liability for cleanup under federal law. Despite the agreements executed with the county and RIDC, federal law might still consider USX as a "responsible party" should EPA decide to issue orders for corrective action and place the site on the National Priority List.[71]

More Investigations, More Responses – 1990

Brooks Robinson followed up on the meeting and subsequent suggestions by writing to Brunwasser and to Chuck Duritsa of the DER to thank them for their participation and comments on the cleanup and demolition plans. He enclosed Kaiser's "Environmental Survey Report," which identified priorities for environmental treatment and development.[72]

By mid-November Kaiser had sampled and analyzed over 300 individual pieces of electrical equipment for PCBs. They had also completed a preliminary investigation of one structure at McKeesport to facilitate a possible lease.[73] They reported bad news: drums and vessels in that structure also contained PCBs.[74] Throughout the month as their investigations proceeded, Kaiser continued to revise their estimated treatment and oversight costs for the two sites, presenting new estimates to Turner and RIDC on November 13 and 19. By late November they had exceeded their contract ceiling. RIDC agreed to extend the limit to allow work to proceed through January 18.

With better environmental data in hand, Kaiser, NISI, and Turner met and divided the sites into several demolition bid package areas—eight for McKeesport and nine for Duquesne. Kaiser also began preparing the first two bid packages for removing asbestos from both sites.

Work was publicly bid at the state's required "prevailing wages," and the contract was awarded in January.[75]

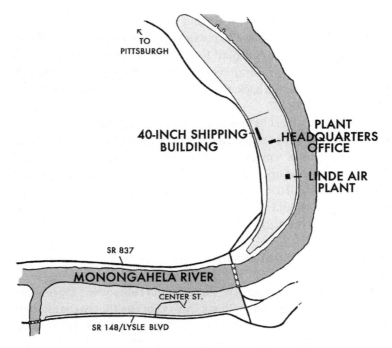

First contract for asbestos removal

Robinson was anxious to find ways to keep environmental treatment costs to a minimum. To that end he sought out innovative treatment methods and competitive prices from environmental contractors, as reflected in a letter RIDC received from Rochez Bros., Inc., regarding disposal of asbestos. Using state-of-the art equipment, with proper planning, Rochez anticipated being able to cut costs from $3.75 million to between $2.575 and $2.7 million, a saving of at least $1.275 million over five years.[76] With removal of asbestos underway, RIDC began removing the PCBs.

Assessing Progress on Site Preparation and Development – 1990-1991

Completion of the McKeesport building for Aluglas—later renamed Metallized Paper Corporation—was now scheduled for January 1, but construction on Center Street to serve the plant hit delays. The administrative law judge responsible for making a recommendation to the Public Utility Commission on the rail crossing had supported expanding it, with the four involved railroads paying 30% of the $410,000 cost, plus maintenance, and the city of McKeesport paying 70%. The railroads balked and appealed. The commission's timing for settling the matter was uncertain. Fortunately, the railroads had already approved the gas, water, sewer, electrical, and telephone lines through their rights-of-way, so that work could still proceed. Although alternative access was possible from the east via Locust Street, vehicles would have to drive through the area where demolition and environmental work was going on. Aluglas would still be able to open, but the situation was far from ideal.[77]

Toward the end of the year, Brooks Robinson wrote to RIDC's general counsel to share progress and plans. He hoped to have the first phase of infrastructure bid by July—committing the state's funds to build it—and raise money at the same time for the next phase. As to environmental issues, he had no plan to address the problem of contaminated soils. RIDC had delayed sampling and testing in favor of bringing down the buildings, so the extent of the problem was unknown. He noted that the regulatory agencies might criticize his approach, but RIDC was going to "endeavor to make the case that this work will be undertaken in a responsible manner as our schedule permits." On the other hand, RIDC did plan to marshal and take care of all drums and other vessels and would complete the cleanup of transformers containing PCBs ahead of construction.[78]

In early January of 1991, Brooks Robinson received another critical letter, this one from Al Brunwasser of the County Health Department reacting to Kaiser's environmental surveys and demolition plans. He expressed concern about possible water contamination from pollutants in the ground and also about airborne pollutants, particularly asbestos. He asked for a far more detailed action plan to guide cleanup, including a surveillance and monitoring program for both groundwater pollutants and airborne emissions. Brunwasser summarized his concerns by saying, "The complexity of this project will require a well coordinated and integrated corrective action plan that is easily read and understood by all parties involved."[79] At this point in the process this statement was fairly obvious.

A Search for Better Approaches, and a New Cleanup Plan – 1991

Kaiser's work on preparing the bid packages for environmental cleanup continued. In early January, RIDC and Turner reviewed a draft work plan and requested a meeting to discuss changes and comments before sending a final copy to the DER.[80] Subsequently, representatives of the county—Turner, Kaiser, and RIDC—met to discuss the draft plan. In the meantime, RIDC authorized Kaiser to clean up two sites at the Duquesne Works at a cost of $87,000—a cleanup that stemmed from the EPA's inspection.[81]

The enormous costs of removing and disposing of contaminated material, not to mention the liabilities this approach entailed for the "generator" of the waste (RIDC), led the RIDC, Kaiser, and Turner to engage in a continuing search for approaches to cleanup that would be less expensive and would incur less future liability. They engaged a transformer consultant to make recommendations on whether to destroy transformers containing PCBs or take them to a landfill.[82] They explored technologies that would reduce the cost of removing asbestos by using a dust-tight barrier system to cover piping that could then be removed with the asbestos intact.[83] In late January they sought advice on regulatory requirements relating to the beneficial reuse of residual waste.[84] Finally, late in the year they asked the Pittsburgh-based National Environmental Technical Applications Corporation to consider supervising a test of new technologies that would employ microorganisms to consume petroleum hydrocarbons and PCBs in contaminated soil.[85]

Prompting RIDC's search for advice on this matter was yet another environmental problem. Construction of the access road to the Duquesne site, the East Grant Avenue extension, required removal of railroad tracks and excavation of the slag on which the railroad was located. Kaiser had tested the slag and found that it contained total petroleum hydrocarbons (TPHs, commonly found on railroad beds because of emissions from coal-fired locomotives) in concentrations of up to 2,000 ppm. Excavation, transportation, and disposal of this material in the closest permitted landfill, in West Virginia, would cost several million dollars. RIDC wanted to explore whether this material could instead be recycled and used as structural support and fill for the reconfiguration of the railroad.

Robinson sought legal advice about this troubling new problem from attorney Steven Faeth, who sent him a confidential "Memorandum of Law Examining the Regulatory Requirements Applicable to the Beneficial Reuse of Residual Waste." The memorandum included an extensive analysis of pertinent federal and Pennsylvania regulatory requirements. Unfortunately, as with much else in the world of environmental regulation and protection, his advice was inconclusive and nondirective. While it could be argued that the roadbed material was not waste because it had never been discarded or thrown away, and while its use as structural fill would not harm human health or the environment, the mere presence of TPHs could cause the DER to classify the slag as a residual waste subject to regulation under the state's Solid Waste Management Act. RIDC could seek DER's approval before excavating the roadbed, or it could not. Contact with the DER could be formal through preparation of a detailed analysis and a preprinted form.

Alternatively, it could be merely an informal discussion, which, hopefully, might afford greater flexibility if DER were willing to enter into the discussion.[86] RIDC would have to untangle the indefinites itself.

Brooks Robinson wrote to USX Realty on January 17, before submitting RIDC's proposed cleanup plan to the DER and EPA. He expressed concern that the agencies might view the plan as "being too management focused and not specific enough at this particular stage; nevertheless, it appears to be a responsible and thoughtful approach to the tasks that would reduce or eliminate risks due to accidents and would permit the phased removal of material which present the most significant exposure." However, the phased plan would permit demolition and site clearance. Monitoring of groundwater would be done as separate phases were undertaken. Further planning would be required to address soil contamination. He expected to send a final document to the EPA and DER in approximately one week.[87]

Kaiser delivered its revised "Work Plan for Environmental Remediation" to RIDC in late January, and Robinson forwarded it to the Health Department, the DER, and the county's Development Department. The work plan detailed RIDC's proposed approach to numerous problems: asbestos, PCBs, electrical equipment, drums, residual waters, solid waste, raw materials, liquid waste, vessels and tanks, soils, and groundwater. It addressed the Environmental Remediation Contract Work Plan requirements and included a quality assurance plan, a health and safety program, and a project plan and schedule.

In his letter to the Health Department, Robinson expressed his belief that the revised plan addressed all the concerns the department had raised earlier in the month regarding the original plan. The priority of the new plan was to address those areas where contaminants could threaten domestic water sources. RIDC would monitor the quality of groundwater throughout the project. The plan also included provisions for safe containment or removal of asbestos and marshaling of drums, vessels, and transformers for testing and disposal.[88] Meanwhile, asbestos analysis, abatement and air monitoring, and cleanup of PCB spills continued at the Duquesne site.[89]

Questions about RIDC's Role – 1991

The complex dance of coordinating serious environmental problems with cost containment and the need to keep making progress was unrelenting. RIDC's persistence and skill under these unremitting pressures were remarkable, but their efforts were not unquestioned in the political arena as well as in the regulatory.

Despite RIDC's leadership on the Mon Valley projects, voices began to claim that the organization's true loyalties were to its own financial strength and its suburban office and industrial parks, which had been the organization's initial focus and the basis of its success.[90] In addition, industrial realtors were troubled that RIDC—as a nonprofit, state-designated Industrial Development Corporation—could take advantage of public funds not only to develop infrastructure but also to construct multitenant buildings, and, with these public subsidies, could dominate the market for industrial and commercial space in the region.

In February 1991 state representative Tom Murphy, who would become mayor of Pittsburgh three years later, led a small group of legislators from western Pennsylvania in calling for a state-sponsored investigation of RIDC's role in the region's economic development.[91] The following month the House approved a bill to appoint a seven-member committee, which proceeded to hold hearings in September in Pittsburgh and Harrisburg.[92] As Pittsburgh's Director of Economic Development, I testified at those hearings, noting the role RIDC was playing both in the city and in the Mon Valley and reinforcing the importance of their efforts in those areas hardest hit by the loss of manufacturing. In fact, RIDC was playing a crucial role in the region's economic recovery, and, at least in Duquesne and McKeesport, without RIDC little might have happened at all.

More from the Health Department and DER – 1991

In early March both the Allegheny County Health Department and the DER responded to RIDC's proposed environmental work plan. The Health Department asked RIDC to consider conducting a geophysical survey, using ground-penetrating radar or terrain conductivity measures, to detect buried tanks, piping, or drums not previously identified by other means. They noted the need for a safety plan that met OSHA's regulations (including the contractor's ability to respond to spills, fires, and other environmental hazards). They asked for additional planning and notification to avoid water pollution, and they asked for continuing involvement to control airborne contaminants, including asbestos.[93]

The DER's comments were more detailed and extensive. They required clarification or correction of a long list of the plan's provisions and, because of the projects' size and complexity, requested a meeting with the RIDC and Kaiser.[94] They began with a fundamental criticism that RIDC had bid on and begun cleanup before the DER had approved the work plan, and they rejected RIDC's attempt to shorten the process by simultaneously demolishing structures and treating environmental problems. DER wanted demolition and cleanup done consecutively.[95] They would also require additional soil testing and analysis following demolition and would require the DER's further review before implementing treatment. They did not agree with the plan's focus on substances that were governed by federal regulations, reminding RIDC that the DER required cleanup to background levels (essentially zero contamination), with certain exceptions that the DER would have to approve. DER would require a comprehensive groundwater investigation, with their prior approval, and at least quarterly sampling and testing of groundwater. The letter included a myriad of additional specific concerns and instructions and finally asked that RIDC submit a copy of the plan to the EPA for their review of the proposed approach to treating the PCBs.[96] Robinson sent a copy of the letter to Joe Hohman at the Allegheny County Department of Development and reported on the environmental situation to William Kiser of USX Realty.[97]

Progress Reports, First Developments, More Problems – 1991

Robinson followed up the letter to USX Realty with a comprehensive progress report on the projects in late March. Along with the letter, he requested a release of USX's mortgage on a portion of the property at Duquesne that RIDC proposed to deed to the city of Duquesne for the new access road.[98]

In McKeesport, Metallized Paper Corporation of America and Camp-Hill Corporation, the manufacturer of steel pipe that had taken over the former Electric Resistance Weld facility, had moved into their new buildings, making them the first new manufacturers on the site. Construction of the first segment of the access road—the Center Street extension—had been interrupted by winter and the dispute with the railroads, but it was scheduled to begin again in April, with completion and conveyance to the city of McKeesport expected by June. Construction of the second phase, lengthwise through the site toward the Locust St. entrance, was also scheduled to begin in April or May, but progress would be constrained initially because RIDC had insufficient funds to complete the cleanup and remove buildings within the alignment. Railroad crossings and traffic signals were scheduled for installation in 1991, and discussions were continuing with the McKeesport Connecting Railroad to relocate lines to permit more development while continuing their rail service.

Work was also extensive in Duquesne. The main entrance had been relocated and would soon be in service. Construction of the East Grant Avenue extension was to begin in April and be completed in 1991. A new railroad embankment and a rail service line would be constructed at the upstream end to provide for the Union Railroad so that they could retain access to McKeesport to serve Camp-Hill Corporation, an outgrowth of ongoing discussions with Union to relocate its service. As funding became available to continue cleanup and demolition, the work on East Grant Avenue would be extended to provide service to properties cleared for development. By separate contract, work was to begin at once on the restoration of the pedestrian bridge between the Duquesne Business Innovation Center, located in the restored former plant headquarters office building, and the Duquesne site, permitting pedestrian access to the site over Duquesne Boulevard and the railroad tracks.[99]

The complications of developing the sites had had a significant impact on Metallized Paper. The difficulties of demolition, EPA, problems in relocating the rail lines, and "a host of other problems" delayed start-up, making it impossible for the company to bid on yearlong contracts with major breweries for 1991. Although they were in their building, all the delays drastically reduced their revenue for the year. The company had closed its Chicago plant in January in anticipation of opening the McKeesport plant, but by March the plant in McKeesport was still some months from being in actual operation.[100]

Kaiser was extremely active throughout March. They tested equipment for PCBs and oils in anticipation of demolition and sales. They continued to oversee cleanup of spills in Duquesne and negotiated discharge of residual water into the McKeesport water system. They rewrote the technical portion of the first eight asbestos bid packages, prepared for a meeting with the Health Department on air monitoring for asbestos removal, and researched federal regulations in an effort to provide a basis for soil cleanup targets. The bill for their work climbed almost $150,000 in two months, to $737,393: $273,018 for McKeesport and $464,375 for Duquesne.[101]

In early April, following public bidding, RIDC awarded a contract to remove PCBs from the sites.[102] Concurrently, RIDC ran into a thankfully small complication relating to asbestos removal. A Philadelphia law firm representing the owners of the patented technology that RIDC planned to use cautioned that RIDC's contractor must be appropriately licensed. Robinson passed the word to Turner Construction and to Kaiser to follow up and ensure that licensing was granted.[103] At the same time, RIDC selected Chester Labnet to perform analyses of soil and water samples collected at the two sites.[104]

Railroad Relations – 1991

In April, RIDC accomplished a swap of land and right-of way with the Union Railroad at both McKeesport and Duquesne, a win-win outcome that created both better development parcels for RIDC and a better location for the railroad's tracks and staging areas along the river, assuring the rail service that particularly would be needed in McKeesport.[105] Securing cooperation from the railroads, however, was not always easy. As in Homestead, the Conrail line at Duquesne cut off access to the site, leaving the only crossing at East Grant Avenue. Mayor Mel Achtzehn remembered how even the governor suffered from that limitation:

> The railroads were a big problem. That's another area that we worked with, with RIDC and they would set up the meetings and we just could not get anything done with that railroad. Nothing. We wanted to move the tracks. We wanted to lower the tracks. Any number of different ways that we tried to eliminate that situation where you can't get in and out of the site because of the railroad, and, boy, I'll tell you something that happened with that. Governor Casey came in. We were dedicating Linden Street, one portion of it, and we asked the governor to come in to dedicate it, put the sign on it, you know. And lo and behold, he's leaving the mill site and what happens? He gets caught with a freight. And the chauffeur had pulled the car up too far, and the gate come down on the car. Heaven helped us, because he knew what our problem was, and he knew what we were trying to do, and I thought, just maybe the state would find a way to help us. But unfortunately it didn't. But it was as if it had been planned.[106]

More Asbestos, More PCBs, More Analyses – 1991

During April and May, Kaiser continued to work on the problem of removing asbestos. They presented test results on Galbestos siding to representatives of the Allegheny County Health Department, DER, and EPA.[107] The test data supported Kaiser's proposed variance for Galbestos from the usual regulations, but theory and practice did not always coincide. Don Horgan of the Allegheny County Health Department remembered one early demolition on the McKeesport site that went awry: "At the National, McKeesport, we had an area that they decided they were going to knock down a building with all this Galbestos on it. We set up all these pumps around it, they knocked the building down, the cloud of dirt was so thick, so black that people on the highway, on the road, were slamming on their brakes, and it was going right to the top. And the Galbestos all flew right off the building, so we put a stop to that. We made that mistake once."[108]

Kaiser was also trying to negotiate a permit to discharge residual water from both sites into the McKeesport sewage system.[109] During the same period, work began on the two site-wide priorities Kaiser had identified in their assessment: marshaling and testing of oil drums and treatment of PCBs. Autumn Industries completed construction of a holding area and moved the drums into it for testing, at a cost of some $250,000 between April and May. In McKeesport alone, the contractor collected approximately 800 drums containing various types of debris, oil, and waste. Kaiser field-tested over 500 drums, designating them as either "recyclable" or "further analysis required," and they sent recyclable oil to an oil recycling firm.

Barrels and drums at Duquesne, marshaled and awaiting analysis and disposal

Kaiser also took over 100 samples of residual water, liquid waste, soils, sludge, solids, and tank contents from the first four bid package areas and sent them to Chester Labnet for analysis.[110] Chester's work was slow, however, and by mid-summer Kaiser suggested hiring Wadsworth/Alert Laboratories and keeping Chester Labnet as a secondary laboratory.[111]

Kaiser also oversaw the $450,000 removal of approximately 150 PCB-contaminated pieces of electrical equipment. Aptus drained them on-site and collected and sent the PCB-containing fluids to a permitted incinerator for disposal. Cases were decontaminated and disassembled for scrap iron at another facility. The work began in late May and was completed by late

July. Tedious removal of PCBs and asbestos continued throughout the summer, including the draining of transformer oils and removal of transformers, capacitors, and lightning arresters, all of which were disposed of in an approved facility. More asbestos was discovered in the roofs of two buildings in Duquesne and were added to the work in progress.[112]

In an effort to attract companies to the McKeesport site, the city council in July directed the redevelopment authority to come up with a plan to use tax increment financing to supplement RIDC's funds to construct access roads and place utility lines.[113] The state legislature had approved this type of financing for Pennsylvania just the previous year.

Additional site planning and development also continued. In August RIDC went to Duquesne's city council with the request to designate and begin construction of Linden Street, the main access road through the Duquesne site. Running north to south, parallel to Duquesne Boulevard and the river and dividing the site lengthwise, the street would be four lanes wide and require considerable excavation to construct. At the same meeting, RIDC made the council aware of the discovery of a fuel tank with unknown contents. No one knew yet whether the tank had leaked or not. RIDC estimated that construction of the road and removal of the tank would cost $530,000.[114]

Much of the developer's and its contractors' attention for the remainder of the year focused on problems associated with removing asbestos from the sites. Although the Allegheny County Department of Health was in the lead in regulating this activity, the EPA was also involved for a number of reasons, including the federal government's sovereignty in environmental matters and the EPA's greater ability to assess the health risks involved. Also included in the reasons were that the EPA needed to rule on whether the Galbestos on the site would be considered "friable asbestos" and that the project would set precedents that could well have future national regulatory implications.[115] Some of the techniques used for this cleanup were developed at the Pittsburgh Technology Center, but this project would set the precedent for future amelioration of asbestos-contaminated sites.

Observations – 1991

The process of clearing and cleaning the sites was far more difficult than originally anticipated, a lesson foreshadowed by the complex work at both Herr's Island and the Technology Center. In September the *Pittsburgh Press* ran a Sunday front-page article about the McKeesport and Duquesne sites titled "One Step forward, Two Steps Back" in which it summarized the problems that had arisen since the county and RIDC had taken control of the sites three years previously. The article also expressed the feelings of residents in the valley: "It's taking too long"; "This town's going to recover, but it will take time, time, time"; "I had no idea of the frustration that would be involved in clearing these sites. It's been one problem after another"; and, finally, "'Maybe my kids are going to profit, but not us.'"[116]

Demolition at Duquesne, December 1992. RIDC had originally planned to retain the historic cranes in the ore pit, but when concerns over liability arose, the Historical and Museum Commission gave permission to take them down. This photo, taken from the ore pit looking north, with the furnace stoves standing on the right, documents the demolition of the first crane.

Even after RIDC had assumed ownership of the properties in the belief that it would be able to move more quickly, problems had continued to delay efforts. There was more asbestos than expected, and cleanup was slower. Relying on raising money from the sale of scrap also constrained the process. Although some $9.7 million had been generated from sales, less than originally expected, the total expected cost of demolition and cleanup had risen to $18 million.[117]

McKeesport mayor Louis Washowich observed

I never thought it would come to that magnitude and how much of the requirements that we would actually have to live by. I mean that same site worked thousands of guys over a long period of time. How many of them were actually affected by the contaminated soil, or the pipes, or. . . . I can't answer that. But they became so difficult, and I find them as difficult today. I think it's mind-boggling. I sometimes don't understand that part of it. I look at what happened. I think sometimes we get caught up in our own world. I think sometimes they're looking for things to do, and say, and hold you to that really don't need to be done. I do know this: it was a nightmare for Brooks [Robinson], who handled the demolition down there, trying to sell the steel off, and all the other things that went with it, requirements, actually removing soil. I think sometimes they just go a little bit too far.[118]

Duquesne mayor Melvin Achtzehn recalled the city's effort to draw firms to Duquesne back in 1984 when the mill had closed. Of the 200 companies they had contacted, several had expressed interest in the site, including trucking firms, machine shops, a bus manufacturer, and even a company that made missiles for the U.S. Navy, but most had lost interest in the intervening seven years. "They couldn't wait for us," Achtzehn said.[119]

On the bright side, in McKeesport, Metallized Paper was in operation and was employing some fifty people. In late 1991 Earth Products Recycling, a company that crushed scrap rock and concrete into various grades of sand and gravel, became the first company to take space at Duquesne. The company had been successful in marketing their products to the Pennsylvania Department of Transportation and Department of Environmental Resources. Once they were established in Duquesne, Brooks Robinson took the initiative to write to the county's Department of Engineering and Construction, hoping to encourage them to use those products as well.[120] With work progressing on cleanup, demolition, and public improvements, RIDC had plans to award a marketing contract for both sites before the end of the year.

On the other hand, the press reflected some tension between the county and RIDC over their respective commitments and investments in the projects. Joe Hohman suggested that RIDC should invest some of its own resources to keep the projects moving along. Brooks Robinson countered that RIDC had invested its funds in Keystone Commons (another Mon Valley project) and that "it's time for the county to start putting its own capital" into the sites. Hohman indicated that it was the county's intention to invest $3 million in capital bonds there within the next year and a half.[121]

Progress with Cleanup – 1991-1992

The highest-priority asbestos abatement activities began in April 1991 and were completed in early December at a cost of approximately $500,000.[122] Concurrently, other contractors removed underground storage tanks in McKeesport and soil containing PCBs from Duquesne. Other asbestos removal continued. The highest-priority soil and water cleanup activities began in November, as removal of the asbestos was coming to an end, and continued until March 1992, at a cost of approximately $250,000.[123]

In November the Duquesne Business Advisory Corporation, led by Chuck Starrett, completed work on an ambitious plan to create a 10-acre riverfront park, including a stage, picnic area, playground, boat launch, and walkway to help attract businesses to the site. The city council, county officials, and RIDC all endorsed the plan, but there was no money to cover the estimated cost of $3.9 million.[124]

The contractors cleared asbestos from one building in December, from six more in January, and from another six in February. Additional asbestos turned up in old stoves.[125] In March, Kaiser applied to begin removing Galbestos from the building where limestone had been ground for use in the blast and basic oxygen furnaces at Duquesne.[126]

Prospects for Development – 1992

In January 1992 RIDC received a $1 million loan commitment from the Pennsylvania Industrial Development Authority (PIDA) to help fund a $2.7 million renovation of two buildings at McKeesport.[127] In March RIDC received a second loan from PIDA, for $800,000, to add 30,000 square feet to the building RIDC had built for Metallized Paper, which RIDC was now calling McKeesport Industrial Manor I. RIDC proposed to market the new space for light manufacturing, high technology, distribution, or research and development.[128]

Brooks Robinson was optimistic that 1992 would mark the beginning of significant development on both the sites. He expected "to have between 60 and 70 acres of land ready for development at each of [the] sites" and "a number of buildings that will be available to be rehabbed," together with new infrastructure—"access roads, utility lines and things of that nature—to support that development."[129]

With expectations that portions of the sites would be available for development by summer, RIDC planned to hire a firm to produce marketing materials. An aggressive marketing strategy would be important because growth and development in the region were slow to begin with, there was an abundance of industrial space, and there would be competition from the Park Corporation at the Homestead site just down the river and closer to the central business district and airport. On the other hand, Park was planning a development that included more commercial than industrial space. To prepare the way for the hoped-for development, the city of Duquesne passed a new zoning ordinance early in the year.[130]

Allegheny Recovery Corporation – 1992

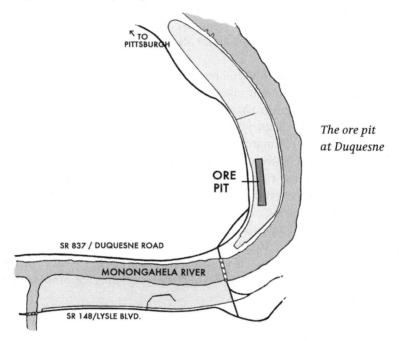

The ore pit at Duquesne

In another move both to attract development and to reduce costs, in early 1992 RIDC pursued Allegheny Recovery Corporation (ARC), a consortium of twenty-seven foundries in western Pennsylvania and an affiliate of Process Recovery of eastern Pennsylvania, to locate on the site. RIDC's interest was in securing the company as a tenant; the company could also provide foundry waste—sand and slag from its affiliated foundries—to fill the former ore basin at Duquesne, a pit that covered 12 to 14 acres, 30 feet deep.

News conference announcing Allegheny Recovery Corporation's commitment to Duquesne, 1993. Among those present in the photo were (in the group on the left) Bill Flanagan (KDKA, in sunglasses) talking with Brooks Robinson, and (in the central group, right) State Representative Tom Michlovic (striped shirt) and Duquesne's Mayor Mel Achtzehn.

Then it was learned that DER had fined Process Recovery $15,000 for leaving a quantity of similar material—consisting of slag, sand, and dust used for metal castings—in a basin in central Pennsylvania when it was to have been taken to the company's landfill. The state's Solid Waste Management Act required that such material be placed in a lined landfill to protect groundwater. Process Recovery contended that they had removed the material. The incident, with the implication that there had been an illegal action or at least impropriety, caused some embarrassment for those who had been working to bring ARC to Duquesne, including state senator Albert "Bud" Belan and the Duquesne Business Advisory Council.

In the end, however, RIDC reached an agreement to bring ARC to the site, in the process solving—at least so it appeared at the time—the problem of how to fill the ore pit and prepare that large portion of the property for development.[131]

Assessing Progress – 1992

To witness the progress of the developments, state and local officials toured the two sites in mid-April.[132] Governor Casey commented during the visit, "These centers once were components of Steel City, but soon they'll make this area home to advanced manufacturing and high tech industry that will serve the international marketplace of tomorrow."[133]

The state had already invested nearly $24 million in McKeesport (including the investments in Metallized Paper Corporation) and $5.7 million in Duquesne. Thus far, however, each site had attracted few tenants.

McKeesport had only Metallized Paper and Camp-Hill Corporation. Apart from the several business development and job training organizations that were tenants in the Duquesne Business Innovation Center, Duquesne had attracted only Earth Products Recycling.[134]

Poignantly, Mayor Louis Washowich of McKeesport lamented, "I became mayor of McKeesport in 1980, and USX had 4,500 employees here at the National Works in 1981–82. I never dreamed I would see this plant close. But by 1985, the city of McKeesport had lost 10,000 jobs. People are looking around this country now and saying we're in a recession. Let me tell you, this area has been in a recession since 1981. The rest of the country doesn't know what a recession is."[135]

Apart from the omnipresent evidence of environmental problems, many leaders were especially frustrated by the aggravating difficulty caused by not having been able to secure a right-of-way across CSX's railroad tracks at Center Street in McKeesport, making the newly constructed street to Metallized Paper Corporation unusable and requiring a detour of several blocks to reach the plant.[136] Brooks Robinson of RIDC, however, was optimistic. "By the fall of this year, the major phase of the rehabilitation will be complete and a marketing effort will be in full stride," he reported.[137]

Cleanup Continues – 1992

Asbestos removal continued through the spring, with satisfactory inspections of seven buildings in March, thirteen in April, and two more in May. Work began on a second phase of asbestos cleanup in McKeesport in April. Concurrently, WMMC removed from Duquesne some 220 tons of material containing PCBs.[138]

The specter and potential stigma of EPA's deeper involvement was always present. In May, attorney Steven Faeth wrote Brooks Robinson to express concern that, without care, reports from McKeesport could unwittingly lead the EPA to place the site on the Superfund National Priority List. Such a designation would make marketing and financing development on the sites much more difficult, since lenders and tenants or purchasers would view the site as far riskier. Designation would also entail higher scrutiny from the regulators and could involve a state or federal cleanup, which would be even costlier than the present, expensive efforts. RIDC would be well advised to stay as far as possible from any of this by taking greater initiative to satisfy the agencies' demands as completely as possible.[139]

In late May RIDC let a $375,000 contract to ENSR—a national environmental services company with offices in Pittsburgh—to complete the second phase of environmental cleanup at Duquesne with completion expected by July. Brooks Robinson was now estimating that the total costs of cleanup for the Duquesne site alone would exceed $9.3 million. On a positive note, however, the recently completed first phase of cleanup had made 50 acres of the Duquesne site available for development.[140]

Simultaneously, RIDC let two contracts, totaling $490,000, for the second phase of demolition at both Duquesne and McKeesport. Robinson noted that the sale of equipment and scrap had so far covered the costs of demolition. Although the first phase of demolition was still not complete, RIDC intended to begin the next stage immediately and to finish the new phase of work by October.[141]

In July Kaiser reported that the first two phases of asbestos removal had been completed and the third begun, representing an estimated 35% of the total to be done at a cost, to date, of $2.5 million. They estimated that 40% of other environmental cleanup was done. All together, environmental cleanup, including analytical costs of $636,000, had so far cost $5.65 million, not including Kaiser's professional services.[142]

In July the DER acquiesced to a request RIDC had made in May to use soil and slag at the McKeesport site to fill machinery pits. In approving this, however, the DER also required RIDC to place a notice in the deed describing the use and location of the waste material. It warned that "RIDC's decision to proceed with this phase of the pipe mill building renovation and site remediation is at their own risk, primarily because an overall groundwater assessment for this site has not yet been completed." In addition, DER would require a formal consent order and agreement that would set forth the results of site assessments, establish cleanup levels, and identify responsibilities and liabilities.[143]

Groundwater in McKeesport was, in fact, already a concern for RIDC. In late July, Kaiser reported on its review of information collected from monitoring wells. Five monitoring wells installed in 1988 showed elevated levels of at least some contaminants, including lead, chromium, and cyanide, although only one well was of real concern. Most of the wells were no longer serviceable, and Kaiser recommended installing three new wells to replace them.[144]

On July 29 Charles Haefner of Kaiser sent RIDC a comprehensive report of environmental activities to date, focusing particularly on McKeesport, so that RIDC could respond to a request from the EPA to visit the site once again. The two highest-priority site-wide activities—holding-area construction and marshaling of drums; and removal, transport, and disposal of PCBs and PCB-contaminated electrical equipment—were complete, as were first- through third-priority asbestos removal and first- and second-priority environmental cleanup.[145] In the end, however, EPA canceled its visit to the site, a cause for some relief.[146]

A Quest for Risk-Based Standards – 1992

So far, efforts to convince the Department of Environmental Resources to establish risk-based standards for acceptable levels of contaminants in the soil had failed. DER had taken the position that the only acceptable standard was the background level of a contaminant. The soil had to be as clean as soil around it that had not been contaminated. RIDC wanted the DER to accept a different standard—one that took into account the actual risk that different levels of contaminants posed to human health, given assumptions about land use and consequent exposure. Brooks Robinson asked Kaiser to develop such standards.[147]

By October, Kaiser had completed this work and sent Robinson a set of tables that proposed acceptable cleanup standards in parts per million of soil for a long list of contaminants, including heavy metals, PCBs, cyanide, and various organic compounds. The proposed standards were based on the assumption that both the Duquesne and McKeesport sites would continue to be zoned for industrial use. They also assumed that vegetation or paving would reduce exposure and allow standards to be raised accordingly. Only additional evaluation would be able to determine if these levels would affect groundwater.[148]

More Cleanup and Demolition – 1992-1993

In the meantime, RIDC's efforts to clean up the sites continued without interruption. In addition to the special projects they had undertaken on standards and waste "generation," Kaiser was developing standards for removal of the underground storage tanks and drums at both sites, specifications for the phase-3 areas for both asbestos and other cleanup, and specifications for monitoring the groundwater at McKeesport that had been a particular concern for the EPA.[149]

In mid-December RIDC and Kaiser met to review the resources available to continue cleanup activities and to set priorities for their use. In some cases costs were difficult to estimate. Was a particular waste pile or a drum hazardous or not? To the best of their ability, they specified which piles, drums, cans, pails, and spills most warranted immediate attention.[150]

Disposal of the hundreds of drums on the sites was a major undertaking over which the DER exercised continuous and careful oversight. Kaiser marshaled the drums in locations set aside and marked for that purpose—"Hazardous Materials Exist, Authorized Personnel Only." Then they sampled the contents and had the samples analyzed. There were concerns about permits for storage areas themselves (not required unless drums accumulated for more than ninety days), labeling of the drums, leakage, security, protection from the weather, possible effects on groundwater, inspections and the actions they required, transportation, documentation (photographs before and after, with manifests), removal, destination, condition of the ground where they had sat, and regulations (of DER, Transportation, etc.) relating to all the above. The list of requirements was exhaustive. During the first part of the year, RIDC, Kaiser, and other contractors patiently worked through the process.[151] Brooks Robinson was careful to keep the DER informed of their plans and progress.

In a February 1, 1993, letter to Chuck Duritsa of DER, Robinson gave his opinion that "on both sites the remaining environmental remediation will be substantially completed by the fall of 1993." Funds were on hand to complete the cleanup, after which RIDC could clear the sites, with Governor Casey's administration having granted much of the money needed for this task. "Our goal," Robinson emphasized, "is to prepare these sites to be able to receive a new generation of industrial development with employment opportunities in a more diversified economy. Your cooperation and understanding in this challenge is very much appreciated."[152]

Three days later, Robinson met with the DER's Joe Chnupa to review the status of cleanup and demolition, and he received a positive response. He was at the DER again on February 9 to discuss groundwater monitoring, having prepared beforehand to assemble a case to restrict both the area to be monitored, based on information about historic uses, and the chemicals to be sampled.[153] Simultaneously, RIDC continued demolition. It awarded a contract in late January for 22 acres on the western end of the McKeesport site right next to both sides of the Duquesne-McKeesport Bridge, thus opening a complete view of the site from the bridge. Work was to be completed by mid-year.[154]

A Prospect for Fill – 1993

An unexpected opportunity presented itself in the form of an offer from the Army Corps of Engineers to make fill available—soil and gravel recovered from the elimination of locks and a dam in Elizabeth. The Corps had planned to dispose of the material nearby, but that would have resulted in having to relocate houses. The possibility of using the material at the Duquesne and McKeesport sites could be beneficial to all parties, but it was not without complications. A spokesman for the Corps was quoted as saying that "it would take about a year to determine if the land is appropriate for the disposal of excavated material. The Corps will conduct hazardous-waste tests and other environmental and safety studies. The sites then must be approved by the state Department of Environmental Resources."[155]

By April, however, the Corps had found another site, in Washington County, that it preferred because it could take the entire quantity of fill, whereas it was unclear whether Duquesne and McKeesport could take the full amount. In addition, to place fill at Duquesne would require construction of a road from the river and put a strain on Duquesne's water filtration plant.[156]

Cleanup Costs – 1993

The costs of cleanup continued to mount, and complications continued to arise. In February, Kaiser asked to raise its expenditure limit by $53,000, to $245,000, in part because of litigation regarding a PCB spill at the Electric Power House in Duquesne.[157] In March they asked to raise the limit by another $41,000, to $286,000.[158]

The Johns-Manville Asbestos Property Damage Settlement Trust rejected claims for costs of asbestos removal because USX, an approved creditor, had not incurred them.[159] USX wrote and asked for reconsideration based on the facts that USX was sharing 50% of the costs of the removal with RIDC and that the presence of the asbestos had affected the price of USX's sale to RIDC.[160] However, at the end of April, Johns-Manville again disallowed USX's claim.[161] After two refusals, RIDC decided to let the matter drop.[162]

A March 10, 1993, article in the *Pittsburgh Post-Gazette* asked, "Why is redevelopment taking so long?" and then answered the question by quoting Dennis Pittman, McKeesport's Director of Community Development: "Because the problems turned out to be much bigger than anyone imagined even a few years ago." Still, the two sites had some 50 acres each available for development at this point. RIDC had engaged Mid-Atlantic Realty Advisors as a marketing agent, and they had completed a presentation kit to market the sites as "RIDC River Place."[163]

In mid-April RIDC awarded contracts for additional demolition at McKeesport, including the portion of the site needed for completion of Center Street and buildings near Locust Street.[164]

A Tiff with the DER – 1993

On April 15, 1993, the *Pittsburgh Post-Gazette* carried an article reporting Brooks Robinson's criticisms of staff members at the DER. Speaking at a Chamber of Commerce luncheon, Robinson had said, "They still believe that industry is evil and (that) everybody is dragging their feet on the cleanup—which we all want. They treat me as if I was the person who created this problem." He believed that higher-level officials in DER, including Secretary Art Davis and Regional Director Charles Duritsa, were cooperative. His complaint was about the rank-and-file of DER officials and the demanding tone and substance of correspondence, which "reads as if it were some kind of a demand for me to go to court." He revealed that RIDC had recently received a letter from DER, stating that if a specified number of drums were not removed by April 18, RIDC would be subject to fines of $25,000 a day. "I can't afford to take $25,000 a day. I [will] drop everything I'm doing, rearrange all my financing and get rid of those drums." He predicted that DER's approach would have to change if the state were going to make any real progress in cleaning up its many abandoned industrial sites.[165]

That same day, Robinson wrote to Wilbert Hanna of RIDC, Mayor Lou Washowich of McKeesport, and Mayor Mel Achtzehn of Duquesne, explaining his motivation for using critical language. He stated first that the paper had reported his remarks out of context, making them appear more confrontational than they had been. He apologized if the remarks were offensive to any of the parties and expressed hope that they would do no damage to the projects. "On the other hand," he continued, "I elected to take this risk because our projects are far enough along that there may be little retaliation that can be rendered to us, and having gone on the record about this issue, DER may be at risk themselves with any retaliation. My view on issues like this is that when problems that are apparent and that have to do with structural matters such as legislation, liability, legal constraints, etc. arise, these should be addressed quietly[;] however, when problems have to do with personalities and perceptions they need to be exposed."[166]

The *Post-Gazette* reported that Robinson's response took DER by surprise. Joseph Chnupa, Assistant Regional Director, stated that the agency's regulations required them to send the notice to RIDC to remove unlabeled drums—about 2,200 remained on the site—but "that doesn't mean we will fine them. We have discretionary authority." Robinson responded that he had nothing else to add.[167] Apparently, the threat of fines had been a bluff.

Comparisons with Homestead – 1993

Mayor Achtzehn contrasted RIDC's experience with the Park Corporation's in Homestead:

> Homestead, when Park Corporation went in there, private, bought it, tore it down, cleaned it up. They didn't have the restraints that we had, because we were dealing with governments, County Health, DER. They didn't have to do that. They moved in and cleaned up, then all of a sudden DER comes down and says, "Whoa-whoa-whoa-whoa. You can't do that." One big barrier was environmental liability. When Kelly Park moved in they didn't have it. Now we've got it.[168]

Mayor Washowich of McKeesport made a similar comparison:

> The most discouraging thing that I saw along the way was what it was taking to clear that area and how long and how much money was involved. It took me by surprise. I watched the Homestead site, and how fast that went and I guess I probably somewhat in my mind thought we could do it, maybe not as quickly, but within a time frame that we would have the land developed or have it in a position that we could bring in developers to show them and try to encourage them, because there were some state programs involved. You had tax credits, Keystone area, and all those other things that the state offers. We felt that it would help us encourage people to come.

> Over the years you've seen what happened at the Waterfront. There's a couple of reasons. The first reason is that it was bought by Park Corporation. We're a governmental agency, and we didn't have sufficient capital. And secondly, we're going to live to the letter of the law. And I'm talking about the county and RIDC, trying to clean that environmentally, so the cost escalated a hundred-fold. Park Corporation went in there and God only knows, I mean, as a private company. Hey, I give them credit down there.[169]

Others in the community drew the same conclusion. Augie Carlino, who was active in both Duquesne and Homestead in his work with the Steel

Industry Heritage Task Force, observed

> Because [RIDC is] a public-private non-profit [Brooks Robinson is]
> dependent on public funds. . . . He can't compete necessarily with
> organizations like Continental [developer of the Waterfront, which
> purchased a major portion of the Homestead site from the Park
> Corporation for commercial development], who can bring in Target,
> because they're putting their own private money into this stuff.
> Brooks has to go through a lot more hoops and channels. And it
> makes it more complicated for him. I mean, all that mitigation
> work . . . , none of that had to be done here, in Homestead, because
> they didn't use a cent of public money in tearing the site down. So
> that's why this site could be prepared for redevelopment a whole
> lot more quickly. So the bureaucracy burdens him, and I think he's
> frustrated. I've talked with him a number of times. Even in the
> work we've done, where we've tried to help him, where some of
> the impositions required by mitigation have burdened him, and
> there's nothing I can do about it—I don't make the law; I can just
> follow it like he does—but I kept trying to stress to him, "Look,
> Brooks, I'll try and work through this with you, but, you know, the
> people who are saying this are state officials."[170]

Some acknowledged that the environmental conditions on the two sites
might not have been exactly the same. Duquesne and McKeesport might
indeed have been more contaminated. Mel Achtzehn observed

> Homestead was not into production like we were here at Duquesne.
> Duquesne was basic; Homestead was more the rolling mills thing.
> And they didn't contaminate the area as much as we did, with the
> oils and the different alloys and metals and stuff that was buried
> in the ground. Homestead didn't have that problem. We shipped a
> lot of our metal to Homestead to be rolled and put into bars and
> things to go on into different products. So they didn't have the
> problem that we had here.[171]

Still, the contrast between the agonizingly slow cleanup process in
Duquesne and McKeesport and the comparatively effortless process in

Homestead caused a certain amount of bewilderment and resentment. Gene Capristo, who served on Duquesne's city council during this period, observed

> I'm not an official brownfields person. I only can tell you what I've heard and what I know. It seems to me that they [in Homestead] do it differently. That steel mill had to be just as, what do you want to call it, dirty, but I don't think they went through all the problems that we did. It's been an ongoing battle of cleanup. We've been cleaning up for 15 years.

> Homestead didn't go through any of this—because we're government, and they're not. That's private money. It's public/private money. If they would have sold this property like they did that one, and a company would have come in and just poured everything down, you wouldn't have any process of remediating. I don't know why. I think it's like two different standards, to me. Maybe I'm wrong, but I feel that that's what it is.[172]

To Chuck Duritsa of the DER, the explanation of the difference was much simpler: "in many cases we became involved . . . when we became aware of a problem, and unless there was some reason for us to go into a site to investigate it, in many cases we didn't." Apparently, the Park Corporation had given DER no reason to question what they were doing in Homestead.[173]

More Cleanup, More Demolition, and a Question about Suitable Development – 1993

By late April 1993, RIDC had removed 600 of the 1,000 drums that had remained on the two sites in February. Another 300 would go soon. The final 100 contained PCBs, and RIDC was soliciting bids for their removal. RIDC expected all drums to be gone by mid-June.[174] At a regular project meeting on May 18 Robinson expressed his frustration with the protracted cleanup process. Kaiser was taking entirely too long to clean the PCBs at one building at Duquesne. "Is ICF making an academic career out of this thing?" he asked. Mindful of his commitment to the DER to have all drums out by July, he also expressed concern about the pace of that process.[175] But progress on cleanup did continue steadily through early summer.[176]

Vacant electric furnace at Duquesne, June 1993

The costs of removing asbestos were over budget, particularly for McKeesport. RIDC had to eliminate buildings from the contracts to bring the costs in line with the funds available.[177] Over the next months RIDC ended up in a dispute with one of the asbestos contractors on the sites. In July, Spacecon Abatement claimed to find additional asbestos, which would increase costs still further.[178] RIDC and Kaiser disputed the claim.[179] Then, after an inspection in August, Kaiser complained to Spacecon about their work, stating that critical barriers had come down and that there was a great deal of both bagged and unbagged asbestos material within the work area, creating violations of the county code and federal regulations that could result in fines of $1,000 per day, or $25,000 per day if the EPA got involved. Although Spacecon and RIDC had a dispute over the scope of the work, they were still responsible for keeping the work area in order. In the end, everyone calmed down, and Spacecon completed its work.

In May another controversy arose over a proposal RIDC had received from the Union Railroad Company to place a coal-blending operation on 25 acres at the far western end of the Duquesne site. New environmental regulations required that high-sulfur coal be mixed with low-sulfur coal before being burned. The idea behind the facility at Duquesne was to receive coal by river, blend it, and then send it by rail and truck to utility companies throughout the Northeast. However, residents of Duquesne, including the prospective mayor, George Matta, had concerns about the environmental impact of the facility, both for coal dust from the open-air operation and for runoff that would result from spraying the coal to reduce the dust. Besides, the facility would employ only ten workers, hardly worth the negative side effects.[180] City Council would vote on the proposal at the end of the summer.

In early June RIDC awarded contracts totaling almost $1 million to six companies for asbestos removal at both sites. RIDC estimated that the contracts would complete 95% of the asbestos cleanup at McKeesport, and 75% at Duquesne. The *Post-Gazette* quoted Brooks Robinson as saying that so far asbestos removal and environmental cleanup, underway now for two years, had cost $10 million.[181]

At the end of June, ARC began operations at the Duquesne site. It was in the process of seeking DER's approval to fill the ore pit—which was 1,800 feet long, 300 feet wide, and more than 30 feet deep—with its foundry sand wastes; it estimated that this operation would take ten to fifteen years. Once filled, however, that portion of the site could then be developed at some time in the future. Mayor Mel Achtzehn was pleased. "This is the first large enterprise coming in. It's been a long time coming, over two years." Employment prospects at the firm, however, were small: ten or so jobs in the first year and a few more in the next.[182]

Allegheny Recovery Corporation's first delivery of foundry sand and waste to Duquesne, June 1993. The photo is taken in the ore pit, looking south, with remaining blast furnace stoves on the left.

Development of infrastructure was proceeding concurrently. In July RIDC awarded Zottola Construction the contract ($84,500) to complete the third phase of construction of South Linden Street.[183]

Between July and October contractors removed nine underground storage tanks from Duquesne, first pumping out and disposing of residual material. In four cases the contractor had to excavate and dispose of contaminated soil from under the tanks as well.[184]

USX Realty, concerned about their possible financial exposure for environmental problems and wondering when the sites would begin to pay off in sales of parcels for redevelopment, inquired about those matters in August. With his experience to date, Brooks Robinson had to respond that to answer those questions would require looking into a "crystal ball." Any opinions could only be best guesses. He reassured them, however, that because of the large infusions of funds from the state and, later, from Allegheny County and the money generated from the sale of machinery and scrap, RIDC had been able to push the cleanup forward far more rapidly than if those sources had not been available. In addition, he stressed, RIDC had followed all governmental regulations, which had "caused the schedule to be more extended than anticipated." Both in McKeesport and in Duquesne, most of the cleanup was complete, so Robinson did not anticipate that USX would incur liability.[185]

In late August, Duquesne's city council voted down the Union Railroad's proposed coal-blending facility by a vote of 3 to 2. The council had received a petition signed by 279 citizens opposing the operation. Although it would have brought needed revenues and some economic activity, the majority of the council, and apparently of residents, felt that the noise, dust, and traffic it would generate outweighed the benefits. They would prefer to wait for more attractive light-industrial uses, which they hoped would employ more workers.[186]

Taking Stock as 1993 Ends – 1993

In a comprehensive and impressive report dated September 19, Kaiser reported that during the ten months from November 1992 to August 1993, they had overseen the work of six different asbestos-removal contractors, six environmental contractors, and four demolition contractors. During that period they had removed 9,350 gallons of hazardous liquids (mainly PCBs); 92,500 gallons of nonhazardous liquids (mostly oils and water); 155 tons of hazardous solids (mostly soil contaminated by PCBs and furnace dust); 1,190 tons of nonhazardous solids (mostly petroleum-contaminated soil excavated from around underground storage tanks); 1,355 drums (most containing nonhazardous oil-and-water mixtures); 1,200 cubic yards of asbestos; and 14 underground storage tanks.[187]

In late September RIDC awarded a contract of $41,164 to Jaskolski

Contracting Company of Clairton to demolish five buildings on the Duquesne site over the following month. Their demolition would enable construction of the new access road and development of several acres at the corner of South Linden Street and East Grant Avenue.[188]

RIDC finished out the year by continuing to implement their strategy of asbestos removal, followed by other environmental cleanup, demolition, testing, and, finally, inspection by the regulatory agencies. The last known drums left the sites at the end of November. The DER received the final "closure" report on the elimination of underground storage tanks the first week of December.[189]

In a front-page feature article published by the *Pittsburgh Post-Gazette* near the year's end, Brooks Robinson observed, "I knew it was going to take time, but I underestimated the problems with the DER. I assumed the commonwealth would step in and help." Kevin Grice of Clairton, who had lost his job at McKeesport's National Works ten years before, observed, "The thing that really depresses me is all those dinosaurs. I just wish they'd hurry up and get them torn down."[190]

Interior of the pipe mill in McKeesport, September 1994, after equipment was gone, looking northwest toward the Monongahela River. The crane rail traverses the building in the center.

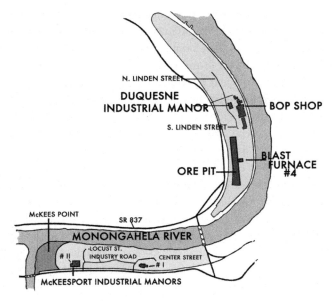

1994–95 Milestones

A Chapter Closes – 1994-1995

Early in 1994 McKeesport Industrial Manor II, a refurbished complex of buildings totaling 131,000 square feet near the Locust Street entrance, attracted its first tenant, Quality Check Metals, a small manufacturing firm.[191]

On Friday, May 13, RIDC demolished the Basic Oxygen Plant (the "BOP Shop") at Duquesne. The demolition was not uneventful. The *Post-Gazette* reported that steel fragments from the imploding plant damaged buildings up to a mile away.[192] Electric Motor Services, the contractor responsible for the demolition, was not even aware that the procedure had gone awry until reports began to come in. Dennis Pittman recalled the drama of the event:

> They have a marvelous table in [the conference room of the RIDC office building, the former plant manager's office, across Route 837 from the mill site]. It was probably the plant manager's table, and the room has a little private bathroom and it's got mahogany walls, and it's a spectacular room. And you, if you look out the window, you look across 837 and you look at the mill site. And the bridge is kind of right next to it. When they were demolishing the [BOP Shop] they imploded it. They didn't gauge the dynamite right, or whatever

they put in there. And a projectile, a piece of the blast furnace, came through the window, across the street, several hundred yards away, just like a howitzer shell, through the window, scarred the top of this marble table—the scratches are still in it—like a prehistoric glacier went through there, out through an oaken door, and into the wall. There were pieces that went up Grant Avenue, another three or four hundred yards and jammed in telephone poles. Nobody was killed, absolutely amazing.[193]

The McKeesport site received an impetus in December, when Governor Casey announced a state grant of $1.8 million for McKee's Point, a proposed 14-acre commercial and recreational complex at the confluence of the Monongahela and Youghiogheny rivers. It was expected to include a Gateway Clipper river excursion vessel, a full-service marina, and retail trade.[194]

In January 1995, RIDC imploded blast furnace number 4 at Duquesne, leaving three and a half of the original six blast furnaces still to be demolished.[195] George Braun, the new director of the Allegheny County Department of Development, reported the same month that more than $8 million had been spent for environmental cleanup at Duquesne alone. "And we're far from completion there."[196]

Idle stoves at Duquesne. These eight and another seven, lined with asbestos, were still standing in 2005. Though they were beginning to list, RIDC had not had the funds to take them down.

239

In February, officials reported that demolition on the two sites was more than 90% complete, and environmental work about 70% complete. The focus had shifted to marketing the sites. Local officials in both Duquesne and McKeesport were optimistic about the potential to attract industrial tenants. Both Duquesne and McKeesport had been designated as State Enterprise Zones some ten years earlier, when steel collapsed—McKeesport in 1985 and Duquesne in 1987. The renovated Duquesne Industrial Manor, with 27,000 square feet of space, was available for lease, as was the 131,000-square-foot McKeesport Industrial Manor II. The expected completion of the Mon Valley Expressway would make the sites even more attractive and competitive.[197]

Duquesne Industrial Manor, July 1994. The former machine shop, this building was the first one renovated at Duquesne. RIDC retained windows and the clerestory.

Passage of the state's Industrial Site Recycling legislation in mid-year also gave the projects a boost, even though by this time environmental cleanup on the two sites was largely complete. As Chuck Starrett of RIDC's Policy Committee observed

> The PA Land Recycling Act not only from the practical standpoint, but also psychologically, started turning things around for people. All of us were so naive to think that this could happen more quickly. We've had lots of battles, and there's been lots of frustration on the part of the local officials, and citizens are very frustrated with how slowly things have gone there.

I know how the paperwork and the red tape and how long things take, and so I can sympathize a little bit with RIDC, but at the same time, looking back, I don't think any of us anticipated we'd have so many obstacles. We've had pretty much the view that not only these sites were dead, diseased sites, abandoned sites, but the reputation and capacity of the towns to stand on their own any more has been quite at risk. The cost of tearing down and cleaning up, incredible costs, and then you find, when they start digging in the ground, that there are foundations, steel plates, and all sorts of things. And there's no sewer lines, there's no water lines, there's nothing. You have to start all over again.[198]

Brooks Robinson simply said, "It involved a great deal more time and money than anybody could have imagined."[199]

LESSONS

As in Homestead and Munhall, community participation in the process of redeveloping the Duquesne and McKeesport sites was crucial. Loss of employment and tax revenues from the mills was devastating both to families and to the municipalities. Allegheny County addressed the concerns of Valley residents early on by forming the Mon Valley Commission. Then, within a year of acquiring title to the Duquesne and McKeesport properties, the county presented draft site plans that allowed residents to express their views of what the sites should become. RIDC, upon assuming title to the properties, followed suit by forming a broadly representative policy committee to guide their development.

RIDC also engaged excellent technical help to maneuver the projects through the uncertainties of evolving environmental regulations and enforcement, similar to the manner in which the URA had been careful to hire excellent technical expertise for the projects in the city. RIDC's management team expanded well beyond its own employees to include its trusted environmental and engineering contractors, who frequently acted as RIDC's agents in managing relations with the DER and the Health Department, and in overseeing the firms that performed cleanup and demolition.

RIDC's and its professional contractors' efforts notwithstanding, relations with the environmental regulators were frosty at best, hostile at worst. Again, I will have more to say about this issue in the concluding chapter of this book. Suffice it to draw two conclusions for now: First, regulators use the state's police power to enforce, and must be expected to act accordingly. Second, there surely is a better way to achieve environmental goals than the combative, punitive approach these projects exemplify. In fact, these projects directly contributed to development of just such a better approach in Pennsylvania.

Finally, it is helpful to contrast the projects in Duquesne and McKeesport with those in Homestead and Pittsburgh. In a word, these projects had none of the benefits of location that the others enjoyed. Washington's Landing had the benefit of being an island, with a beautiful view and in close proximity to Pittsburgh's downtown. The Pittsburgh Technology Center had the benefit of proximity to major research universities. The Waterfront had retail market centrality. Duquesne and McKeesport had none of these advantages. They are relatively isolated, with poor access to population and economic centers. As locations for manufacturing, they have poor access to the interstate system and to labor.

As a result, private development, which was already difficult for the other sites, was impossible in Duquesne and McKeesport. No private entity would take them on. The risks were simply too high, with no prospect of profit to be made. Asking whether a public or a private organization would have done better as a developer suggests that there was a choice, when such was not the case: only a public entity such as Allegheny County or a public-supported nonprofit like RIDC would take on these properties. Residents of Duquesne and McKeesport looked longingly downriver to Park Corporation's relatively quick progress in Homestead, failing to see that no private corporation was going to step forward with the same enthusiasm over prospects for making a profit in their towns.

Sculptural tribute to the vanished steelworkers at City Center of Duquesne, 2016

6

OBSERVATIONS IN CLOSING

INTRODUCTION

In the history of transforming Pittsburgh's abandoned industrial sites, 1995 marked the end of one era and the beginning of another. On May 19, 1995, a new governor, Tom Ridge, sat at a long table in one of the refurbished mill buildings at the Industrial Center of McKeesport, surrounded by many of the leaders of the arduous efforts to renew the industrial properties of the Mon Valley. Then and there, he signed into law a group of acts that established the Industrial Land Recycling Program, thus creating a new legal framework for redeveloping contaminated industrial land in Pennsylvania. RIDC soon took advantage of the program in Duquesne and McKeesport. (The other projects were far enough along that the new laws did not benefit them.) With the program's incentives and new leadership at the DER, developers and public officials across the state launched projects to put abandoned industrial properties back into use.

Governor Tom Ridge, with newly appointed McKeesport Mayor Joe Bendel on his left, shaking hands with Brooks Robinson at the signing of the bills that created the Industrial Land Recycling Program, May 19, 1995

244

This year also brought important changes in local political leadership. Tom Murphy became mayor of the city of Pittsburgh, bringing in new faces to replace many who had been influential in the city's redevelopment efforts through the Caliguiri and Masloff administrations. That same year, Tom Foerster ended his fifteen-year term as chairman of Allegheny County's Board of County Commissioners. Another significant change in county administration occurred in 1998, when an elected county executive and county council replaced the three-commissioner system.

Nonetheless, the projects I have described in this book continued their transformation. In Homestead, not long after the close of my story, the Waterfront shopping district and adjacent housing emerged seemingly overnight, dramatically transforming that property. Changes in the other projects were more gradual and evolutionary, building on the character that had been set from the start. Undoubtedly there are stories to be told about these later developments, but they are beyond my scope here. Rather, by way of conclusion, I offer some final observations on these early industrial redevelopment projects and on the themes that emerge from the stories I have related.

SIGNIFICANCE OF THE PROJECTS

The projects chronicled here were important for at least two reasons. First, as I have described, they were central to economic recovery in their respective communities. But second, beyond their importance to their particular communities, they led public officials to develop more effective ways to encourage and support reuse of contaminated industrial land. Here my purpose is to explain the pertinent environmental issues so that the reader can understand how they came to bear on the projects, how they led both developers and regulators to take the actions they did, and how their experience contributed to changes in the way our society approaches recovery of contaminated industrial properties. My focus is on the projects, however, not on environmental policy, because this book, as I state in the preface, is not an environmental study.

Importance for Pittsburgh's Economic Development

The declining economic growth rates of the 1970s, followed by the recession of 1981–82, were hard on American industry, and especially hard on Pittsburgh.[1] This was the era when Japan grew to dominance in the U.S. consumer market for automobiles and electronics; when Brazil and Korea were rapidly expanding their steel production, with heavy public subsidies, and "dumping" steel on the world market; when "just in time" and "total quality" became household words.[2] These trends precipitated a crisis in Pittsburgh.

In 1954 well over half of all manufacturing employment in the Pittsburgh region was in the primary metals; food; and stone, clay, and glass products industries. All three of these industrial sectors declined nationally between the mid-1950s and mid-1980s. Their decline in Pittsburgh was even worse than in the nation as a whole because of population and market shifts to the south and west and Pittsburgh's aging plants. Between 1954 and 1987 Pittsburgh lost 175,000 manufacturing jobs, of which 73%—128,000—were in food or primary metals.[3]

The jolt that Pittsburgh received from the loss of its basic industries moved the entire region to question its future.[4] Communities suddenly had to imagine new economic roles for themselves. Civic leaders went to other cities in search of new economic models and ideas to help Pittsburgh compete for capital and to attract and retain the highly educated workforce that growing economies required. Pittsburgh's research universities grew in importance as seedbeds for new technologies and companies that would promote the region's future well-being. The structure of local government became a widespread topic of discussion.

The abandoned industrial properties had a special place in these considerations. They had been important economic generators, employing thousands of people and supporting municipal budgets with large tax contributions. The thought that those jobs and taxes had simply disappeared was difficult to accept. Replacing those jobs and tax revenues became a high priority for both officials and the general public.

Adding to the importance of the properties was that they were so large and so prominently located. Hulking, abandoned, and deteriorating, they were dangerous and constant reminders of the losses the municipalities had sustained and the economic difficulties through which they were passing. Putting them back into use was not only economically but also symbolically compelling.

Perhaps most significant, however, was that there were no other major tracts of land available to offer new employers. The communities in which they were located were fully developed and landlocked, and if they were to compete with other localities to rebuild their economic base, these were the only large sites they had to offer.

For all these reasons the derelict plants loomed large in the communities' development plans. These considerations gave the projects a special importance to the places where they were located.

Importance for Environmental Recovery Efforts

Beyond these local considerations, however, were the important roles these projects played in the development of approaches to recover and reuse the thousands of contaminated industrial sites that were the legacy of America's industrial age.

When the city of Pittsburgh began to redevelop Herr's Island, in 1976, environmental problems relating to asbestos and contaminated soil were just beginning to enter the public's consciousness. Laws to protect the public from exposure to these conditions were new, and many more remained to be written. Environmental matters were therefore not an early consideration in planning or budgeting these projects. The communities' and the planners' focus was on economic recovery, not environmental recovery.

The country's outlook on this changed during the very time that these projects were in process of development. Rachel Carson's *Silent Spring*, published in 1962, had galvanized the citizenry of the United States to take action on environmental contamination and had led to public initiatives at both state and federal levels. Between 1967 and 1971 Pennsylvania adopted numerous new environmental laws and created a new Department of Environmental Resources.[5] Federal action included formation of the Environmental Quality Council and Citizens Advisory Committee on Environmental Quality in 1969 and passage of the National Environmental Policy Act, which President Nixon signed on January 1, 1970, inaugurating "the environmental decade." The first Earth Day was celebrated April 22, 1970, and the Environmental Protection Agency started operation December 2 of the same year. The first federal laws specifically to address the control of toxic substances and hazardous wastes (TSCA and RCRA), however, were not passed until 1976, the same year work on Herr's Island began, but these laws focused more on prevention and regulation than on cleanup and site recovery.[6]

Those issues came to the fore later in the decade, when work on Herr's Island was well underway, with the Love Canal, an abandoned dump for toxic chemicals near Niagara Falls, New York. The Love Canal dump sickened people who lived in the houses and attended the school that were later built on top of the contaminated property. "Love Canal exposed a gap in [the] new blanket of protection [created by TSCA and RCRA]. Toxic chemicals did not need to be newly introduced to provide a threat to a community. Wastes that had been buried long ago—and mostly forgotten—could suddenly prove to be dangerous."[7]

Love Canal and other environmental catastrophes resulting from past disposal of toxic waste led to passage of the Comprehensive Environmental Response, Compensation, and Liability Act of 1980 (CERCLA, or Superfund law), which gave the government the authority to intervene in the event of a "release or substantial threat of release into the environment" of a "hazardous substance" or "any pollutant or contaminant which may present an imminent and substantial danger to the public health or welfare."[8] The law gave EPA authority to take or require others to take remedial actions to clean up a site. It established a trust fund to finance its activities and appropriated public funds from general revenues and special taxes.[9] It also assigned responsibility for cleanups and held "responsible parties" liable for the cost. "Potentially responsible parties" included former or current owners or operators of the affected property and anyone who arranged for disposal, treatment, or transportation of hazardous substances on the property—regardless of whether they had been responsible for the contamination or not.

Under these provisions the most innocent and even altruistic owners—like the URA, Allegheny County, or RIDC—could be held responsible for cleaning up sites they had had no hand in polluting.[10] Regulatory approaches and court opinions throughout the country reflected the Superfund law's approach to establishing liability. In Pennsylvania the courts ruled that under the Clean Streams Law, "fault is not prerequisite to establishing liability" of landowners and tenants to correct conditions where pollution or a danger of pollution exists on land they own or occupy.[11]

These liability provisions became a strong deterrent to undertaking redevelopment of sites whose former uses could have resulted in contamination. Rather than stimulating cleanup and redevelopment, the Superfund law had the opposite effect: developers and prospective users avoided any connection with those sites. It was far less risky to choose sites that had never been developed. The approach encouraged sprawl by reinforcing the trend to develop greenfields in the suburbs rather than redevelop brownfields, the abandoned and contaminated sites in the cities and river valleys. However, new industrial use on greenfields only created new contaminated areas for future concern.

The Superfund Amendments and Reauthorization Act (SARA) of 1986 did nothing to address this problem, but instead only strengthened enforcement and required state involvement in implementation. Pennsylvania responded by adopting the Hazardous Sites Cleanup Act in 1988.[12] This act replaced the Solid Waste Management Act of 1968 and directed the Department of Environmental Resources to "develop, administer and enforce a program to provide for the investigation, assessment and cleanup of hazardous sites" and to "cooperate with ... the Federal Superfund Program" under regulations to be promulgated by the Environmental Quality Board.[13] The act took note of the fact that there were many sites in Pennsylvania like the projects in Pittsburgh that did not qualify as Superfund sites but yet "pose[d] a substantial threat to the public health and environment."[14]

By 1988, when this act became law, the projects described in this history were all underway, and one after another their development collided with the new environmental concerns.[15] Issues about health and safety arose, regulators became involved, delays and costs increased, financing became difficult to obtain, prospects turned away, and frustration and disappointment grew, along with dissatisfaction with the regulatory approach.[16]

There were several aspects of the approach that troubled, bothered, or angered the URA and RIDC, the public-spirited organizations that were trying to clean up the sites.

Cleanup Level

Standards for cleanup often seemed arbitrary and irrational, and, as written, they did not allow for reasonable discussion or debate. In Pennsylvania, the standard was "background," the level of the pollutant in the general environment, which, for most pollutants, meant no measurable contamination.[17] Such an approach "places emphasis on evaluation and technology to remove that last part, whether it was needed or not."[18] Still, regulators were responsible to enforce the standard, although in practice its unreasonableness often led them to back down in the end.

A striking example of the resulting conflicts involved the cyanide discovered on the site adjacent to the University of Pittsburgh's building at the Pittsburgh Technology Center. The cyanide, buried under the mill's massive foundations some 10 to15 feet below the surface, apparently had had no adverse effect on the thousands of laborers who had worked in the mill. Removing the cyanide would have cost millions of dollars for a dubious benefit. In the end DER did not require its removal but only monitoring to ensure that it was not entering the river. Still, the very real legal possibility that the DER could require its removal caused CMU to relocate its building and caused the site to sit vacant for years.

Another example involved construction of the East Grant Avenue extension in Duquesne. RIDC did not want to spend millions of dollars to send soil contaminated with oil, which had been deliberately placed there to control dust, to a landfill. Rather, they wanted to use it as fill under a relocated rail line, where it would have negligible, if any, contact with people.

Initially, DER indicated it would require the soil to be excavated and sent to a landfill in Alabama, and by law it could, and perhaps should, have done so. However, after much back and forth, DER finally allowed the contaminated soil to be placed under the road.[19]

Liability

Superfund and its companion laws held innocent owners—who had had no hand in polluting property they acquired—responsible for the pollution, essentially treating them as criminals. Similarly, those who lawfully placed nontoxic waste in landfills that were later found to be contaminated were responsible for the pollution they did not create and did not even know about.[20] Every owner in a chain of title—whether a polluter or not—was fully liable for cleanup.[21]

The liability entailed in ownership determined the location of both Pitt's and CMU's buildings at the Pittsburgh Technology Center. Concern for liability led to the URA's difficulties in finding private financing for development at the same project. The same concern led Brooks Robinson of RIDC to take extreme precautions to protect both himself and others in his organization:

> You could say that . . . because of the legal liabilities that occur with all of these undertakings, all this getting in and becoming the "generator," I declared that there was nobody in this office that was going to sign any documents that had to do with any of this, so that their names and their families and all of their things would not be in the paper trail. I signed everything. Then I promptly went down and had my entire estate planning reset, so that in the event anyone got mischief, and the black robes decided that they were going to support that (they could, by the way the law reads) they could wipe me out personally. So we had it protected to a degree by having it in a Growth Fund, but then I had to protect the individuals, and so that's why in your research you get so much "Brooks Robinson," whereas in fact it's RIDC.[22]

Cleanup as Pollution

As Brooks Robinson alluded above, the laws and regulations defined the developers—those who were trying to return the properties to productive use—as "generators" of pollution because they dug up and removed previously contaminated soil for proper disposal or because previously contaminated groundwater from the sites they owned was entering public waterways.[23]

Police Power

The regulatory approach of Superfund and its derivatives relied on the state's police power, making it adversarial and punitive.[24] Meetings were combative. Letters from regulators were terse and legalistic. Rather than fostering a spirit of collaboration in accomplishing common objectives, the approach created an environment of intimidation and fear in the relations between the regulators and the developers they were regulating.[25]

With the exception of Homestead, all of the Pittsburgh projects illustrate this problem. The subjects of regulation (the URA and RIDC), working, as they were, in the public interest, understandably found the antagonistic position of the regulators baffling; felt unfairly treated and aggrieved; and sought, to the greatest extent possible, to avoid involvement with them. Although many regulators sympathized with the goal of redeveloping the contaminated sites and wanted to contribute to that effort, they responded in turn according to the laws and regulations they were charged with enforcing.[26]

Uneven Enforcement

Application of the standards was uneven. In practice, regulators had the resources only to control what came to their attention and what they had the time and personnel to reach. "The rules are so complex that there cannot be enough environmental police to do the job," one observer commented.[27] Thus, one property owner might bear the full brunt of regulatory enforcement, while another owner, with land just as polluted, might receive no oversight and might incur no penalties simply because the regulators were not aware of or did not have the resources to investigate.

The Pittsburgh cases illustrate the issue in the difference between the regulators' attention to the Duquesne and McKeesport sites, where RIDC, the publicly sponsored developer, came under intense regulatory scrutiny, and Homestead, where the private developer, the Park Corporation, cleared the site with practically no regulatory oversight or involvement. While I have no evidence of any illegal or improper action on Park's part, and in fact employees of Park indicated that they fully complied with environmental laws and regulations, the DER appears to have had no involvement in or oversight of the matter. This apparent lack of uniform application fostered a sense of arbitrariness and unfairness in the application of the regulations and contributed to pressure for change.[28]

Public officials in old industrial areas throughout the country felt these same concerns, and they became increasingly frustrated and angry. In response, beginning with Minnesota in 1988 and Illinois in 1989, states one by one began to adopt voluntary cleanup programs to increase flexibility, limit liability, and reduce uncertainty and costs.[29] Some did this by law, others by regulation. By the end of 1993, ten states had adopted voluntary cleanup programs. Another six adopted programs in 1994; and five more, including Pennsylvania, in 1995.[30] The redevelopment projects in Pittsburgh played a big part in the Pennsylvania story, where creative administrative initiatives came first, followed later by legislative and regulatory changes.

Chuck Duritsa, DER's regional director at the time, recalled

I encouraged [my staff] . . . to get together and try to work up a framework for cleanup standards, . . . with my encouragement. We were trying to find ways to make it reproducible for the next piece of property that would want to be developed, but it was a struggle. It took time. It took too much time, quite frankly, for every individual project. . . . But it was all trial and error. It truly was. And in many cases it was not conforming with what the guidelines and regulations were at that time. But it ultimately got to the point that we got to have a site redeveloped and it was in a condition that would not be harmful to the public health and safety.

To give you an inside perspective of the department, I was often criticized because of the things we would do in Pittsburgh. We were leaders in brownfields redevelopment. And these were things that they were not doing in other parts of the state. Quite frankly, they were on the verge of not meeting state regulatory and legal requirements. But we took pride in what we were doing in Pittsburgh, with brownfields. We thought we were doing it better than the other parts of the state, who were not using the same type of instruments that we were.[31]

Joe Chnupa, working under Duritsa, spoke of the motives that prompted him to pursue those steps outside of his agency's traditional approach. "That's what catches your attention. What could be done to bring this up to a sustainable, viable community? In pushing these key projects, you had a wider community watching. We had a major industrial collapse. We had to find a way to work with [the public redevelopers]. We built on some, clean closure, flexibility in permitting, evolution of soil and water standards."[32]

Kenneth Bowman, DER's assistant regional council, recalled, "It was starting from the bottom up, and this region led the way. The process was evolutionary.... Consent agreements were among the first [responses]. They took the place of permits, to the extent they could by law."[33]

> And so it's the old method of trial and error. You know, you [RIDC and the URA] come in, and you're not quite sure what we want to do, and we're trying to engage you, and we're trying to work out whatever cleanup standards when our goal at the time was "clean up to background," and yet recognizing that's very difficult to do and yet a medium ground would be some kind of structured agreement where we recognize that and work with the development agency to cobble together what is an appropriate response and put that in a document that is basically transferable to other people [that is, the early consent agreements for Washington's Landing and the Pittsburgh Technology Center]. We didn't have liability protection ... , but at least with an agreement you would absolve yourself of the "what if's," you knew what you had to do, and hopefully it fit with your design plan.[34]

The innovations that Chnupa and Bowman described were small steps, made by individuals who were at a level to recommend policy for their agency, to begin to resolve the conflicts, but they went only so far. Living in Pittsburgh, they, and undoubtedly others at DER, wanted to be part of the solution, and they could appreciate far better than most the problems of the prevailing environmental regime. They tried to be creative and to be as flexible as possible, working to change the framework within and then beyond.

In 1993 officials in the DER and Commerce announced administrative changes that they termed a "Greenfields Policy" (although in fact it was a brownfields policy). I recall being invited, along with others at the URA, to an announcement and briefing on the new program at the DER's new regional headquarters at Washington's Landing. The program included (a) limits on environmental liability for purchasers of industrial properties where the original polluter could not be found; (b) public funds for assessments; (c) a proposal for legislation to limit the liability of publicly sponsored redevelopment; and (d) clarification of DER's role in private property transactions. However, without changes in the law, these efforts could make only a marginal difference.

In the 1994 gubernatorial campaign, Republican candidate Tom Ridge made industrial land recycling an issue. Once elected, he chose James M. Seif—an attorney who had worked in the legal branch of the EPA's Philadelphia regional office from 1973 to 1975, and later as EPA's regional director from 1985 to 1989—to be secretary of the DER. Even before he took office, Seif criticized the DER as "insular, bureaucratic, overlawyered, slow and insulated from other parts of Pennsylvania life, such as economic growth." He charged that DER had a "gotcha attitude" and said, "We shouldn't be stuck using 1970 environmental solutions."[35]

Once in office, Ridge and Seif immediately championed the package of three Senate bills sponsored by Senator David "Chip" Brightbill that had passed the Senate in spring of 1994 but then had died. Brooks Robinson, who as president of RIDC had been working on the Duquesne and McKeesport sites since 1990, had played an important role in drafting those bills.[36] DER, with Seif in the lead, promoted the bills as a "bipartisan package that would eliminate barriers to the cleanup and reuse of [abandoned industrial] sites by establishing a framework of realistic cleanup standards based on health and environmental risks and would end an owner's liability when those standards are met."[37] The Senate adopted the bills unanimously on March 1 and sent them to the House of Representatives, urging prompt action.

There was controversy, however. The regional administrator of EPA alleged that the bills might create a conflict with federal laws. DER answered that while the new laws did not prevent the state from enforcing existing laws, "the excesses, expenses and impracticality of the federal Superfund" had in fact caused many of the problems the proposed laws would correct.[38] Some environmental groups and all the state's major newspapers, fearing that less stringent standards would lead to pollution of undeveloped land, voiced opposition.[39] Proponents stressed that the proposed laws maintained criminal and civil penalties against polluters. Farm organizations, business organizations, and many local political leaders voiced strong support of the bills.

In late April, Secretary Seif reminded House members that in "September 1993, two state Senate committees heard 67 witnesses and solicited comments from more than 2,000 individuals, businesses and citizen and environmental groups" before completing work on the bills. He went on to say that criticisms appear to be based more on what is believed to be the intent of [the] bills than on what they actually say. These criticisms also reflect a misunderstanding of the land development process and a lack of knowledge about how cleanups have been conducted in Pennsylvania in the past. Our past policy of requiring cleanups to an unachievable pristine standard helped cause the abandoned properties [the bills] are trying to reclaim.[40]

On May 2 the House voted 163 to 36 to approve the package of bills, and Governor Ridge signed them into law at the Industrial Center of McKeesport on May 19. In signing the bills, he said, "We are here today because this valuable site must be returned to productive use for the benefit of this community and this region that worked so hard to give our Commonwealth and our nation the steel we needed to build our country."[41]

By the time the acts took effect sixty days later, DER had already prepared helpful manuals, handbooks, and fact sheets for public use; made information electronically available; and appointed members to the new Cleanup Standards Scientific Advisory Board.[42] The following week the governor announced the first grants to conduct environmental assessments under the new Land Recycling Program.[43] Six months after the laws went into effect, thirteen contaminated sites had been cleaned up, and cleanup was underway on forty-seven others in twenty-nine counties.[44] At the end of the first year of operation, Secretary Seif reported

In its first year, 100 sites have been enrolled in the Land Recycling Program, with 35 successful cleanups to date. The one-year record of the program compares favorably with the state Hazardous Sites Cleanup Program, which has so far yielded only two permanent cleanups in eight years, and the federal Superfund program, which has removed just eight of the 103 sites from the National Priority List in 16 years.

The Land Recycling Program is simply a case of government making sense. We have fundamentally transformed Pennsylvania's cleanup program from a "government knows best" philosophy to one that encourages creativity and innovation from the private sector.[45]

Mike Dawida, a Pittsburgh attorney who served as a Pennsylvania state legislator during the period that the Mon Valley sites were being developed, later commented on the Land Recycling Program's profound impact:

The steel mills that were on all those pieces of property dumped all kinds of crap there, and until the state passed a law making it easier to develop land that is not environmentally pristine—and I played a role in that, by the way, as a legislator—that kept private money from ever wanting to come in there, because you never knew what your liability might be. You will find buried some stuff.

Because of the nature of the fact that even a little bit put a black mark on the title, you couldn't move. Nobody would move, because they didn't know what it meant. So the law got changed at the state level, and now we can move on these lands much more efficiently.[46]

Experiences with the early recovery projects in Pittsburgh led directly to that change.

CONFLICTING PRIORITIES: ECONOMIC DEVELOPMENT VS. ENVIRONMENTAL PROTECTION

A corollary question that often perplexed local officials was, How could Commerce and Community Affairs give millions of dollars to develop Herr's Island, the Pittsburgh Technology Center, and Duquesne and McKeesport while DER was simultaneously adding costs and stopping the projects in their tracks? Mayor Lou Washowich of McKeesport put it this way: "On one hand the state's giving you *x* dollars; on the other hand they're taking it away from you."[47] The conflict first became evident during Governor Robert Casey's administration (1987–94), when environmental concerns came to the fore. Governor Casey toured the devastated Mon Valley on his first day in office and promised to help rebuild the valley. Yet subsequent events demonstrated that environmental officials in his administration would time and again obstruct or delay attainment of that goal.

Ray Christman and David Donahoe, who both served as executive director of the URA and then afterward in Governor Casey's cabinet (Christman as Secretary of Commerce and Donahoe as Secretary of Revenue), were perhaps uniquely able to comment on this issue and to speculate about why the state did not resolve the conflict earlier. For both Christman and Donahoe, the answer lay in the role that Casey and other important public officials had played as leaders in the environmental movement. They had been among those who, in response to past environmental abuses, had been energetic proponents and creators of the legal and regulatory approach that characterized the early environmental movement. Another approach to the problem would probably never have crossed their minds. Christman observed that

> during the Casey administration you had at DER a guy who . . . was a dear friend of mine, a former boss, Art Davis, who was and is a strong environmentalist, strong. . . . . Art is a very balanced guy, who believes in jobs and growth and is a guy who believes in all the diversity of economic and urban life and metropolitan life, but in his core he's an environmentalist. And I really think that the permit-granting processes within DER during the Casey period—now don't forget Casey was also a guy who said, you know, I have three priorities, . . . education, economic development, and the environment, and he was a guy who said, I believe in a strong environment and a strong economy, and I'm going to do both; the two aren't necessarily in conflict.

> But of course they would come into conflict from time to time, and I think when they did he was not . . . inclined to intervene to push the Department of Environmental Resources to do things differently than they normally did, in the interests of the economy. And if things got slowed up in the interests of environmental concerns, well, then that was probably appropriate, and he was not going to order DER to do anything that DER, within its own department, didn't want to do. And Art was there for the full eight years of the Casey administration, from day one till the last day when they turned out the lights, and he was, you know, very strong on making sure that decisions were made only when all the evidence was in and everything was going to be handled just the right way.[48]

David Donahoe also noted the influence of Secretary Davis's environmentally conservative voice: "Casey . . . had a very strong environmental secretary who was, in addition to being strong in that area, was a friend of the governor's . . . and so he had more the ear of the governor. . . ."[49]

Even the most ardent supporter of redevelopment in the Mon Valley, Commissioner Tom Foerster, had made his mark as a state legislator by championing environmental legislation. David Donahoe, who worked closely with Commissioner Foerster for many years, noted

He actually was elected a commissioner as an environmentalist. That's how his name became known to the county, was through his efforts for environmentalism, Clean Streams, and all of those sorts of things. . . . It just strikes me I'm not sure people in those years really thought there was a solution. In other words, nothing was going to really happen that was affordable, or that would make a good investment. So I don't think they felt the need to focus on that issue as precisely as [our] focusing on it in retrospect. And they had other things that they could do. I'm just not sure they knew that if they risked their reputations as environmentally concerned, and so on, that it would have a payoff anyhow, that it would actually pay off in something, that it would result in investment.[50]

Based on their experience, it was difficult for these environmental veterans to see a way out of the impasse. It would take a shift of power to a new generation of leaders who could conceive of new approaches for fundamental change to occur. David Donahoe observed, "People came into power and the legislature changed significantly so that people who had, during the '70s and early '80s, particularly, who were either environmentalists by nature or by political persuasion, a lot of those people disappeared over time. So you didn't have the same resistance."[51]

By the time Governor Ridge took office, the situation was ripe for change, and the new leadership was able to bring change about quickly. Ray Christman saw it this way:

Ridge had Jim Seif as his DER secretary. And Jim Seif, who I've worked with both before then and after then, was a—I would describe him as a guy who was less passionate, sort of emotionally, if you will, about the environment, but more of a guy who prided himself on being a problem-solver. . . . I don't think he . . . betrayed the environment or just undermined environmental standards, in general, but I think he was more of a neutral sort of a person, I guess I would describe him, as someone who felt that you could move forward on the development front without sacrificing unduly environmental standards. And I think he took on the industrial site redevelopment issue early in the Ridge administration as a priority and said, you know, we can figure out a way to make this work, and took it on.[52]

In a way, this was ironic because, if anything, the Democratic Casey administration had been more sympathetic to the concerns of the Mon Valley's distressed communities and unemployed laborers and had invested more in the valley's redevelopment than did the Republican Ridge administration. This irony only underscored the influence of the older environmental paradigm, which, although well intentioned, had proved stifling. Christman observed

> The Casey administration had as strong as or stronger focus on economic development than the Ridge administration, . . . I mean Casey had such a focus on trying to help distressed communities, I mean, much more than Ridge, so, ironically enough, that wish to help distressed communities was stronger under Casey than it was under Ridge, but nonetheless it got done under Ridge, and I think the real reason was that the people who held the cards were the people at DER, and you had a secretary there, in Seif, who was more inclined to figure out a way to implement that kind of a program, more than there had been previously.[53]

Notwithstanding the pain of the cities and towns devastated by the loss of basic industry, the competing public priorities of environmental purity and economic development were unequally matched, with the environmental claim being dominant.[54] Despite the earnest desires of the participants, no true resolution of the conflict was possible until the issue had fully matured and people had gained experience. Only then could a new generation of legislators and administrators develop and adopt a more nuanced approach to environmental law and regulation.[55]

PUBLIC CONCERN AND INVOLVEMENT

The impact of the loss of Pittsburgh's manufacturing base varied enormously from one part of the region to another. In some areas the impact was huge; in others it was not as great. Thus there were different responses in the different locations.

In the city of Pittsburgh the impact of the collapse of the steel industry was not felt as directly, immediately, or acutely as in the mill towns of the Mon Valley. Relatively few mill workers actually lived in the city: with their high union wages most had moved out to suburban areas, and they were not a significant force in the city's politics. Too, from the standpoint of

259

neighborhoods, the abandoned sites in the city were relatively isolated: Herr's Island was an island, and topography and a rail line separated LTV's Pittsburgh Works from Oakland on the hill above the site and from Hazelwood farther upriver.

As a result, there were practically no community interest or involvement in the redevelopment of these properties. The only exception was the North Side Civic Development Council's participation in Washington's Landing, which was motivated not by widespread popular interest in the island but rather by the opportunity the Council saw to assert its control, become involved in real estate development, and earn fees.

In addition, the properties in the city, although important, did not constitute nearly as large a proportion of the city's employment or tax revenues as had the steel plants in the mill towns up the Monongahela River. While city officials had compelling reasons to undertake the projects—to strengthen the tax base, increase employment, and improve the city's image and quality of life—and the public at large generally supported the projects, they were not at the center of the public's concerns.

In contrast, in Homestead, Duquesne, and McKeesport the loss of the mills was devastating both to many individual families and to the corporate municipalities. Here thousands of workers and their families lost their livelihoods and their traditional way of life when the mills closed. They were desperate to return to work, fearful that they would be unable to regain what they had lost, nostalgic about the loss of the mills, and anxious to reestablish their comfortable and accustomed patterns of life. For the municipalities the closing of the mills was a tremendous financial loss, requiring them to adopt—quickly—a painful fiscal discipline.

In these places the citizenry at large had strong views about the future of the sites. Fearful, angry, and impatient, they expressed their feelings and views forcefully in demonstrations, in community meetings, on advisory boards, in the newspapers, and to their elected representatives.

DECIDING ON USE

Interestingly, and perhaps understandably, the impulse with all the sites was to try to hold on to the region's industrial past. The difficulty, even futility, of trying to do so, in light of emerging societal needs and wants and the accompanying inexorable change in the region's economy, ultimately led political leaders and the sites' developers to explore and then to embrace and pursue new visions, including new uses more in keeping with the changing times.

RIDC's initial plans for Herr's Island included factories and warehouses, developed by The Buncher Company and supplied by rail, covering both the island and land created by filling the back channel. When Ed deLuca took charge of City Development, his concept for the island was the same—hence his turning to the industrially oriented Economic Development Administration for financial support.

While these plans would have undoubtedly been feasible given the demand for industrial land in the city, Paul Farmer and Bob Lurcott of City Planning saw a different future for the island, based on their familiarity with housing and amenities on waterfront sites in the more dynamic regions of New England and the New York metropolitan area. They saw the attractiveness of the island as a unique amenity and pushed for a variety of uses that would take advantage of the island location while also minimizing traffic congestion—flex office buildings, riverfront trails and a park, a conference center, a marina, and housing. These choices and others that followed—the rowing center, the purchase of Buncher's property, and the expansion of parkland—turned Washington's Landing entirely from its industrial past to new and progressive uses.

The vision for the Pittsburgh Technology Center likewise shifted from one still rooted in the past to one that fully embraced a new identity for the city. The briefing book that the URA prepared in November 1984 for the Urban Land Institute's advisory panel referred to a proposed "Pittsburgh Industrial Park" at the site. Although the URA had wanted to develop the site for high-technology uses (and had included substantial information about the research strength of the universities in the briefing book), in their report the advisory panel went further, renaming the development the "Technology and Industry Park." The panel pushed the city to consider more seriously that it should take advantage of the universities' research strengths to position and market the site for development: "The proximity of [the universities] and the university health/medical complex is an attribute of the site that offers unique marketability."[56] Later, when the RIDC sought zoning that would allow generic office and industrial uses, City Planning took the position that research should be the focus of the project, despite the greater challenge that it would create for marketing the property. The city adopted the more restrictive zoning, and the URA renamed the project the Pittsburgh Technology Center.

In both cases—Washington's Landing and the Pittsburgh Technology Center—the arguments over uses—old or new—were largely among expert professionals: planning and development officials in the city, professional planners, and real estate professionals. Such was not the case in the Mon

Valley sites, where public opinions about uses were widely and strongly held.

Of all the projects, the process of defining a new vision for Homestead was probably the most difficult and contentious. Here, as in all the Mon Valley cases, the community resisted change: people wanted the mills to reopen. Every effort was expended to achieve that goal, but it was not to be. As Commissioner Foerster observed, however, going through the process of trying to revive steel was necessary in order for people to be able to put the past behind them and move on. In Homestead, however, that did not mean abandoning the industrial past but rather enshrining it. Thus, for many additional years and even to the present, elements in the community sought to preserve the old buildings and machinery as a memorial to the way of life they had lost. Finally, through extraordinary effort they were able to do this at the site of the Homestead Strike landing and on the portion of the site across the river to the northeast where the Carrie furnace stood. The eastern end of the site, too, where Park had left the old mill buildings standing, retained its industrial character. (In fact, industrial uses were Park's initial vision for the entire site.) However, Park's desire for flexibility in marketing the site and resulting market opportunities intervened and led to a vastly different outcome for the bulk of the site.

Sandcastle and the Waterfront, which occupy the largest portion of the site, are emblematic of America's twenty-first-century entertainment and consumer culture and pay no homage to the industrial past beyond the row of chimneys at the Waterfront that remind visitors that a steel mill once stood there.[57] Sandcastle's developers saw the commercial opportunity of the riverfront site for entertainment from the start, and they acquired their property directly from USX and immediately put it to the use they intended. The proposal for the Waterfront shopping center did not arrive until after the site was fully prepared. This dramatic transformation in use became a possibility only because, in the end, Park made the decision to clear the site completely, foundations included, so that any use was possible.[58] What presented itself at that point was a large retail shopping center and adjacent rental housing. The public had not foreseen nor did it dictate these uses, but the municipalities accepted and approved them when they appeared. Now the community seems to embrace the modern uses fully and to take pride in the fact that they bring people from throughout the region to live, shop, and enjoy themselves.

Duquesne and McKeesport, in contrast, retained their industrial character more fully. In these cities the displaced workers were as desirous as in Homestead to revive the mills, and they suffered the same disappointment when it became clear that the mills would never open again. Unlike in

Homestead, however, no private developer saw a compelling commercial future for the properties. RIDC toiled over the years to attract new industrial users, and they succeeded in landing a number. In the end, however, even here many of the most prominent new uses were not in the image of the sites' industrial past but rather representative of the new century—the Pittsburgh Community Food Bank in Duquesne and EchoStar Communications in McKeesport being notable examples.

ROLES FOR THE PUBLIC SECTOR

The early Pittsburgh industrial redevelopment projects allow us to examine the public sector in a number of roles, including those of funder, promoter, regulator, and developer. Each merits discussion.

Funder

Public funding was essential to all the Pittsburgh projects; none would have succeeded without it. Even the least expensive for the public—Homestead—required millions of dollars for construction of bridges and road improvements.

Local public resources were entirely inadequate, especially in light of the economic crisis that had created the need for the projects in the first place. The Commonwealth of Pennsylvania thus became the largest contributor, investing tens of millions of dollars in the projects over the period I have chronicled. Fortunately, there was sympathetic leadership in both the state administration and the legislature, as well as a tradition of state investment in local development projects. Still, the level of state investment required the sustained support of the legislature, the governor, and the secretaries and staffs of the Department of Commerce and Department of Community Affairs.

Promoter

Obtaining and maintaining such broad public support required attention and effort. The developers of all the projects constantly needed to reassure the public of the projects' desirability and success. Thus, the press became extremely important, and cultivation of the media and their views of the projects a constant concern. Developers also expended considerable time in keeping the projects and their progress before state legislators. The URA began publishing a quarterly newsletter especially to report progress on its state-funded projects in an attractive way to its supporters in the legislature. Developers and local officials often took state legislators and officials on tours of the sites and invited them to participate in press conferences, ground breakings, and other public events as another means of keeping the projects in front of them and ensuring the state's continued financial support.

Regulator

Having previously discussed regulation of environmental cleanup, I now turn to the other major relevant public regulatory function, regulation of land use. Zoning was a critical factor for all the sites, but its role differed considerably among them.

In the city, the Department of City Planning was competent and persuasive and generally had the mayor's confidence. Additionally, because the projects were publicly developed, city officials had to resolve questions of land use internally and then present a unified front at zoning hearings. This is not to say there was unanimity. As I noted above, Ed deLuca and City Planning were at loggerheads over land uses on Herr's Island, with the old-timer deLuca advocating the industrial uses he was accustomed to supporting, and the younger, more progressive planners advocating mixed uses. When Mayor Caliguiri decided to dismiss the difficult, entrenched deLuca, and it was clear he believed that the planners were better informed about the options and their consequences, their ideas prevailed. Similarly, for pragmatic marketing purposes, RIDC pushed for general office uses at the Technology Center, while City Planning wanted to restrict use to research and development. Since the city, with the URA as developer, was ultimately in charge, the planners prevailed. For the city projects, City Planning dictated land use.

The Homestead project produced an innovation: collaboration among three municipalities on land use planning and taxation. The idea for collaborating in zoning arose in the early years, as I have described in the history. Park initially encouraged the idea but then later rejected it when the municipalities proposed higher development standards than Park had expected. The issue lay dormant until 1997 when Park and Continental Real Estate Companies announced the Waterfront. This galvanized the three municipalities—Munhall, Homestead, and West Homestead—to collaborate on a joint land use, zoning, and revenue-sharing plan. They agreed to allocate specific shares of the revenues from the entire site—20% for Munhall, 50% for Homestead, and 30% for West Homestead—regardless of the assessed values developed in each municipality. This agreement made it possible for them to work cooperatively with the developers of the Waterfront to adopt a land use plan and zoning that would be the most advantageous for the site without their having to worry about the amount and value of the development located in the respective municipalities.

The issues of land use and zoning in Duquesne and McKeesport were more straightforward. There, the developments were confined to a single municipality. RIDC and the communities both wanted and pursued industrial development from the start, and RIDC had established a cooperative decision-making process involving community leaders. Use was never a question, and site planning was public and collaborative.

A discussion of the public sector's regulatory (policing) role would be incomplete without at least a mention of the public's power of eminent domain for redevelopment purposes. In fact, eminent domain was not exercised in any of the projects I have described, despite its being considered for both Herr's Island and Homestead.

Developer

The Pittsburgh cases highlight the strengths and limitations of public real estate development, allowing us to contrast a public developer (the URA) with private nonprofit developers (the RIDC and the universities) and private for-profit developers (The Buncher Company, Park Corporation, and the developers of Sandcastle).

Washington's Landing involved all three types of organizations: public (the URA), nonprofit (the RIDC), and private (The Buncher Company). At points in the process it appeared possible that each of these three might develop the island. In the end, the URA served as the developer. The outcome would likely have been different had the RIDC or Buncher been the developer.

For one thing, neither RIDC nor The Buncher Company had experience with the kind of mixed-use development that Washington's Landing became. The experience of both was in developing industrial parks, and their aspirations for the island conformed to their experience: they viewed the island's potential largely as an office, manufacturing, and distribution center, although RIDC's initial plan for the island did include a marina. Public access to the riverfront would not have been a priority. They might well have filled the back channel, as RIDC proposed, to improve access, cut development costs, and increase land area. The Rowing Center would likely not have found a home on the island, nor would the trail system have been built. Housing would never have been a consideration. It is unlikely they could have secured the large amount of public funds that made the extensive public improvements and the cleanup possible. Without Buncher's sale to the URA, however, the PCBs might never have been discovered and might have remained in place, with no one the wiser.

In this case the public developer created a better product than either Buncher or the RIDC would have produced, although the public cost was high. In a stronger market, undoubtedly other for-profit developers would have taken interest in the island, would have capitalized on its location, and would have developed it more quickly and with less need for public investment. At the time, however, Pittsburgh's economy was depressed, and thousands were leaving the region. Attracting private capital to develop the island was not realistic.

The Pittsburgh Technology Center is also an interesting case because of the number of possible development scenarios. Here, the candidates were the private Park Corporation, the URA, the RIDC, and the two universities with their own private developers. Perhaps the Park Corporation's decision to sell the property implies they had concluded that they could not prepare and sell the site profitably. As seen in Homestead, however, Park was not so much a developer as a scrapper, making profit from selling machinery and scrap and preparing land for others to develop. The deal with the URA might have given them more profit, in their judgment, than they would have made had they retained the property. At least it gave them greater certainty of profit: they had found a buyer for the prepared site.

Once the URA had bought the property, there was still the question of who should develop it. While the real estate experts from the Urban Land Institute were intrigued by the potential of for-profit development, in the end they recommended the nonprofit RIDC, rather than the URA, in light of RIDC's experience in developing industrial parks, its dominance in the market, and its access to financial resources from the state. The panel also recommended, however, that the two research universities be involved in the development to exploit what the panel judged to be promising private interest in the universities' commercially valuable research, although they did not recommend them as developers.

The project took a turn when the presidents of the universities asked the mayor for the opportunity to undertake the real estate development themselves, with their private, for-profit developer-partners, and pushed the RIDC aside. Their involvement slowed the process considerably, but it came to a standstill with the discovery of the cyanide, which would probably not have become an issue if the universities had not been involved as developers and the state had not been Pitt's landlord. Once that occurred, however, the universities went from wanting total control of the site to wanting as little as possible to do with it. The URA was left holding the bag.

The URA had already secured millions of public dollars, mostly from the state, for the roads and green spaces, the plazas and overlooks, and widening of Second Avenue, exceeding what any private developer, for-profit or nonprofit, would have received. On the other hand, the combination of the URA's own limited financial resources, inexperience, and vulnerability to political considerations; the universities' continued involvement because of their obligation to repay the state's investment in their buildings; and the environmental problems, all made progress difficult. RIDC would have had fewer limitations. A for-profit developer would have pushed for speedier, denser, less encumbered development in order to realize a greater financial return on the substantial investment in infrastructure the site required.

The Homestead site provides the contrast. There, the Park Corporation saw—and realized—potential for profit by preparing the land fully for private development. Although there had been much discussion of a public role in saving the mill, there was never serious discussion of public redevelopment. The Park Corporation stepped forward with an offer and negotiated a deal with USX. Allegheny County did not intervene. With an offer in hand from Park, USX had no reason to pursue the county's involvement, nor did the county have strong reasons to take the project on. Park prepared the land with no public assistance other than the substantial amount for access improvements, and they sold the prepared land for private development.

Duquesne and McKeesport were different in that no private developer stepped forward, even though the need to redevelop the old steel mills there was just as urgent. As described above, the difference was the market for the property. As time has shown, Homestead's location, closer to the region's population center and surrounded by more affluent communities, gave the site a tremendous advantage. Slow as it was, the process of redeveloping Homestead was far quicker than for Duquesne or McKeesport, which are more remote, more difficult to reach, and farther removed from the more prosperous parts of the region. In Duquesne and McKeesport, the county and its agent, the RIDC, were necessarily the developers. No for-profit interest was forthcoming.

As with Washington's Landing and the Pittsburgh Technology Center, however, publicly sponsored development brought high public scrutiny and heavy reliance on public investment. The resulting process in Duquesne and McKeesport was agonizingly slow and tortuous. Requirements for environmental compliance were high, and financial resources were severely constrained, far more so than in Homestead, which advanced more quickly both because Park provided the financing and because public regulators did not get involved.

In summary, the projects in Pittsburgh raise interesting questions about public and private development of large contaminated sites. In Pittsburgh, at least over the time covered here, the public necessarily played an important leading or supporting role. In another region, with a more dynamic economy and correspondingly higher demand for land, private initiative could well have been more prominent. In Pittsburgh, however, battered as it was by the loss of its basic industries, public initiative and public support were crucial.

In January 2011 a delegation of private and public leaders from Detroit 2020 visited Pittsburgh and "found there were lessons [they] could learn." The committee reported, "Pittsburgh has demonstrated resilience and a willingness to act. City leaders, donors with deep pockets and the brainpower of universities drew up a battle plan for reinvention." Detroit city council president Charles Pugh was enthusiastic about the application for Detroit: "One thing I love about what Pittsburgh has done: they've gone from being a town where steel was 70% of their economy and now it's less than 20%. Experts say the same must be done in the auto industry."

In response, Dennis Yablonsky, CEO of Pittsburgh's Allegheny Conference on Community Development, commented on the process that had taken place in Pittsburgh, saying, "The problems developed over a long time here and the solutions took a long period of time. So you just have to set your targets, work together and be persistent about it and you'll see incremental progress, but it takes a while to get through all this."[59]

The projects I have chronicled here were an integral part of the economic reinvention that so amazed the visitors from Detroit. The lessons that can be learned from the process of reclaiming these properties left behind by economic upheaval can be important in the future as other regions suffer other economic dislocations and lose key industries. The projects in Pittsburgh teach the importance of civic leadership, public–private partnership, resourcefulness and flexibility, and, above all, patience and persistence. Their transformation confirms that with those elements in place, success is possible.

ACKNOWLEDGMENTS

Many individuals contributed to this book. Andrew McElwaine, formerly of the Heinz Endowments, provided the initial impetus. Dr. Constance D. Ramírez, as dean of Duquesne University's McAnulty College and Graduate School of Liberal Arts, under whom I worked for ten years, allowed me the time and gave me the encouragement to work on this project in the midst of my administrative duties for the College. Her successors, Dean Francesco C. Cesareo, Acting Dean Albert C. Labriola, Dean Christopher M. Duncan, and Dean James Swindal, continued that support and encouragement.

Alan Lang, Adam Rabiner, and Angelo Taranto helped to assemble data on economic change in Pittsburgh. Mark Jablonski and Michael Knehr, research assistants in Duquesne University's Graduate Center for Social and Public Policy, spent hours poring over and extracting information from project files at the RIDC and the URA. Hiroaki Mori, a visiting fellow from the Matsushita Institute of Government and Management, also assisted in collecting the historical data, motivated by his belief that his native city of Kitakyushu, Japan, which faced the same problem of reusing abandoned industrial sites, could benefit from Pittsburgh's experience. Maureen Ford at the RIDC and Dana Michael O'Connor, project manager at the URA, spent time orienting Messrs. Jablonski and Knehr to the projects, made files available for examination, and answered many questions. Ms. Ford helped me identify buildings and photos and read portions of the manuscript. Brooks Robinson, at the time still president of RIDC, and his son Brooks, Jr., also of RIDC, gave their full support and cooperation and shared helpful resources, insights, and conclusions. Jerome Dettore, at the time deputy executive director of development at the URA, likewise shared his experiences in managing the environmental problems and physical development of the URA's sites and provided access to files. Others at the URA, including Madeline Augello, Anita Stec, and Kathleen Tkachik, also made files and minutes available for review. Dr. Mulugetta Birru, executive director of the URA at the time the research was done, lent his full support and cooperation. David

Donahoe and George Whitmer, former executive directors of the URA, reviewed portions of the draft and shared their recollections. Former executive director Raymond Christman also shared his recollections, as did my old URA colleagues Jerry Dettore and Jack Noonan. I thank Jack Bell of the Park Corporation and Mark Patrick of the Allegheny County Department of Development for sharing their memories. Kenneth Bowman, Joseph Chnupa, Charles Duritsa, John Matviya and Carl Spadero of the Pennsylvania Department of Environmental Resources, later the Department of Environmental Protection (Chnupa and Duritsa retired), shared memories, made project files available and made helpful corrections. Donald Horgan of the Allegheny County Health Department did the same. Former chairman of the Board of County Commissioners of Allegheny County Tom Foerster, before his death, and Joseph Hohman, former director of the county's Department of Development, provided helpful information on the county's early efforts in the Mon Valley. Joe Hohman's project files were an invaluable source of information about the former U.S. Steel sites. Deborah Lange of Carnegie Mellon University's Brownfields Center (now the Steinbrenner Institute for Environmental Education and Research) opened the center's files and made available the taped interviews conducted by the Brownfields Systems Group. Indirectly, I thank all those whose interviews they recorded. Mel Achtzehn, former mayor of the city of Duquesne, and Lou Washowich, former mayor of the city of McKeesport, gave interviews. Jennifer Wyse transcribed some tape-recorded interviews. Randy Harris and Herb Ferguson graciously gave me permission to use their slides. Ron Baraff of Rivers of Steel kindly provided maps and photographs of the Mon Valley plants and projects.

Dr. Ralph Bangs, Charles Duritsa, Dr. Douglas Harper, Joseph Hohman, Dr. Gerard Magill, Cynthia Miller, Dr. Charles Rubin, Christopher Shea, Anita Stec, Susan Wadsworth-Booth, and Steven Zecher each read drafts of sections and offered helpful suggestions. Brooks Robinson, Sr., read an entire draft and made many helpful comments. My wife Janet read and commented extensively on various drafts, offering many helpful suggestions. She also cleaned and prepared the photographs and made all the maps. My son-in-law Robert Bennett suggested using maps to introduce sections of the text. My friend Doug Harper worked his magic to improve—vastly—the quality of the photographs, bringing back the historic ones that otherwise would have been problematic to use. The talented Maggie Diehl ably edited the entire manuscript, raising questions along the way. Our discussions of the issues she raised clarified many points and helped me to fix problems I had not seen. Taylor Tobias skillfully designed and typeset the book, including the striking cover. "Collaborative" should be her middle name.

Of course, having acknowledged the contributions of all these, I accept full responsibility for the contents and conclusions of the work, including any errors and omissions.

This study would not have begun without the support of the Howard Heinz Endowment, its board and staff, which made a grant of $15,000 in 1995 that got the project started and paid miscellaneous costs of supplies, research, and editing. The Howard Heinz Endowment is one of the Pittsburgh-based Heinz Endowments, which together form one of the nation's largest philanthropic organizations. The Endowments' mission is to support progress in community development, the arts, education, health, human services, and the environment.

NOTES

Preface

1. These redevelopment efforts were one significant element of what became known in Pittsburgh as *Renaissance II*. "Renaissance II, usually associated by Pittsburghers with the onset of the Caliguiri mayoralty (1977), gave birth to a flock of new office buildings in the Golden Triangle, as well as a new level of commitment to neighborhood revitalization (already launched during the Flaherty administration). . . . It would be useful . . . to define it . . . as an effort to reconstruct Pittsburgh's economy, its system of neighborhood citizen organizations, and its cultural image." Roy Lubove, *Twentieth-Century Pittsburgh, Volume 2: The Post-Steel Era* (Pittsburgh: University of Pittsburgh Press, 1996), vii–viii.

2. LTV Corporation (formerly Ling-Temco-Vought) was a Texas-based conglomerate with wide-ranging business interests. In 1968 it acquired a controlling interest in the Jones & Laughlin Steel Company, which had built the Pittsburgh Works.

3. After the United States Steel Corporation, which owned the Homestead, Duquesne and National Works, acquired major oil and gas interests in the 1980s, the corporation changed its name to USX Corporation in 1986.

4. Alexi Mostrous, "Pittsburgh Shows How the Rust Belt Can Be Polished Up," *Washington Post,* September 24, 2009.

5. The Urban Redevelopment Authority of Pittsburgh (URA) was incorporated in 1946, pursuant to the Urban Redevelopment Act passed by the Commonwealth of Pennsylvania the year before, to undertake redevelopment of the portion of downtown Pittsburgh (Gateway Center) immediately adjacent to the proposed Point State Park. The act gave the Authority power to acquire private land by eminent domain for private reuse. Mayor David Lawrence served as the Authority's first chairman, and John P. "Jack" Robin as its first executive director. The Authority is an independent governmental body, but under the city's control. It has its own budget and operates through "cooperation agreements" with the city to undertake development on the city's behalf. In the 1970s, and more so in the 1980s, the Authority added important financing functions for both housing and economic development, becoming a public lender of some importance for low-income housing and small and mid-sized businesses. Some of the Authority's important early projects (and their starting dates) during the "urban renewal" period of the so-called Pittsburgh Renaissance (Renaissance I) were Gateway Center (1950), the Civic Arena (1951), East Liberty (1955), Allegheny Center (1959), and Three Rivers Stadium (1964).

For a history of the URA's first fifty years see Bessie C. Economou, *Urban Redevelopment Authority of Pittsburgh Fifty Years: Forging the Pittsburgh Renaissance* (Pittsburgh: Urban Redevelopment Authority of Pittsburgh, 1997).

6. The term *brownfield* first came into use in the early 1990s to refer to an abandoned industrial or, at times, commercial site, in contrast with a greenfield, which is a site that has never been previously developed. The U.S. Environmental Protection Agency defines a brownfield site as "real property, the expansion, redevelopment, or reuse of which may be complicated by the presence or potential presence of a hazardous substance, pollutant, or contaminant." "Brownfields and Land Revitalization," U.S. Environmental Protection Agency, accessed March 5, 2014, http://www.epa.gov/brownfields.

Chapter 1. Washington's Landing

1. URA, invitation to "Completion Celebration on Washington's Landing," September 30, 1999. See Lubove, 55, for a brief history of the project.

2. Nathaniel Cox, "Washington's Landing: A Case of Brownfield Remediation," unpublished paper for Dr. Joel Tarr's Carnegie Mellon University class, "Perspectives on the City and the Natural Environment," April 29, 1999; E. Kenneth Vey, "Small Strip of Land Changed from Industrial Site to Community," *Pittsburgh Post-Gazette*, August 29, 2001.

3. Fred R. Herr, "Herr's Island," *The Western Pennsylvania Historical Magazine* 53 (July 1970): 214–15; Randy Rieland, "Herr's Island: From Cattle Yard to Central Park?" *Pittsburgh Press*, October 24, 1974, 2.

4. "It Happened 25 Years Ago," *Pittsburgh Post-Gazette*, August 2, 1990, D12.

5. "It Happened August 20," *Pittsburgh Post-Gazette*, August 20, 1990, C4.

6. The Regional Industrial Development Corporation of Southwestern Pennsylvania (RIDC) was created in 1955 as an offshoot of the Allegheny Conference on Community Development (originally the Allegheny Conference on Post War Community Planning), founded in 1943 to improve the city as a business location. By the 1950s changes in the nation's industrial structure and the trend toward suburban business development were already evident. The Conference concluded that competition for employers required a more focused approach, and they formed RIDC to stimulate economic growth, promote industrial diversification, and retain and create jobs in the nine-county region around Pittsburgh. In 1962 RIDC reorganized as a full-fledged, nonprofit real estate development and finance company. Over the next three decades it came to dominate the industrial real estate market with its industrial parks, offering inexpensive land and special state financing in three strategic corners of Allegheny County. Beginning in the 1980s RIDC turned its attention to the city and the Monongahela River Valley. It established business incubators in Oakland, near Carnegie Mellon University and the University of Pittsburgh, to capture commercial development of innovations arising from the universities, and in 1988 it acquired the abandoned Westinghouse plant in East Pittsburgh, renamed Keystone Commons, where "traditional types of industry—machine shops, pipe and generator facilities—would be followed by offices, high-tech companies, and research and development laboratories." Frank Brooks Robinson, "Testimony," Select Committee of the Pennsylvania House of Representatives Investigating Industrial Development Corporations, September 12, 1991, 8, quoted in Lubove, *Twentieth-Century Pittsburgh*, 38.

7. The following table lists the owners of property on the island, with their corresponding uses and areas, at the time the city began considering the island's redevelopment.

Owners and Uses on Herr's Island, 1976

Owner	Use	Area (in acres)
Penn Central Railroad	stockyards, tracks	24.54
City of Pittsburgh	ash dump	7.11
The Buncher Company	rail-car recycling plant	4.85
Inland Products, Inc.	rendering plant	2.87
Chessie System	railroad tracks	1.53
Western Packers	meat-packing plant	0.49
Total:		41.39

8. David Warner, "Herr's Island a Boon, Study Says," *Pittsburgh Press,* January 25, 1976, A2; "Last Roundup for Herr's Island?" *Pittsburgh Press Roto,* November 6, 1977, 2–3.

9. *Pittsburgh Press,* "The Prolonged Transformation of Herr's Island," November 6, 1977, *Roto* magazine section.

10. The Urban Redevelopment Law of 1945 had found that "there exist in urban communities in this Commonwealth areas which have become blighted because of the unsafe, unsanitary, inadequate or over-crowded condition of the dwellings therein, or because of inadequate planning of the area, or excessive land coverage by the buildings thereon, or the lack of proper light and air and open space, or because of the defective design and arrangement of the buildings thereon, or faulty street or lot layout, or economically or socially undesirable land uses" (35 P.S. §1702(a)). These became the criteria that planning commissions used to "certify" an area as "blighted." The act provided that a redevelopment authority, established by a municipality pursuant to the act, was "to procure from the planning commission the designation of areas in need of redevelopment and its recommendations for such redevelopment" (35 P.S. §1709(a)). The authority was "to study the recommendations of the planning commission," "make its own additional investigations" (35 P.S. §1709(b)), and then "prepare a redevelopment proposal for all or part of any area certified by the planning commission to be a redevelopment area and for which the planning commission has made a redevelopment plan" (35 P.S. §1710), for approval by the municipality's governing body after a public hearing.

11. The cost of the study, conducted by General Analytics Corporation, was $120,000. URA, minutes of the meeting of April 6, 1978; Eleanor Chute, "City Moves toward Herr Island Plan," *Pittsburgh Press,* April 7, 1978, B-8.

12. The board authorized the URA to pay Buncher $420,000 for the railroad land. URA, minutes of the meeting of March 8, 1979; Eleanor Chute, "Herr Island Industrial Park Plans Gain," *Pittsburgh Press,* March 9, 1979, A-19. Concurrently, we were negotiating with Buncher on another project. Gary Fry and I had made a proposal to the city to purchase the old Pennsylvania Produce Terminal in the Strip District, between 16th and 21st streets. (See Evan Stoddard and Gary Fry, "Expanding the Role of Pittsburgh's Strip District as a Food Distribution Center: An Action Proposal," Department of City Planning, May 17, 1979.) Buncher owned the land between the Produce Terminal and the Allegheny River, and we wanted a sliver of that

land to improve access to the Produce Terminal. In my journal I recorded one frustrating episode from this negotiation that gives insight into Buncher's personality and approach: "Friday, November 11, 1979, Gary [Fry] & I spent most of the afternoon with Jack Buncher & Herb Green. I never remember how worn out I am going to be by those meetings. They go on forever, & Buncher is so intense. . . . Today we had to listen to 'the grand PLAN for the Strip District.'"

13. GAI's initial fee was $69,748. URA, minutes of the meeting of August 2, 1979.

14. Jerome Dettore to Ronald J. Chleboski, September 30, 1980.

15. URA, minutes of the meeting of March 6, 1980.

16. The funds for Herr's Island would take most of the $4.5 million total the Department of Environmental Resources had for these purchases. Presciently, Jack Robin envisioned that "a picture of a park-edged area on both sides of the Allegheny River [would] materialize." Minutes of March 6, 1980.

17. Conditions of the state's grant were that the URA would dedicate the land for a park and that it would determine that "no deleterious substances exist on the island." URA, minutes of the meeting of June 12, 1980.

18. The cost was not to exceed $70,000. URA, minutes of the meeting of June 12, 1980, resolutions #127–28.

19. Carl Morris, "Caliguiri Says Island Has Room for Waste Plant, Industries," *Pittsburgh Post-Gazette,* December 10, 1980; "What Uses for Herr Island?" *Pittsburgh Post-Gazette,* December 11, 1980, A6. The plants were owned by Allegheny Steam Heating Company (ASHCO), a division of Duquesne Light. To address the problems, the downtown businesses formed the nonprofit, cooperative Pittsburgh Allegheny County Thermal Limited (PACT) to buy ASHCO. PACT then converted ASHCO's coal-fired boiler on Ft. Duquesne Boulevard to a modern gas-fired steam plant.

20. URA, minutes of the meeting of January 14, 1982.

21. URA, minutes of the meetings of March 12 and April 9, 1981.

22. URA, minutes of the meeting of November 12, 1981. By September 1982 the design of the new bridge was sufficiently complete that the URA issued an invitation to bid on the drilling and soil sampling.

23. Relocation of Inland Products' plant was an issue, since it was the only rendering plant in the region. Although noxious, it gave businesses and institutions from a wide area an outlet to dispose of their waste animal byproducts.

24. James O'Toole, "State Buys Site on Herr Island for Park, Marina," *Pittsburgh Post-Gazette,* December 10, 1981, A4.

25. I had raised this issue three years earlier. An additional concern was that many costs were unknown. For example, one long-standing element of the plan was a marina, but a marina on Herr's Island would be the first to be attempted in the Pittsburgh pool (the stretch of river between the locks upstream and downstream of downtown). The economics of such a venture were unexplored. The Port Authority was in the midst of a study of marina locations in the region, but that study would likely not provide the details of what placing a marina on Herr's Island would entail. With an offer from the Allegheny County Planning Department to pay half the cost, up to $25,000, the URA decided to undertake an economic feasibility study that would estimate the amount of public financing that a marina on the island might require. Minutes of the meeting of June 11, 1981, resolution #159.

26. The uses proposed in the application to the EDA were 300,000 square feet of office space, 315,000 square feet for distribution, and 230,000 square feet for light manufacturing, together with a small marina for seventy boats.

27. Robert Lurcott, memorandum to John P. Robin and Hiram Milton, December 15, 1982.

28. The Harlan Company, land-use recommendations for Herr's Island, August 1983, in URA, Planning and Engineering, Washington's Landing, box 25. However, there had been much discussion leading up to that. I recorded the following entries in my journal:

Tuesday, March 29, Spent the morn. on Herr's Island with the team of us who have been working on it—reevaluating land use alternatives and possibilities one last time.

Tuesday, May 17, Morning trying to come to agreement on a tentative land use plan for Herr's Island.

29. Jerry Dettore to Jack Buncher, September 22, 1983.

30. GAI Consultants, "Waste Materials Investigation for Herr's Island Development Project, Pittsburgh, Pennsylvania: Report of Findings," September 1983; and "Washington's Landing Environmental Summary," January 13, 1993.

31. The URA, in contrast, estimated that remaining land acquisitions and site preparation would cost $11 million beyond the $9.2 million in federal, state, and city monies that had already been spent on acquisition and site improvements.

32. URA, minutes of the meeting of October 13, 1983.

33. By February the spine road was 90% complete, the design of the bridge 90% complete, and the design of the River Avenue ramp 70% complete. The URA had applied to the Pennsylvania Department of Community Affairs for a grant of $2.3 million (approved in February of the following year) to supplement the 1978 grant from EDA secured through Pittsburgh County-wide Corporation ($2.27 million) and Community Development Block Grant funds from the city ($1.81 million from 1978 to 1981). Together, they would meet the projected cost of $6.38 million to build the road, bridge, and ramp.

By June the spine road, including water and sewer lines, lighting, grading, and seeding, was complete. In the process the contractors had discovered one waste-materials lagoon that temporarily stopped construction until it could be tested and cleaned up. Designs of the bridge and of the ramp were practically complete. The designs had taken longer than expected because the city's Department of Public Works had rejected the initial design because it had placed the bridge's piers in the back channel. In August, in preparation for constructing the bridge, the URA approved a budget to upgrade electrical and gas service and to oversee demolition of the old 30th Street Bridge once the new bridge was in place. URA, minutes of the meeting of August 3, 1984.

In December the URA approved purchase of some 2 acres from Conrail on the north side of the back channel to accommodate the new ramp that would bring River Road up to the new bridge. The old ramp had been in some danger of collapsing. Construction of the new bridge and ramp would solve that problem. URA, minutes of the meeting of December 19, 1984.

34. Paul Maryniak, "A Dream?: $5.2 Million, Decade Later, Herr's Still Fantasy Island," *Pittsburgh Press,* April 7, 1985, A1, 16.

35. URA, minutes of the meeting of May 9, 1985.

36. The Council, whose board of directors came largely from the North Side's business community, was seeking to expand employment opportunities on the North Side. To this end

the Council had created a development fund for new businesses, using state Enterprise Zone funds, and formed an affiliated, state-certified North Side Industrial Development Corporation that could serve as a conduit for low-cost business financing from the state. State Representative Tom Murphy, who, before being elected to the state legislature, had been the Council's president, was a vocal critic of Pittsburgh-based Regional Industrial Development Corporation (RIDC), which was the oldest and by far the most successful Industrial Development Corporation in the Pittsburgh region. These state-certified corporations were uniquely able to borrow money from the Pennsylvania Industrial Development Authority (PIDA) at very favorable interest rates—3%—for construction of industrial and commercial buildings for lease, and to serve as conduits for PIDA loans to industrial firms that built and occupied their own buildings. RIDC had used these funds to good effect in its industrial park developments in O'Hara Township (RIDC Park) and the North Hills, earning substantial fees in the process. Tom Murphy and the leaders of North Side Civic Development Council were critical of RIDC's historic commitment to development in the suburbs that they believed had enticed many firms to leave the city. They wanted a city organization that they believed had greater concern for the city's economic well-being so that they would be able to use these attractive state resources to keep firms in the city and on the North Side, which led to their efforts to have the state certify the council to compete with RIDC for PIDA business in the city.

37. URA, minutes of the meeting of June 12, 1986; Tom Barnes, "Herr Island to Get Market Help," *Pittsburgh Post-Gazette*, June 13, 1986, A5.

38. Ellen M. Perlmutter, "Herr's Island Plan Faces 2-week Delay," *Pittsburgh Press*, September 10, 1986, B5; Tom Barnes, "No Herr's Rezoning, Island Remains Idle," *Pittsburgh Post-Gazette*, September 10, 1986, A4.

39. Jack Buncher to Paul Brophy, September 22, 1986.

40. Pittsburgh Planning Commission, minutes of the meeting of September 23, 1986; "Planners OK Herr Zoning," *Pittsburgh Post-Gazette*, September 24, 1986, A4.

41. URA, minutes of the meeting of December 11, 1986.

42. The building would be built to be able to expand to 58,000 square feet. The developer could lease the land for up to sixty years, or purchase it after six years for $200,000, equating to $55,555 per acre, or $1.28 per square foot, about the going rate for industrial land in the region at the time.

43. URA, minutes of the meetings of October 8, 1987, resolution #345, and November 5, 1987, resolution #382.

44. GAI Consultants, "Final Report, Phase 2 Study—Highway Improvements, Herr's Island," which identified "the costs and benefits of long-term, capital intensive highway improvements" around Herr's Island. URA, minutes of the meeting of August 20, 1987.

45. URA, minutes of the meeting of October 8, 1987, resolutions #343–44.

46. Virginia Linn, "URA Ready to Buy Key Parcel on Herr," *Pittsburgh Post-Gazette*, October 7, 1987, 1; URA, minutes of the meeting of December 10, 1987, resolutions #423–26.

47. URA, minutes of the meeting of December 10, 1987, resolution #414; Virginia Linn, "Herr Island renamed; redevelopment begins," *Pittsburgh Post-Gazette*, October 24, 1987, A5.

48. URA, minutes of the meeting of January 14, 1988, resolution #11.

49. David L. Donahoe, interview with the author, April 30, 2003.

50. Concentrations of PCBs (polychlorinated biphenyls) in the samples ranged from under 0.1 part per million (ppm) to 200 ppm, where background levels were less than 0.1 ppm. Concentrations of PAHs (polynuclear aromatic hydrocarbons) ranged from 0.4 ppm to 430 ppm, compared with background levels of 0.01 to 13 ppm.

51. Donahoe, interview.

52. Donahoe, interview.

53. Donahoe, interview.

54. David Guo, "Toxic Waste Found on River Island," *Pittsburgh Post-Gazette,* April 27, 1988, 1, 4.

55. URA, minutes of the special meeting of April 28, 1988, resolutions #161–65.

56. Donahoe, interview.

57. The article went on to say, "The Urban Redevelopment Authority announced yesterday that hazardous wastes have been found on part of Washington's Landing, creating a costly problem that could impede plans to create a riverside marina, housing and retail complex." David Guo, "Toxic Waste Found on River Island," *Pittsburgh Post-Gazette,* April 27, 1988, A1.

58. Dettore, memorandum to the files, April 29, 1988.

59. Dettore, memorandum to the files, May 5, 1988.

60. Gariti, memorandum to the files, May 4, 1988.

61. Donahoe, interview.

62. Jack Robin to Jack Buncher, June 17, 1988.

63. Donahoe, interview.

64. That study established a 100-foot sampling grid, decreasing to 50 and then 25 feet at the margins of the contaminated area. It included a risk assessment, meetings with the DER, development of a remedial design (assumed to be excavation, transportation, and disposal of the contaminated soil at an approved landfill), and cost estimates. In its proposal ICF's Jim Nairn stated, "At present, it is assumed that remediation will involve excavation of soils, transportation, and disposal at a landfill licensed by EPA to accept PCB." In transmitting its report, ICF stated, "The Urban Redevelopment Authority feels that their development plans are flexible enough to locate commercial buildings in this area of the island, or to exclude the plan for backyard areas with townhouse development. . . . If DER feels that the removal of some contaminated soil is absolutely necessary, we would like to explore other cleanup levels with you which may be higher than 10 mg/kg, but which will afford equal protection to public health and which will also enable URA to develop the island for the benefit of the City of Pittsburgh." James Nairn to Robert J. Finkle (Solid Waste Specialist, DER), July 11, 1988.

65. Letter from Anthony Orlando, DER, to David L. Donahoe, URA, September 9, 1988

66. URA, minutes of the meeting of September 8, 1988, resolution #316.

67. URA, minutes of the meeting of October 13, 1988.

68. ICF Kaiser Engineers, "Environmental Summary, Washington's Landing, October 7, 1988.

69. Donahoe, interview. Joseph Chnupa, former Assistant Regional Director, Department of Environmental Protection, remembered, "Art Davis came out to the regional office and I covered the issues that were coming out with him. Unfortunately, that was close to the end of

his term as secretary. It struck a chord with him, but it could not be dealt with in the time remaining to him." Interview with the author, August 19, 2003.

70. Charles Duritsa, interview with the author, Pittsburgh, Pennsylvania, June 7, 2005.

71. URA, minutes of the meeting of January 12, 1989.

72. Andrew Sheehan, "Washington's Landing Development Pact Near," *Pittsburgh Post-Gazette,* March 1, 1989, A1.

73. Anthony Orlando to David L. Donahoe, March 1, 1989.

74. The URA planned to use a combination of funds from the Pennsylvania Department of Commerce, already on hand, and a $2.3 million loan from Pittsburgh National Bank to pay for the property and dispose of the contamination, the latter to be repaid upon receipt of a new grant from the Appalachian Regional Commission, secured through Commerce. In addition, the URA transferred $650,000 from an old, inactive redevelopment project account, Reedsdale Ridge (not coincidentally another North Side project) to help pay for the cleanup and to provide cash flow for the project. URA, minutes of the meeting of March 9, 1989; Ellen M. Perlmutter, "Waste Cleanup Accord Spurs Island Project," *Pittsburgh Press,* March 8, 1989, B1.

75. "Summary of Completed Field Construction Activities," Environmental Summary, Washington's Landing, March 9, 1989; URA, minutes of the meeting of March 9, 1989.

76. URA, minutes of the meeting of July 13, 1989, resolution #280; Ellen M. Perlmutter, "City Extends Washington's Landing Pact," *Pittsburgh Press,* July 14, 1989, B3.

77. The cell would consist of a 12-inch layer of sand bedding for the liner; a 40-mil HDPE liner (secondary liner); MiraDRAIN® (a single mat of drainage netting for the leachate detection system); a 60-mil HDPE liner (primary liner); a double mat of drainage netting, one for the leachate collection system and one for added protection of the 60-mil HDPE liner; filter fabric; a 12-inch layer of sand and gravel for protection of the liner; and an additional layer of woven filter fabric for protection of the liner.

78. "Report of Investigation, Herr Island Buncher Property," Environmental Summary, Washington's Landing; Anthony Orlando to Jerry Dettore, August 18, 1989. The URA proceeded to submit its detailed plan for disposal of the PCB-contaminated soil on the Buncher property to the DER on January 11, 1990, outlining a phased excavation and temporary storage, and the DER approved the plan on February 6.

79. URA, minutes of the meeting of August 10, 1989, resolutions #298–99.

80. "Consent agreements were among the first [responses]. They took the place of permits, to the extent they could by law." Kenneth Bowman (Assistant Regional Counsel, Southwest Regional Office, PA Department of Environmental Protection), interview with the author, August 19, 2003.

81. URA, minutes of the meeting of January 11, 1990, resolution #29.

82. URA, minutes of the meeting of October 12, 1989. Interestingly, the only local developer beside Haulover to submit qualifications was the O'Loughlin Company, whose principal, David O'Loughlin, had played an early role in Mayor Flaherty's administration as an advocate for the island's redevelopment.

83. URA, minutes of the meeting of November 9, 1989, resolution #391.

84. Jim Gregory, former president of Calgon Corporation, and his brother Dick owned the

Haulover Resort Marina in Miami Beach, Florida. Jim later formed Washington's Landing Marina, Inc., to develop the marina on Herr's Island.

85. As required by DER, to pledge fulfillment of the environmental responsibilities it was agreeing to assume on the island, the URA, at its September 1990 board meeting, authorized a bank letter of credit or surety bond, payable to DER, in the amount of $216,578 "to guarantee ... that the Authority, for a period of ten years, will conduct all activities required by the Consent Order and Agreement for the Washington's Landing Project." URA, minutes of the meeting of September 13, 1990, resolution #364.

86. URA, minutes of the meeting of October 12, 1989, resolutions #376–78.

87. "Toxic Fears Halt Washington's Landing Work," *Pittsburgh Post-Gazette,* November 5, 1989. Other aggravations plagued the project. The URA had thought there was a single underground gas tank on the Buncher site. In fact, there proved to be two, the second almost twice as big as the first, requiring a crane, the excavation of additional soil, and another $4,500. GAI, the URA's traffic consultant, encountered unforeseen complexities in working with PennDOT on designing the traffic improvements. Costs went from $21,000 to $68,000. URA, minutes of the meeting of November 9, 1989, resolutions #392–94.

88. The Planning Commission adopted the URA's plan for the park on December 12, including tennis courts (over the containment cell), nature trails, river overlooks, parking for sixty cars, and a 2.5-acre parcel for an office/research and development/light industrial building.

89. ICF's letter reported the discovery and its immediate impact on the project:

Work to remove the assumed animal rendering waste was started on Monday, November 6, 1989, with eight dumpsters being loaded that day containing 125 cubic yards of material. On Tuesday, November 7, 1989, only 3 dumpsters were available at the site and were loaded within a few hours during the morning. . . . Work was stopped for the remainder of Tuesday and all of Wednesday due to the unavailability of dumpsters at the site. After exhausting all reasonable sources to supply dumpsters, it was apparent that they were not available in the necessary quantity to complete the removal.

ICF Engineers to Pennsylvania Department of Environmental Resources, November 16, 1990.

90. The change orders to Atlas's contract for the months of November and December, for excavation and storage of the newly discovered animal wastes, were $228,981.77. January added another $121,213.56, and February another $131,375.12. URA, minutes of the meetings of January 11, 1990, resolution #29, February 8, 1990, resolution #60, and March 8, 1990, resolution #114. The original contract was for $994,717, the final contract for $1,476,287.45.

91. To help finance the construction cost of over $3 million, the URA agreed to apply for grants from the state's departments of Commerce, for site improvements ("Business Infrastructure Development"), and Community Affairs. Urban Redevelopment Authority of Pittsburgh, minutes of the meetings of January 11, 1990, resolutions #8–9, and May 17, 1990, resolution #186. The Business Infrastructure Development Grant from Commerce was $85,000. The Enterprise Zone Competitive Grant from Community Affairs was a $500,000 grant to the URA, but became a low-interest loan to Sports Technology Group, passed through North Side Civic Development Council.

92. On January 29 the URA got a revised cost estimate for ICF's engineering services through 1989. Where the original budget was $230,760, they had actually incurred costs of $665,233.

93. URA, minutes of the meetings of February 8, 1990, resolutions #61–62, 76–77; and April 12, 1990, resolution #139.

94. Jerry Dettore of the URA gave a detailed explanation of the discovery of the rendering waste and its consequences for the project:

> Jerry states that the Washington's Landing-Herr's Island Project, Site Remediation and Soil Encapsulation Cell budget was initially estimated at $850,000 and now stands at $1,200,000 to cover extras. Low bid was $1,000,000 and the present estimates were at $1,300,000. Jerry stated that the estimated cost of off-site disposal of the rendering waste was in the range of $850,000 to $1,000,000. Jerry stated that the URA may have to stop the job as it does not have the money to complete it if off-site disposal is necessary and would have to store the rendering waste on-site until funding was available. Jerry stated that the URA's objective and purpose at this meeting was to resolve the issues of on-site vs. off-site disposal and that the URA wanted the least costly alternative. Jerry stated that on-site disposal had been estimated at $250,000 to $350,000 which represented a $500,000 savings to the URA.
>
> When the rendering waste was first discovered, it was assumed that approximately 400 cubic yards of rendering wastes were buried which had come from surface stockpiles of rendering waste that were discovered on the island in 1983–1984. Those stockpiles were to be removed by Inland Products Company[,] the former property owner. Upon discovery of the rendering waste during earthwork for construction of the encapsulation cell, it was assumed by all involved, that those stockpiles of rendering waste had simply been buried at the site. It became apparent after several days of remediation efforts, that more material was present than the 400 cubic yards. ICF KE began to excavate exploratory trenches to determine the extent of the rendering waste. At the time of the November 21, 1989, meeting, the trenches were still being excavated and a preliminary estimate of materials was given at approximately 4,000–4,500 cubic yards. Since that meeting, an additional 3,000–3,500 cubic yards of material has been discovered along with considerable other amounts of construction debris, machinery, old foundations and random layers of rendering waste product.

URA, minutes of a meeting at the Department of Environmental Resources, February 23, 1990.

95. "Council Criticizes Pace of Island Development," *Pittsburgh Press,* March 14, 1990.

96. ICF Engineers, "Environmental Summary, Washington's Landing."

97. On May 11 the EPA's David Kregenow determined that soil contaminated above 500 ppm would have to be incinerated, while soils with levels between 50 and 500 ppm would go to the landfill. The subsequent excavation unearthed a total of forty-five capacitors, which the URA disposed of according to these guidelines. ICF Engineers, *"Environmental Summary."*

98. ICF Engineers, "Report of Investigation, Herr Island Buncher Property," *"Environmental Summary."*

99. The developers agreed to pay the URA $235,224 for the first parcel, retaining options on the remainder. Tom Barnes, "Pleasure Boat Dock Planned for Island," *Pittsburgh Post-Gazette,* May 17, 1990, 6; URA, minutes of the meeting of May 17, 1990, resolutions #181, 187.

In June, Schneider Engineers reported on its subsurface environmental investigation of the mainland property. Expectedly, they found slightly elevated levels of metals, likely the result of the former scrap-metal operation that had been on that site. (It was, in fact, the site of Jack Buncher's father's original scrap dealership—hence Buncher's emotional attachment to the island.) On the other hand, there was no evidence of groundwater contamination. Since Schneider did not consider removal of the soil to be a reasonable option, they recommended containment in the form of treatment with lime and capping. In mid-July the DER agreed with this approach. Gale Campbell to Jerome Dettore, July 18, 1990; Washington's Landing Development Environmental Consent Order.

Another problem impeding development of the marina was the sunken barges on the north shore. The plan for the marina called for using that property for boat storage and repair, requiring removal of the barges and other junk. The URA had addressed the issue of the barges three years previously and had contracted with the Army Corps of Engineers to remove them. The URA and Corps had then traced ownership of the barges to two firms—River Salvage, and Harry Zubik's Marine Contractors. After attempts to dislodge them, the city finally sued in Common Pleas Court to evict them from the property, claiming, in Finance Director Ben Hayllar's words, that they are "literally turning it into a junk yard, in the water and on the land." Zubic, taking his case to the press, "said he runs a nice and clean contracting business and does not store junk on the property," a comment anyone looking at the property might have disputed. But Zubik, undoubtedly looking for compensation, replied that he had operated on the site for forty years, and argued, "I've fixed up the riverbanks, cleaned it up when the city didn't do anything. I never received a dime for it." In the end the URA picked up the $272,000 cost of removing the barges. Jon Schmitz, "City Moves to Evict 2 Firms on Riverfront," *Pittsburgh Press,* October 8, 1990, A7; "City Says 2 Firms on Allegheny Create Eyesore near Marina Site," *Pittsburgh Press,* October 9, 1990, B4.

100. J. H. Waters Systems, Inc., began capping the cell June 29, installing and welding a 40-mil HDPE cap to the primary liner and installing a 40-mil HDPE liner on the cell's east and west sides for construction of the cap's drainage system. Drainage netting, filter fabric, and a 6-inch layer of sand were then placed over the liner, and the cap drainage system was installed, followed by 2 feet of soil, which was placed over the cap liner system and compacted before installation of a red plastic warning grid over the entire cell to serve as a mark for future excavators who might be working in the area. On top of this came 9 to 36 inches of soil. ICF Engineers, *"Environmental Summary."*

101. Ellen M. Perlmutter, "Developers to Launch River Project This Fall," *Pittsburgh Press,* July 11, 1990, B9.

102. Ellen M. Perlmutter, "Washington's Landing May Get Tennis Complex, Marina," *Pittsburgh Press,* July 25, 1990, B1. The URA's proposal noted that "while the goals and objectives of the Redevelopment Plan have remained the same, the manner in which they will be implemented has changed due to site and market characteristics." URA, minutes of the meeting of August 9, 1990, resolution #338.

103. "1800 Rowers Expected 9/29 for Head of the Ohio Crew Race," *Pittsburgh Press,* August 5, 1990, A4; and "Picnickers Welcome to Riverbank to Watch 4th Head of the Ohio Race," *Pittsburgh Press,* September 23, 1990, B7.

104. Drawing samples from soil borings and groundwater monitoring wells on parcels 13 and 14, SE Technologies tested for a variety of contaminants, including heavy metals (arsenic, cadmium, chromium, copper, lead, mercury, selenium, silver, and zinc), pesticides, PCBs, volatile organic compounds, and TPHs (total petroleum hydrocarbons). The tests discovered elevated levels of heavy metals and TPHs, the latter due to the presence of a 550-gallon underground storage tank. The URA had the tank drained and removed it and the soil it had contaminated

to an acceptable dump. The DER expressed concern that concentrations of the heavy metals might leach into the groundwater. Taking the URA's proposed use and the DER's concerns into consideration, SE Technologies suggested raising the grade with clean fill, treating the soil with lime, and then compacting the soil. Crushed stone would then cover the site for its ultimate use for boat storage and parking. The DER reviewed SE Technologies' design and approved it for parcel 14, but added an asphalt cap for parcel 13 and required quarterly sampling and testing of the groundwater for a year, which disclosed no leaching.

105. State funds included both grants (BID from Commerce and Enterprise Zone funds from Community Affairs) and loans, from an alphabet soup of Commerce's programs, PIDA, MELF, PCLF, and EDPF.

106. "Riverside Hiking, Bike Trail Proposed for City," *Pittsburgh Press*, December 6, 1990, C1.

107. The building would have been about 50,000 square feet in size and housed about seventy-five employees. Bernie Kohn, "Microbac Considers Washington's Landing," *Pittsburgh Press*, January 4, 1991, B9.

108. URA, minutes of the meeting of March 17, 1991, resolution #82.

109. URA, minutes of the meetings of June 13, 1991, resolution #189; and September 12, 1991, resolution #338.

110. George Whitmer observed, "We're still in a better position now than we are normally in on 99 percent of our loans." URA, minutes of the meeting of April 30, 1991, resolution #139; and "Financing for Marina Approved," *Pittsburgh Press,* April 30, 1991, A6.

111. Ralph Haurwitz, "DER Moving to Former Site of Toxic Dump," *Pittsburgh Press,* June 21, 1991, D1.

112. Charles Duritsa, interview.

113. The DER needed 65,000 square feet, and Washington's Landing Associates' first building could provide only 44,500. Urban Redevelopment Authority of Pittsburgh, minutes of the meeting of July 11, 1991, resolution #225. The new building was to have a total of 26,000 square feet. URA, minutes of the meeting of October 10, 1991, resolutions #365–66.

114. URA, minutes of the meeting of September 12, 1991, resolutions #336–37. Strategy 21 was the city's, county's, and universities' joint request to the state for financial support of their most important major economic development projects. See Lubove, 49–50, for a brief explanation.

115. URA, minutes of the meeting of October 10, 1991, resolution #367.

116. Ralph Haurwitz, "DER Set for Move to Washington's Landing," *Pittsburgh Press,* December 18, 1991, B1.

117. The URA helped the Rowing Association with a grant of $25,000 to address the unusual site preparation costs that the project entailed. URA, minutes of the meeting of February 13, 1992, resolution #74.

118. Charles Duritsa, interview.

119. URA, minutes of the meetings of December 12, 1991, resolution #465, and April 9, 1992, resolution #129.

120. URA, minutes of the meeting of June 11, 1992, resolutions #205, 251–55.

121. URA, minutes of the meetings of December 10, 1992, resolution #517, and February 11,

1993, resolution #50; "Rubinoff Building Planned," *Pittsburgh Post-Gazette,* March 10, 1993, B10.

122. URA, minutes of the meeting of March 11, 1993, resolution #85.

123. Tom Barnes, "Washington's Landing: The Smell of Success," *Pittsburgh Post-Gazette,* October 5, 1993, A1. In 1997 the URA calculated that it had spent $26.5 million of public funds for the development of Washington's Landing, not including public loans and grants to individual business and housing development projects. Following is the URA's accounting, by source:

Appalachian Regional Commission	$1,850,000
City of Pittsburgh Bond Funds	$3,248,000
City of Pittsburgh CDBG	$4,400,000
PA Capital Budget (Strategy 21)	$3,000,000
PA Department of Community Affairs	$2,300,000
PA Department of Commerce	$2,400,000
Pittsburgh Water and Sewer Authority	$1,200,000
Port Authority Transit	$800,000
U.S. Economic Development Administration	$2,280,590
Urban Redevelopment Authority	$1,301,000
Urban Redevelopment Authority Program Income	$585,500
Total:	$26,505,090

By 1995 this public investment had resulted in private development of over $44 million:

Washington's Landing Associates I	$2,400,000
Washington's Landing Associates II	$2,900,000
Three Rivers Rowing Association	$1,500,000
Sports Technology Group	$3,288,000
Washington's Landing Marina	$3,000,000
600 Riverfront Drive	$2,600,000
800 Riverfront Drive	$2,900,000
Automated Healthcare	$4,590,000
The Village at Washington's Landing	$21,000,000
Total:	$44,178,000

124. URA, minutes of the meeting of December 9, 1993, resolution #562.

125. Tom Barnes, "Island Townhouses Next Year: Work to Start in the Fall," *Pittsburgh Post-Gazette,* July 15, 1994, B1; "Life on the Rivers: Murphy Uses Riverfront Housing to Attract New Residents," *Pittsburgh Post-Gazette,* July 18, 1994, B2; Joyce Gannon, "A Smooth Landing," *Pittsburgh Post-Gazette,* July 24, 1994, L1.

126. Donahoe, interview. In February 2007 the *Pittsburgh Business Times* reported that one 5,000 square-foot, double-unit, four-story townhouse with an elevator was on the market for $1.15 million. CEOs and Steelers football players owned nearby units. Ben Semmes, "For Panoramic View of the River, Try Looking from One of Four Decks," *Pittsburgh Business Times,* February 23–March 1, 2007, 26.

Chapter 2. Pittsburgh Technology Center

1. Lubove includes a brief history of the project, 52–55.

2. See Vagel Keller, "Anatomy of a Brownfield: A Retrospective Look at the Pittsburgh Technology Center's Infrastructure," unpublished paper, September 1, 1999, in possession of the author. A 1961 report on soil conditions, commissioned by J&L in preparation for constructing a proposed annealing facility and conducted by the firm of A.C. Ackenheil & Associates of Pittsburgh, recommended piles bearing on bedrock to carry the foundation due to large estimated settlements, shallow depth of the bedrock, and the fact that the level of the groundwater would make caissons difficult. A.C. Ackenheil & Associates, Inc., *Jones & Laughlin Steel Corporation, Pittsburgh Works Division, Pittsburgh, Pennsylvania, Step 1* (Pittsburgh, Pennsylvania, December 4, 1961), in URA Engineering & Construction Box 45.

3. Bob "Ike" Eisengart, former hot-mill electrical department foreman and galvanizing department master mechanic, in Mark Perrott, and John R. Lane, *Eliza: Remembering a Pittsburgh Steel Mill* (Charlottesville, Virginia: Howell Press, Inc., 1989), 39.

4. Historical information is drawn from Sanborn Map Company, *Pittsburgh, 1893,* Perrott and Lane, 102–3 (Mark Perrott's photographic essay of the abandoned Pittsburgh Works, with images taken between 1979 and 1983, the year in which the URA acquired the property from the Park Corporation); Joel A. Tarr, "The plume is gone. But we can't forget Hazelwood," *Pittsburgh Post-Gazette,* May 27, 1998, A-13; Keller, "Anatomy of a Brownfield"; Johnna Pro, "A sad day for steel workers," *Pittsburgh Post-Gazette,* June 22, 2004, B-1, 4.

5. Park had purchased its first Pittsburgh property, a vacant Wean United plant in Lawrenceville, in 1973. He liquidated the machinery, renovated and leased the buildings, and then sold the property. Park had taken on other Pittsburgh projects as well: liquidation of machinery from a Heppenstall plant in Pittsburgh and reuse of a rail car plant in Glassport that had sat vacant for three years.

6. URA, minutes of the meeting of August 25, 1983.

7. URA, minutes of the meeting of September 22, 1983. The URA's Jack Noonan remembered that Park was happy to sell the property. Their main interest was the profit to be made from the equipment and scrap; they did not have interest in developing the land. Initially, the Metaltech property was part of the sale, but then Park pulled it out. Jack remembered that at first relations with Park were "adversarial, till they found out Joe [Gariti] and I weren't so bad." Jack said he "had to push like heck to get the URA to do it. Jack Robin didn't want to do it." Of course, Mayor Caliguiri did. John L. Noonan, telephone interview with the author, March 7, 2007.

8. URA, minutes of the meeting of October 25, 1984. Since the city's grant was to come from bonds that were to be sold in the following year, the URA borrowed $1 million from Pittsburgh National Bank to finance that portion of the cost and, when the sale of the city's bonds was delayed, had to extend the term of its loan into 1985.

9. URA, minutes of the meetings of February 9 and July 12, 1984.

10. URA, minutes of the meeting of March 15, 1984, resolution #72.

11. URA, license agreements to contractors to enter onto the site to place fill, and letters to Dick Enterprises, April 26, 1984; Noralco Corporation and Repal Construction Company,

March 1985; Argo Construction, May 1985; S.J. Groves & Sons, June 26, 1985; and Arthur Lubetz, July 12, 1985.

12. Funding for the panel came from the Pittsburgh Foundation, the Pennsylvania Department of Community Affairs, the Westinghouse Corporate Foundation, and the URA. The chairman of the panel was Willard G. Rouse III, with other members representing private and public developers and a planning firm.

13. ULI Panel, press release, November 16, 1984, in URA Engineering & Construction Box 45.

14. Frank Brooks Robinson to Claude M. Ballard, November 20, 1984, and Ballard to Robinson, December 14, 1984, in URA Engineering & Construction Box 45.

15. Donald Horgan, interview with the author, Pittsburgh, Pennsylvania, September 10, 2004.

16. Horgan recalled

I learned a lot from Park in those jobs, because this was new for us, too. These are big, huge facilities. . . . When you had negative air we came up with something we called directional negative air, which means you moved all the negative air to [the] section you were working at, kind of sealed that off, and then moved it along, because you'd have to have a couple hundred negative air machines to do a facility that big plus seal everything up. So, like I said, I learned a lot from that; that was a learning experience for us. There were things we said had to be done that we later modified a bit. Most of the stuff we made up ourselves as we went along.

Horgan, interview.

17. URA, minutes of the meeting of March 2, 1985, resolution #63.

18. "Pittsburgh Technology Center Environmental Chronology," May 17 and June 5, 1985.

19. URA, *Urban Redevelopment Works in Pittsburgh,* Fall 1985. Carnegie Mellon wanted to build a home for its National Center for Robotics in Manufacturing. URA, task force agenda, September 9, 1985, in Engineering & Construction Box 45. By the end of the year the URA had revised its projection of expected tax revenues down to $1.2 million. URA, draft "Statement of Projected Public Benefits from the Pittsburgh Technology and Industry Park," December 19, 1985, in Engineering and Construction Box 45.

20. URA, minutes of the meeting of October 10, 1985, resolution #237.

21. September 3, 1985, Engineering & Construction Box 47.

22. The soil was segregated and hauled to an approved landfill. The water was treated with an oil separator and discharged into a storm sewer, while a licensed waste hauler removed the oil. "Proposal to Provide Pre-construction Environmental Assessment for PTC, CMU."

23. Agreement between the URA and RIDC, April 21, 1986.

24. URA, minutes of the meeting of May 8, 1986, resolutions #125 and 126.

25. URA, *Urban Redevelopment Works in Pittsburgh,* Spring 1986.

26. URA, minutes of the meeting of June 12, 1986.

27. John Coyne, memorandum to the files, July 11, 1986.

28. URA, minutes of the meetings of June 12, 1986, resolutions #183 and 184, and October 9, 1986, resolutions #357 and 358.

29. February 22, 1989. URA, Engineering & Construction Box 39. By the time they completed

their work, in 1989, Casciato had placed a total of 96,802 cubic yards of fill on the site.

30. Rich Gigler, "Transforming J & L site: High-tech facility to emerge," *Pittsburgh Press,* October 7, 1986; URA, minutes of the meeting of October 9, 1986.

31. URA, *Urban Redevelopment Works in Pittsburgh,* Winter 1987.

32. See Lubove's discussion, 43–49, of the important role of nonprofit organizations, and particularly Carnegie Mellon University and the University of Pittsburgh, in the region's strategy for economic diversification, and the context for their involvement in the Pittsburgh Technology Center:

CMU (along with Pitt) would exemplify the emergence of the entrepreneurial nonprofit entity in the realm of higher education. Responding to a perceived market for advanced technology and applied research, both universities aggressively pursued contract research opportunities from public and private sources. Their explosive entrepreneurship and its economic implications for Pittsburgh . . . helped the city make the transition from a manufacturing to a diversified service economy. (44)

Like Cyert, Posvar represented a new breed of university administrator—one who viewed higher education as a form of entrepreneurship, a provider of services to government, business, and the local community. (46)

33. URA, minutes of the meeting of May 14, 1987, resolution #154.

34. The URA had found no significant concentration of priority pollutants or "tentatively identified compounds" in the soil—no PCBs, only low concentrations of phenols, and cyanide and heavy metals that were bound tightly to oils, rendering them harmless. As for the groundwater, they had again found no PCBs; very low phenols, base-neutral compounds and metals below the standards for drinking water; and low levels of cyanide (0.56 ppm). URA, "Pittsburgh Tech. Center Environmental Chronology," January 1987.

35. Deborah Barman, memorandum, May 20, 1987.

36. Federal regulations obligated the URA to inform Casciato Brothers, the contractor that was constructing the sewer in the area of the suspected oil dump, of the potential of encountering unsafe environmental conditions and to take the necessary precautions. A meeting with the contractors resulted in the withdrawal of one subcontractor from the job and suspension of construction on the storm sewer pending completion of the environmental investigation. Project manager Deborah Barman expressed some frustration with this outcome in her memo to her associates: "Given that the area below the old mill has been determined to be free of environmental hazards as well as the fact that it is the waste from the old mill which was supposedly dumped in the area near the storm sewer construction, it is difficult to believe that the site of the former waste dump will contain hazardous materials." At the same time the study would delay completion of work on the storm sewer and the start of work on the next phase of site improvements by four to six weeks. ICF drew and analyzed samples in April and May to define the chemical characteristics of the various oils, sludge, and liquids that had accumulated on the site. They drilled core borings, installed monitoring wells, and took soil samples. Utilizing the existing stormwater system, they also assessed the quality of water that was draining from the various pits throughout the site. Finally, they looked for better information on former users and uses of the site. Deborah Barman, memorandum to Ray Christman, Jerilyn Donahoe, E. Stoddard, Joe Gariti, Jack Noonan, and Jerome Dettore, May 20, 1987, discussing in rather lengthy detail the "Phase II Environmental Analysis of PTC." (However, penciled in on the memo was a message, "never sent per Steve, 5/21/87.")

37. URA, "Pittsburgh Tech. Center Environmental Chronology," May 15, 1987, in URA, PTC Environ. General file.

38. Phase A would include monitoring the groundwater. If the tests proved negative, no additional testing would be warranted. In fact, based on the tests so far completed, the report concluded, "A purposeful and diligent effort by the RIDC/URA to identify environmental hazards at the site has indicated that none exist." Phase B would identify and determine the nature of the "material dump site" near the new western entrance, conduct further investigations of the cyanide cleaning tank on the former C.G. Hussey site, install groundwater monitoring wells at selected locations on the site, and correct any other problems found in phase A.

39. Information included in the attached (it was missing from the file) was "Report of Findings: Preliminary Environmental Assessment, Pittsburgh Technology Center," prepared by ICF/SRW. It included collection and analysis of fourteen samples taken at twelve locations throughout the site included in contract 2A. Tests for priority pollutants, priority pollutant metals, priority pollutant base neutral compounds, phenols, and PCBs identified only a limited amount of metals in the sludge at the manhole into which most of the facility located on the site of contract 2A drained. These sediments were not identified as a potential problem "unless an acid water was introduced into the sewer system." Former J&L employees whom Wilbur Smith interviewed included four engineers, a manager, and a security guard. Wilbur Smith was unable to gather any specific information pertaining to the cyanide cleaning tank identified on the site plan of C.G. Hussey's former facility. When contacted, Hussey's attorneys commented that there had been several changes of ownership since the operation closed. Based on limited comments, tests and the site plan, the consultants gave their opinion that "when the Hussey facility was shut down, the tanks were drained (drain lines were shown on the site plan) and then the structure was demolished down to the floor slab and that the site was then covered with slag for future use as a parking lot."

40. URA, minutes of the meeting of July 16, 1987, resolutions #270 and 271. Strategy 21 was the city's, county's and universities' joint request to the state for financial support of their most important, major economic development projects. See Lubove, 49–50, for a brief explanation.

41. *Pittsburgh Technology Center: Development Policies,* July 10, 1987.

42. Although the PAHs were in concentrations considerably above those recommended for drinking water, this did not seem problematic since groundwater was not used, nor was it planned to be used for drinking. "1987 Summary of Environmental Testing," in URA, PTC Env. General DER.

43. August 14, 1987. That fall the site preparation contractor uncovered additional oily water and sludge in concealed pits. These materials were segregated and stored on-site to allow site preparation to continue. URA, "Pittsburgh Technology Center Environmental Chronology," in PTC Environ. General file.

44. Brooks Robinson to Joseph Gariti, August 18, 1987.

45. URA, minutes of the meeting of August 20, 1987, resolution #310.

46. Compensation was projected to be $150,000. Contract between URA and Urban Design Associates, October 23, 1987.

47. Donahoe, interview.

48. April 5, 1988. Construction was to begin within a week. URA, Engineering and Construction Box 39.

49. URA, minutes of the meeting of July 17, 1988, resolutions #261–62.

50. URA, *Urban Redevelopment Works in Pittsburgh,* Summer 1988.

51. Evan Stoddard to Jack E. Freeman (Executive Vice President, University of Pittsburgh) and Frederick Rogers (Vice President for Business Affairs, Carnegie Mellon University), September 7, 1988.

52. Evan Stoddard to Jack Freeman and Fred Rogers, November 2, 1988.

53. Jack Freeman to Evan Stoddard, November 11, 1988.

54. David Matter to David Donahoe, November 10, 1988.

55. Evan Stoddard to Jack Freeman and Fred Rogers, November 23, 1988.

56. URA, minutes of the meeting of September 8, 1988, resolution #314.

57. URA, "Pittsburgh Technology Center," September 27, 1988, in PTC-DGS Environmental Gen file.

58. ICF/SRW reported October 31, according to their chronology. J. McCann to John Coyne and Jon Jackson to S. Knapik (Department of General Services), October 21 and November 1, 1988.

59. Jerry Dettore to Jack Freeman, November 15, 1988, in PTC-DGS environmental test file.

60. December 2, 1988, according to URA, "Pittsburgh Technology Center Environmental Chronology," in PTC Environ. General file. The URA's Jerry Dettore explained

> While Pitt recognizes that the testing already conducted by URA/RIDC indicates no significant environmental degradation, they desire additional testing to ease the concerns of financial institutions that will be involved in the financing of projects on the site. Because the Development Policies agreed to by all parties state that "the development ... of the university development zones is conditional upon ... assurances satisfactory to the universities that the development zones are free of environmental ... conditions which could impair their development and use," the URA offered the $10,000.00 for environmental work. Pitt has received a proposal from ICF/SRW Associates to place four monitoring wells and undertake testing of water and soil samples to further characterize the environmental status of their development zone. This service will cost approximately $27,000.00 and the proposed approach is to enter into a three party agreement (URA, Pitt, ICF/SRW) whereby the URA and Pitt will pay a proportional share with the URA's share not to exceed $10,000.

"Pittsburgh Technology Center," January 9, 1989, in PTC-DGS Environmental Gen file.

61. URA, minutes of the meeting of January 12, 1989, resolution #11.

62. Eisenman Architects, "Reshaping the Technological Landscape" (folder with enclosed plans and text), Pittsburgh: Oxford Development Company, January 26, 1989.

63. Donahoe, interview.

64. URA, *Urban Redevelopment Works in Pittsburgh,* Spring/Summer 1989

65. March 1989. URA, "Pittsburgh Technology Center Environmental Chronology," in PTC Environ. General file.

66. They found no volatile organic compounds, PCBs at detection limits, no priority pollutants, and low TPH levels in the soil. In the groundwater they found no organic compounds, heavy metals below the ambient water quality, and cyanide at 4.5 ppm (contrasted with the ambient water quality standard of 0.2 ppm). "Summary of Environmental Testing," June 13,

1989, in PTC Env. General DER.

67. URA, "Pittsburgh Technology Center," June 13, 1989, in PTC-DGS Environmental Gen file; W. Kosco to Ana Guzman, August 22, 1989, in PTC-DGS environmental test file. This letter was also forwarded on to URA for action.

68. "URA submits ICF Env. Report to DER," September 5, 1989, in PTC-DGS environmental test file.

69. In September or October. URA, "Pittsburgh Technology Center," in PTC-DGS Environmental Gen file.

70. October 20, 1989. URA, "Pittsburgh Technology Center"; Jerry Dettore to Gale Campbell, October 19, 1989, transmitting additional information requested by DER, and October 31, 1989, in Pittsburgh Technology Center–DGS Environmental Gen file.

71. Specifically, DER called for two additional soil borings for monitoring wells on parcel 4 to determine the extent of the cyanide problem; analysis of soil and groundwater taken from these two borings at 2-foot intervals for TPHs, total and free cyanide, and volatile organic compounds; similar analysis of groundwater taken from other wells; and collection and analysis of samples of the fill the URA had placed over the site for metals. Gale Campbell to Jerome Dettore, November 7, 1989, in PTC-DGS environmental test file. Kenneth Bowman, Assistant Regional Counsel, Department of Environmental Protection, described the prevailing mind set in the department as "'Just keep studying it and we'll get back to you. I'd rather postpone making decisions, and we'll get back to you.' The evolution of a thought process was developing in these early years." Interview with the author, August 19, 2003.

72. URA, minutes of the meeting of November 9, 1989, resolution #402.

73. December 21, 1989. URA, "Pittsburgh Technology Center" in PTC-DGS Environmental Gen file; and Civil and Environmental Consultants, "Summary of Environmental Testing, Parcels 3 & 4," December 20, 1989, submitted to DER the same date, in PTC Env. general DER file. See chapter 6 for a discussion of "safe" levels of contamination.

74. G. Campbell to Jerome Dettore, January 12, 1990, in PTC-DGS Environmental test file.

75. URA, minutes of the meeting of February 8, 1990, resolution #79.

76. URA, minutes of the meeting of March 8, 1990, resolution #92.

77. "University of Pittsburgh Center for Biotechnology and Bioengineering: Fact Sheet," March 1990.

78. Dettore noted that the DER had received and reviewed all the environmental studies and reports on the site, which had involved 19 borings, 138 soil samples, and 7 monitoring wells. While samples from parcels 3 and 4, to the west of Pitt's proposed development, had total cyanide exceeding 50 ppm, generally the level of cyanide contamination, even in those areas where it was highest, was less than 20 ppm, and there was little evidence of reactive cyanide (0.59 ppm) in the groundwater. On the western end of the site, near MetalTech, the consultant had found one concentration of VOCs. Jerome Dettore to Gale Campbell, April 9, 1990, including "Summary of Environmental Testing" and "Report of Findings, Contamination Assessment, Pittsburgh Technology Center." Concurrently, based on the findings of the investigation, Rob Pfaffman of Pitt's architectural firm wrote to General Services, outlining Civil & Environmental Consultants' proposal for environmental monitoring services during construction, at a cost of $24,650. Pfaffmann to S. Knapik, April 9, 1990, in PTC-DGS Environmental test file.

79. Years later Chuck Duritsa of DER observed

In fact, we deserve criticism for the length of time it took us to review projects, which we're like any other industry; we have more to do than we have staff to do it. That is one of the key things that changed under the action in '94–'95, which set a time line for our review, something that was needed. That was needed. I think the department deserved criticism for the amount of time it did take us to review the projects.

Duritsa, interview.

80. Evan Stoddard to Raymond Christman, May 18, 1990, in Pittsburgh Technology Center, PTC-DGS Environmental Gen file.

81. The relevant federal law was 40 CFR 261.3. James P. Nairn to George Whitmer, "Status of Cyanide Contamination, PTC," May 24, 1990.

82. On the basis of this and related experiences, Roy Lubove observed

How far can institutions dedicated to education and research pursue economic development objectives? How much capital can universities afford to risk? Pitt's and CMU's experience in marketing the Pittsburgh Technology Center suggests that the institutions were not overendowed with commercial knowhow. (49)

83. Aetna made annual loans of some $4 billion. Rachel Handel of Aetna Realty Investors, Inc., to Jon Pelusi of Carey, Kramer, Pelusi & Company, Inc. Further, Handel advised that statements such as "additional ground water and soil testing will be required, deed notices will be required for the environmental protection of past, present and future owners and insistence that ground water on the site not be used for any purpose" did not lead Aetna to believe the property could pass an environmental audit. Here, the officials at Aetna appear to have been following an observable pattern, though clearly that was not evident to the URA, or to Aetna at the time. Yount and Meyer observe that

uncertainty about environmental pollutants may well lead to an exaggerated estimation of the actual risks involved in brownfield investments and may arouse considerable anxiety. In efforts to reduce anxiety, people frequently avoid having to contend with the uncertainty by inflating the risk to the point that the risk-bearing activity is deemed unacceptable.

Kristen R. Yount and Peter B. Meyer, "Bankers, Developers, and New Investment in Brownfield Sites: Environmental Concerns and the Social Psychology of Risk," *Economic Development Quarterly* 9, no. 4 (November 1994): 340.

84. Campbell's letter also noted the following facts:

- The cyanide waste on the site had been covered with earth and is in the complex, nonreactive state; gas generation should not be a concern, but, in keeping with the consultant's recommendation, air should be monitored during the building's construction.
- An area of approximately 1,000 feet long by 300 feet wide, located 10 to 14 feet below existing grade on parcels 3 and 4, contains cyanide waste.
- Groundwater data is variable and difficult to interpret. Additional monitoring was necessary to further evaluate these variations.
- Volatile organic compounds, most notably chloroform and other chlorinated solvents, were located near Metaltech.

In response to the URA's statement that removal of waste material on parcels 3 and 4 was not a feasible option, since the cyanide-containing waste was dispersed over a large area at varying depth, the DER "does not believe that the impact on the ground water by these waste materials has been adequately demonstrated." The DER reiterated a previous worker safety requirement and required that waste materials excavated during foundation or footing construction be disposed of at an approved site. Further investigation at the MetalTech facility had to be performed and a remediation method proposed for the DER's approval. (The URA's consultant had already proposed and the DER had verbally approved additional investigations in this regard.) Gale Campbell to Jerome Dettore, August 8, 1990.

85. Remediation Technologies, Inc., "Preconstruction Environmental Assessment for a Proposed Building Site at the Pittsburgh Technology Center," ReTeC Project No. E30–739–400, prepared for Carnegie Mellon University, undated, c. December 1991.

86. Richard G. Luthy, "Evaluation of Contamination at the Pittsburgh Technology Center Site," Department of Civil Engineering, Carnegie Mellon University, undated, after April 1990.

87. Remediation Technologies, Inc., "Preconstruction Environmental Assessment."

88. "As it turns out," Chuck Duritsa of the DER later remembered, "the cyanide was not coming from the LTV operations on the site. It came from a previous operation, a coal gasification facility. And with hindsight if we had consulted the proper materials, historical materials such as the old insurance map, we could have picked up earlier exactly where the problem was coming from." Duritsa, interview.

89. The combined bids came in at $11.7 million. Ellen M. Perlmutter, "Bids Opened, Work May Start Next Month at Tech Center," *Pittsburgh Press,* August 17, 1990, B5.

90. Jon Schmitz and Mary Niederberger, "Troubled Pittsburgh Tech Center Gets Boosts from State, CMU," *Pittsburgh Press,* November 27, 1990, A1; "High-promise High-tech," *Pittsburgh Post-Gazette,* November 28, 1990, C2. In light of the environmental problems it had encountered on Pitt's site, the URA contracted with Civil and Environmental Consultants to perform the same kind of intensive tests east of Bates Street "to assure developers and financial institutions [of] the suitability of the site for development" (although, in fact, that site would not be developed for another ten years). URA, minutes of the meeting of January 16, 1991, resolution #13.

91. Ana Guzman to George Whitmer, August 20, 1990.

92. Referring to indemnification, a pledge of the state's full faith and credit, and abrogation of the state's police powers, he said, "In my opinion, if any of these are requirements for development, we can close the books on this project now." Instead, he offered the following possibilities:

- an agreement that the state would clean up the site, if necessary, by declaring it a priority site for the state Superfund program, and transfer of this commitment to future owners or occupants of the site;
- identification of the appropriate legal mechanism (e.g., memorandum of understanding or consent agreement) that would give the development community comfort as to the enforceability of this commitment;
- consideration of separating title for surface and subsurface property;
- creation of a dedicated fund (perhaps through tax increment financing) to provide partial funding (say, 10% to 20% of $20 million) for monitoring or cleanup;
- reconfiguration of the site plan to put public uses like parking lots and open spaces on polluted areas; and
- identification of areas where limited cleanup could be done immediately, thereby reducing the problem.

Raymond Christman to George Whitmer and Joseph Gariti, October 29, 1990.

93. Bill Zlatos, "Scientist at Helm: Mehrabian Surprised by CMU's $50 Million Debt," *Pittsburgh Press,* August 16, 1990, A1.

94. Karen Miller to George Whitmer, November 11, 1990.

95. Evan Stoddard, memorandum to George Whitmer and Joseph Sabino Mistick (executive secretary to Mayor Sophie Masloff), September 12, 1990.

96. Gerald M. McLaughlin (Oliver Realty/Grubb & Ellis), letter and request for proposals to Richard D. Irwin (National Development Company), September 25, 1990.

97. Richard Irwin to Gerald McLaughlin and Roger Edwards (Oliver Realty/Grubb & Ellis), October 26, 1990.

98. "It had always been our intention," Whitmer reasoned, "to transfer portions of the site to the universities at no cost, to serve as an incentive for development. Therefore the necessity of a land contribution to assist in the developer's financial package for Legent is an option we have previously considered for development of the site." George Whitmer to Gerald McLaughlin, November 2, 1990.

99. URA, "Legent Parking Proposal," October 23, 1990.

100. Jon Schmitz, "Bridge May Tie Oakland, South Side," *Pittsburgh Press,* October 18, 1990, B1.

101. Jerry Dettore to Gale Campbell, December 4, 1990.

102. Two wells were involved, 1 and 6, which exceeded the maximum cyanide standard of 0.2 ppm. Additionally, DER requested an explanation of the wide disparity of pH levels among the monitoring wells. Gale Campbell to Jerome Dettore, January 3, 1991.

103. In all, the Department of General Services awarded $11.6 million in contracts for Pitt's building, including $7.3 million to Tedco; $2.5 million to W.G. Tomko & Son of Pittsburgh for heating, ventilating, and air conditioning; $576,000 to Ruthrauff, Inc., of McKees Rocks for plumbing and fire protection; $1.2 million to Lighthouse Electric Company of Monroeville for electrical work; and $60,000 to Marshall Elevator Company of Pittsburgh for elevators. URA, *Urban Redevelopment Works in Pittsburgh,* Spring 1991.

104. This led CMU, in March, to reapply to the state through URA for the funds for its building. URA, minutes of the board meeting of March 14, 1991, resolutions #83–84. In May CMU reviewed a proposal from RETEC, also submitted to the DER, to provide a preconstruction environmental assessment for their specific building site "to gain information on subsurface conditions and to perform an assessment of potential human health risks during and after proposed construction."

105. Chriss Swaney, "Northeast Notebook: First Glimpse of Tech Center," The *New York Times,* July 28, 1991. The article mistakenly described the cyanide as "residue from the steel mill's plate-bathing process." It reported the URA's original (1983) estimate that the Center would generate $260 million in private investment, 11,000 new jobs, and $3 million in annual tax revenues for the city; but it also noted that Carnegie Mellon had scaled back its plans for the Center from two buildings to one, whose construction "was also delayed by the cyanide discovery, as well as a change in design and an inability to attract tenants."

106. License agreement between URA and RETEC for sampling, August 14, 1991, in PTC General Correspondence file; and Stephen A. Schillo (CMU) to D. Morgan (RETEC), August 26,

1991, in PTC General Correspondence file. Schillo confirmed CMU's acceptance of RETEC's revised scope of work, which was submitted by RETEC on August 12. This is an addendum to the work described in the proposal (PEN-985) of May, 1991 and in the May 31 letter to A. Middelton.

107. Items located in "Papers Introduced in Council and Referred to the Committee on Finance," items 3147 and 3148, October 2, 1991.

108. The memorandum also provided that the universities would negotiate with the taxing bodies regarding payments for public services (URA, minutes of the meeting of September 12, 1991, resolution #343). George Whitmer formally notified Brooks Robinson of the change of approach in a letter dated October 30.

109. George Whitmer to Brooks Robinson, February 6, 1992, terminating the Site Plan and Final Land Development agreement between the URA and RIDC, dated October 23, 1987, which also served as the basis for RIDC's agreement with UDA (Urban Design Associates) Architects to perform all the planning and site development on the URA's behalf. Under it, the RIDC had let and managed all planning and site improvement contracts related to the Center. At this point, however, the only remaining contract that RIDC had open for the Center was the master planning contract with UDA Architects, for master planning. Since only $17,897 of the original amount of $300,000 remained in the contract, and since the URA had effectively managed the relationship with Urban Design Associates for some time, Whitmer proposed that the URA assume the remainder of that contract, and it took the formal step of sending a letter to terminate the agreement early in 1992.

110. His concern was warranted, for, concurrently, the DER wrote to question the details of RETEC's sampling, monitoring, and risk assessment procedures, even while RETEC's regular sampling of soil, soil gas, and groundwater from the contaminated area west of Pitt's building site continued to show no change in the levels of cyanide or other contaminants. See Gale Campbell to George Whitmer, October 22, 1991, and D. Morgan (RETEC) to O. Mayer (DER), November 13, 1991, in PTC General Correspondence file; and D. Morgan to O. Mayer, December 19, 1991, in CMU environmental testing file.

111. The Department of General Services had committed $14 million for the University of Pittsburgh Center for Biotechnology and Bioengineering. Through the city's Strategy 21 program, the Department of Community Affairs had pledged approximately $25.3 million: $17 million toward the construction of the CMU Research Institute and $8.3 million toward site preparation and improvement activities. The Department of Commerce had granted $10 million for site preparation and marketing activities. The city's funds came from a general revenue bond for marketing, management, and open space construction for the site. The foundations contributed toward planning and design activities.

112. Evan Stoddard, internal memorandum to the Pittsburgh Technology Center file, March 17, 1992.

113. George Whitmer, memorandum to Dana Michael, March 18, 1992, transmitting news from Dave Chittester, Pennsylvania Department of Community Affairs. The URA submitted a revised application to Community Affairs for the funds in May, as construction on Pitt's building reached 80% completion and full enclosure. Unidentified notes, May 4, 1992; and Evan Stoddard to David Chittester (Chief, Community Development Division, Department of Community Affairs), May 8, 1992, with a revised application form for funds in the amount of $16,107,144, and showing a private match of $17,002,195, which was the original amount committed in the grant to RIDC. The audit CMU and RIDC would conduct of the grant to RIDC would

document not only the expenditure of $895,051 of state funds but also the expenditure of private funds as well.

114. Raymond Gindroz (UDA Architects) to George Whitmer, April 1, 1992; Brooks Robinson to Evan Stoddard, April 14 and 22, 1992; and Evan Stoddard, memorandum to Joseph Gariti, requesting preparation of a contract with UDA Architects for an amount not to exceed $6,000 for the preliminary design of a third building at PTC, July 21, 1992.

115. Gale Campbell to Jerome Dettore, April 3, 1992.

116. Ken Bowman explained

So you need some kind of understanding, at least in that early 90's period, to resolve the legal liability for the fact that you, as a landowner, have ground contamination. And so a binding document was the tool that was used at the time to analyze that, come to conclusions, and develop a control system, if you like, that dealt with your Clean Streams liability. And the vehicle chosen was a C.O. and A. [consent order and agreement] with the department.

Basically, your control strategy was, don't use the ground water for drinking water purposes. I think the department was satisfied that whatever releases were going into the river were *de minimus*, and not causing a problem. And that was the vehicle we were using at the time, under the ground water strategy, to work out the responsibilities of a property owner. Whether he caused the problem or not, you have the liability. That's a form of warranty or covenant not to sue which is now embodied in Act 2. You're starting to see the evolution of how to give some kind of warranty, if you like, or covenant not to sue, from our standpoint, now embodied by statute, and then, when can that warranty or covenant be retracted?

Kenneth Bowman, interview with the author, August 19, 2003.

117. *Pittsburgh Post-Gazette,* April 13, 1992.

118. Joyce Gannon, "Family Owned Firm Leaving City for O'Hara," *Pittsburgh Post-Gazette,* April 8, 1993, B-14.

119. URA, minutes of the meetings of October 8, resolution #434, and December 10, 1992, resolution #545, amended by resolutions #61–63, adopted at the meeting of February 11, 1993.

120. See Lubove, 19, regarding the attempt to save the Swissvale plant.

121. Joyce Gannon, "Union Switch Finds High-Tech Home," *Pittsburgh Post-Gazette,* March 7, 1993, B-16.

122. "High on 'Tech' the Pittsburgh Technology Center Lands a Private Business," *Pittsburgh Post-Gazette,* March 6, 1993, B-2.

123. Donald Miller, "Building the Future on the Past Pitt's Biotech Center, Built on the Site of the Former J&L Mills on Second Avenue, Is Just the Beginning of a New Era for This Post-Industrial City," *Pittsburgh Post-Gazette,* March 2, 1993, D-1.

124. "News Digest," *Pittsburgh Post-Gazette,* June 11, 1993, B-4.

125. "Chairman Robin and former Executive Director Brophy took the idea to the State and testified before a committee of the State legislature and the State offered the Authority $1 million at the time." URA, minutes of the meeting of March 11, 1993, resolutions #78–84.

126. URA, minutes of the meeting of May 13, 1993, resolution #187.

127. URA, minutes of the meeting of June 10, 1993, resolutions #244–46.

128. URA, minutes of the meeting of July 8, 1993, resolution #306.

129. URA, minutes of the meeting of July 8, 1993, resolutions #304–5.

130. Joseph Chnupa, former Assistant Regional Director, Southwest Regional Office, Pennsylvania Department of Environmental Protection, observed that the provision in the agreement to "ensure that waste materials will not be disturbed and ground water will not be used" illustrates DER's beginning to address "pathway elimination, elimination of the pathway of exposure, which is now part of standard operating procedure." Interview with the author, August 19, 2003.

131. "I didn't negotiate the agreement," Ken Bowman remembered, "but I'm sure you'd ask for something like that because you wanted to know that these other parcels were done, and I think that was part of the chemistry of the negotiations, because you needed to know that." Bowman, interview. The department lifted restrictions on development two years later, after seven quarterly monitoring reports revealed no problems. "In the meantime," the *Pittsburgh Post-Gazette* editorialized, "momentum for development was lost. . . . The fact that development may now take place is due in large part to the decision by the Ridge administration to allow the city to move forward once it was clear that no harm was posed." The editorial concluded by saying, "If the governor's actions toward the technology center are any indication of the stance his administration will take in managing the delicate relationship between state regulations and economic development, we can all be encouraged about the future." "A Ban Lifted: The State Gives a Green Light for the Technology Center," *Pittsburgh Post-Gazette*, October 14, 1995.

132. Evan Stoddard to Michael Weber (Provost and Academic Vice President, Duquesne University), September 16, 1993. The letter included a copy of the state capital budget of 1988 (Act 1988–113), including the $20 million line item for "Monongahela Valley redevelopment projects," and a copy of H. B. 1261 of 1993, which governed the use of these funds. URA was already the intended applicant for the Warhol Museum, the Cultural District, and the Library Center.

133. The plan provided for repayment of what was actually $5.5 million in tax increment revenue bonds over twenty years, in 2013, but in fact sufficient revenues had accumulated by September 2001 to retire the bonds early, meaning that thereafter the city, county, and school board would begin to benefit financially from the new development. Gregor McGavin, "URA to Pay Off Bond for Technology Center Early," *Pittsburgh Tribune-Review,* September 14, 2001.

134. URA, minutes of the meeting of August 12, 1993, resolutions #356–60.

135. Jim McKay, "Union Switch Showing Strength," *Pittsburgh Post-Gazette,* September 24, 1993, B.

136. Councilman Gene Ricciardi commented, "It seems much, much too low when you consider the value and location of that land." Tom Barnes, "Pitt, CMU Tech Center fees called too low," *Pittsburgh Post-Gazette,* October 7, 1993, B-4.

137. Robert Mehrabian, "The Technology Center got a slow start, but it's on its way," *Pittsburgh Post-Gazette,* November 19, 1993, C-2.

138. Ron DaParma, "Slow Going, But Technology Park Taking Shape," *Pittsburgh Post-Gazette,* July 17, 1994.

139. DaParma, "Slow going."

140. DaParma, "Slow going."

141. Ron DaParma, "Identity Crisis Over, Researchers Reassembled," *Pittsburgh Post-Gazette*, April 9, 1995. The original neoclassical Mellon Institute building on Fifth Avenue in Oakland had grown increasingly inadequate for the research units that occupied it, and as departments at the university had grown and competed for space in the building, the institute's research units had scattered or grown up at various locations on campus or had been housed in rented space in Oakland. The Institute's administrative headquarters were located in rented space across Fifth Avenue from the original building.

142. Paul Furiega, "A New Address Brings a New Mission," *Pittsburgh Business Times*, September 18–24, 1995.

143. Ron DaParma, "Consortium to Be Housed at Center," *Pittsburgh Post-Gazette*, May 19, 1995.

144. Kris, B. Mamula, "URA Targets Drug Market," *Pittsburgh Tribune-Review*, June 8, 1995.

145. Scott Stephens, "Pittsburgh's Renaissance Holds Lesson for Cleveland," *The Plain Dealer*, November 23, 2008, accessed June 13, 2011, http://blog.cleveland.com/plaindealer/2008/11/pittsburghs_renaissance_holds.html.

Chapter 3. Rise and Fall of Steel

1. One excellent history is John P. Hoerr's *And the Wolf Finally Came: The Decline of the American Steel Industry*, Pittsburgh: University of Pittsburgh Press, 1988.

2. Joseph Frazier Wall, *Andrew Carnegie*, Pittsburgh: University of Pittsburgh Press, 1989, 474–76, 486–88.

3. Joel Tarr et al., *Brownfields Revitalization Systems Project: A Study of Stakeholder Roles in Development Decision Making*, Pittsburgh: H. John Heinz III School of Public Policy and Management, Carnegie Mellon University, May 12, 2000, 11.

4. Jim McKay, "Homestead Works Sold to Park," The *Pittsburgh Post-Gazette*, April 1, 1988.

5. Historical and geographical information is drawn from *United States Steel Duquesne Plant: National-Duquesne Works* and *United States Steel National Plant: National-Duquesne Works*, Pittsburgh: United States Steel Corporation. n.d., and from Regional Industrial Development Corporation.

6. Wall, *Andrew Carnegie*, 497–99.

7. Brownfields Center, Carnegie Mellon University, "Chapter IV: Brownfield Redevelopment in the Mon Valley: A Comprehensive Outlook for Three Sites," undated photocopy, c. 1997–2000, 41–42.

8. City of Duquesne, "Duquesne's Silver Jubilee" (September 10–16, 1916). Belying the rhetoric, "a house-to-house survey conducted by 22 WPA field workers" in 1941 "built a gloomy statistical picture of Duquesne housing conditions … showing 2,211, or better than 50 per cent of all houses in Duquesne, were substandard. Only 207 of these 2,211 had bathtubs. Half of [those without bathtubs] had no toilets as well." Charles B. Holstein, "City 50 Per Cent Slums despite Defense Prosperity, Experts Disclose," *Pittsburgh Post-Gazette*, November 1, 1941.

9. The seamless mill produced pipes ranging in size from 4½ inches to 24 inches. The submerged arc weld mill, which was built to meet the demands for large-diameter pipe, produced 24-inch to 36-inch pipe in 41-foot lengths. The electric resistance weld mill produced pipe of

longer length, thinner walls and greater strength.

10. Only the Number 1 blast furnace remained in operation in McKeesport, producing ferro-manganese steel.

11. Change in Municipal Population, 1930–1990

	1930	1940	1950	1960	1970	1980	1990
Homestead	20,141	19,041	10,046	7,502	6,309	5,092	4,179
Munhall	12,995	13,900	16,437		16,674	14,532	13,158
W. Homestead							2,495
Whitaker					1,697	1,615	1,416
Total							21,248
Duquesne	21,396	20,693	17,620		11,410	10,094	8,525
McKeesport	54,632	55,355	51,502		37,977	31,012	26,016

Mike Dawida, who served both as a state representative and a senator from the Mon Valley, and later as a county commissioner, observed

A lot of these communities had begun to fail even before the steel mills left. Braddock, for example, is considered one of the worst communities in Allegheny County and still a failed community in many ways, and the mill still operates there. But the mill operates with a technological expertise that requires one-tenth of the people that it did twenty years ago. So fewer people, the people working there live in other places, because they have the mobility and the money to live elsewhere, and so the communities around them died before the mill left. So you had this mixture of older people who had worked in the mills, thinking it would come back; they couldn't comprehend that even if the mills came back the communities were in a failure to begin with.

Michael Dawida, interview with the Brownfields Revitalization Systems Project, Carnegie Mellon University, January 13, 2000.

12. ICF Kaiser Engineers, Inc., "Executive Summary," in "Groundwater Quality Assessment Summary Report, Industrial Center of McKeesport, McKeesport, PA," August 1993, prepared for RIDC Southwestern Pennsylvania Growth Fund. At its peak the Duquesne plant had employed 3,200 workers. When it closed in May 1984 about 1,200 were working there.

13. Melvyn Achtzehn, interview with the author, Duquesne, Pennsylvania, June 22, 2005.

14. Louis Washowich, interview with the author, Duquesne, Pennsylvania, June 22, 2005.

15. Washowich, interview.

The loss of steel and manufacturing in this area was apocalyptic, incredible, the loss of business, the volume of business, the tonnage, every scale, wages and taxes and fees and spinoffs, an incredible loss, and nobody outside of Pittsburgh even knows about it. And I think over the years people just kind of got tired of the Mon Valley. It's not been a high priority.

Charles Starrett (Duquesne-McKeesport-Clairton Enterprise Zone Coordinator, McKeesport Redevelopment Authority and member, Duquesne-McKeesport Policy Committee), interview with the Brownfields Systems Group, Carnegie Mellon University, January 10, 2000.

16. Tom Foerster, interview with the author, March 13, 1997.

17. Jim McKay, "Factory Fixers? Regional Authority Needs a Victory in Fight to Salvage Jobs," *Pittsburgh Post-Gazette,* April 12, 1988. See Lubove, 18–23 and 165–66, for a history of the beginnings of the Tri-State Conference on Steel and the Steel Valley Authority.

18. See Lubove, 19, for additional context. Mel Achtzehn remembered
We had a number of people who had worked in the plant, thought that they could reevaluate, rejuvenate some of the departments. The blast furnace was one, Dorothy. They felt that they could operate Dorothy furnace much easier and much better than U.S. Steel did. Well, I can remember sitting at the table at city hall, council chambers, and this group of people there asking our help to get this portion to operate again. And in the course of the discussion I asked them their feelings about how they were going to operate this particular furnace. They said they could operate it with 50% less men. And my question to them was, why didn't you do that earlier? Why didn't you go to U.S. Steel and say that we can do this? You would have probably still been working because if they would have been able to do it with 300 men as opposed to 600 men that the unions demanded that they had, look at the cost factor. That was one of the big items that caused U.S. Steel to close the plant down, and I said, why didn't you bring that up earlier? Well, we felt that jobs were a big, important thing for them, and they had to featherbed. They had to make sure there was enough work there for the different people that they were looking forward to putting on.
Achtzehn, interview.

19. Don Hopey. "Duquesne Marches in Step to Efforts to Save Steel Industry," *Pittsburgh Press,* May 19, 1985.

20. Washowich, interview.

21. Foerster, interview.

22. Virginia Linn, "Firms Want to Set Up Operations at Former USX Corp. Sites," *Pittsburgh Post-Gazette,* June 2, 1988, 13–14. Mike Bilcsik, a steelworker and community organizer who represented the dissenting viewpoint, that all efforts should be focused on reopening the mill, said
It was my travel trailer, matter of fact, that sat across from the mill gate to make sure they weren't cannibalizing the plant. Elected leadership in Duquesne was against what we were doing. We wanted to keep the plant open. Duquesne's the only company town, the only town I know that's a company town after the company's gone. And it's amazing. As a matter of fact, when we went head to head with Duquesne the respect was there between U.S. Steel and myself—and I only speak for myself—the respect was there between each other. I mean we had different points of view, but we did respect each other. It wasn't between Duquesne, I mean elected officials of Duquesne called me Communist, called a lot of people Communist, I mean really baited us. The mayor of Duquesne said they had five companies, five major manufacturers [his tone was incredulous], that wanted to move into Duquesne as soon as we left [pause for effect]—2,000 jobs. It was all in the newspapers.
Michael Bilcsik, interview with the Brownfields Systems Group, Carnegie Mellon University, January 21, 2000.

23. Carlino spoke for those who saw that the mills would not reopen and wanted to move forward:

And quite honestly we helped in that sometimes, because as we were coming up with plans for trails and riverfront reuse of those mill sites and maybe some historical interpretation there, and that would meet resistance, we would find people in the community, as we always would, to work with, but they were impeded as much as we were by them. What it did was it created in some of these communities a drive for people to sort of get the old dead weight out of there. And that happened in Duquesne, it happened in Homestead, it happened in Munhall, in their public offices, be it borough council or the mayors. So I was really frustrated with the local governments and I would say at the outset, when they were in their old mode of thinking, I couldn't even read them. Everything that you read and hear about the stereotypical Pittsburgher, Mon Valley, old way of thinking, "we can't do that here because it's never been done before," it was all there, like that. But then there was a younger generation, people, say, in their fifties, young fifties and younger, who started to see a need to rethink that. And those were the people that got involved either at a local government level, or started to get involved with some of these local non-profits, either creating them or infusing their board with new people, as volunteers or board members, and so that's why the satisfaction level changed over the course of time.

August Carlino, Steel Industry Heritage Task Force, interview with the Brownfields Systems Group, Carnegie Mellon University, January 21, 2000.

24. Carlino, interview.

25. Jim McKay, "'It Was like Watching a Friend Die,'" *Pittsburgh Post-Gazette*, August 2, 1988.

26. Achtzehn, interview with the author.

27. "'Steel Valley' Veterans Help Preserve History," *Pittsburgh Tribune-Review*, July 17, 1994.

28. Virginia Linn, "Mon Valley Officials Urge Brock to Help End Steel Dispute," *Pittsburgh Post-Gazette*, October 9, 1986.

29. McKay, "Factory Fixers?"

30. Lou Washowich remembered the hopes for the dog track:
I loaded sixteen buses out of McKeesport. I put people on buses who probably hadn't been on a bus for thirty years, old-timers that loafed in downtown McKeesport. I took them to Harrisburg. We tried to lobby them. The study that was done—it was done out of some company in Texas that does these kinds of studies—it was paid for by Allegheny County. They said that if there was a dog track put on the National Tube site—which would only have been part of it—it would have been the most profitable dog track in the country. And what we were looking at in terms of the dollars that they said would be coming out of that to pump into the development of—other communities also. There would have been a $10 million economic development fund coming out of that, that we could have put, to help other communities in this valley if we could have ever got the legislation passed that we were never able to do.

Washowich, interview.

31. Carol Waterloo and Karen Popp, "Grants Boost Revitalization Efforts," *Daily News*, October 24, 1986; Ron Gruendl, "Mon Valley Group Airs Concepts," *Daily News*, January 1987.

32. Mark Patrick, interview with the author, July 1, 2003.

33. Ron DaParma, "Group Sees Progress in Steel-Plant Talks," *Pittsburgh Tribune-Review*, March 9, 1991.

34. Virginia Linn, "Vandals Endanger Legacy of Steel Mills" and "Man, 25, Is Killed at Old Mill," *Pittsburgh Post-Gazette,* April 23, 1987, 1ff.

35. Linda S. Wilson, "Steel Mill Towns Told to Consolidate Services," *Pittsburgh Post-Gazette,* June 5, 1987.

Mayor Mel Achtzehn of Duquesne observed

We were a one-horse town, and the horse died, and the wagon was not being pulled any more. We lost one-third of our budget when the mill site came down, between the taxes and between the water rents, and things like that, we lost a million dollars in revenues. Now a small town like Duquesne, when you take one-third of your budget and you lose it, you've got some big, big problems.

When I took the office of mayor [in 1990] I had an eight-man police department, and we had 23 men at one time. Trying to work seven days, three turns every day, with eight men to schedule is tough. And there were days that the only officer we have on duty was the chief. And, of course, sitting and talking with the men, asking for their help and assistance if we needed help we could call on them at any time, and they would be there to help us.... But that devastation of losing one-third of our budget, and trying to maintain the municipality, and meanwhile working from the Duquesne Business Advisory Corporation. I was mayor. I was also president of this organization. We're trying to rehab the houses, we have small business loans, rehab for resale, we had a home equity conversion program going, trying to maintain this side of the site to have proper housing, working with the school district, trying to maintain a decent school district. It was—I lost a lot of hair and I lost my teeth over it.... We knew something was happening and when it hit, it hit so hard at that particular time that we didn't know whether we were going to survive or not.

Achtzehn, interview.

Mayor Lou Washowich of McKeesport gave the following account:

Sitting as an elected official and trying to move a city forward, I went out and hired some people I thought would be aggressive and help us, ... We were stuck financially. I brought some graduate students in from GSPIA in Pittsburgh, finance director, administrators, I mean these were kids right out of college. I couldn't afford to pay people. I brought them in.... I had sense enough to know that if I put good people around me then I'm going to keep the city functioning. And fortunately, if you look at the entire valley, McKeesport was the only community that didn't go Act 47. The Duquesnes, the Homesteads, the Braddocks, the Rankins, they all went Act 47. We hung in there.

I went in. Getting away from the steel mills, when I became mayor we had 300 employees. I went through a childhood raised by grandparents that my grandfather worked in a place that became the Kelsey-Hays site over in Liberty Borough on the Yough River. He spent 39 years there, and when they closed the door he got this [zero]. He was 68 or 69 years old. So I was always a strong believer in the unions. I was always sympathetic to the workers. And when I became mayor I [saw] the position that I was being placed in. I had to make some very difficult decisions, but I said at the time, I will not lay these people off. We offered some incentives, through attrition, and it took me I guess in about five years I reduced the work force from 300 down to 150. We had a police force when I became mayor, a big fire department that was literally killing the community. We were never able to do what I wanted to do with the fire department, but the police department I finally got them to a point where we had maybe 35 full-time police officers, then I hired part-timers. And I could hire three part-timers for the price of one full-timer. And what I was looking at, and the obligation I had, was to put the uniformed man out on the street. So that part of it really worked out for us. And those were just some of the things that we tried to do.

Washowich, interview.

36. Dennis Pittman (former Community Development Director, City of McKeesport, and member, Duquesne-McKeesport Policy Committee), interview with the Brownfields Systems Group, Carnegie Mellon University, January 11, 2000.

Chapter 4. Sandcastle and the Waterfront

1. Mary Kane, "Steel Valley Panel Facing Rough Road in Plant Takeover," *Pittsburgh Press*, December 13, 1987.

2. Don Hopey, "Historic Homestead 'Big Shop' in line for comeback," *Pittsburgh Press*, March 1, 1987.

3. Bernie Kohn, "'Liquidator' Park Takes Pride in Its Developments," *Pittsburgh Press*, November 22, 1987.

4. Kohn, "'Liquidator' Park."

5. Kane, "Steel Valley Panel."

6. Mary Kane, "Mill Deal Delay Rebuffed," *Pittsburgh Press*, December 9, 1987.

7. Kane, "Steel Valley Panel."

8. Jan Margo, "Eminent Domain Urged for USX Homestead Land," *Daily News*, December 11, 1987.

9. Kane, "Steel Valley Panel."

10. Kane, "Steel Valley Panel."

11. "Spinning Straw into Steel," *Pittsburgh Press*, December 13, 1987.

12. Peter P. Scolleri, "Romanelli Backs Plant Closing," *Pittsburgh Tribune-Review*, January 23, 1988.

13. Mary Kane, "Firm Seeks Local Support for Redevelopment of Homestead Works," *Pittsburgh Press*, January 24, 1988.

14. Allegheny County Department of Development, "Mon Valley Draws International Attention as Subject of the Remaking Cities Conference," *Development*, vol. VI, no. 4 (Winter 1988): 1–2.

15. Barbara Davis, editor. *Proceedings of the 1988 International Conference in Pittsburgh: Remaking Cities* (Pittsburgh: Pittsburgh Chapter of the American Institute of Architects, distributed by University of Pittsburgh Press, 1989), 51.

16. This was Commissioner Tom Foerster's feeling, at least. Foerster, interview.

17. David Lewis remembered, "The conference was an enormous success. After it was all over I had a sinking feeling that nothing would happen." David Lewis, interview with the Brownfields Systems Group, Carnegie Mellon University, January 24, 2000.

18. For a history of the Mon Valley Initiative, see Lubove, 159–73.

19. Linda S. Wilson, "West Homestead Wants Mill Sites Cleaned," *Pittsburgh Post-Gazette*, March 10, 1988, 1, 5.

20. Ron DaParma, "USX Sells Homestead Works to Cleveland Firm," *Pittsburgh Tribune-Review*, April 1, 1988.

21. Jim McKay, "Homestead Works Sold to Park," *Pittsburgh Post-Gazette*, April 1, 1988.

22. Continuing, DeBolt remembered

Even the *Post-Gazette* had an editorial cartoon, because one of the things we were proposing was an interim use of that site as a garden festival, you'd plant flowers down there between [then] and the time you'd demolish the mill. So the mind set in the community is, that's a mill. And the first folks to suggest that that be something other than a mill get creamed, get hammered, people talking in bars, in the newspapers, TV, everything else. You see one steel worker talking to another, "They want us to plant roses." So, if you were talking about anything other than a mill here, you were almost ostracized. But some of us took on that, said, "Doggone it, let's get the planning done. Let's look ahead."

George DeBolt, interview with the Brownfields Systems Group, Carnegie Mellon University, January 11, 2000.

23. Ron DaParma, "Park's Plan for Homestead: Demolish Old Steel Facilities," *Pittsburgh Tribune-Review*, April 3, 1988, C1–2.

24. "Scrapping Historic Homestead," *Pittsburgh Post-Gazette*, April 6, 1988.

25. Ron DaParma, "Park's Plan for Homestead: Demolish Old Steel facilities," *Pittsburgh Tribune-Review*, April 3, 1988, C1–2. Lubove, 249–54, explains much more about the context of the formation of the Steel Industry Heritage Task Force and project.

26. Ed Blazina, "Roddey Plans Sports Center for Closed Mill in Homestead," *Pittsburgh Press*, April 13, 1988.

27. Blazina, "Roddey Plans Sports Center"; Virginia Linn, "Olympians to Test Mettle on Mill Site?" *Pittsburgh Post-Gazette*, April 14, 1988.

28. "More Steel-Site Disputing," *Pittsburgh Press*, April 17, 1988.

29. Mary Kane and Ed Blazina, "Developer to Study Restarting Homestead Works Shop," *Pittsburgh Press*, April 29, 1988; Ron DaParma, "Big Plans in Works for Idle 'Big Shop,'" *Pittsburgh Tribune-Review*, April 30, 1988, A1, 4.

30. Linda S. Wilson, "Retired USX Plant Workers Seen as Key," *Pittsburgh Post-Gazette*, June 3, 1988.

31. "Shop Reviewed," *Pittsburgh Business Times*, July 8, 1988.

32. Linda S. Wilson, "Ex-Steel Workers Would Return to Homestead Shop," *Pittsburgh Post-Gazette*, July 28, 1988; Reverend Pierre Whalon, letter to the editor, "The Good News," *Pittsburgh Post-Gazette*, August 18, 1988; Pamela Gaynor, "Park Studies Homestead Works Uses," *Pittsburgh Post-Gazette*, c. 1989, A-25.

33. Linda S. Wilson, "End Near for First 2 Mon Blast Furnaces," *Pittsburgh Post-Gazette*, July 28, 1988.

David Lewis remembered

I began, in 1987. At that time all the mill buildings were standing, and the first step, of course, was to try to reuse the mill buildings. But the Park Corporation that had bought the mill buildings from USX had—was forced by USX—to sign a covenant that they would not be reused for steel making, which cut us out completely from reusing what the buildings were actually designed for. It soon became clear that we couldn't reuse the buildings. I mean we tried everything you can imagine: hydroponics and growing food, to entertainment complexes, ice skating rinks and things like that, but of course the costs were enormous. It wasn't just simply the structure, but there were enormous costs and not only that, but it became clear that the soil was all polluted and all the remedial work had to be done before any recycled use could take place. And meanwhile, . . . their taxi meter was running, they had to pay their mortgages and all the rest of it, so they were anxious to get some type of return on their expenditures. So they began to pull the buildings down and recycle them for scrap.

Lewis, interview.

34. Linda S. Wilson, "Ex-Steel Workers Would Return to Homestead Shop," *Pittsburgh Post-Gazette,* July 28, 1988; Linda S. Wilson, "Historic Ruins on the Mon," *Pittsburgh Post-Gazette,* August 2, 1988.

35. Linda S. Wilson, "Mill Site May Have Edge as Museum," *Pittsburgh Post-Gazette,* August 4, 1988, A1, 3.

36. Linda S. Wilson, "U.S. Funds Sought for Mill Conversion Plan," *Pittsburgh Post-Gazette,* August 18, 1988.

37. Ron DaParma, "Park at Work on Homestead Works," *Pittsburgh Tribune-Review,* October 16, 1988.

38. Linda S. Wilson, "End Near for First 2 Mon Blast Furnaces," *Pittsburgh Post-Gazette,* July 28, 1988; DaParma, "Park at Work."

39. Patricia Lowry, "Sandcastle Hopes to Bolster Numbers with New Attractions," *Pittsburgh Press,* July 20, 1990, D1.

40. Gaynor, "Park Studies Homestead Works Uses."

41. Jack Bell, Chief Engineer, Park Corporation, telephone interview with the author, January 9, 2003.

Don Horgan of the Allegheny County Health Department recalled
I worked in those mills. I worked in the 160-inch mill. That was the last facility they kind of knocked down, because even then the government wanted that to stay open because they made military plating there. As they were knocking everything else down, that particular building stayed there because even to the end they were hoping that somehow they could get it activated again. The Navy and the Air Force wanted it because they were making this armored plating there, and it was one of the few places in the United States that still made it. That was one of the facilities I worked at.

Donald Horgan, interview with the author, Pittsburgh, PA, September 10, 2004.

42. Donald Dombrosky, "Area's Vacant Steel Mills Transforming into Productive Job Sites," *Allegheny Business News* 4, no. 11 (November 1989): 16.

43. Bell, interview.

44. Barbara White Stack, "State Aids Mills' Reuse," *Pittsburgh Post-Gazette,* February 2, 1990, A1, 6; "Mon Valley Momentum," *Pittsburgh Post-Gazette,* February 5, 1990; "Summary of State Grant to Mon Valley Sites," February 16, 1990, Casey file, Allegheny County Department

of Development.

45. Christine Vorce, *Pittsburgh Post-Gazette,* June 24, 1990, A20. No article title given.

46. "Plan to Save Rolling Mill for Museum Bogs Down in Sheer Enormity of Task," *Pittsburgh Post-Gazette,* June 7, 1990. In March of 1991 the Steel Industry Heritage Task Force, joined by representatives of the National Park Service, honored the group of firms and individuals who had helped to preserve the 48-inch rolling mill and the steam engine that powered it. Now in storage at RIDC's Keystone Commons, it was still to be a centerpiece of the planned steel heritage center that they hoped would also include the Carrie blast furnace and the riverbank where the Pinkerton guards had landed during the Homestead steel strike. Ron DaParma, "Group Sees Progress in Steel-Plant Talks," *Pittsburgh Tribune-Review,* March 9, 1991. Kelly B. Casey, "Museum Plans On Hold; Site Owner Stalls Land Sale," *Pittsburgh Tribune-Review,* July 17, 1994.

47. "200-Ton Mill to Be moved Piece by Piece by Task Force," *Pittsburgh Post-Gazette,* November 15, 1990; "Preservation of Historic Mill Begins," *Pittsburgh Post-Gazette,* December 30, 1990.

48. "It's History Now: Roll Shop Comes Down despite Museum Plans," *Pittsburgh Post-Gazette,* June 30, 1990.

49. Christine Vorce, "West Homestead Enterprise Expanded to Include 2 Neighborhoods," *Pittsburgh Post-Gazette,* August 2, 1990, S4. Years later, former Senator Mike Dawida would observe

> I would say, one of the things that, I was very down on the Park Corporation, because they aren't real developers in my mind, and I'm still right about that, but they did something that was probably the most critical, at least in the Homestead site, and that is they did clear the site. They liquidated the site, and until the site was clean, the people in the community couldn't comprehend what it could be used for.... I opposed ... getting Park to own the land. But that turned out to be effective, because they were good liquidators, and that was necessary for the community psyche.

Michael Dawida, interview with the Brownfields Revitalization Systems Project, Carnegie Mellon University, January 13, 2000.

> David Lewis recalled
> I joined the board of HERC and we fought bitterly, and then I realized that there was no point in fighting. It was so stupid, so counterproductive. Why would we want to go into confrontation with the Park Corporation? Why would we regard them as the enemy? What was the solution? The only solution, I felt and still feel, was that we had to join forces and develop a vision for where we were going to go.
> HERC got into a ... progressively confrontational mode. So I left the board. I felt that my role had to be to try to mend the fences. I began to work with the Park Corporation to see whether or not we couldn't prepare the site for recycling in some form. I persuaded the Park Corporation to keep the chimneys. It cost them thousands, the chimneys. They all had to be reinforced. I got them to keep the station. We formed a little small group. We made friends with Ray Park and particularly with his son, Kelly Park.

Lewis, interview.

50. "Park Corp. Begins Study of Museum Costs, Foerster Says," *Pittsburgh Post-Gazette,* July 26, 1990.

51. "Two Towns Cool to Steel Museum, Park," *Pittsburgh Post-Gazette,* August 16, 1990.

52. "Homestead Works Zoning Review Tonight," *Pittsburgh Post-Gazette,* May 31, 1990; "Here's How to Comment on Zoning at Mill Site," *Pittsburgh Post-Gazette,* June 14, 1990; "Residents Favorable to Plans for Mill Site, *Pittsburgh Post-Gazette,* July 5, 1990.

53. Ed Blazina, "Uniform Zoning Unlikely for Homestead Works Site," *Pittsburgh Press,* October 11, 1990, S1.

54. Horgan, interview.

55. "Homestead Works Towns Hit Bottom after Reassessment," *Pittsburgh Post-Gazette,* January 10, 1991; Christine Vorce, "Assessment Settlement in Jeopardy," *Pittsburgh Press,* January 17, 1991, S5; Christine Vorce, "Park Corp., Homestead at Loggerheads on Taxes," *Pittsburgh Press,* February 21, 1991, S1.

56. Vorce, "Park Corp., Homestead at Loggerheads."

57. "New Rules for Millsite Face Long Review," *Pittsburgh Post-Gazette,* May 23, 1991; "Homestead Zoning Hearing Set to Resume," *Pittsburgh Post-Gazette,* July 3, 1991; "Piecemeal Approach to Land Use Irks Owner of Homestead Millsite," *Pittsburgh, Post-Gazette,* August 15, 1991.

58. "Stores Envisioned on Part of Mill Site," *Pittsburgh Post-Gazette,* February 21, 1991; "USX Site Guidelines Face Veto," *Pittsburgh Post-Gazette,* December 5, 1991; "Zoning Called Obstruction for Planned Supermarket, *Pittsburgh Post-Gazette,* December 19, 1991; "Supermarket Not Ruled Out for Homestead," *Pittsburgh Post-Gazette,* January 2, 1992.

George DeBolt explained the strange dynamics that had led the Park Corporation to request uniform zoning for the site only later to reject the resulting product:

The Park Corporation wanted uniform zoning from the three boroughs for the mill site. So Park Corporation goes to the local municipalities and says, "We want you guys to come up with a common zoning ordinance, land use plan for the mill site," thinking, these are three uninformed, uneducated, unsophisticated borough councils that have been kind of like just sitting there for a hundred years, and they won't do much. Well, there were a couple of [professionals] in Homestead at the time . . . who had a lot of experience with land use planning and zoning, and they came up with what I've been told was perhaps one of the most comprehensive zoning ordinances in the state of Pennsylvania, which the Park Corporation didn't expect, which the Homestead Borough Council didn't understand at all, and what's worse, couldn't appreciate. I mean, they're looking at all these old rusty steel mills, and these folks are talking about view corridors, they're talking about tree plantings, green space, paths along the river, this kind of stuff. And the community is just, "What are you talking about?" But you were able to convince enough people on Homestead Council to pass this thing.

The mayor vetoed that. And the thinking was, that's somebody's private property. They should be able to do with it what they want. You know, the steel mill did what they wanted to do on it, and it worked out well for everybody here, so we shouldn't be trying to tell them how many trees to plant, how wide the streets should be, how tall the buildings should be.

So, on the one hand you have this mindset of people still thinking it should be a mill. On the other hand you have these people saying it's private property, they should be able to do what they want to. And then you've got this small, progressive, visionary group, saying that what happens on that mill site is very important and is directly related to the rest of the community, and there should be a real relationship there.

The mayor vetoes the zoning ordinances. Council takes up the overriding of the veto. Then Park, who's the head of the Park Corporation, lobbies the community to support the mayor's veto, because he doesn't want his hands tied. He doesn't want to be told how many trees he has to plant and this kind of thing. He sent a letter to the voters in Homestead, asking them to talk to their council to uphold the mayor's veto, because this is Homestead, folks. This isn't Beverly Hills. This isn't New York City. This isn't Los Angeles. This is Homestead, and who do you think you are to expect an attractive site down here, an attractive development? But the visionaries, whom I'll call the good guys in this case, lobby council enough that council unanimously overturns the mayor's veto, great victory for land use planning, great victory for the future, great victory for the vision.

Now, as Park begins to get serious about developing, they went back and had some of these things amended, but I don't think there were any critical revisions. For example, the public space along the river, which we had specified be 100 feet, they got reduced to 50 feet. The view corridor on McClure Street, coming down the hill, got reduced. Whereas before there was no idea of a view corridor. You know, they could put up a mill if they wanted to, or a warehouse or something. So they didn't gut them, but they did amend them, they did adjust them, and nobody opposed that. So once they basically got their adjustments and amendments to the zoning ordinances, they basically went on their own.

After 1992 or 1993 there were fewer and fewer opportunities for ordinary citizens to have a say as to what was going to happen on the mill site. And for the powers that be, that was fine. It's private property. Let them do what they want to on it. Fortunately, though, we had fought that battle in the early 90s, to make sure the development was going to have some quality to it.

DeBolt, interview.

59. At the same time, Dindak was amazed at the rapid progress once the site had been cleared and Continental Real Estate's development of the site—Continental purchased portions of the site from Park in 1997—was underway: "I never envisioned this, what is happening today. I figured there would be a building here and a building there, you know. There were a lot of people coming in . . . , but money was always a problem, for an independent private developer to come in, till Continental came in. And it's just beyond my wildest dreams, all that is going on down there, will be there within the next year or so. It's just happening so fast." John Dindak, interview with the Brownfields Revitalization Systems Project, Carnegie Mellon University, January 13, 2000.

60. Tim Vercellotti, and Christine Vorce, "'One Step Forward, Two Steps Back,'" *Pittsburgh Press,* September 29, 1991, A4.

61. Kenneth Bowman, Assistant Regional Counsel, Southwest Regional Office, PA Department of Environmental Protection, remembered

We had no involvement with the supervision of the cleanup. That's my understanding. We can check the records. "Manifests" is a term of art that deals with off-site disposal of hazardous wastes. I'm sure if they disposed of hazardous waste that was excavated there it would be manifested, and those records would be turned in to the department. If they removed tanks and they were regulated tanks they would file the various reports that would be required for regulated tanks, but I don't know that we had any other involvement in that.

Bowman, interview.

According to Carl Spadero of the DEP "manifests" meant "hazardous waste manifests" to DEP, which would entail assignment of an EPA identification number as a "small waste generator," but he had no record of such operations at the Homestead site. "If he meant hazardous waste manifests," Spadero said, "I don't know who he sent them to, but he didn't send them to us" (telephone interview with the author, January 26, 2004). After investigating further, Spadero reported that DEP had one file from the late 1980s to the early 1990s with the name "USX Homestead Hazardous Waste File," about 0.5 inch thick, which indicated there had been some hazardous solvents, perhaps in connection with a pickling line that was removed in 1990, and removal of a gas line. "Nothing was in the ground. There was no evidence of soil testing." Telephone interview with the author January 27, 2004.

John Matviya, Program Manager, Environmental Cleanup at DEP, found two accordion files from the mid-1990s containing closure reports for eighteen underground storage tanks containing gasoline and heating oil, but no chemicals. Matviya commented that "most of our involvement is due to the buyer's wish." Telephone interview with the author January 28, 2004.

Bell may have been referring to manifests connected with the removal of asbestos, which was overseen by the Allegheny County Health Department, rather than the DER. In that respect, Donald M. Horgan, Asbestos Inspection Supervisor at the Allegheny County Health Department, stated that "Park, whatever we asked them to do they did." Horgan, interview.

62. Bell, interview.

63. Tim Vercellotti and Christine Vorce, "'One Step Forward, Two Steps Back,'" *Pittsburgh Press,* September 29, 1991, A1, 4.

64. "Declining Property Values Lamented," *Pittsburgh Post-Gazette,* December 12, 1991.

65. "Homestead Mulls Distressed Status," *Pittsburgh Post-Gazette,* November 27, 1991.

66. Maureen Morrissey, "Developers to Vie in Marketing Millsites," *Pittsburgh Press,* January 23, 1992, S1.

67. Maureen Morrissey, "Park Corp. Appeals Homestead Assessment," *Pittsburgh Press,* March 26, 1992, S4.

68. Clifton B. Parker, "Cleanup at Mill Won't End Soon," *Pittsburgh Post-Gazette,* March 3, 1993, S2.

69. Parker, "Cleanup at Mill."

70. Eric Heyl, "State Grant Will Provide Funds for New Span to Former USX Site," *Pittsburgh Tribune-Review,* August 25, 1993.

71. "Mill Site Viewed as Key to Recovery," *Pittsburgh Post-Gazette,* May 19, 1993. When Homestead Borough emerged from the program almost fourteen years later, Mayor Betty Esper credited the redevelopment of the site as the reason. "'Thank God for The Waterfront,' she told a news conference . . . , referring to the shopping and entertainment mecca that has played a large part in restoring the financial health of the former steel-dependent community." Ed Blazina, "Homestead Emerges from 'Distressed' Status," *Pittsburgh Post-Gazette,* March 29, 2007, B1.

72. "Steel Valley Zone Gets State Funds," *Pittsburgh Tribune-Review,* July 13, 1993.

73. Eric Heyl, "State Grant Will Provide Funds for New Span to Former USX Site," *Pittsburgh*

Tribune-Review, August 25, 1993.

74. Kelly Casey, a reporter for the *Pittsburgh Tribune-Review,* summarized the history:
The project originated in 1987, only two years after U.S. Steel workers were laid off for the last time. That year, the federal government started the America's Industrial Heritage Project—but initially ignored the nation's largest industrial area.

"Overlooking Homestead and Pittsburgh on a story about steelmaking is tantamount to overlooking Detroit when telling the story of the automobile industry," [the Steel Industry Heritage Corporation's executive director August] Carlino said.

U.S. Rep. John P. Murtha, D-Johnstown, and the late Sen. John Heinz acted quickly at the urging of local congressmen to amend the legislation. Nine southwestern Pennsylvania counties then became part of the national project.

A task force soon formed and four years later this group of local historians, educators, steelworkers and community leaders completed an inch-thick industry heritage concept plan. During that time, two years of negotiations with Park proved fruitless when the company told the task force in June 1990 it would not sell any property for a project it did not deem feasible. When the task force disbanded, the Steel Industry Heritage Corporation formed to make the concept a reality.

Kelly B. Casey, "Museum Plans On Hold; Site Owner Stalls Land Sale," *Pittsburgh Tribune-Review,* July 17, 1994.

75. Don Horgan of the Allegheny County Health Department described Park's approach to demolition in these words:
The one thing I learned from Park, though, in doing a demolition, is, he said, you always start from the back to the front. You want the front to look like there's nothing going on because if you remember you had the DMX, or whatever those guys were called, oh, the mills were going to come back and this and that, so they wanted the front to look like there was nothing going on as they moved everything behind it and kept on moving to the front, then at the end that was gone and there was nothing you could do about it.

Horgan, interview.

76. Todd Gutnick, "'Big Shop' Demolition Miffs Historians," *Pittsburgh Tribune-Review,* February 7, 1994.

77. Casey, "Museum Plans On Hold."

78. "Protestors Halt Demolition of USX's 'Big Shop,'" *Pittsburgh Post-Gazette,* January 28, 1994; "'Big Shop' Gets Stay from Wrecking Ball," *Pittsburgh Post-Gazette,* February 2, 1994; "'Big Shop' Fate On Hold," *Pittsburgh Post-Gazette,* February 9, 1994.

79. Linda Wilson Fuoco, "Park Corp. Says Museum Deal Is Needed Soon," *Pittsburgh Post-Gazette,* February 23, 1994, S1; "'Big Shop' Demolition Permit Advised," *Pittsburgh Post-Gazette,* February 23, 1994; "Steel's 'Big Shop' Now Pile of Rubble, *Pittsburgh Post-Gazette,* February 27, 1994.

80. Bohdan Hodiak, "Pending Land Sale Gives New Life to Steel Museum," *Pittsburgh Post-Gazette,* November 3, 1993, S1; Linda Wilson Fuoco, "Park Corp. Says Museum Deal Is Needed Soon," *Pittsburgh Post-Gazette,* February 23, 1994, S1.

81. Gutnick, "'Big Shop' Demolition."

82. William Opalka, "Davis: No Property Tax," *Pittsburgh Tribune-Review,* April 30, 1994.

83. "Shop 'n Save Plan a Marketing Coup," *Pittsburgh Post-Gazette*, April 6, 1994; "Approval of Supermarket May Bring Mill Site Renewal," *Pittsburgh Post-Gazette*, July 27, 1994; "New Food Market Isn't Much Like Depot," *Pittsburgh Post-Gazette*, August 10, 1994; "Council Backs Shop 'n Save Project," *Pittsburgh Post-Gazette*, August 24, 1994; Eric Heyl, "Officials Hope Homestead Works as Store Site," *Pittsburgh Tribune-Review*, August 10, 1994.

84. Heyl, "Officials Hope Homestead Works as Store Site."

85. Martin Kinnunen, "Amusement Firm Willing to Gamble on Gaming," *Pittsburgh Tribune-Review*, July 31, 1994.

86. Ron DaParma, "Business Bargains Thrive in the Mon Valley," *Pittsburgh Tribune-Review*, February 12, 1995.

87. "East Fly-over Work to Start in Spring," *Pittsburgh Post-Gazette*, March 15, 1995.

88. Mark Patrick, interview with the author, July 1, 2003.

89. "Bridge Ramp Project Survives Cost-Cutting," *Pittsburgh Post-Gazette*, June 12, 1996.

90. Kelly B. Casey, "Restoration Under Way at Heritage Park," *Pittsburgh Tribune-Review*, May 7, 1995. After ten more years of planning and negotiation, in August 2005 Allegheny County finally purchased a total of 137 acres from the Park Corporation, including the entire Carrie Furnace site (approximately 125 acres) and a small strip of land across the river in Munhall and Whitaker, at the tail end of the Waterfront site, for $5.75 million. A feasibility study made by the county's Department of Economic Development envisioned (from west to east) a mixed-use development of housing in Swissvale, the national historic park around the remaining blast furnaces, a hotel and conference center, and an office park. See Andrew Conte, "Rebirth of Carrie Furnaces Site Likely," *Pittsburgh Tribune-Review*, January 20, 2005, A1, A7; Dan Reynolds, "Highway's Growth May Stymie Plans for National Park at Carrie Furnace," *Pittsburgh Business Times*, May 13–19, 2005, 4; Glenn May, "Cleaning Carrie Furnace Site Could Be Easier than Expected," *Pittsburgh Tribune-Review*, September 22, 2005, 1, 9.

91. Ron DaParma, "Business Bargains Thrive in the Mon Valley," *Pittsburgh Tribune-Review*, February 12, 1995. For background on Strategy 21 see Lubove, 49–50.

92. "Shop 'n Save Opens This Week," *Pittsburgh Post-Gazette*, May 24, 1995.

Chapter 5. Duquesne and McKeesport

1. Cristina Rouvalis, "State Rejects Renewal Projects," *Pittsburgh Post-Gazette*, January 17, 1987; Vince Leonard, "County Told to Reapply for Strategy 21 Funds," *Pittsburgh Post-Gazette*, January 18, 1987; Linda S. Wilson, "As Promised: Casey visits Mon Valley, Speaks of Restoring Economic Health," *Pittsburgh Post-Gazette*, January 22, 1987; Virginia Linn, "Funding Hold-up Delaying Projects," *Pittsburgh Post-Gazette*, April 13, 1987; Virginia Linn, "Strategy 21 Focuses on Remaking Four Industrial Sites," *Pittsburgh Post-Gazette*, February 11, 1988. For background on Strategy 21 see Lubove, 49–50.

2. Virginia Linn, "200 Jobs: Public Works Program among Report's Proposals for Mon Valley," *Pittsburgh Post-Gazette*, March 26, 1987.

3. Carol Waterloo, "Mon Valley Report Eyes Steel Facilities," *Daily News*, March 25, 1987, 1, 4.

4. Ed Blazina, "$333 Million Plan for Economy Renews Hope, *Pittsburgh Press*, March 26, 1987.

5. "Leaders Ready to Move Ahead," *Daily News,* March 26, 1987.

6. "Leaders Ready to Move Ahead."

7. David Roderick's younger brother Bill had played football for Foerster from 1948 to 1949. Foerster, interview. USX was represented on RIDC's board of directors.

8. Brooks Robinson remembered

At that time USX, David Roderick, was marketing, if you can use that term, both McKeesport and Duquesne as a package, and Homestead. Roderick was the chairman of the board. And so he made a package of USX McKeesport and Duquesne to us, and he sold Homestead to the Park Corporation.

Getting the property in the first place was certainly not an easy thing. USX was very concerned about the precedent among all their other properties should they make a sweetheart deal with us as a community agency for these two sites.

Frank Brooks Robinson, Sr., interview with the Brownfields Systems Group, Carnegie Mellon University, January 5, 2000.

9. Ed Blazina, "USX Will Sell County 2 Plants for Development," *Pittsburgh Press,* March 25, 1987.

10. The note provided further that the total price paid to USX would not exceed $3,662,800 and that if the sale price exceeded $30,000 per acre, RIDC would pay USX half the difference. See Allegheny County Department of Development, "Mon Valley Starts 90's with New Image and New Progress," *Development* VI, no. 5 (Spring 1990): 1.

11. Joseph Hohman, interview with the author, December 9, 1998.

12. Allegheny County Department of Development, "Mon Valley Starts 90's with New Image and New Progress."

13. Virginia Linn, "Firms want to set up operations at former USX Corp. Sites," *Pittsburgh Post-Gazette,* June 2, 1988, 13–14.

14. Virginia Linn, "Strategy 21 Focuses on Remaking Four Industrial Sites," *Pittsburgh Post-Gazette,* February 11, 1988.

15. Albert J. Neri, "$156 million is sought for jobs," *Pittsburgh Post-Gazette,* January 28, 1988.

16. "Ditching the Dinosaurs," *Daily News,* February 2, 1988.

17. "District Expressway Fund Plan Proposed," *Daily News,* February 10, 1987; Albert J. Neri, "New Funding Plan Proposed for Mon Link," *Pittsburgh Post-Gazette,* February 10, 1987.

18. In January 1988 the Southwestern Pennsylvania Regional Planning Commission released SAI Consulting Engineers' study of the State Route 837 corridor (running along the western bank of the Monongahela River through the valley), which explored options for an expressway that would improve access to the Mon Valley, with the cost estimated to exceed $100 million. Part of the region's total of $425 million requested of the state under Strategy 21 was $89 million to link Route 837 with the Parkway East and $35 million for Mon Valley redevelopment, including Duquesne and McKeesport. See Allegheny County Department of Development, "Foundation Set for County Action on Commission Recommendations," *Development* VI, no. 4 (Winter 1988): 2–4.

19. Albert J. Neri, "Mon Valley Expressway a Top Priority, Casey says," *Pittsburgh Post-Gazette*; "Casey to Speed Expressway," *Daily News,* March 27, 1987; Ken Fisher, "The Fast Lane: Mon Valley Expressway Plans Speeded," *Pittsburgh Post-Gazette,* March 27, 1987; Albert J. Neri,

"Mon Valley Toll Road Gets Federal Funding," *Pittsburgh Post-Gazette,* June 25, 1987.

20. Wes Cotter, "Lysle Project Given May 1 Starting Date," *Daily News,* April 20, 1987.

21. "Foundation Set for County Action on Commission Recommendations," *Development* VI, no. 4 (Winter 1988), Allegheny County Department of Development.

22. Virginia Linn, "Water Purity a Concern at Two USX Plant Sites," *Pittsburgh Post-Gazette,* July 22, 1988.

23. See Virginia Linn, "Water Purity a Concern at Two USX Plant Sites," *Pittsburgh Post-Gazette,* July 22, 1988. Commissioner Foerster remembered that RIDC succeeded in raising some $15 million from the sale of machinery and scrap, but then the scrap market took a downturn (Foerster, interview). RIDC then had to turn to the state as a source of funds for cleanup. Mel Achtzehn remembered

> The problems that we ran into, with the cleanup down there, all that cleanup, we ran into some big problems on that. We hired a firm to come in and do a study, as to what it was going to take, in moneys, to clean the site up, and the firm was Duncan Lagnese. They came up with the figure of 15 million dollars. Well, at the policy board meeting we discussed this and Brooks felt that, something wrong with that figure, because of what we had at that time. Too low. Too low, because the ground itself had to be remediated, I mean with all the chemicals and stuff that went into that site. And so we hired another firm, called Kaiser Corporation. Kaiser Corporation came in and they gave us a figure of 30 million dollars. Well, now we're getting really into a big problem. So U.S. Steel had given to the county, which went to Brooks, the equipment and the mill site. So those revenues could be used to clean up the site. Well, our best customer was U.S. Steel. They wrote it off, and then they're buying everything back 25 cents on a dollar. That's not bad business. Then we had a customer. So actually U.S. Steel was helping us to remediate the site. Well, we went through that 30 million, and we have problems down there right now, and we're still not done with cleaning the site up, and here we are 2005, and we still have the stoves standing down there, which is another big problem.

Achtzehn, interview with the author.

24. Linda S. Wilson, "Mill Site May Have Edge as Museum," *Pittsburgh Post-Gazette,* August 4, 1988, 1ff.

25. Dennis Pittman (former Community Development Director, City of McKeesport, and member, Duquesne-McKeesport Policy Committee), interview with the Brownfields Systems Group, Carnegie Mellon University, January 11, 2000.

26. Wes Cotter, "Accord Paves Way for Site Development," *Daily News,* August 9, 1988.

27. Mark Belko, "County's IDA Votes Today to Acquire Old Steel Plants," *Pittsburgh Post-Gazette,* August 10, 1988; "Duquesne and National Works Transferred to Public Ownership," Allegheny County Department of Development, *Development* VI, no. 2 (Fall 1988).

28. Tax records valued the land in McKeesport at $3 million and the land in Duquesne at $5.48 million. July 26, 1988, agreement of sale and development between USX Corporation, Regional Industrial Development Corporation of Southwestern Pennsylvania and Allegheny County Industrial Development Authority, executed August 10, 1988.

29. Ed Blazina, "Developer Showing Interest in Mill Site Acquired by County," *Pittsburgh Press,* August 11, 1988.

30. "Pennsylvania Makes New Bid to Get Jobs for Depressed Area: Two Abandoned Steel

Mills, Converted to Public Use, Will Be Industrial Parks," *Wall Street Journal,* August 12, 1988, 17.

31. July 26, 1988, agreement of sale and development. Mayor Lou Washowich of McKeesport later commented incredulously

Can you imagine back then, before they would have done that, if somebody would have said to U.S. Steel, you can walk away from this, but you're going to be held liable for the contamination here? But the deal was struck. We really had nothing to say about it. The only thing we really got out of the deal over a period of time they paid us, and I don't even remember what the numbers were, x number of dollars that decreased over a period of time until a point in time when they didn't pay us anything. But if they would have been required to tear that and clean that site environmentally by federal regulations I think they would have thought a hell of a lot different. But the deal was struck. No question about it. Do I think it was a bad deal? Most certainly I do. I sure do. But we knew we had to move on.

Washowich, interview.

Reacting to this and similar provisions, Chuck Duritsa of DER said

I'll add something that did bother me to no end, and it's how ... public agencies went in and purchased these and indemnified the people who caused the contamination. That was a tremendously tough issue. I mean if they hadn't indemnified them we could have gone after the people who caused the pollution, but to a person these public agencies indemnified the people they took the property from. To me, that made it very difficult to go back to the U.S. Steels and LTV's and say, look, even if I sued them they were going to get the money out of the people who bought it since they were indemnified. In hindsight, I always questioned, why the hell did you people do this? I can't even go help you by suing the company now because you've indemnified them. That bothered me a lot. That was my perspective on it. Why did you do that?

Duritsa, interview.

32. Jan Bamford, "Rehabilitation of USX Mill Sites One Step Closer," *Pittsburgh Business Times-Journal,* July 25, 1988, 1sff.

33. Mark Belko, "County's IDA Votes Today to Acquire Old Steel Plants," *Pittsburgh Post-Gazette,* August 10, 1988.

34. Allegheny County Department of Development, "Duquesne and National Works Transferred to Public Ownership," *Development* VI, no. 2 (Fall 1988): 1.

35. Mark Belko, "Developers Interested in Old Mills," *Pittsburgh Post-Gazette,* August 11, 1988.

36. Ed Blazina, "Developer Showing Interest in Mill Site Acquired by County," *Pittsburgh Press,* August 11, 1988.

37. Foerster, interview.

38. At this point the estimated value of the scrap and equipment was between $16 million and $22 million at prevailing prices. Mark Belko, "Mon Valley Mills' Scrap, Equipment Is Worth Millions," *Pittsburgh Post-Gazette,* August 19, 1988.

39. Allegheny County Department of Development, "Mon Valley Commission Update," May 12, 1989.

40. Mary Kane, "Mon Valley Development Panel Plans Public Report," *Pittsburgh Press,*

June 8, 1989.

    41. RIDC, Mon Valley Policy Committee, minutes of the meeting of January 13, 1989.

    42. Ed Blazina, "Mill Site Demolition Contracts Due Soon," *Pittsburgh Press,* c. March 1989.

    43. RIDC, Mon Valley Policy Committee, minutes of the meeting of February 10, 1989.

    44. Achtzehn, interview with the author.

    45. Carmen J. Lee, "Plans for Former USX Plants Presented," *Pittsburgh Post-Gazette,* June 13, 1989; James Rankin, "County, RIDC Outline Plans for USX Site Development," *The Daily News,* June 14, 1989; Bill Steigerwald, "Plans for Mill-Site Renewal Unveiled," *Pittsburgh Post-Gazette,* June 14, 1989, 1, 7.

    46. Allegheny County Department of Development, Duquesne/National Project Bid Tabulations, undated, with attached note dated August 21, [1989].

    47. Ed Blazina, *Pittsburgh Press,* c. May 2, 1989.

    48. Ed Blazina, "New Process Lets Firm Pay County, Still Turn Profit on 2 Steel Mills," *Pittsburgh Press,* c. May 9, 1989.

    49. Ed Blazina, "County to Change Bonding Plan for Mon Valley Mill Demolition," *Pittsburgh Press,* c. August or early September 1989.

    50. Tom Barnes, "Only Bidder Offers to Pay County to Demolish 2 Former USX Mills," *Pittsburgh Post-Gazette,* October 24, 1989.

    51. Tim Vercellotti and Christine Vorce, "'One Step Forward, Two Steps Back,'" *Pittsburgh Press,* September 29, 1991, A1, 4.

    52. Allegheny County Department of Development, "Mon Valley Starts 90's with New Image and New Progress," *Development* VI, no. 5 (Spring 1990).

    53. Looking back ten years later, Dennis Pittman reflected on the problem the county faced and what actually came to pass.

U.S. Steel said they would walk away, and they reached in their pocket and gave us the keys and said, "You can have what's there. You can dismantle and sell, you can take scrap. If you have a remediation problem our value of scrap is about 17 million, and the value of remediation by report done by Duncan Lagnese was about the same. And therefore we'll leave it in your hands, because we're not good at that." That, on the surface of it, seemed to make sense. Well, when the Allegheny County Industrial Development Authority, which was very ineffective because of public policy, the way you have to bid and move, not quite as quick as the private sector, nowhere near as quick as the Park Corporation, really the private sector, and it made sense. That was the good news. The bad news was that the actual cleanup was probably double that. Double, 33 million. So that brought you back to the funding table, and the grants and all that, and doing this incrementally, which is the reason Homestead is now cleared and building movie theaters and other things, and we're still struggling with buildings.

Pittman, interview.

Lou Washowich remembered

The state naturally only had so much money going out. We're out there begging and borrowing, and, you know, trying to do everything humanly possible through our elected officials and, you know, trying to garner money through the state. But it was a very difficult time.

Washowich, interview.

54. Mel Achtzehn remembered

We went to the federal government, Lou Washowich and I went to Washington, DC. John Heinz, Senator, he got us some people to see and we went down and we discussed it, try to get revenues sent back here to try to help us get this site cleaned up, and it was, yes, the nod, but we never did get it; we never got the revenues we wanted. That was 1989, before I took office as mayor, we went down.... And we needed these revenues, because we didn't have the money. The moneys we were getting from our taxes and stuff just wasn't here, and we needed help desperately. And we went down to Washington, they listened to our story, and nothing ever developed. It was a wasted trip, is what it was.

Achtzehn, interview with the author.

55. Their lease-purchase agreement with the county, for $20,000 per acre, had them paying for the property over ten years. Rick Teaff, "Financing Set for Mckeesport Factory," *Pittsburgh Business Times,* 9, 13 (November 6–12, 1989), 1, 15.

56. Allegheny County Department of Development, "Mon Valley Starts 90's with New Image and New Progress."

57. The other projects that received funds from this grant were Keystone Commons ($4.84 million), and Homestead Industrial Park (the former USX Homestead Works), $2.1 million for an extension of Martha Street for better access to the site). Coincidentally, the same day as the governor's announcement, USX announced it would build a continuous caster at the Edgar Thomson Mill in Braddock, the first major investment in steel in the valley in many years. See also Barbara White Stack, "State Aids Mills' Reuse," *Pittsburgh Post-Gazette,* February 2, 1990, 1, 6.

58. "Mon Valley Momentum," *Pittsburgh Post-Gazette,* February 5, 1990, 6.

59. ICF Kaiser Engineers, Inc., Executive Summary, in *"Groundwater Quality Assessment Summary Report, Industrial Center of McKeesport, McKeesport, PA,"* prepared for RIDC Southwestern Pennsylvania Growth Fund, August, 1993.

Robinson described RIDC's approach as follows:

From a concept standpoint, because RIDC is involved with business and industry, our concept has been that we would develop these two sites as payroll and real estate tax generation, but that it would not compete with the rebuilding of the retail commercial, residential and housing energies of the community. Had we decided to put a shopping center, either in whole or in part, on those sites, we would kill the retail capacity of the cities of McKeesport and Duquesne.

So, with that concept, we had to meet with, not only the political leaderships of McKeesport and Duquesne, but with the community, in order to explain to them what we were going to do and what we were not going to do. That was reflected in doing, first, a master plan, which had a public disclosure in both McKeesport and Duquesne. There were public hearings, so that the community, to the extent they wanted to be involved, could have input or could comment on it, and it was followed along by ... what we call a policy committee. It meets once a month. It is comprised of the mayors of each of the two cities, and then there are two other people that each mayor may appoint, and the hope here was that they would appoint somebody who was an advocate for the community. In the case of Duquesne, when we started, it was a preacher, and in the case of McKeesport, when we started, it was the director of the McKeesport Hospital. So that there was a way in which communication could go not only into the political realm, through council, but there was also a way of getting to the community, across the pulpit or whatever. We meet every month, and have since 1990, when we started this project. So that is our way of getting our information into the community, but it's also our way of being able to show to the leadership how complicated some of these issues are, and how expensive they are, which is part of the problem that was occurring at the same time in Homestead, where the community of Homestead, both political and community itself, was very anxious about what Park was doing, not that he was not doing it correctly; it's because he wasn't telling anybody what he was doing. And so under that kind of an organization you think the worst. We elected to go the other way. It's been total interaction, with the political, with the community.

When we first started . . . there was resistance. "Why aren't you doing it faster? Why aren't you doing it more? Why aren't you getting me a job?" A lot of what we did for the first five years was really very technical, so it was outside of the realm of interest or expertise of the people we were communicating with, but we did it anyway.

One of the first things that I said when we spoke in these public hearings about starting this thing, to people from McKeesport and Duquesne, whose lives had been completely disturbed by the loss of the steel industry, I said, if we are even marginally successful here it's not going to help you. We can't promise you a job. We may not even be able to promise your children jobs if you don't get them into schools. But what we will do is we're going to rebuild the economy of this region in a diversified way so that if there is an economic hiccup it's not going to take out the whole system as it would if there was a shutdown of the steel industry.

Robinson, Sr., interview with the Brownfields Systems Group.

Commenting on RIDC and the process of redevelopment, Lou Washowich said
I really got familiar with RIDC. But I think over the years I learned to respect RIDC more each year as time went on, knowing and finding out what a tough job it was and the amount of dollars it was taking, and I have the utmost respect for Brooks Robinson. He was the kind of fellow that, when he would sit across the table from you, he would never try to B.S. you. I always respected him for that. And on the other hand I would think that he always thought that we had to learn and I had to learn to have a little more patience than I originally had.

Washowich, interview.

Mel Achtzehn of Duquesne also enjoyed a good working relationship with RIDC:
Brooks and I, we sat down many, many times, during the meetings, after the meetings, and before the meetings, and discussed different things that we would like to see happen on the site, and there were times that I wasn't happy with the progress, I have to say that. And we would suggest certain items that we would like to see happen with the real estate. . . .
There were times that we felt that RIDC wasn't moving good enough, wasn't moving fast enough or going in the right direction. We did overflies, studies with pictures. We made videos to try to sell the site. And we, the DBAC [Duquesne Business Advisory Council] at that time, had revenues, we still have some today, that we could advance to firms for small business loans, to help them put their program together, help them

with their marketing, and in some cases help them get special revenues to do some construction work. There's three or four firms down there right now are paying us back, every month, for moneys that we had loaned to them to get their operation started. We had this available, and sometimes Brooks or his staff would meet with somebody and wouldn't mention that we were available to help them. And so that was a step backwards. And we kept asking Brooks, let 'em know we're here. We'll work with you. You have this available; let's use it.
Achtzehn, interview with the author.

60. Vercellotti and Vorce, "'One Step Forward, Two Steps Back,'" A4.

61. The RIDC's Brooks Robinson, Jr., explained how the management team operated: NISI would come in and say, inside this building you have about x amount of dollars of resalable tools, equipment and stuff, whatever the market was, and you could generate that, okay? Then Kaiser would say, and it's going to cost you this much to clean it up, and then Turner through a demo. contractor would say, you're going to get this in the way of scrap when it's done. And through that there was a way in which they evolved this plan. Now with that process in place, which was the only process we could think of doing it financially without a lot of subsidy. The problem with that process was that it took an inordinate amount of time, a lot of time, certainly more time than the elected officials had and the community had, but it was the way in which we had to proceed.
Frank Brooks Robinson, Jr., interview with the author, July 6, 2004.

62. Killam Associates Consulting Engineers to Wilbert Hannan (RIDC), May 21, 1990, describing a May 18, 1990, meeting and inspection of documentation in Killam's possession from the environmental assessment performed in 1988, which includes a PCB transformer inventory, a PCB equipment location map, and a copy of USX's PCB inspection in August of 1987. In addition, EPA requested USX's 1985 registration of PCB equipment with the local fire department, 1988 and 1989 annual reports, and quarterly inspection reports from August 1987. Art Riley of USX Realty Development was notified of the inspection by USX's representative, Bob Zimmer, and of the information needed.

Killam agreed to take a number of actions. They would prepare EPA's "Notification of PCB Activity" form and receive an ID number from EPA, which any "generator" needed to process, store, dispose of, or transport PCB-contaminated waste. They would attempt to obtain documentation on PCBs from USX Realty's files, the local fire department, and Allegheny County. They would inspect the property; assess and verify the numbers, locations, and conditions of equipment containing PCBs (transformers and capacitors); and assemble an inventory, a map, previous inspection documentation, the required inspection forms, a schedule for maintaining compliance with applicable regulations, and a site evaluation narrative, including recommendations for treatment or disposal of equipment with PCBs, all at an estimated cost of $7,000. Thomas E. Artman (Environmental Specialist) and James P. Hannan (Manager, Geotechnical Services); Killam Associates, to Wilbert Hannan, June 8, 1990, in reference to RIDC's needing assistance in developing a program for record keeping and monitoring of PCBs in accordance with the US EPA's regulations, 40 CFR Part 761, for McKeesport. RIDC needed to develop a PCB management program to meet EPA's final rules promulgated December 21, 1989. Since ownership of the property had transferred from USX to Allegheny County and subsequently to RIDC in May of 1990, activities on the site had apparently resulted in changes from the original PCB electrical equipment listings. Existing information was therefore not accurate. An April 1988 inventory cited 38 PCB transformers throughout the site. RIDC needed clarification of the location and number of PCB transformers and potentially regulated capacitors present on the site.

63. Killam also noted that their original cost estimate of $7,000 for their services was not going to be enough now. They requested an increase of $5,000, to $12,000. Thomas E. Artman and Paul Wojciak (Killam Associates) to Wilbert Hannan, August 24, 1990.

64. Brooks Robinson explained why RIDC, rather than Turner Construction, had the contract with Kaiser:

> In the team that we put together . . . , with Turner Construction and NISI, obviously we had to have an environmental outfit in there. That's where Kaiser came in. Turner's board of directors would not subcontract to Kaiser for fear again of the chain of litigation that could follow environmental remediation. So we had to contract with Kaiser for all of that. It turned out fine.

Frank Brooks Robinson, Sr., interview with the author, August 27, 2004.

65. Charles Haefner, Jr. (ICF Kaiser), to Brooks Robinson, July 29, 1992.

66. Campbell went on to say

This problem is compounded further by the fact that the environmental assessment is a very cursory type document which appears to be based primarily on a walk through audit rather than any in depth analysis or sampling program. Numerous drums and tanks of "unknown" materials were identified in the report in various areas of both plants. Visible soil contamination was identified in many areas; however, the extent and concentration of contaminants was not well defined and potential subsurface contamination was not addressed. In areas where oily contamination was obvious, it was not determined if this might be due to PCB type oil.

DER enumerated twenty concerns with Killam's study, among them the following:

- The magnitude of the project, along with the many gaps in information in the study, would require more than one engineer. They recommended hiring an "oversight contractor" with expertise in all the pertinent statutes. The oversight contractor would review all contracts to ensure compliance with applicable regulations.
- "Obvious hazardous wastes at the site, and those hazardous materials which, if they cannot be sold, will be hazardous wastes, must be transported by a licensed hazardous waste transporter to move these materials off site with a properly completed manifest." As already known, RIDC, as the new owner of this material, would have to obtain an ID number as a "generator" of hazardous waste.
- DER agreed with the idea of establishing a marshaling area for drums potentially containing hazardous wastes. There, determinations could be performed and the containers properly identified as to contents, hazard, and so forth.
- Disposal of any soil containing PCBs above 50 ppm must comply with federal requirements, and testing of all unknown oils for PCBs (not just those in electrical equipment), particularly those from hydraulic systems or those used in high heat.
- DER noted that cleanup levels for spilled PCBs were 25 ppm for "restricted" areas and 10 ppm for "nonrestricted," but since the future use of the property had not been determined, the stricter standard would apply. Additionally, the DER noted that it did not concur with the levels acceptable to the EPA. The DER required cleanup to "background" levels.

- Killam had recommended a cleanup level of 1,000 ppm for total petroleum hydrocarbons. The DER normally considered 50 ppm as clean. A demonstration that oil was not present and would not migrate to surface or groundwater was necessary to justify the proposed level.
- Killam had proposed cleanup levels for eighteen contaminants in the soil. The DER found no justification for the proposed levels and believed some were too high. Since they considered only background levels to be clean, RIDC should take a sample of soil near the facility to determine background levels. Sampling should then be performed after cleanup to verify results. Alternate concentration limits might be permissible, depending on proposed use of the area and on effects on public health and the environment.
- All underground tanks should be closed, and the Department's Bureau of Water Quality contacted.
- All friable asbestos should be removed prior to demolition.
- Additional testing and more monitoring would be needed in several areas.
- It appeared groundwater was contaminated near two 50,000-gallon fuel tanks at the National Plant and that treatment might be needed. Additional monitoring might also be needed near other underground tanks if evidence of leakage was noted.

Gale Campbell to Mary Klich (RIDC), July 3, 1990, "in re: Environmental Assessments USX National and Duquesne Works Allegheny County."

67. "Company Gets Early Start on Access Road at Mill Site," *Pittsburgh Press,* July 26, 1990, S7; Maureen Ford, RIDC, interview with the author, Pittsburgh, July 6, 2004.

68. Brooks Robinson to Gale Campbell, regarding DER's July 3, 1990, letter to Mary Klich.

69. Charles Haefner, Jr. (ICF Kaiser), to Brooks Robinson, July 29, 1992.

70. RIDC, minutes of the meeting of October 29, 1989.

71. Brunwasser speculated that as the RIDC moved forward to clean the site, the EPA might want to claim the development as a success for themselves, and for that reason have a motive to get involved. EPA would be most concerned about potential threats to public water supplies and would likely emphasize the importance of steps to protect groundwater serving the city of Duquesne and surface water supplying the Pennsylvania American intake at Beck's Run. Assurance that these supplies were protected from contamination might be enough to keep the two sites off the EPA's National Priorities List. Albert H. Brunwasser to Joseph M. Hohman, November 1, 1990.

72. Brooks Robinson to Albert H. Brunwasser and Charles A. Duritsa, November 12, 1990, regarding Priority 1, 2, and 3 Environmental Survey Reports prepared by ICF and dated November 5, 1990. Kaiser's work was two weeks ahead of schedule. They had spent 77% of their authorized budget: $140,000 to investigate the McKeesport property and $187,000 on the Duquesne site. They expected to spend another $100,000 by the end of January.

73. Designated as A-10.

74. ICF completed this work on November 11. In structure A-10 they collected five drums and three vessels from the oily wood flooring that contained concentrations of 1.34 to 5.50 ppm of PCBs.

75. Ford, interview. "Prevailing wages" refer to state-mandated wages for construction workers on state-funded projects. They were significantly higher than market rates, and often higher than normal union rates. American Asbestos Control Company was responsible for five

structures in Duquesne and one in McKeesport: U-8 (Linde Air Plant), T-26 (40-inch Shipping Building), T-23 (Conv. Building), and T-21 (Conv. Building), in Duquesne; and D-3 (Blowing Room), in McKeesport. Allegheny Asbestos Analysis monitored the air during abatement. Charles Shutrump & Sons provided support service, such as drum and transformer relocation to facilitate the asbestos removal and structural demolition. A second January asbestos contract, for Duquesne, went to Remcor. ICF Kaiser Engineers, "Monthly Progress Report No. 3 (Period 10/28 to 11/24/90)," December 5, 1990.

76. Joseph Rochez, Jr. (Vice President, Rochez Bros.), to W. Hannan, November 28, 1990.

77. Joseph Crumb, "Railroad Crossing Dispute Blocks Main Access to National Tube Site," *Pittsburgh Press,* December 6, 1990, S6.

78. Brooks Robinson to Thomas Snyder, with accompanying graphic, December 17, 1990.

79. For asbestos removal the Health Department particularly singled out the need to develop a written operations plan to establish specific work practices and procedures for contractors. They called for the plan to delineate staging areas, storage facilities, pumping or treatment facilities, and transportation routes for removal of materials. They requested "an overall spill detection, prevention, and emergency response plan" and indicated that "a compliance program should be developed in cooperation with the County's consultant and all contractors to ensure that the handling, storage, transportation, or disposal of hazardous materials is carried out in a manner consistent with federal, state, county or local requirements." Albert H. Brunwasser to Brooks Robinson, January 3, 1991.

80. Bruce H. Laswell, P.E., letter, January 3, 1991.

81. Unsigned note at RIDC, dated January 4, 1991.

82. S. D. Meyers and Randy Stebbins (the transformer consultants) to Joseph Switala (Turner Construction). This information then went to RIDC.

83. John A. Stahl (Barrier Systems, Inc.) to Penrose R. Wolf (Project Engineer, Turner Construction), January 10, 1991. The Asbestos NESHAP Revision issued by the EPA November 20, 1990, permitted asbestos-containing material to be left on items such as piping and taken away from the demolition work site if covered with leak-tight coverings, meaning that solids (including dust) or liquids could not escape or spill out. RIDC and Turner reviewed technologies known as Staytex Asbestos Encasement Systems and materials manufactured by Barrier Systems, Inc., Cleveland, Ohio. These materials were used for encasing asbestos on pipes, boilers, tanks, and equipment for subsequent transportation and burial. A January 23, 1991, letter from Penrose Wolf to Mark Stiffler, ICF, expressed two concerns. First, a portion of the work could be eliminated if the owner used the shredding and disposal method proposed by Rochez Bros. Second, while the Staytex encasement system manufactured by Barrier Systems or an equivalent might be an acceptable method for containing the asbestos, the contractor was concerned about application of the product at below freezing temperatures or to wet material.

84. Steven F. Faeth, "Privileged and confidential attorney-client Memorandum of Law Examining the Regulatory Requirements Applicable to the Beneficial Reuse of Residual Waste, prepared by Steven F. Faeth, attorney at Eckert, Seamans, Cherin, & Mellott, for RIDC," January 21, 1991.

85. Brooks Robinson to V. Fishman (National Environmental Technical Applications Corporation), November 27, 1991.

86. Brooks Robinson to V. Fishman, November 27, 1991.

87. Brooks Robinson to William Kiser (USX Realty), January 17, 1991.

88. Bruce Laswell (Senior Vice President, ICF Kaiser) to Brooks Robinson, with attached "Work Plan for Environmental Remediation," January 25, 1991. The work plan reflects the bid package approach suggested in the meeting of December 12 and incorporates input from a meeting of January 17 (Brooks Robinson to Albert Brunwasser, January 28, 1991, responding to Brunwasser's letter of January 3, 1991). Robinson apologized for delaying the response, but explained that he thought the "Work Plan" would address the department's concerns (Brooks Robinson to Charles Duritsa, to Gale Campbell, and to Joseph M. Hohman, with accompanying "Work Plan for Environmental Remediation," January 28, 1991). RIDC believed it was on schedule to correct the conditions threatening groundwater by mid-1991. The matter of handling drums, vessels, and transformers was of special importance to RIDC because of the risk of accidental contamination or exposure.

89. Kaiser solicited proposals, again at "prevailing wages," for marshaling of drums and transformers early in January and by the end of the month had received bids from thirteen companies. Kaiser anticipated developing cost estimates to perform sampling and analysis of residual water, liquid wastes, solid wastes, and tanks and vessels in the first four bid package areas for each site, and they began correspondence with local authorities to secure the permits that would be required to discharge residual water from the sites. By the end of January 1991, Kaiser had billed a total of $589,548.18 for their efforts on the sites—$224,991.47 for McKeesport and $364,556.71 for Duquesne. RIDC labeled buildings in both sites for easier identification according to zone. The McKeesport site was divided into zones A through E, from west to east. The Duquesne site was divided into zones P through V from north to south. In this instance, asbestos analysis and abatement and air monitoring were on structure T-20, and cleanup of PCB spills in buildings T-5 (the Electric Distribution Building, the T zone being the first area RIDC wanted to prepare for development, adjacent to the new East Grant Avenue) and U-10 (Sub Station). ICF Kaiser, "Monthly Progress Report No. 5—12/30/90 through 1/26/91," January 30, 1991.

90. Chuck Starrett, a member of RIDC's Policy Committee for its Duquesne and McKeesport projects, observed

There's been a lot of criticism of RIDC. I think they've done somewhat of a capable job in the demolition and the cleanup without a tremendous amount of resources. But let's face it, the situation between here and Homestead has been quite dramatic. It would be much better if you had somebody with lots of money like the Park Corporation come in and just do things. Everything with RIDC's been hand to mouth, and I think to a great extent they've done a good job in what they've done and I know the limitations of what they've done, but maybe their time has passed, and maybe they need to turn the torch over and open it up for private development. I understand there's a payment in lieu of taxes with USX and there's environmental issues and there's liability, and there's lots of things. But the fact of the matter is for RIDC, this is a back-burner project for them. They're not an investor here. They don't have anything at stake. They don't have their own money in this. Things need to change dramatically if you're going to see development. They used basically government money, too. They haven't invested any of their own equity in this.

Charles Starrett (Duquesne-McKeesport-Clairton Enterprise Zone Coordinator, McKeesport Redevelopment Authority and member, Duquesne-McKeesport Policy Committee), interview with the Brownfields Systems Group, Carnegie Mellon University, January 10, 2000.

Brooks Robinson felt such criticisms were unfair:

You probably know that when you get a grant for doing remediation, or doing demolition, or doing road construction, from the Commonwealth of Pennsylvania, they do not cover any of the engineering, or any of the testing, all the soft costs. So it's a fifty-fifty thing. If I get a $3 million grant from the Commonwealth of Pennsylvania RIDC has to put $3 million of our capital or our in-kind service into that project to make it work.... RIDC put an enormous amount of our "coin of the realm" into these projects, with the anticipation of being able to recapture it through land sales, and we're yet not there.

Robinson, Sr., interview with the author, August 27, 2004.

91. Ellen M. Perlmutter, "Officials Critical of RIDC Practices Question Use of Public Funds," *Pittsburgh Press,* February 7, 1991, B-1.

92. Ellen M. Perlmutter, "Inquiry on RIDC Approved by House," *Pittsburgh Press,* March 21, 1991, and "RIDC Chief Says Agency 'Flexible,'" *Pittsburgh Press,* September 13, 1991, C-10.

93. Albert Brunwasser to Brooks Robinson, March 6, 1991, with a copy to Bruce Laswell (ICF Kaiser) "in re: comments on the work plan for remediation at Duquesne and Mckeesport."

94. The meeting took place on April 22, and a revised plan went to the DER on May 13. ICF Kaiser, "Monthly Progress Report No. 9, April 28,–May 31, 1991."

95. As time passed, RIDC saw merit in DER's sequence, but for very different reasons than the DER's. Brooks Robinson explained

We didn't do any testing of anything below the surface of the ground until after we had removed the buildings. We could have gone in there and done the ground water testing. I focused entirely on clearing everything from the ground up, and then let that land sit for several months, rain or snow or whatever, to see if, when we did test it, whether nature had cleansed itself, and it's remarkable what nature does. Nature has a wonderful way of recovering from all the abuses we put on it.

Robinson, Sr., interview with the author August 27, 2004.

96. Joseph Chnupa to Brooks Robinson, March 6, 1991, "in re: the issues requiring clarification and correction following DER's review of the Work Plan for Environmental Remediation, USX National and Duquesne Works Demolition Project."

97. Brooks Robinson to Joseph Hohman, March 19, 1991; Brooks Robinson to William Kiser (President, USX Realty Development), March 22, 1991.

98. Brooks Robinson to William Kiser, March 27, 1991.

99. RIDC, "RIDC Awards Contract for Pedestrian Bridge in Duquesne," March 27, 1991.

100. Wes Cotter, "Plant Delays End Firm's Bid for Brewery Contracts in '91," *Pittsburgh Business Times,* March 4–10, 1991, 4.

101. Kaiser tested twenty pieces of equipment for NISI and took another thirty-one samples for Turner. Spills cleaned were in buildings T-5 (Electric Distribution Building) and U-10 (Electric Power House) on the Duquesne site (ICF Kaiser, "Monthly Progress Report No. 7," 10 April 1991). Maureen Ford reported that cleanup of the spills started out very small but grew to cost over $1 million (Ford, interview).

102. After reviewing the bids, ICF recommended Aptus Environmental Services to RIDC

on March 8, 1991. On March 27 Penrose Wolf wrote RIDC's Frank Brooks Robinson, indicating that they were prepared to award the contract to Aptus. Robinson wrote back on April 3, approving the award.

103. Lawrence Michaels and Associates, Philadelphia, to Brooks Robinson, March 28, 1991. The "Reduced Pressurization and Filtration System" was owned by GPAC, Inc. Brooks Robinson to Penrose Wolf (Turner Construction), April 2, 1991, informing him that Rochez Bros.' use of the system could constitute a patent infringement, and giving instructions for securing the license.

104. Kaiser recommended Chester from eight laboratories that submitted proposals (of eleven invited), and RIDC concurred, while specifying a review of their performance and written recommendations for their continuance at six-month intervals. Brooks Robinson, memorandum to P. Wolf, T. Mckinney, and W. Hannan, April 3, 1991.

105. Karen Schmidt, "Land Swap to Aid Millsite Development," *Pittsburgh Press,* April 11, 1991, S-3.

106. Achtzehn, interview with the author.

107. ICF Kaiser Engineers, "Monthly Progress Report No. 9, April 28–May 31, 1991." By the end of May RIDC was ready to award three contracts totaling $726,293 for asbestos treatment and a fourth for monitoring during removal. The three firms were American Environmental Consulting Co., $82,901; American Asbestos Control Company, $243,597; and Kleen All of America, $399,795. As always when state funds were involved, these bids were at the state's "prevailing wages." Kaiser recommended Allegheny Asbestos Analysis for the air-monitoring work during asbestos removal because it was a woman-owned business, had done excellent work at sites in the past, and was the lowest bidder (Thomas McKinney [Kaiser] to Penrose Wolf [Turner Construction], May 6, 1991). On May 28 RIDC Southwestern Pennsylvania Growth Fund indicated its intention to award these "lump sum contracts for asbestos abatement at the City Center of Duquesne and Industrial Center of McKeesport sites for the work identified in asbestos abatement specification City Center of Duquesne/the Industrial Center of McKeesport-A-3 with the exception of package City Center of Duquesne-A-4."

108. Horgan, interview.

109. The permit would cost $12,000. Monthly payments of $1,000 to the municipal authority would cover their independent testing of water samples, inspections, and preparation of reports and documentation for the EPA. T. McKinney (ICF Kaiser), to Wilbert Hannan, May 21, 1991.

110. Located under roof, in a secure building, the McKeesport holding area was designed and built to meet all applicable standards. It was constructed in a building with a dirt floor and was designed with nine 12-foot-by-80-foot cells complete with synthetic liners and collection sumps. ICF Kaiser, "Monthly Progress Report No. 9, April 28–May 31, 1991."

111. T. McKinney to Wilbert Hannan, July 15, 1991.

112. The PCBs went to TSCA-permitted facilities, including S.D. Meyers, which received the cases. Asbestos was discovered in the roofs of buildings T-12 (Boiler Shop) and T-15 (Air Compressor), in Duquesne. ICF Kaiser, "Monthly Progress Report No. 10, June 3, 1991–August 10, 1991."

113. Bill Grattan, "Council Endorses Strategy to Attract Millsite Investors," *Pittsburgh Press,* July 11, 1991, S-4.

114. "New Access Road to Millsite Sought," *Pittsburgh Press,* August 8, 1991, S12.

115. A. Brunwasser to Louis Washowich, August 28, 1991.

116. Tim Vercellotti and Christine Vorce, "'One Step Forward, Two Steps Back,'" *Pittsburgh Press,* September 29, 1991, A1, 4.

117. Vercellotti and Vorce, "'One Step Forward, Two Steps Back.'"

118. Washowich, interview.

119. Washowich, interview.

120. "Industrial Waste Firm Interested in Former Mill Site," *Pittsburgh Press,* March 19, 1992, S1; Brooks Robinson to Herbert Higginbotham (Allegheny County Department of Engineering and Construction), March 24, 1992.

121. "Industrial Waste Firm Interested in Former Mill Site."

122. Charles Haefner, Jr. (ICF Kaiser), to Brooks Robinson, July 29, 1992. According to Maureen Ford, all four of the contracts began low and ended up with much higher costs. Ford, interview.

123. The asbestos contractors removed asbestos from buildings A-6 (Boiler Shop); C-4 (Scrap Department/Pouring Pads); C-5 (Walker Thickner) in McKeesport; and T-6 (Mold Conditioning Building) and T-10 (Mixer Building) in Duquesne. Concurrently, other contractors removed underground storage tanks near buildings C-15 (Locker Room) and C-17 (Antenna) in McKeesport, and removed soil containing PCBs near building T-5 (Electric Distribution Building) in Duquesne. ETSS, Inc., was responsible for tank cleaning, removal and disposal of hazardous and non-hazardous liquids and soil wastes, and treatment and discharge of residual water. Thomas Snyder (Eckert, Seamans, Cherin & Mellott) to Joseph Hohman, October 16, 1991; ICF Kaiser, "Progress Report, November 11–December 14, 1991."

124. Maureen Morrisey, "Duquesne Mayor Sees Future in Waterfront," *Pittsburgh Press,* November 27, 1991, S4.

125. ICF Kaiser, "Monthly Progress Report No. 15 to RIDC, Feb. 20, 1992." T-20 (Inspection Building) in Duquesne in December; in January D-3 (Blowing Room) in McKeesport, and T-17 (Roll Shop), P-4, P-5, and T-18 (Brick Shed) in Duquesne; and by February B-24 (Office), B-29 (Office) and B-30 (Drawing Storage) in McKeesport, and S-10 (Continuous Furnace), S-12 (Clarifying Control Building), and W-7 (Brick Shed #3) in Duquesne.

126. The Galbestos was in building U-1 (Lime Building). C. Haefner (ICF-Kaiser) to J. Stanko (Allegheny County Health Department), March 31, 1992.

127. "Loan to Help Renovate McKeesport Millsite," *Pittsburgh Press,* January 16, 1992, S12; Ford, interview.

128. "RIDC Gets Loan," *Pittsburgh Press,* March 6, 1992, B6.

129. Ron DaParma, "Progress Seen in Pittsburgh-Area Projects—Enterprise," *Pittsburgh Tribune-Review,* February 16, 1992.

130. Maureen Morrissey, "Developers to Vie in Marketing Millsites," *Pittsburgh Press,* S1.

131. "Industrial Waste Firm Interested in Former Mill Site," *Pittsburgh Press,* March 19, 1992, S1; Maureen Morrissey, "Leader of Firm Pursuing USX Tied to Dumping Fine," *Pittsburgh Press,* March 26, 1992, S1; Bohdan Hodiak, "Lagging Renewal Tied to Pollution," *Pittsburgh Post-Gazette,* March 10, 1993, S-1.

Mel Achtzehn, who served on the Duquesne Business Advisory Council, remembered
The people that I had worked with, originally, came in with the plans, we liked them,
we thought we could do something because we're going to get the site prepared for

entrepreneurs to move in and build. They were supposed to put in a building. They were supposed to do some recycling for us. They were going to have the garages, their labs and things on the site. That never materialized. Then the materials that they were putting in at the old ore pit weren't to our liking, because originally they were supposed to put a liner in, fill it, and develop it. That never happened.

Achtzehn, interview with the author.

132. Tim Vercellotti, "Casey Praised for Aid to Former Mill Sites," *Pittsburgh Press,* April 15, 1992, B4.

133. Scott Robertson, "Renovations at Mill Sites Signal Mon Valley Renaissance," *Allegheny Business News,* May 27–June 9, 1992.

134. Ron DaParma, "Officials Know It Will Take Years to Replace Steel Mills," *Pittsburgh Tribune-Review,* April 15, 1992.

135. Scott Robertson, "Renovations at Mill Sites Signal Mon Valley Renaissance," *Allegheny Business News,* May 27–June 9, 1992.

136. Robertson, "Renovations at Mill Sites Signal Mon Valley Renaissance."

137. Robinson still projected that between 50 and 75 acres at both sites would be available for development by that time. Ron DaParma, "Officials Know It Will Take Years to Replace Steel Mills," *Pittsburgh Tribune-Review,* April 15, 1992.

138. Buildings B-25 (Oil House), B-26 (Stores Building), and B-29 (Office Building) in McKeesport, and S-7 (Sub Station), S-9 (Steel Conditioning), U-15 (Blowing Engine House #3), and Q-11 (Metallurgical Lab) in Duquesne were completed in March; U-17 (Central Boiler House), Q-11 (Metallurgical Lab), S-19 (Heat Treating and Finishing Building), S-10 (roof of the Continuous Furnace), and U-5 (Linde Air Plant) in Duquesne, and A-10 (Machine Shop), B-25 (Oil House), A-9 (Coupling Blank), B-29 (roof of an Office Building), C-21 (Office), B-22 (Locker Room), B-23 (roof of the Die Shop), and C-19 (Smith Shop) in McKeesport in April; C-20 (Roll Shop) and C-16 (Spare Parts Storage) in McKeesport in May. PCBs came from T-5 (Electric Distribution Building) in Duquesne. ICF Kaiser, "Monthly Progress Reports Nos. 16–18," April 14, 1992, May 18, 1992, and July 10, 1992.

139. He reasoned that Kaiser's wording of test results of the slag samples from Metallized Paper's site sounded less than convincing that the slag was free of contaminants. Although the sample analyzed by Kaiser was free of hazards, their wording could invite the DER to require more samples, which the EPA might subject to its Superfund Hazardous Ranking System, a complex formula that would yield a score that, if high enough, could place the site on the National Priority List or a comparable state list. S. Faeth (Eckert Seamans Cherin & Mellott) to Brooks Robinson, May 18, 1992.

140. This would entail cleanup of ten pits: removal of 250,000 gallons of contaminated water; 500 tons of debris, sludge, and oils; 5,000 gallons of nonhazardous recyclables; and 2,500 gallons of acid. "RIDC Hands Down Trio of Contracts for Cleanup Effort at Shuttered Mills," *Pittsburgh Business Times,* May 25–31, 1992.

141. "RIDC Hands Down Trio of Contracts for Cleanup Effort at Shuttered Mills."

142. Mark Stiffler (Director, Site Restoration, ICF Kaiser) to Brooks Robinson, July 13, 1992, detailing the environmental summary of the City Center of Duquesne and Industrial Center of McKeesport. This is an update by Kaiser of the environmental summary tables included in the Priority Reports 1, 2, and 3, dated September, 1990.

143. Joseph Chnupa to Brooks Robinson, July 23, 1992.

144. Mark Stiffler to Brooks Robinson, July 28, 1992. Their work plan to accomplish this, submitted in August, estimated costs of some $62,000. Charles Haefner (ICF Kaiser) to Brooks Robinson, August 17, 1992.

145. Charles Haefner to Brooks Robinson, July 29, 1992.

146. Brooks Robinson to Michael Giuranna (EPA, Philadelphia), September 22, 1992, recognizing Guiranna's cancellation of a visit to the McKeesport site.

147. Robinson explained his rationale to RIDC's attorney Steven Faeth, saying, "Sometime ago I asked ICF to develop a recommended level of environmental cleanup for the McKeesport and Duquesne sites where the proposed reuse and zoning are for industrial purposes. What I am trying to obtain is some standard that can be negotiated with DER as the acceptable background which if and/or when achieved, would get them to pass on." Brooks Robinson to Steven Faeth, October 27, 1992.

148. Mark Stiffler to Brooks Robinson, October 19, 1992, including tables of nominal soil cleanup standards, derived by applying general health-based risk criteria, with supporting rationale for potential uses at industrial site restorations. Robinson forwarded the report to Steven Faeth for examination on October 27.

Shortly after, he wrote Faeth again with another concern about the DER, namely, their classifying RIDC as a "generator" of waste because of their cleanup activities. While Robinson did not feel that what they were doing should constitute the RIDC as a generator, he expressed concern about what the classification might entail (Brooks Robinson to Steven Faeth, November 6, 1992). A December report from Kaiser indicated that to date, RIDC had removed approximately 165 tons of solid waste and 56,000 gallons of liquid waste from McKeesport, and approximately 2,100 tons of solid waste and 243,000 gallons of liquid waste from Duquesne (Mark Stiffler to Brooks Robinson, December 4, 1992). Robinson immediately forwarded this report to Faeth as well, again expressing his concerns over RIDC's uncertain status as a generator.

149. This program included reconditioning old wells, installing new wells, and sampling and analysis of all monitoring wells (Scot Lewis [Kaiser project engineer] to Maureen Ford [RIDC] November 17, 1992). RIDC expected to receive bids for construction of the new wells by the end of the year and to award a contract for drilling in early January. If the wells could be in place by the end of January, samples could be drawn, analyzed, and evaluated by the end of March. Wilbert Hannan, draft letter to Michael Giuranna (Hazardous Waste Management Division, EPA), December 10, 1992.

150. RIDC, minutes of a meeting concerning the Duquesne and McKeesport demolition projects, December 15, 1992. Attending were Brooks Robinson, Thomas Mckinney (ICF Kaiser), and others.

151. Mark Stiffler to Brooks Robinson, January 25, 1993, with answers to forty-three questions and comments Robinson had registered with Kaiser.

152. Brooks Robinson to Charles Duritsa, February 1, 1993, attaching a copy of Robinson's questions to Kaiser and their answers and a Development Plan Schedule.

153. Brooks Robinson to Mark Stiffler, February 4, 1993.

154. "Buildings Razed at Industry Center," *Pittsburgh Press*, S-5.

155. Patti Murphy, "Soil, Gravel from Dam May Go to Ex-Mill Sites," *Tri-state Sports & News Service*, February 14, 1993, W-2.

156. Nonetheless, Brooks Robinson said in a letter to the Corps that he was still hopeful that some or all of the fill could be used to raise the elevation of the two sites. Patti Murphy, *Tri-state Sports & News Service,* April 7, 1993, S-2.

157. The spill was at building U-10. "Task Order No. 6A Cost for Engineering Services for 1/31/93–1/27/93," February 5, 1993.

158. Task Order of March 5, 1993, for February 28, 1993, to March 27, 1993, for a total of $41,216, increasing the expenditure limit to $286,131.

159. Steven Faeth to Brooks Robinson, February 9, 1993.

160. That is, USX could have cleaned it up prior to the sale and secured a higher price. USX's claim was for $1,316,405 (W. L. White [Senior General Attorney, USX Corporation] to Johns-Manville Asbestos Property Damage Settlement Trust, March 30, 1993). The RIDC proceeded regardless, opening bids for additional asbestos removal February 12. By early March Kaiser had analyzed the bids and recommended American Environmental Consultants, Kleen All, Spacecon, and American Industrial to do the work.

161. Johns-Manville contended that RIDC had not submitted "proof of payment documentation." Johns-Manville Asbestos Property Damage Settlement Trust, April 30, 1993.

162. W.L. White to Steven Faeth, May 7, 1993, asking if RIDC wanted to request binding dispute resolution regarding the asbestos claim, and May 14, 1993, response from Brooks Robinson concluding there was no reason to pursue further a claim against Manville.

163. Bohdan Hodiak, "Lagging Renewal Tied to Pollution," *Pittsburgh Post-Gazette,* March 10, 1993, S-1; Ford, interview. Hodiak's article estimated that environmental cleanup had already cost over $30 million and that many millions more would be required to complete the job. This appears to be an error. In an article four months later the same journalist quoted Brooks Robinson as saying that cleanup to date had cost $10 million. Bohdan Hodiak, "Asbestos Removal Contracts Awarded," *Pittsburgh Post-Gazette,* June 9, 1993, S-6. Eight months earlier, ICF Kaiser had reported that cleanup to date had cost $5.65 million, exclusive of their fees (Mark Stiffler to Brooks Robinson, July 13, 1992). In early 1995 George Braun estimated that environmental cleanup costs at Duquesne alone had been $8 million. Eric Heyl, "EPA Will Pay for Cleanup Costs for Industrial Sites," *Pittsburgh Tribune-Review,* January 20, 1995.

164. "Demolition Work Set in McKeesport," *Pittsburgh Post-Gazette,* April 14, 1993, S-5.

165. Tom Barnes, "RIDC Chief Criticizes DER Staff Attitudes," *Pittsburgh Post-Gazette,* April 15, 1993, B-4. It was just such experiences that led Robinson to become an active participant in drafting the legislation that would become the state's Industrial Land Recycling Program two years later.

166. Brooks Robinson to Wilbert Hanna, Louis Washowich, and Mel Achtzehn, April 15, 1993.

167. Bohdan Hodiak, "DER Says It's Satisfied with Cleanup Pace," *Pittsburgh Post-Gazette,* April 21, 1993, S-2.

Mayor Mel Achtzehn described the difficulty of working with the DER. He recalled the problems of getting the main road constructed into the Duquesne site.

It wasn't necessarily the construction. It was the cleanup. We had to deal with DER, DEP now, and they were tough. They came in and said, "You have to take all the dirt out," from the site where that road was going to go in, to at least five feet, pretty close, to get the road in. In the earlier part of our cleanup we were taking the hydrocarbons and things like that out of the site. We had to send it to Alabama, in barrels and drums. That was expensive, very expensive. Well, finally, after a number of meetings, they finally realized that it wasn't necessary to take these contaminants out, because the type of contaminants we had were nothing more than hydrocarbons, oils and things like that. When we had dust we spread oil to keep the dust down. We did that all the time; your back street ways, your back alleys, had oil put on them to keep the dust down. So then they came to the conclusion that if we encapsulate the dirt that we were fine, and that's exactly what we did. We went down far enough—our road down here right now is built and constructed to sustain any large vehicle you can think of without damage, and we've got a three-foot base under that road, so we're in good shape, and that encapsulated the rest of the dirt and saved us a tremendous amount of money trying to put this street in.

Melvyn Achtzehn (former mayor, City of Duquesne, and member, Duquesne-McKeesport Policy Committee), interview with the Brownfields Systems Group, Carnegie Mellon University, December 7, 1999.

Don Horgan of Allegheny County Health Department explained more about the practice of spreading oil on roads at the mills to reduce air pollution:

When I used to work for Energy Impact Associates we did road dust emissions for U.S. Steel Homestead Works and that area. And the idea was, the EPA went to what they called the bubble system. So rather than just taking all the emissions that came out of the stack, you would take emissions that were coming off the roads. And they had found out that if you cleaned your roads there were less emissions, and not only that, a lot of the roads were dirt and they put creosote or whatever they were putting on them to keep them hard and to keep the dust down. The government went out of its way to help these plants.

That became the standard. We did Chenango and that's what we would do. You'd go in and that's just how we'd work. You'd come in with these tires, basically four high-balls on a tower, and you'd have cars run by, and you'd have to make them speed, and then you'd see how high the plume was going and you'd capture all that, and you'd figure out a trail and how much was getting off the plant, and then you'd trade that, you'd subtract that out, from the total that they were getting, so you could actually put more out of the stack if you were saving this much in fugitive emissions. That's exactly what would happen. As soon as you would do it you'd take all these tests with no controls and then they'd go in and they'd pour oil over it, and you'd go back and retest it and you'd find out how much you were saving by doing this.

Horgan, interview.

168. Achtzehn, interview with the Brownfields Systems Group. Some years later he had much the same to say:

We were unfortunate. When Homestead went down Park Corporation came in and they moved immediately. There was nobody there to stop them. They started tearing buildings down, they started getting the site cleaned up and everything else, with no problems, problems with the site, with the scrap and stuff. But then when we started County Health came in, says, you can't do that. Before we could do anything, with any building, we had to get a permit from the county to come out. And trying to get a permit from them would take upwards of six months.

Kelly Park moved in right away, and they immediately started. We didn't have that ability here. We didn't have those people on board to do that on our site. This is private enterprise. Now Brooks had to do things in a certain way that Kelly Park didn't have to worry about. The Park Corporation moved in too fast for them. They came in, took over, and immediately leveled it, immediately. . . . a private enterprise like that, coming in and moving immediately, I think they took them by surprise, they really did. We didn't have that. We didn't have a private realtor come in and immediately find a way to dispose of the equipment, the buildings, and get the ground ready for new construction like they have down there now. That didn't happen.

Achtzehn, interview with the author.

Don Horgan of the Allegheny County Health Department saw the situation differently. Describing his experience, he said

It's funny, Park, whatever we asked them to do they did. RIDC was just the opposite. We don't want to do this. We want to knock this building down. We're going to do this. I mean they were actually coming in and telling us what we were going to do. It's because they contracted out to an oversight company that thought they could come in and tell us how we were going to do our job.

And, believe it or not, we had to get EPA involved because of RIDC. They went, and Brunwasser was the head of the Health Department at the time, and he turned around and said, we're going to knock these buildings down with all this asbestos in it, that's what RIDC proposed. He kind of went along with it, and he may have been given some false information, too, because one of the guys said, uh, EPA in Ohio gave us permission to do this, and we have all these numbers, and I called EPA in Ohio. To begin with it wasn't the EPA Federal, it was the state of Ohio—they called themselves the EPA, too— and they said, no, we never gave permission to knock those buildings down. We gave them permission to bury it at the site, and that's where those numbers are from, so someone was. . . . And EPA came in and said, if you think you're going to knock those buildings down we're going to cite you. And Brunwasser to his credit came right back and said, you'll follow every regulation that Allegheny County tells you to do.

It's funny. Two different groups, and you see the difference. One's down, gone, something in its place, the other one, just hemmed and hawed, we're going to do this, no, we don't like how you want to get on me. I don't know why that is, other than, I think, one is a private corporation, went in with a plan, we're going to knock this down, we're going to develop it, and the other was always looking for money before they did the next phase of it. Plus Park was scrapping everything.

Horgan, interview.

169. Washowich, interview.

170. August Carlino (Steel Industry Heritage Task Force), interview with the Brownfields Systems Group, Carnegie Mellon University, January 21, 2000.

171. Achtzehn, interview with the author.

172. Gene Capristo (member, Duquesne City Council), interview with the Brownfields Systems Group, Carnegie Mellon University, March 11, 2000.

173. In contrast, in Duritsa's mind RIDC was looking for the department's assurance of relief from liability:

We were being asked for a blessing on those sites. Specifically, they came to us. Ultimately, they wanted a blessing from us to say we can use it for the purpose we propose. Well, that set a mechanism for us to give that specific blessing.

That was the issue that we most often dealt with groups who wanted to develop brownfields, was the issue of liability relief. Although they came to us to discuss the cleanup, I always felt it was a challenge for my staff and me to work with them to come to some reasonable understanding of what cleanup they'd have to do and under what circumstances. But probably the issue they were most concerned about was legally how they would be held responsible after the cleanup. Would there be any release from the Commonwealth as far as any future cleanup actions or even a threat from third-party law suits. That issue seemed to be paramount in their minds, even more so than what the cleanup would entail.

[Park] never came to us, asking us for any blessing, pre-Act 2 or post-Act 2. They just did not think that release from liability was important to them. They could get the funding and proceed, where others felt they had to have it, much to the chagrin of our central office and political people, who told everybody that nothing will ever proceed unless one goes and gets the liability relief that's offered under the state legislation, and that's not true. You can do it without that.

Duritsa, interview.

174. Brooks Robinson to Joseph Chnupa, April 23, 1993.

175. Building T-5 had the PCBs that were taking so long to clean. RIDC, minutes of a project meeting held May 18, 1993.

176. At the end of June the contractors reported that in McKeesport they had excavated five underground storage tanks, taking soil samples (results pending) before backfilling; pumped over 30,000 gallons of oil from one oil tank (in the C-10 Fire Foam building and tank), leaving it ready for asbestos abatement; were preparing eighty-five drums containing PCBs for disposal (in the C-2 Pipe Storage marshaling area); were validating groundwater samples; and were removing asbestos from outside tanks and piping (in the C-9 Water Softener Plant). In Duquesne they were awaiting the approval from a landfill for the disposal of some seventy-five drums (from the S-1 Shipping Building #3 marshaling area); working on a decontamination area and work plan for a PCB spill (in the U-10 Electric Power House); had finished cleanup of PCBs and had removed the asbestos roof material from the T-5 Electric Distribution Building (although the county still had to inspect the work before the building could be demolished); and were 70% to 75% complete with the removal of two other roofs (70% off the S-4 Bar Stock/Finishing/Slow Cool Building and 75% off the S-16 Electric Furnace Plant), with approximately three more weeks of work remaining. RIDC, minutes of an update and planning meeting on environmental remediation held June 29, 1993.

177. RIDC, minutes of a project meeting of ICF Kaiser and RIDC held June 9, 1993.

178. T. McCormick (Spacecon Abatement) to Richard Easler (ICF Kaiser), July 15, 1993.

179. Brooks Robinson and Richard Easler to Timothy McCormick, August 5, 1993.

180. Tom Barnes, "Plan for Coal Blending Facility Has Friends, Foes in Duquesne," *Pittsburgh Post-Gazette,* May 31, 1993, B-1.

181. Bohdan Hodiak, "Asbestos Removal Contracts Awarded," *Pittsburgh Post-Gazette,* June 9, 1993, S-6.

182. Ron DaParma, "Officials Know It Will Take Years to Replace Steel Mills," *Pittsburgh Tribune-Review*, April 15, 1992; "Foundries Open Landfill," *Pittsburgh Post-Gazette*, June 26, 1993, B-10; Jack Markowitz, "Sand Pit Spells Hope in Mon Valley," *Pittsburgh Tribune-Review*, June 27, 1993.

183. "For the Record," *Pittsburgh Press*, July 23, 1993, C-11.

184. ICF Kaiser, "Underground Storage Tank Closeout Report," December 7, 1993.

185. Brooks Robinson to William W. Kiser (President, USX Realty), August 12, 1993.

186. Tom Barnes, "Duquesne Rejects Coal Blending Depot," *Pittsburgh Post-Gazette*, August 20, 1993, B-7.

187. Mark Stiffler (ICF Kaiser), *"Update Report"* addressed to Wilbert Hannan for the purpose of reviewing the environmental and demolition activities performed at the Industrial Center of McKeesport and City Center of Duquesne from November 1992 to August 1993, September 17, 1993.

188. The affected buildings were the Pattern Storage Building, Production Planning Building, Heat Treating Laboratory, General Office Building, and one other structure. "Contract Awarded," *Pittsburgh Tribune-Review*, September 26, 1993.

189. RIDC, minutes of the environmental remediation update and planning meeting, November 30, 1993.

190. David L. Michelmore, "Can Mill Towns Revive? Areas Decimated by Demise of Industry Seek New Assets," *Pittsburgh Post-Gazette*, November 29, 1993, A-1.

191. Ron DaParma, "Business Bargains Thrive in the Mon Valley," *Pittsburgh Tribune-Review*, February 12, 1995.

192. "Blast Hurls Shards a Mile[,] Pieces of Steel Hit Buildings, Apartment, in Furnace Demolition at Old Duquesne Mill," *Pittsburgh Post-Gazette*, May 15, 1994.

193. Pittman continued

We're having a meeting in the room after that. There's these big globes that are in the ceiling, bigger than basketballs, that illuminate the room. And Mel [Achtzehn] is sitting at that end of the table and I'm sitting at this end of the table, and the lights are one, two, three across. We're in the middle row. Right in the middle of the meeting—we didn't realize how much this thing had been shaken—one of those globes dislodges itself and hits the floor. Glass goes everywhere. Had someone been sitting under that, had to have been killed—like a big street light. No one will ever forget that day. Whenever I go in that room today I always look up, because they're on spindles, and then these big globes.

Pittman, interview. Maureen Ford corrected Pittman's memory that this occurrence was in connection with the demolition of Dorothy and stated that the damaged table was not marble. Ford, interview.

194. DaParma, "Business Bargains Thrive in the Mon Valley."

195. "Big Bang," *Pittsburgh Tribune-Review*, January 14, 1995.

196. Eric Heyl, "EPA Will Pay for Cleanup Costs for Industrial Sites," *Pittsburgh Tribune-Review*, January 20, 1995.

197. DaParma, "Business Bargains Thrive in the Mon Valley."

198. Starrett, interview.

199. Robinson, Sr., interview with the author, August 27, 2004. In 2004 Robinson calculated that RIDC had removed 2,569,000 square feet of asbestos-containing material and 2,081,000 gallons of hazardous and nonhazardous liquid waste in 3,855 drums from the Duquesne and McKeesport sites. Maria Guzzo, "Agreement Encourages Brownfield Development, Clarifies Cleanup," *Pittsburgh Business Times*, May 28–June 3, 2004.

Chapter 6. Observations in Closing

1. After a period of economic expansion in the 1960s, high federal budget deficits and dramatic rises in oil prices led to serious and persistent inflation, beginning in about 1965, that continued for the next twenty years. This inflation, coupled with actions by the Federal Reserve Board to bring it under control and deregulation of the banking industry in 1980, led to rising interest rates, which peaked in the early 1980s. The economy stagnated, leading to periods of recession in 1970, 1974–75, 1980, and 1981–82, with high rates of unemployment.

2. In 1950 American steel had accounted for 47% of the world's total production (96.4 million of 207.9 million tons), but by 1979 it accounted for only 16.5 % (131.5 million of 824.5 million tons). Pittsburgh's steel plants could no longer operate profitably. "By the early 1980's, the beleaguered steel executives and their alter egos in the unions were haunting Washington, D.C., pleading for government protection from foreign competition." Jonathan Hughes, *American Economic History* (Glenview, IL: Scott Foresman and Company, 1983), 591.

Talbot Hiteshew, the vice president of Mellon Bank who ran the Pittsburgh Division of the bank from 1966 to 1977, observed

> As time passed the business of making steel got skinnier and skinnier, and competition became fierce. Union and management in the United States allowed costs to get totally out of hand. Mills in America paid employees $25 an hour while mills in other countries paid $7 to $9 an hour. Steel companies in Pittsburgh simply priced themselves out of the marketplace.
>
> When I was fairly new in the business, Pittsburgh had the top three manufacturers of rolling-mill equipment in the world. I traveled to all of the steel companies in the Pittsburgh area to suggest buying equipment from these manufacturers, who were crying for business, but the mills couldn't justify the cost. They believed the return on their investment wouldn't be there. I tried to tell the mills that it wasn't a question of return on investment, but one of whether they were going to be in business in 10 or 15 years. Other companies were going to buy the modern equipment in the meantime and lower their costs.
>
> That's exactly what happened. The Japanese bought the new technology while Pittsburgh watched the decline of a major industry. It was hard to see in advance. Japan started out as a nineteenth-century country after World War II, but arrived in the twenty-first century before we did. Nothing could have stopped foreign steel progress during that period.

Quoted in Mark Perrott and John R. Lane, *Eliza: Remembering a Pittsburgh Steel Mill* (Charlottesville, VA: Howell Press, Inc., 1989), 33. Part of the picture was also more profitable investment possibilities in other sectors, as in U.S. Steel's 1982 purchase of the Marathon Oil Company, for example. See Lubove, 22–23, on this point.

3. Although manufacturing employment in the United States grew by 21% (from 15.6 million

to 18.9 million) from 1954 to 1987, employment fell off in four industrial sectors, namely, apparel and three that were important to Pittsburgh. In 1954 food manufacturing constituted 7% and primary metal industries constituted 44% of manufacturing jobs in the Pittsburgh region. Over the next generation jobs in food production fell nationally from 1.6 million to 1.4 million; jobs in primary metal industries fell from 1.2 million to 0.7 million. U.S. Department of Commerce, Bureau of the Census, *Censuses of Manufactures, Wholesale Trade, and Service Industries, 1954, 1958, 1963, 1972, 1977, 1982, and 1987, Geographic Area Series.*

Pittsburgh plants had aged: the last integrated steel mill was completed in 1911. Production costs had risen. Markets shifted westward with the population, and firms responded by building new production facilities—employing new technologies—elsewhere. Communication and transportation evolved rapidly, undermining Pittsburgh's traditional market (at one time half of Pittsburgh's steel was produced for the railroads) and changing the economics of the location of production. Still, all of this was in the context of a national decline in Pittsburgh's most important manufacturing industries.

4. Perceptive observers had seen the change coming. In his foreword to the Pittsburgh Regional Planning Association's 1963 report, *Region in Transition: Report of The Economic Study of the Pittsburgh Region,* Streuby L. Drumm, the association's president, had warned

> An industrial area with strong roots in the past inevitably faces a period of massive transition from its traditional pattern of specialization to a kind of economy in which a diversity of lighter industries, automation, communications, research, education, capacity to acquire new skills, and a broader conception of the amenities of community life play a crucial role. The Pittsburgh Region . . . is confronted with a particularly challenging problem of adjustment. The fullest possible recognition of this challenge, and of the strengths which can be mobilized to meet it, is clearly needed.

Pittsburgh Regional Planning Association, *Region in Transition: Report of The Economic Study of the Pittsburgh Region, Vol. 1* (Pittsburgh: University of Pittsburgh Press, 1963), vii. The study was carried out under the direction of the noted regional economist Edgar M. Hoover. In the concluding chapter of *Region in Transition,* "At the Crossroads," the research team summarized

> In coal, in steel, and also in glass, the Region first prospered because here were the natural resources in ample supply. In steel and in glass, the economies of large-scale production further promoted the concentration of these industries in the Region. But the exploitation of these resources, while profitable in the narrow sense of costs and revenues, led to infirmities in the Region's economic fiber which were to take their toll later on.
>
> The Region has exhibited a marked failure to extend its economic domain much beyond its basic specializations. . . . Now Pittsburgh needs the second stage [of diversification] to maintain growth, but it seems lacking in vigor. (420–21)

In his review of the same study, historian Roy Lubove had observed that even by the time of the original Pittsburgh Survey of 1907–08, "Pittsburgh had already entered a long period of economic decline" and that by 1963 the "regional industrial structure which was brilliantly appropriate for the nineteenth century . . . in the electronics and space age appears as flexible and nimble as an elephant dancing a minuet." Roy Lubove, review of *Region in Transition: Economic Study of the Pittsburgh Region, Vols. I and II. Technology and Culture* 6, 3 (Summer 1965), 485–86.

In his retrospective *Twentieth-Century Pittsburgh: The Post-Steel Era* Lubove suggested that

Pittsburgh's industrial transformation was, at least in part, a strategy rather than simply the result of forces entirely beyond the control of Pittsburghers: "Efforts to halt the erosion of the industrial sector in the Pittsburgh region failed through a convergence of market forces and a strong consensus within the civic coalition that the local economy had to be diversified and modernized" (Roy Lubove, *Twentieth-Century Pittsburgh, Volume 2: The Post-Steel Era* (Pittsburgh: University of Pittsburgh Press, 1996), 21). He refers at length to labor historian David L. Rosenberg's view that the Allegheny Conference on Community Development "aspired to attain 'balance and diversity in the regional economy' at the expense of the traditional industrial sector." He quotes Rosenberg as saying, "'The possibility of global overcapacity and competition from foreign imports could not have been entirely unanticipated by conference planners, when, in their role as bank directors, they must have participated in the banks' investment policies.'" Lubove, 17.

Still, all this was too little, and mostly too late. Despite the warnings of academic researchers and the efforts of the civic leadership, most Pittsburghers could not and did not appreciate the forces that in the 1980s would turn their lives and their communities upside down. Nor, perhaps, could anyone have predicted the rapidity of the collapse and the full extent of its impact or have been able to avert it.

5. Pennsylvania environmental protection laws passed between 1967 and 1972 were the All Surface Mining Act; the Coal Refuse Disposal Act; the Air Pollution Control Act; the Comprehensive Clean Streams Act; the Solid Waste Management Act; the Pennsylvania Scenic Rivers Act; the act creating the Department of Environmental Resources, the Environmental Quality Board, and the Environmental Hearing Board; the Land and Water Conservation and Reclamation Act; and the act requiring the Department of Transportation to conduct environmental evaluations in planning highway projects. This activity culminated in passage in May 1971, by a ratio of 4 to 1, of an environmental amendment to the State Constitution, Article 1, Section 27, that declared, "The people have a right to clean air, pure water, and to the preservation of the natural, scenic, historic and esthetic values of the environment. Pennsylvania's public natural resources are the common property of all the people, including generations to come. As trustee of these resources, the Commonwealth shall conserve and maintain them for the benefit of the people."

The 1968 Solid Waste Management Act and the 1970 amendments to the Clean Streams Law were precursors of this new doctrine and preceded comparable federal legislation. The Solid Waste Management Act gave the state authority to regulate both "hazardous" and "residual" wastes. The act directed the Environmental Quality Board to promulgate a list of hazardous wastes, defined as wastes that increase mortality or morbidity or "pose a substantial . . . hazard to human health or the environment." The act empowered the state to issue permits, enforcement orders, and restraints and to impose fines and criminal penalties for failure to conform to the state's rules and regulations on treatment, storage, transportation, and disposal or management of solid wastes. 35 P.S. § 6018.103.

The Clean Streams Law directed that "whenever the department [of Environmental Resources] finds that pollution or a danger of pollution is resulting from a condition which exists on land in the Commonwealth the department may order the landowner or occupier to correct the condition in a manner satisfactory to the department." The law gave power to the state to issue orders for abatement, restraints, and fines, and defined each day of violation as a separate offense. 35 P.S. § 691.316.

6. The Toxic Substances Control Act (TSCA), enacted October 11, 1976, authorized the EPA to catalog industrial chemicals and to "require reporting or testing of those that may pose an environmental or human-health hazard" (U.S. Environmental Protection Agency, "Toxic Substances Control Act," http://www.epa.gov/region5/defs/html/tsca.htm, March 3, 2003). Under the Resource Conservation and Recovery Act (RCRA), enacted October 21, 1976, "the handling and disposal of hazardous wastes, which are generated mainly by industry, will come under Federal/State regulation" (U.S. Environmental Protection Agency, "New Law to Control Hazardous Wastes, End Open Dumping, Promote Conservation of Resources," press release, December 13, 1976).

7. U.S. Environmental Protection Agency, Office of Solid Waste and Emergency Response, *Superfund: 20 Years of Protecting Human Health and the Environment*, EPA 540-R-00-007, OSWER Directive 9200.5-16, December 11, 2000, 4.

8. Comprehensive Environmental Response, Compensation, and Liability Act of 1980, 42 U.S.C.A. § 9604 (1).

9. Authority for those taxes expired in 1995, and thereafter the trust fund was replenished with cost recoveries, interest on the fund balance, fines and penalties, and appropriations from the general fund. See U.S. General Accountability Office, "Hazardous Waste Programs: Information on Appropriations and Expenditures for Superfund, Brownfields, and Related Programs," GAO-05-746R, June 30, 2005.

10. By policy and usually in practice, EPA attempted to be fair about allocating the costs of cleanup among "potentially responsible parties," going after those most responsible for contamination to pay the highest costs for cleanup. Still, the broad liability established by the law encouraged those fingered by the EPA to pull in others in an effort to cut their own costs. Often many parties, including insurance companies and smaller firms, became embroiled in lawsuits over responsibility, which added still more costs.

Assignment of liability to innocent parties, who had had no role in contaminating a property, seemed fundamentally unfair, a case of the end justifying the means, and cried out for reform. A contemporary report of the Reason Foundation summarized, "Current environmental enforcement policy often violates fundamental principles of fairness and justice—by using criminal punishments where they're not appropriate, by abandoning traditional concepts of intent and responsibility, and by eroding constitutional protections." Alexander Volokh and Roger Marzulla, "Environmental Enforcement: In Search of Both Effectiveness and Fairness," Los Angeles: Reason Foundation, 1996, ii.

11. Pennsylvania American Water Company v. Commonwealth of Pennsylvania Department of Environmental Resources, 560 A. 2d 905, affirmed 586 A. 2d 1372, 526 Pa. 443.

12. Forty other states also passed their version of the Superfund law. U.S. General Accounting Office, "State Voluntary Cleanup Programs," GAO/RCED-97-66, 13.

Coming some years after the Superfund law, the Pennsylvania act benefited from recognition of some of the injustices and the ensuing criticism of that act's liability provisions. Presaging the kinds of reforms that would come later in the Industrial Land Recycling Program, Pennsylvania made an exception from "responsibility for the release or threatened release of a hazardous substance from a site" for innocent owners. 35 P.S. § 6020.701.

13. 35 P.S. § 6020.301.

14. 35 P.S. § 6020.102(8). "Many states passed laws with similar liability and enforcement

provisions [to CERCLA's]. The state enforcement programs implementing these laws generally address the thousands of sites that are not risky enough to qualify for federal cleanup, although the state programs may also handle highly contaminated sites. The federal Superfund program and the state enforcement programs establish stringent procedures for cleanups, which can add to their time and costs." U.S. General Accounting Office, "Superfund: State Voluntary Programs Provide Incentives to Encourage Cleanups," GAO/RCED-97-66 (April 1997), 2.

"There are a number of industrial sites in Allegheny and surrounding counties whose soils and/or groundwater are contaminated as the result of past manufacturing activities. Some of this contamination is the result of previously acceptable manufacturing practices. . . . In some cases, the sites were 'built up' using fill from another property which, by current standards, is classified as contaminated. . . . Health effects which were not perceived as a problem have now become major problems, threatening the financial viability and political health of industries and communities. Such examples include: widespread use of asbestos in industrial, commercial and resident environments; PCBs in transformers, lead solder in pipes, paint, glazes. . . ." Steven Ostheim, "White Paper on Liability, Indemnification and Risk Sharing," Pittsburgh: University of Pittsburgh Center for Hazardous Materials Research, WPPSTO/173, December 4, 1991, 1–2.

15. Work on Washington's Landing began in 1976, and on the Pittsburgh Technology Center in 1983. The Park Corporation acquired the Homestead site, and the county acquired the Duquesne and McKeesport sites in 1988.

16. The exception was Homestead, where the regulators did not get involved, and where the Park Corporation moved ahead, apparently unencumbered by the new laws and regulations. See "Comparisons with Homestead" and associated notes in chapter 5.

17. Brooks Robinson commented that "this was an almost impossible demand in most circumstances. It was a control mechanism utilized by the DER, which allowed them to be in control of the level of cleanup. If they didn't have a real interest you were fine, but if they were interested you could be put through regulatory hoops. (This was an extrapolation on my part.)" Frank Brooks Robinson, Sr., interview with the author, July 26, 1995.

18. According to Joseph Chnupa, former Assistant Regional Director, Southwest Region, Pennsylvania Department of Environmental Protection. Chnupa interview.

One observer summed up the situation by saying, "Lofty goals embodied in detailed federal legislation do not translate into effective solutions. Massive expenditures on pollution control do not necessarily result in equally significant improvements in environmental quality" (Bruce Yandle, "Environment and Efficiency Lovers," *Society* 29, no. 3 [March/April 1992], 23). Another concluded, "American society is in fact going to heroic lengths to eliminate supposed cancer causing agents that could well be harmless" (Robert H. Nelson, "How Much Is Enough? An Overview of the Benefits and Costs of Environmental Protection," in *Taking the Environment Seriously,* ed. Roger E. Meiners and Bruce Yandle, The Political Economy Forum (Lanham, MD: Rowman & Littlefield Publishers, Inc., 1993), 14. A 1995 opinion editorial in the *Wall Street Journal* summarized, "Federal environmental regulations, devised by unaccountable bureaucrats, often impose huge costs in return for little benefit" (David Schoenbrod, "On Environmental Law, Congress Keeps Passing the Buck," *Wall Street Journal,* March 29, 1995, A15).

19. As described in chapter 5 for the year 1991 and accompanying notes.

20. Describing the result, Bill Huebner wrote
With marching orders like those, you can easily guess the EPA's standard operating procedure: Track down every company with even the most remote connection to a

Superfund site, force them to pay, or drag them into court. Most companies fight the charges, rather than pay to clean up a problem they had little or no responsibility for creating. All the litigation caused by Superfund's notorious liability scheme is the main reason it now costs $30 million and takes 12 years to clean up the average Superfund site.

Bill Huebner, "My Superfund Nightmare," *Wall Street Journal,* October 25, 1995, A.

Most Americans, however, did not find that a fair approach: "Americans appear to think that those who pollute should pay, and prefer that the public itself contribute. . . ." John M. Gillroy and Robert Y. Shapiro, "The Polls: Environmental Protection," *Public Opinion Quarterly* 50 (1986): 271.

21. Commenting on the motives behind this approach, one observer said
If sites are abandoned and the previous operators are bankrupt, there is only one reason to go after firms that operated legally by contracting to have their waste products moved to disposal sites. The logic is simple. If someone can afford to pay, find a way to make them. But this says little for [a] society that seeks to operate under rules of law. In a similar way, it makes no sense to hold current owners of a site liable for actions of a previous owner, unless the purpose is simply to get money.

Brett A. Dalton, "Superfund: The South Carolina Experience," in *Taking the Environment Seriously,* 136.

Since parties to Superfund projects are not, for the most part, past law violators, there is only one good reason to make them parties to suits: The federal government is unable to obtain the revenues for the program from other sources. Calling for a public works program opens debate about benefits and costs among taxpayers.

Bruce Yandle, "Environment and Efficiency Lovers," *Society* 29, no. 3 (March/April 1992): 30.

22. Interview with the author, Pittsburgh, PA, August 27, 2004. Reacting to this fear, Chuck Duritsa of DER observed
Brooks told me something once that really stuck with me. I had not realized how concerned people were over dealing with these brownfield sites, and he told me, I am so concerned at what you guys in government will do to me that he said I've taken all my personal finances and put them into an account or whatever that I can't be held personally liable, because I fear you're going to sue me personally for these sites. When he told me that, that really stunned me, because in my mind, it never crossed my mind that we would ever do something like this. . . . The thought of going after somebody personally, like Brooks, that just stunned me when he told me that. I'm glad he told me that. It really opened my eyes up.

Duritsa, interview.

23. For Brooks Robinson of RIDC this was one of the "policy stances taken by the DER [that] have seemed to defy logic . . . that a third party such as RIDC could be held to be a 'generator' of waste, that was held to the same liability standard as the person responsible for the pollution." In his mind the motive behind the policy was "more disciplinary than practical or logical" (Robinson, Sr., interview with the author, July 26, 1995). But because of his concern
On at least three occasions that I can recall I literally followed the trucks that were leaving the site to their destination in Ohio, and in some cases West Virginia, to make sure that in my heart that the material was in fact not going to end up on the side of the road. Because I had to sign the transfer documents. I just followed them a couple

of times to make sure they got from point A to point B, not a very sophisticated way of assuring yourself, but you know, a trucker could go halfway, unload it somewhere in a dark alley or in a ravine some place, in order not to spend all that time going the rest of the way and coming back.

Robinson, Sr., interview with the author, August 27, 2004.

24. This approach to environmental regulation was only one manifestation of the nation's more general efforts in the 1960s and 1970s to improve the quality of life through governmental regulation and control. Where previous federal governmental economic regulation had generally been industry-specific, for example, regulation of transportation, banking, communication, or securities, the new wave of regulations—of civil rights, product packaging, traffic safety, truth in lending, safety of consumer products, and the environment—applied to all industries and had power over all violations. Their "motivation was clear enough: The free market, left to its own devices, either could not or would not produce a quality of life that satisfied [the public]. So, the force of government was placed at the service of broad reform." Hughes, *American Economic History*, 603.

25. One revealing study described the dynamics as follows:

Environmental inspectors deal with people who may not voluntarily desire their services ... the regulator strives to ... appear tough and credible to industry, government and public—without disabling industry and without straining its own litigation resources. Persuasion and control are "staged" in situationally-specific rituals, where the crafting of emotional display is a key interactional and control tool. . . . It was a widely shared belief amongst inspectors that regulatory outcomes and standards were open to negotiation, but "that's the last thing you'd admit, so you keep your cards close to your chest."

The inspector is prepared for confrontation because of his prior difficulties with the company and their resistance to regulation. . . . He needs to get tough. . . . The inspector adopts the "correct" bureaucratic position, "reminding" the manager that the legal onus is on him to demonstrate that the problem is not a problem. Thus the lines are drawn. The meaning of the encounter is partly determined by its history. Its social-emotional texture is set to be antagonistic; consequently a spikiness pervades the encounter. . . . Terse letters stating legal obligations, together with hints of enforcement and prosecution, provided appropriate leverage.

While inspectors were often unenthusiastic about actual prosecution, the symbols of prosecution were still valued—as a threat, a saber to rattle, something to look serious about. . . . Inspectors were happy to negotiate, but from a position of strength. . . . Except in situations of apparently serious or clear breaches of the law, a delicate balance between being helpful and authoritative—close and distant—was to be struck and composure maintained. . . . Nevertheless, the regulators could draw upon their legal-structural power, and its potential personal and economic costs to industry . . .

Stephen Fineman, "Street-Level Bureaucrats and the Social Construction of Environmental Control," *Organizations Studies* 19, no. 6 (1998): 953–54, 957, 962–63. Although these passages actually describe environmental regulation in another country (Great Britain) and in another context (control of industrial pollutants), they could easily have been written to describe the texture and the behaviors that characterized regulation of cleanup of the early brownfield sites in Pittsburgh.

26. Understandably, regulators viewed the relationship differently. Especially those regulators who, like Chuck Duritsa and other regulators in Pittsburgh, were doing their best within the prevailing regime to encourage cleanup and redevelopment had difficulty understanding the fear and antagonism felt by the regulated. Commenting on this, Duritsa observed,

> The attitude was that the environmental regulatory agencies would be unreasonable in their demands, but in fact I don't see that that was the case at all. We were willing to work with the groups that came before us. And I can't ever recall a failure. If they wanted to work it out we worked it out, to both of our mutual satisfaction—very bureaucratic and very threatening, but end result, once we sat down at the table, I thought we did well.
>
> I always saw myself as more practical and pragmatic, trying to resolve these issues. But it even came from the central office. There's no doubt about it. Some of the staff are zealots. But when you're talking about me, that's not the way I was.
>
> I took and the staff that I dealt with, like my managers, took great pride. It's so funny how it was looked at from one end and how I looked at it: I took pride in it, that we came to resolution and let it move forward. They would probably find it very hard to believe that I felt that way.

Duritsa recognized, but found somewhat baffling, the developers' hesitancy to view the regulators as helpful, since that is how he wanted to be. Still, leaving personalities aside, the system itself inherently made the parties antagonists, led those being regulated to avoid the regulators, and made them hesitant to divulge any information that could be used against them. Duritsa observed

> I'll make a general comment. Many times the negotiations with these types of things would have gone a lot quicker but the problem with the regulated community was that they were reluctant to put all their cards on the table with the regulators. Once I finally found out what they were concerned about it was much easier to resolve it. I guess they came in thinking that we can't tell DEP everything because they'll do something bad with it when in fact once they told us what the real issues of concern were, once they told me that, it made it much, much easier for us to deal with those issues. It would take three or four meetings over months until finally they would say, look, this is the real issue we're concerned about. And it could maybe be resolved right then and there, but we didn't understand that was the real issue that they were concerned about.
>
> With the URA, after dealing with it for years and years, the meetings now with the URA are much different. They are quite willing to tell us immediately what they were concerned about, and we could work with them much quicker than when they were scared of us.

Duritsa, interview.

27. Roger E. Meiners and Bruce Yandle, "Preface," in *Taking the Environment Seriously,* ix. As Joseph Chnupa, former Assistant Regional Director of DER's Pittsburgh office, observed, "The thing we noticed was, under command and control, if we caught the problem, fine. But did we have enough people to investigate?" Chnupa, interview.

28. See "Comparisons with Homestead" and associated notes in chapter 5.

29. U.S. General Accounting Office, *Superfund: State Voluntary Programs Provide Incentives to Encourage Cleanups,* GAO/RCED-97-66, April 1997, gives a good summary of provisions of

state voluntary cleanup programs in effect by that time.

30. By late 1999 over 90% of the states had some form of voluntary cleanup program in place. "State brownfields programs have evolved at an extremely rapid rate, shifting over time towards provision of greater incentives for redevelopment as a means of attracting more private sector capital." ICF Consulting and The E.P. Revitalization Systems Project, Inc., "An Assessment of State Brownfield Initiatives," U.S. Department of Housing and Urban Development, Office of Policy Development and Research, March 1999, i, iii.

The programs targeted the thousands of sites that did not clearly meet the criteria to be placed on the EPA's National Priority List but that were still under the Superfund cloud. They were contaminated, as defined in the Superfund law, but not so severely that EPA would require their cleanup. Still, they were subject to the same cleanup and liability provisions of the most polluted toxic waste dumps. Hence, in the minds of owners or developers, there was great uncertainty and unpredictability as to how the environmental regulators would react to efforts to develop them.

The states' voluntary programs typically provided for flexibility in cleanup levels and methods. In some cases developers could choose among different cleanup levels, for example, opting either for a "background" standard or for a standard designed for a particular future use. In some cases developers could choose a temporary solution to an environmental problem, such as paving a contaminated portion of a site for parking or erecting barriers to prevent human contact. Some states allowed partial cleanups, for example, permitting an owner to clean a portion of a site that was slated for development and leaving the remainder of a site untouched until a later time.

If developers cleaned a site under a voluntary program, the state typically gave some kind of release from state liability. In some states this was done by law, in others by regulation. Some assurances took the form of a covenant not to sue the owner, or even a restriction on the ability of others to sue. Some simply awarded a certificate of completion or issued a letter committing that the state would take no further action to require cleanup of the site.

Finally, several states offered financial assistance to owners for environmental assessment or cleanup, in the form of grants, loans, or tax credits.

A matrix of state programs, including their dates of adoption, is available in Charles Bartsch and Elizabeth Collaton, *Coming Clean for Economic Development: A Resource Book on Environmental Cleanup and Economic Development* (Northeast-Midwest Institute, 1996), 147ff.

31. Duritsa, interview.

32. Chnupa and Bowman, interview. Ken Bowman, former Assistant Regional Counsel in the same office, described similar feelings and the same developmental process:

We were struggling, too, with trying to figure out how to deal with contaminated sites as a policy matter, in an era when we had statutes, obviously, liability for people that buy property, but certainly a desire at that time to get the property back on the rolls for the local municipality.

Well, we were certainly evolving from experience, and we were not unmindful of the fact that Pittsburgh had gone through a tremendous transformation with the demise of the steel industry, and we also work for the people of Pennsylvania, as does the local municipality, and how do you work your role as an environmental agency charged with enforcement to work out a facilitative attitude with remediations, particularly brownfields? The URA didn't cause the problem. They tried to develop it. The steel industry had moved out and was gone, and we needed to work with the local government to get this property going and you see us trying to struggle, trying to figure out how to make this work and fit your plans as a development agency, with statutes that really weren't designed for brownfields development. And we were trying to cobble together, based on the school of hard knocks, through experience working with people, a system of dealing with URAs and other development agencies to remarket this property, all these properties. I mean you're talking lots and lots of land in western Pennsylvania.

Bowman, interview.

Don Horgan described a similar mentality at the Allegheny County Health Department: My thing was I didn't work for the government all my life. I used to work for a consulting firm, so I'll be honest, it's been a philosophy of the county ever since I've been here that we're here to work with industry, we're not here to punish them, and if we come up with an alternative method, and sometimes other people come to us, that's the way we work, and there's plenty of times we've gone out and said, let's try this; if it doesn't work we say no.

Horgan, interview.

33. Chnupa and Bowman, interview.

34. Bowman, interview. In addition to these attempts to help bring closure to the department's oversight through the consent agreements, the department began to experiment with other approaches that would offer protection from contamination while allowing development to proceed, essentially retreating from the standard of cleaning to a pristine level, as Kenneth Bowman described:

And that was another major feature of the time was fitting your design plans for the reuse with the remediation, to save money, so that you could move on to another property and develop it. And you see the evolution, for example, of the site-specific standard. Paving an area which isn't going to be a risk to anybody is a good way to deal with non-media solids and other materials that have been deposited over the years as they fill up these sites; that's an engineering control [an approach that the DER would not consider at Washington's Landing, but later approved for the Pittsburgh Technology Center]. The institutional control is, "don't use the ground water" [which the DER required at the Technology Center in lieu of insisting that the contamination be removed from the ground beneath the old foundations of the mill]. So those...issues were being worked on and thought through several years before Act 2 even came on the books.

It all seems so simple now as you look back over ten years of development when you're given a statute that empowers you to come up with these answers, but just two or three years before that, I mean, it was all brand new.

35. Don Hopey, "I, Too, Am an Environmentalist, DER's New Chief Declares," *Pittsburgh Post-Gazette,* December 12, 1994, A.

36. He recalled, "I sat down in a conference center in our office with Senator Brightbill and wrote Act 2." Robinson, Sr., interview with the author, August 27, 2004.

37. "Abandoned Sites—Top Environmental Priority," *Environmental Protection and Natural Resources Update,* Pennsylvania Department of Environmental Resources, April 14, 1995.

38. "EPA's Kostmayer Criticizes SB1," *Environmental Protection and Natural Resources Update,*

Pennsylvania Department of Environmental Resources, April 14, 1995.

39. "A Patch of Brown: Recycle Old Mill Sites without Degrading Greenfields," *Pittsburgh Post-Gazette,* March 15, 1995, A; "Industrial Reuse: Senate Bill Would Lower the Standard for Pollution at New Industrial Sites, Too," *Patriot-News,* March 22, 1995; "Revolting Development: City and Suburbs Would Reap a Bitter Harvest from Ridge's Latest Try at a 'Brownfields' Bill," *Philadelphia Inquirer,* April 4, 1995, A16; "Betraying Greenfields: A Flawed Cleanup Bill Establishes Too Low a Standard," *Pittsburgh Post-Gazette,* May 6, 1995, A.

40. James M. Seif, "Restoring and Reusing Industrial Sites," Pennsylvania Department of Environmental Resources, April 27, 1995.

41. Pennsylvania Department of Environmental Resources, "Governor Signs Land Recycling Bills into Law," *Environmental Protection & Natural Resources Update,* May 19, 1995. DER's official summary of the bills described them in these terms:

[The Land Recycling and Environmental Remediation Standards Act] establishes a realistic framework for setting cleanup standards based on health and environmental risks, sets up a clear process to standardize state approval of cleanup plans with deadlines for action, ends the now never-ending cleanup liability for sites once they are made safe, and provides opportunities for public review and input into setting cleanup standards.

[The Economic Development Agency, Fiduciary and Lender Liability Act] provides lenders, economic development agencies, municipalities and conservancies protection from environmental cleanup liabilities if they did not cause the pollution on a site.

[The Industrial Sites Assessment Act] establishes a special fund to finance environmental assessments and cleanups of sites in distressed communities.

42. "Pennsylvania Launches Land Recycling Program," *Natural Resources & Environmental Protection Update,* Pennsylvania Department of Environmental Resources, July 21, 1995.

43. "Five Members Appointed to Land Recycling Standards Board," *Natural Resources & Environmental Protection Update,* Pennsylvania Department of Environmental Resources, July 28, 1995.

44. "Act 2—13 Sites Cleaned and 47 Underway in Six Months," *Environmental Protection Update,* Pennsylvania Department of Environmental Protection, March 1, 1996.

45. "Land Recycling Report Is 'Solid Record of Achievement,'" *Environmental Protection Update,* Pennsylvania Department of Environmental Protection, July 26, 1996. In recognition of the innovative nature and the success of its Land Recycling Program, the Commonwealth of Pennsylvania was named a 1997 winner of the Innovations in American Government Awards sponsored by Harvard University's John F. Kennedy School of Government.

46. Dawida, interview with the Brownfields Revitalization Systems Project. The Industrial Land Recycling Program and similar programs in other states returned regulation of environmental cleanup to the states, where it had first begun. Some have suggested, based on experiences such as those in Pittsburgh, that decisions on environmental cleanup should move to an even more local level:

Cleanup of hazardous waste sites is logically the business of communities, counties, and rarely, the joint endeavors of adjacent states. The logic for Superfund is primarily political, not economic.

We conclude that hazardous waste problems are community problems.

Truly hazardous and abandoned waste sites should be cleaned, if the exposed community determines it is in their interests to do so. The exposed community, be it town, county, or state, can then decide how best to resolve and pay for such programs, using ordinary tax revenues. Ideally, the community that gets the collective benefit of risk reduction should pay. In other words, what is now Superfund should become a local public works program, a program that competes with others developed by people to provide services they value.

Brett A. Dalton, "Superfund: The South Carolina Experience," in *Taking the Environment Seriously,* 135–36. Had such a process been available, the progress of the projects in Pittsburgh would likely have been quite different. Mayor Lou Washowich observed

> I think if we had done it, the city of McKeesport, if we would have had the dollars, I think that we would have cleaned it to the point that we felt that we considered environmentally clean, maybe not in terms of what they thought. If you take soil that has some contamination in it, and you cover it with concrete how does the contamination come through the concrete? Those are the types of things that are mind-boggling, but yet you had to go in there and tear everything down and take soil off the top and the oils that penetrated.
>
> Oils! My dad was a body and fender man. He worked in a garage all his life. I mean people that work around cars, is this contamination killing them? Maybe so, but yet if you feed your family, you send your kid to college, you have a house, and you might take a vacation, that's going to keep you alive a hell of a lot longer than if you've never touched any type of contamination but you don't have any money to do any of those things. And that's one of the approaches I looked at it.
>
> I knew and I saw what that site meant to McKeesport, and then once they were out and they were leaving and they were gone I thought we could move the site, not to come back to having the same number of employees that the National Tube, but it would have been a hell of a lot easier bringing these small businesses in there to develop in there, if it would have been 25% of the jobs we once had, and the environment would have been much cleaner. There's no question about it. But that was the approach and the consideration and, well, I believe it could have happened but it just didn't work out that way.

Washowich, interview.

47. Washowich, interview.

48. Raymond Christman, telephone interview with the author, 29 January 2004. Joe Chnupa, in DER's Pittsburgh office, recalled

> Art Davis came out to the regional office and I covered the issues that were coming out with him. Unfortunately, that was close to the end of his term as secretary. It struck a chord with him, but it could not be dealt with in the time remaining to him. . . . I remember calling the chief counsel of the department and said, "You have to look at real risk." He said, "Yes, we are looking at that, Joe, and I think we can work out a reasonable approach to it."

Chnupa and Bowman, interview.

49. David L. Donahoe, telephone interview with the author, January 28, 2004.

50. Donahoe, telephone interview.

51. Donahoe, telephone interview.

52. Raymond R. Christman, telephone interview with the author, January 29, 2004.

53. In defense of Art Davis he added

And, again, I'm not trying to cast Art as somebody who was, it wasn't that he was opposed to it overtly or just that he was standing in the way of it, but he had a different philosophy about how things should get done . . . a more traditional, you know, centralized, regulatory approach to environmental management, as opposed to a more, not just market-oriented approach, but also an approach that involved using incentives, not just command and control and things of this sort, which I think was more what Seif brought to the table.

The developments in Pittsburgh had also contributed to the change, as described in the previous section. Ray Christman observed

It may have been that even with, perhaps, a different kind of natural inclination or mind-set, had Seif been in charge in '87 and the years following, he might not have been able to tackle the problem as expeditiously as he did in '95 because he wouldn't have had the political support, and wouldn't have had the same perspective, perhaps, that he had coming at it seven or eight years later.

Christman, interview.

54. The early history of developing brownfields in Pittsburgh and in other old industrial cities seems to run counter to Professor Samuel Hays's general conclusion that

Environmental thought and action arose in the midst of a previous and continuing overriding national commitment to development, which heavily shaped environmental affairs. In no sense have environmental concerns become overriding or even reached a place of importance in either personal life or public affairs equal to that of development objectives. Public leaders continue to give major emphasis to the overriding value of population growth, jobs, and investments and measure progress in these traditional terms; only in a few localities and in a few instances have environmental factors made their way to a leading place in the society and politics of the United States. While the nation's institutional leaders give favorable expression to the "environment," they continually warn about too much emphasis on it and implicitly affirm that it is subordinate to conventional economic growth. The dominant view is that it is a luxury, affordable only if sufficient economic growth provides means to finance it.

The tenuous role of environmental affairs couched among overriding developmental objectives is emphasized through the continual interaction between widespread affirmation of the importance of the environment on the one hand and limited support and often opposition to specific environmental objectives on the other. Institutional leaders on all sides, whether public or private, affirm the importance of environmental objectives. Yet almost immediately after such affirmations they define desirable policy in such a way as to limit its importance. Individuals also affirm the importance of "the environment" but are prone to divorce themselves from its policy implications when they affect them or to be highly selective, affirming them when they fit into their personal agendas but rejecting them when they do not.

Environmental objectives have arisen within the context of overwhelming development objectives and are still subordinated to them. Moreover, it is doubtful that the balance will be reversed and environmental ways of thinking will subordinate developmental interests. Rather, one can predict more accurately that they will remain in tension and conflict for the long run. Environmental objectives will continue to be advocated and to work their way occasionally into the nation's personal and public agendas, but, at the same time will face the resistance of a dominant developmental agenda.

Samuel P. Hays, *A History of Environmental Politics since 1945* (Pittsburgh: University of Pittsburgh Press, 2000), 228–29, under the heading "Environment and Development in Tension." Perhaps these are among the instances he had in mind in saying that "only in a few localities and in a few instances have environmental factors made their way to a leading place in the society and politics of the United States." Or perhaps his general conclusion was wrong with reference to the subject of contaminated properties.

55. Commenting on the conflict from a national perspective in the years when people around the country were exploring and adopting such approaches, one scholar wrote as justification that

it is precisely in designing policies to serve both economic and environmental goals effectively that our past efforts have all too often failed. The nation has frequently made much greater expenditures than were necessary to attain the environmental goals sought, diverting scarce resources from other areas of pressing national need. The allocation of our environmental resources has often shown little relationship to the true severity of our environmental problems. Environmental policies often impose complex and time-consuming regulatory regimes, stifling entrepreneurial energies on which the American market system depends. If we are serious about efforts to make the American economy more productive and efficient, improved policies for the environment must command one of the highest priorities.

Robert H. Nelson, "How Much Is Enough? An Overview of the Benefits and Costs of Environmental Protection," in *Taking the Environment Seriously,* ed. Robert E. Meiners and Bruce Randle, 1. Such a statement, made in 1993, could not have been made without the experience of the ten years that had gone before.

56. ULI—the Urban Land Institute, Technology and Industry Park: An Evaluation of Development Potential and Strategies for the Urban Redevelopment Authority of Pittsburgh, A Panel Advisory Service Report, November 11–16, 1984, 17.

57. Architect David Lewis talked the Park Corporation into retaining the chimneys. See Chapter 4, note 49.

58. David Lewis explained how Park came to that decision:

We formed a little small group. We made friends with Ray Park and particularly with his son, Kelly Park. And then came the big persuasion, which was to get them to invest literally millions of dollars in remediating the site, taking out all the concrete caissons the steel mills had sat on.

Now, an object lesson for all of that is actually down at Second Avenue, where the Technology Center is. That was a steel mill site. And on that site also it had caissons and also belonged to the Park Corporation. And when that site was due to be recycled the state or city, I can't remember which, which acquired the site from the Park Corporation, said, "Oh, they will take the concrete caissons out and remediate the site," because the Park Corporation said the price as is is so-and-so and the price if we do this remediation will be such-and-such. So they said, "Oh, well, we'll take it at the lower price." The result is they never took the concrete caissons out, and as result that's why the buildings are placed the way they are. They're placed where the concrete caissons are not. And that's why the landscaping is like that, with the concrete caissons underneath them. [Note from author: This is not correct. The foundations of the mill at the Pittsburgh Technology Center actually cover practically the entire site. The URA covered the entire site, including the foundations, with sufficient fill that gravity sewers could be run under the buildings built atop the fill, which in turn is on top of the old foundations.]

So, with that lesson in mind, and that was important for Homestead because the Parks looked at what happened down there and said, if we leave those concrete caissons in there we're going to have to live with the results. We're not going to be able to have a free canvas. They hadn't got a buyer for their land or anything like that at the time, and they needed every kind of advantage that they could get. So they went and they remediated, and the cost of remediation is a tremendously important part of the equation, because when redevelopment begins to occur, that redevelopment of course has to absorb the cost of the preparation of the site. So the Park Corporation did all that, and then they formed a liaison with Continental [to develop the Waterfront].

Lewis, interview.

Park and Continental Real Estate Companies announced plans to develop the Waterfront in 1997, and Park sold land for the Waterfront to Continental the following year.

59. "Learning from Pittsburgh," Detroit 2020, January 6, 2011, accessed June 14, 2011, http://detroit2020.com/2011/01/06/learning-from-pittsburgh/.

NOTES ON SELECTED PARTICIPANTS

Joseph M. Barr was mayor of the city of Pittsburgh from December 1959 to January 1970.

Mulugetta Birru became executive director of the Urban Redevelopment Authority of Pittsburgh in July 1992 after serving as executive director of Homewood-Brushton Revitalization and Development Corporation. He was still serving in 1995, when the stories in this book end.

Paul Brophy was executive director of Action-Housing from 1976 to 1979, when he was appointed director of the city of Pittsburgh's short-lived Department of Housing. He served in that capacity through December 1981, when Mayor Caliguiri reassigned the staff of the department to the Urban Redevelopment Authority and made Brophy executive director of the Authority. He served in that capacity until November 1986.

Jack Buncher was president of the Buncher Company from 1935 until his death in 2001. Originally a scrap and junk collection business, The Buncher Company became a leader in demolition and salvage and then in industrial real estate development. Buncher created the state's first industrial park, in Leetsdale, in 1954.

Richard S. "Dick" Caliguiri was a member of Pittsburgh's city council from 1970 to 1977 and was elected its president in March 1977. He assumed the office of mayor in April 1977, when Pete Flaherty resigned to go to Washington, D.C. Caliguiri served as mayor (elected in 1977 and reelected in 1981 and 1985) until his death in May 1988.

Robert P. "Bob" Casey served two terms as the Democratic governor of Pennsylvania, from January 1987 to January 1995. Prior to serving as governor, he had been the state's auditor general.

Raymond R. Christman was director of economic development for the Allegheny Conference on Community Development from 1981 to 1985. From January to November of 1986 he was deputy executive director of the Urban Redevelopment Authority of Pittsburgh. Upon Paul Brophy's resignation, Christman was appointed executive director and served until November 1987, when he became Pennsylvania's secretary of commerce. He served in that capacity until April 1991, when he resigned and returned to Pittsburgh to head the Technology Development and Education Corporation, a nonprofit organization charged with promoting growth of small and medium-sized manufacturing and high-technology firms, later renamed Southwestern Pennsylvania Industrial Resources Center (SPIRC), and later Catalyst Connection. In 1996 he assumed the additional role of president of the Pittsburgh High Technology Council.

Selected Participants

Thomas Cox was North Side coordinator at the Urban Redevelopment Authority of Pittsburgh from 1971 to 1973, director of development of Manchester Citizens Council from 1973 to 1979, and president of North Side Civic Development Company from 1979 to 1989. From 1989 to 1993 he was in Cleveland, Ohio, as president and executive director of Neighborhood Progress, Inc., a nonprofit community development organization. He returned to Pittsburgh in 1994, when he was appointed deputy mayor for policy and development by Mayor Tom Murphy.

Richard M. Cyert served as president of Carnegie Mellon University from 1972 to 1990.

Edward D. deLuca was director of the city of Pittsburgh's Department of City Development from April 2, 1979, until Mayor Caliguiri eliminated the department and sent its staff, except for deLuca, to the newly created Economic Development Department at the Urban Redevelopment Authority of Pittsburgh on January 1, 1982.

David L. Donahoe was Pittsburgh's city treasurer from 1978 to 1980, Allegheny County's aviation director from 1980 to 1984, executive director of the western division of the Pennsylvania Economy League from 1984 to 1985, and executive secretary to Mayor Dick Caliguiri from 1986 to 1987. He was appointed executive director of the Urban Redevelopment Authority of Pittsburgh in December 1987 and served until April 1989, when he became secretary of revenue for the Commonwealth of Pennsylvania. He left that position in 1995 to became the first executive director of the Allegheny Regional Asset District.

Gloria Fitzgibbons was director of the Urban Redevelopment Authority of Pittsburgh's Economic Development Department from January 1982 until her death in November 1983.

Peter F. "Pete" Flaherty was mayor of the city of Pittsburgh from 1970 until April 1977, when he left Pittsburgh to join the U.S. Department of Justice in the Carter administration. He quit after a year to run for, and lose a second time, the U.S. Senate. He returned to a private law practice and then was elected a county commissioner of Allegheny County, serving from 1981 to 1995.

Thomas J. "Tom" Foerster served a record twenty-eight years—seven terms—as a county commissioner of Allegheny County, from 1968 to 1995, and as chairman of the Board of County Commissioners for the last fifteen of those years. In 1995, he was defeated in the Democratic primary election. Prior to his service as a county commissioner he was elected a state representative in 1958 and served five terms, until 1968. In that office he supported measures to clean polluted streams and abandoned strip mines. He was a prime sponsor of the 1965 Clean Streams Act and the 1966 Mine Subsidence Act. During Tom Foerster's twenty-eight years as an Allegheny County commissioner, the county established four hospitals for the elderly and built a new airport and jail, and Community College of Allegheny County added its three suburban campuses. In November 1999 Foerster was elected to the first Allegheny County Council but was too ill to be inaugurated. He died January 11, 2000, at age 71, a few days after he was to have taken that seat.

Joseph Gariti became the Urban Redevelopment Authority of Pittsburgh's general counsel in January 1982 and served past 1995, when the stories in this book end.

Stephen A. George was executive director of the Urban Redevelopment Authority of Pittsburgh from September 14, 1973, to December 31, 1981.

Arthur V. Harris was an executive with Gulf Oil Corporation until 1975. In 1968 he became president of Three Rivers Improvement and Development Corporation (TRIAD), whose objectives were improvement, development, and beautification of Pittsburgh's three rivers. He was appointed to be a member of the Citizens Advisory Council to the new Pennsylvania Department of Environmental Resources at the time of its creation.

Rebecca A. Lee was director of the Economic Development Department at the Urban Redevelopment Authority of Pittsburgh from January 1984 to April 1986.

Robert H. Lurcott was the city of Pittsburgh's planning director from 1977 to 1989, when he joined the Pittsburgh Cultural Trust as director of development.

Sophie Masloff became a member of Pittsburgh's city council in 1976 and was elected chair in January 1988. Upon Mayor Caliguiri's death in May 1988 she became mayor and served through 1993.

David M. Matter was Mayor Caliguiri's executive secretary from 1977 until he resigned in 1985 to become executive vice president of Massaro Properties, Inc. In September 1990 he became director of development, and later president, of Oxford Development Corporation.

Robert Mehrabian was president of Carnegie Mellon University from 1990 to 1997.

Hiram Milton was president of Regional Industrial Development Corporation from 1967 to 1981, chaired the city of Pittsburgh's Economic Development Committee during Ed deLuca's tenure as the city's director of development, and then served for a number of years as president of the Allegheny Conference on Community Development's Regional Economic Development Committee.

Thomas "Tom" Murphy was executive director of Perry Hilltop Citizens Council and North Side Civic Development Council from 1973 to 1978. He served as a member of the Pennsylvania General Assembly from 1979 to 1993. He was elected mayor of the city of Pittsburgh in 1993, for a term beginning in January 1994.

John L. "Jack" Noonan was director of real estate at the Urban Redevelopment Authority of Pittsburgh from July 1965 to July 1987.

Robert Paternoster was Pittsburgh's planning director from September 1970 through 1976, when he left Pittsburgh to become planning director of the city of Long Beach, California.

Thomas J. "Tom" Ridge was the Republican governor of Pennsylvania from 1995 to 2001, when he responded to President George W. Bush's request that he become the United States Homeland Security Advisor. He became the first secretary of the newly established U.S. Department of Homeland Security in 2003.

John P. "Jack" Robin was the first executive director of the Urban Redevelopment Authority of Pittsburgh, serving from 1948 to 1954. He became Pennsylvania's secretary of commerce and then executive vice president of Old Philadelphia Development Corporation. In June 1973 he returned to Pittsburgh, after an eighteen-year absence, as a professor of public affairs at the University of Pittsburgh and as program advisor to the Allegheny Conference on Community Development. Dick Caliguiri, upon assuming the office of mayor, appointed him to the board of directors of the Urban Redevelopment Authority. He was elected chairman on May 6, 1977, and served in that office until 1994.

Selected Participants

Frank Brooks Robinson descended from a long line of Pittsburghers. He graduated from Yale University in 1954 and received his Bachelor of Architecture degree in 1960 from Carnegie Mellon University. He worked for the Pittsburgh architectural firm of Deeter Richey Sippel before joining RIDC in 1963. He left RIDC to join the administration of Governor Dick Thornburgh in Harrisburg in 1979, serving first as deputy secretary of commerce and then as executive director of the Governor's Economic Development Cabinet Committee. On Hiram Milton's retirement from RIDC in 1981, Robinson was named president of RIDC and served in that capacity until his retirement in 2003. He served as a member of many boards of directors, including the Carnegie Hero Fund, Carnegie Museums of Pittsburgh, Dollar Bank, Phipps Conservatory and Botanical Gardens, Pittsburgh High Technology Council, Pittsburgh Symphony Society, and the Public Auditorium Authority.

Chuck Starrett served as executive director of the McKeesport Redevelopment Authority, coordinator of Duquesne's enterprise zone, and executive director of the Duquesne Business Advisory Corporation.

Evan Stoddard began working in Pittsburgh's Department of City Planning in 1974 and in 1976 was named principal economic development planner. From 1980 to 1981 he was deputy director of the city's Department of City Development and then worked in the URA's Economic Development Department, serving as its director from April 1986 to October 1993. In 1994 he was named associate dean of the McAnulty College and Graduate School of Liberal Arts at Duquesne University.

George Whitmer served as assistant for management and legislative affairs to Mayor Richard Caliguiri, who also appointed him to the Stadium Authority. After Mayor Caliguiri's death he worked as a regional manager for Three Rivers Aluminum Company until he was appointed executive director of the Urban Redevelopment Authority of Pittsburgh in September 1989. He served in that capacity until July 1992, when he became executive secretary to Mayor Sophie Masloff.

Steven M. Zecher first worked for the Urban Redevelopment Authority of Pittsburgh's Economic Development Department as a contracted consultant to develop a business information system in 1984. He then joined the department as a project manager, later becoming manager of its Center for Business Assistance. He served as Pennsylvania's deputy secretary of commerce under Ray Christman and then returned to the URA's Economic Development Department, where he served as deputy director until October 1993.

INDEX

Index

Technology Center, 105, 114; tries to recruit PNB to the Technology Center, 108; tries to recruit Legent to the Technology Center, 109-10; tries to recruit "Corporation X" to the Technology Center, 113; tries to recruit Mine Safety and Health Administration to the Technology Center, 115-16; negotiates consent agreement for Technology Center with DER, 116-17, 123-24; tries to recruit American Thermoplastics to the Technology Center, 118-19; recruits Union Switch and Signal to the Technology Center, 120-22; tries to recruit Duquesne University to the Technology Center, 124

USX Clairton Works, 132, 134, 162

USX Corporation/United States (U.S.) Steel Corporation/Carnegie Steel Corporation, 76, 133-34, 136-38, 140, 143-44, 152-53, 155-57, 159, 162-63, 193-96, 198, 204, 208-09, 213, 215, 229, 236, 267, 272n3, 303n33, 311n7, 311n8, 311n10, 312n23, 313n31, 314n53, 317n62, 327n160

USX Duquesne Works: xiv, 132, 136, 143, 157, 165, 232-33; transformation, xi; history, 134-35, 137, 140-42, 298n12, 299n18, 299n22

USX Homestead Works: xiv, 132, 157-59, 164-65, 168, 181-83, 232-33; transformation to Sandcastle and Waterfront, xi; history, 133-34, 143; early development proposals, 152-54

USX National Works: xiv, 132, 134, 157, 165, 232-33; transformation, xi, history, 136, 138, 225, 237

Wadsworth/Alert Laboratories, 218

Wagner, Jack E., 48, 110

Washington's Landing: 128-29, 167, 182, 219, 247, 253, 256, 260-61, 264-66, 336n15; transformation of Herr's Island, x; costs and benefits, xiii, 11-13, 21-22, 30, 41, 53, 109, 276n31, 276n33, 284n123; conditions in 2005, 6-7; RIDC's plan, 10-12; certified as a redevelopment area, 13; city's initial plan, 14, 16; agreement with RIDC, 14; purchase of Inland Products, 15; demolition, 15, 17; garbage to energy proposal, 17; URA accepts ownership of Walker Bridge, 18; exploration of bridge options, 18; Preliminary Land Development Plan, 19; Redevelopment Plan and Proposal, 21, 282n102; Buncher land swap, 22-25; projected schedule, 24; conference center marketing study, 24; marketing contract with North Side Civic Development Council, 26-27; development agreement with Buncher, 27-28; Herr's Island renamed Washington's Landing, 27; housing study, 28; land lease to Washington's Landing Associates, 28; access issues and improvements, 28, 280n87; sunken barges, 28-29, 281n99; purchase of Buncher property, 29; request for marina proposals, 30; master plan for lower end, 30; streetscape design, 30; discovery of PCBs and PAHs, 30-32; response to discovery of contamination, 34-35; approval of rowing center, 37; cleanup options, 37-38; approval of renegotiated Buncher acquisition, 40; request for qualifications for housing, marina and town center, 41, 43; consent order and agreement, 41-43, 53, 65-66; approval of plan for northern end of island, 43; sale of property to Gamma Sports, 45; revised land development and redevelopment plans, 51; second Washington's Landing Associates building, 56-58

Washington's Landing Associates, 28-29, 32, 55, 58, 68

Washington's Landing, encapsulation cell: proposed by ICF Kaiser, 37; location, 38, 40; approval by DER and URA, 41; contract to Atlas Services, 42; construction, 42, 44, 47-49, 279n77, 282n100; discovery of animal waste, 44, 280n89, 280n90, 281n94; rezoning, 48; completed, 50-51

Washington's Landing, housing: 30, 68, 265, 284n123; in Harlan report, 20; and Buncher, 22, 27, 29; market study, 24, 28; announced, 62-64

Washington's Landing, marina: in RIDC plan, 11, 30, 68, 265, 275n25, 284n123; on Inland Products property, 18; in Harlan plan, 20; in Redevelopment Plan and Proposal, 21;

ABOUT THE AUTHOR

Evan Stoddard earned a bachelor's degree in English and a master's degree in sociology from Brigham Young University, and his Ph.D. from the University of Pittsburgh in Public and International Affairs. During the administrations of mayors Pete Flaherty, Richard Caliguiri, and Sophie Masloff, he worked in the city of Pittsburgh's departments of City Planning, City Development, and the Urban Redevelopment Authority, where he served as director of the Department of Economic Development from 1986 to 1993. From 1994 to 2015 he was associate dean of the McAnulty College and Graduate School of Liberal Arts at Duquesne University, where his favorite classes to teach were the Honors Seminar: Community and University, and Policy Implementation in the Graduate Center for Social and Public Policy. Evan and his wife Janet Gardner Stoddard are parents of six grown children and still live in the same South Side row house they bought when they first came to Pittsburgh in 1971.

The author in front of the offices of the Pennsylvania Department of Environmental Protection (formerly DER) on Washington's Landing, 2016

CPSIA information can be obtained
at www.ICGtesting.com
Printed in the USA
LVOW04s2228201216
518186LV00008B/1878/P